Scottish Christianity
in the Modern World

A. C. Cheyne

Scottish Christianity in the Modern World

Edited by
STEWART J. BROWN
GEORGE NEWLANDS

In Honour of A. C. Cheyne

T&T CLARK
EDINBURGH

T&T CLARK LTD
59 GEORGE STREET
EDINBURGH EH2 2LQ
SCOTLAND

www.tandtclark.co.uk

First published 2000

ISBN 0 567 08765 4

British Library Cataloguing-in-Publication Data
A catalogue record for this book is available from the British Library

Typeset by Waverley Typesetters, Galashiels
Printed and bound in Great Britain by MPG Books, Bodmin

Contents

v

Introduction

Stewart J. Brown and George Newlands

I

THIS volume of essays in modern, mainly Scottish, religious and social history, has been prepared to honour the Rev. Professor Alexander Campbell Cheyne, Professor (Emeritus) of Ecclesiastical History at the University of Edinburgh, and one of the most distinguished Scottish scholar-teachers of his generation. The contributors include only a fraction of the many people – colleagues, friends and former students – who have benefited from Alec Cheyne's scholarship and generosity over the years. While the essays in this collection explore different themes and take different approaches, they are united by the shared view that an understanding of the Church is fundamental to an understanding of the modern world, and that the history of the Church must be comprehended within the broader context of social, political, and intellectual history.

When reference is made to Alec Cheyne's lectures, essays and books, the descriptive term most frequently used is 'elegant'. As an historian, he has above all been committed to the art of history. His historical writing is characterised by polished sentences, an engaging narrative technique, an acute understanding of human motivation, an eye for the telling detail and illustration, a sense of humour and an abiding empathy. His historical essays are well-crafted compositions, to be savoured again and again. He writes with his reader constantly in mind; his aim as an historian has been to inform, to persuade, and to entertain, and always to reach beyond the circle of professional historians to the larger educated public. He has a love for language and especially for the precision of the English language. His historical writings also demonstrate an interest in the development of character; he never neglects history's human actors. It is perhaps no accident that some of his finest essays have been biographical studies, of Thomas Chalmers, Henry Drummond, John Caird, John Tulloch or John and Donald Baillie. In this command of narrative style, Cheyne is in the tradition of the great eighteenth-century Scottish historians, of William Robertson and David Hume, historians who devoted considerable care to style and who viewed history as a form of literature, as an art as well as a science.

A second, frequently mentioned characteristic of Alec Cheyne as historian is his breadth of vision. Trained as an historian at Edinburgh and Oxford Universities, he taught general history at Glasgow University for some years before studying theology and turning his attention to the history of the Church. While his published works have focused on ecclesiastical history, and more particularly Scottish ecclesiastical history, he has never viewed ecclesiastical history as an isolated sub-discipline, separated from the rest of the historical enterprise. For him, the methodology of the Church historian is essentially the same as that of other types of historian. Throughout his career, he has endeavoured to keep up with the literature in political, social, economic and intellectual history, and he has encouraged his students to do the same. His reading has indeed been prodigious, not only in history, but also in novels, essays and poetry – especially the works of his beloved Victorians. Moreover, he has devoted attention to music and the visual arts, appreciating that all of human experience is grist to the historian's mill. The Church, he recognised, has ever been part of human society, and historians of the Church must strive for a broad understanding of its social and cultural context.

Alec Cheyne is rooted in the tradition of liberal historiography, with its emphasis on the importance of human actors, on human dignity and potential, and on respect for human freedom. This is the tradition of Thomas Babington Macaulay and Lord Acton in the nineteenth century, and of Richard Pares and George Kitson Clark in the twentieth. While sharing in the liberal historical vision, however, Cheyne is too good a historian to accept any deterministic interpretations of history, including any simplistic

Whig Interpretation of History with its view of inevitable progress in this world. He has known too much of the darkness of the twentieth century. He is also sceptical of human efforts to claim to know the truth of history or to create sweeping interpretative systems that claim to express the essence of history. No mere human being, he believes, can claim to possess the truth; all we can do is honestly seek the truth with humility and forbearance. Our efforts to understand our past will always be partial and incomplete. His objective as an historian has not been to write a definitive history, were such an achievement possible. Rather he seeks to present plausible explanations of past events and to do justice to the historical actors of the past, to rescue them from 'condescending views of posterity' and assess their actions within the context of their times. He is impatient with those who claim certain knowledge of historical truth, based on some infallible system, whether theological or philosophical. In his writings there is a refreshing tentativeness, combined with a positive view of human potential for toleration, mutual respect and basic decency, and permeated throughout with an abiding appreciation for the rich diversity of human endeavour.

Cheyne's main publications as an historian have focused on the history of the Church in Scotland since the Reformation, with particular attention to the Presbyterian tradition. His emphasis has been on the responses of the Churches to the changing social and intellectual climate of Scotland. He has been particularly attracted to the Victorian Church, and some of his finest work has explored the revolutionary transformations in religious thought during the Victorian era – in social structures and attitudes, in the rise of science, in the new biblical scholarship, in new attitudes to the historic creeds of the Church. Perhaps more than any other scholar, he has directed our attention to the great Scottish liberal evangelical theologians of the nineteenth century, a period when Scotland's religious influence on the larger world was probably at its height, and when such names as Thomas Chalmers, A. B. Bruce, William Robertson Smith, John and Edward Caird, Henry Drummond and James Denney were respected throughout the Protestant world. Alec Cheyne is primarily a historian of Scotland, but his Scotland was an outward-looking nation, committed to playing a role on the global stage.

II

The aim of the authors in this collection has been to contribute to our understanding of Christianity and the Scottish people since the eighteenth century, building on Alec Cheyne's pioneering scholarship. The book opens with D. W. D. Shaw's appreciation and brief biographical account of Professor A. C. Cheyne as teacher, scholar and Church leader. The bulk of the contributions are then organised into two main sections – 'Faith and Doubt' and 'Church, State and Society' – which correspond to the major emphases in Alec Cheyne's historical contributions.

The first section, on 'Faith and Doubt', opens with two linked chapters that explore the religion and religious doubt of the Scottish author, Thomas Carlyle, and his circle. In chapter 1, Ian Campbell considers the religion of the young Carlyle, particularly in relation to the strict piety of his father and his community of staunchly independent Scottish Seceders in early-nineteenth-century Ecclefechan. Kenneth Fielding follows up this theme in chapter 2, 'A Carlylean Elegy in Auchtertool Kirkyard', which offers a poignant account of the visits of the mature Carlyle and his wife, Jane Welsh Carlyle – by now long-time residents of London – to their native Scotland, and especially to Auchtertool, where one of Jane's relatives was minister. It is a haunting study of loss of faith, loss of community and loss of innocence among urbanised intellectuals in the mid-Victorian years.

In chapter 3, William Ferguson continues with the theme of the crisis of faith, providing a wide-ranging survey of 'Christian Faith and Unbelief in Modern Scotland'. Beginning with the Reformation, he describes the gradual spread of religious doubt among the educated classes in Scotland, giving particular attention to the challenges of science and the impact of the new biblical scholarship. The Scottish identity has been strongly linked with Scotland's Christian faith. And yet, as Ferguson notes, Scots also played a leading role in the development of the geological science, the new biology and the Higher Criticism of the Old Testament – all of which served to undermine traditional Christian beliefs. The tensions between faith and doubt, Christian tradition and scientific progress, were thus particularly acute in Victorian Scotland, as Ferguson's survey demonstrates. Barbara MacHaffie continues this exploration of the Victorian crisis of faith, focusing in chapter 4 on the challenges of Old Testament Criticism, and how the results of the Old Testament Criticism were treated in literature intended for use in schools and Sunday schools. She demonstrates that many writers of such literature were able to present the results of the Criticism to children in a creative and thoughtful manner. A considerable number of such writers were women, and their contributions indicate that women often took the lead in intelligent engagement with the new Criticism and its challenges to the traditional faith.

In chapter 5, 'Transforming the Creed', Peter Matheson shifts our attention from Scotland to the Scottish diaspora, and considers the career of the Scottish Presbyterian clergyman and theologian, William Salmond, who left Scotland for New Zealand in 1876, becoming the first professor of the recently founded theological hall of the Synod of Otago and Southland. A minister in the United Presbyterian Church while in Scotland, Salmond's efforts to introduce the liberal evangelical ethos of that Church in New Zealand soon brought a severe backlash from the more conservative elements of colonial Presbyterianism. The essay thus explores the contrasts between Scottish and colonial Presbyterianism, and between liberal and conservative interpretations of the historic creeds of the Church.

George Newlands moves in chapter 6 to the period of the First World War, and the impact of that cataclysm on the early development of Scotland's eminent twentieth-century theologian and Church leader, John Baillie, who served with the YMCA in France during the war. Drawing on his research among the Baillie papers, Newlands provides an intimate view of Baillie's pre-war friendships and visits to Germany, and demonstrates how the war devastated those pre-war associations. The experiences of the war, however, also drew the young Baillie into regular association with a wide spectrum of humanity. While the horrors of the war shattered the faith of some, and brought doubt, disillusionment and despair, in Baillie's case, the war matured and deepened his faith, and helped to forge the theologian who in the post-war world would be associated with the movement of 'Christian realism' and the struggle for social justice and ecumenical co-operation among Christians.

In the second section, the book moves from issues of 'Faith and Doubt' to the relations of 'Church, State and Society'. In chapter 7, John McCaffrey considers the impact of the Irish Famine of 1845–51 on Scottish society. The massive migration of impoverished and traumatised Irish Catholics into Scotland, coming as it did at a time of major change associated with the growth of heavy industry and rapid industrialisation, represented one of the most formative events in modern Scottish history. The migrants changed the social and religious composition of Scottish society, undermining the Presbyterian ascendancy and bringing new challenges of ethnic and sectarian division to a nation already struggling with the problems of class divisions, extreme inequality and working-class suffering.

In chapter 8, 'The Sacrament at Crathie, 1873', Owen Chadwick explores the problems of inter-communion and Church establishment in mid-Victorian Britain. In 1873, Queen Victoria, still in mourning over the loss of Albert and finding solace and a sense of belonging in her Balmoral retreat, resolved to take the sacrament of the Lord's Supper in the Church of Scotland parish church of Crathie. Her proposal led to a crisis. Although the Church of Scotland was an Established Church and the Queen was a member of this Church when travelling north of the Tweed, the Church of England did not recognise shared communion with the Church of Scotland, and the Queen's Anglican advisers argued strenuously against her taking such a step. The affair, as Chadwick demonstrates, revealed the continued tensions between the Anglican and Presbyterian religious establishments within the United Kingdom.

David Thompson continues with the theme of religious establishment and inter-Church relations. In chapter 9, he provides a study of the movement of Presbyterian Church union which led to the union of the Established Church of Scotland and the non-Established United Free Church in 1929. At the time, the Scottish Church union of 1929 was viewed as an early achievement of the twentieth-century ecumenical movement, and there were hopes that it would be the beginning of a world movement that would gradually re-knit the torn fabric of Christendom. As Thompson demonstrates, the Church union of 1929 was a great achievement. But at the same time, he suggests, it was also too much a matter of the Established Church of Scotland absorbing the non-Established United Free Church, while retaining most of its identity as a national establishment. In that sense, it did not provide a satisfactory model for the larger ecumenical movement.

In chapter 10, Keith Robbins explores the theme of religious establishments through a comparative study of the history of the Established Churches of Wales and Scotland. In Scotland, as Thompson argued in the preceding chapter, the Established Church was preserved, even strengthened, in part by union with its major non-Established rival. In Wales, on the other hand, the Established Church was disestablished in 1919, after a prolonged campaign by the Welsh Nonconformist Churches. Robbins explores the different experiences of Wales and Scotland, and considers the impact of the constitutional changes of the late 1990s on the future of the Established Church of Scotland.

In chapter 11, 'Presbyterians and Catholics in Twentieth-Century Scotland', Stewart Brown takes up the theme of sectarian tensions and the re-shaping of Scottish identity – surveying the changing relations between Presbyterians and Catholics in a century which witnessed the transformation of Scotland from an overwhelmingly Presbyterian nation into one in which membership of the Catholic Church is almost equal to that of the Church of Scotland. The waning of the idea of Scotland as a Presbyterian nation was, not surprisingly, a difficult one for many Presbyterians, as demonstrated in Brown's account of the Church of Scotland's campaign against Irish immigration in the 1920s and 1930s, or of the controversies surrounding the appointment of a Roman Catholic scholar to the chair of divinity at the University of Edinburgh in 1979. Yet, on the whole, Scotland followed a peaceful path towards a more pluralist society, a not inconsiderable achievement.

The Scottish missionary outreach receives attention from Andrew Ross, who in chapter 12 provides an overview of the special relationship between Scotland and Malawi, which had for many years been the main mission field of the Scottish Presbyterian Churches. The relationship between Scotland and British imperialism in central Africa, as Ross shows, was an ambiguous one. Scottish missionaries and the Scottish Churches at home were prepared to call on imperial power in the nineteenth century to advance what they perceived as the cause of Christianity. Yet during the years 1948 to 1964, the Scottish people demonstrated an impressive solidarity with the people of Malawi in their struggle for independence from both the empire and the Central African Federation.

A. C. Cheyne:
An Appreciation

D. W. D. Shaw

SCHOLAR, churchman, teacher – no one epithet will do for Alexander Campbell Cheyne. So it is as well to begin with the bare bones of his career thus far. A son of the manse, he was a pupil of Kirkcaldy High School and took his first degree at the University of Edinburgh, graduating in 1946 with First Class Honours in History. National Service followed, first in The Black Watch and then in the Intelligence Corps. Post-graduate study followed, at Oriel College, Oxford, culminating in the BLitt degree in 1950. The University of Glasgow was the first to exploit his gifts and potential and for the next three years he lectured in the Department of History. All academics, whether they admit it or not, know the frightening experience of being thrown in at the deep end and having to lecture with minimum time for preparation to large classes of critical undergraduates. Alec Cheyne not only survived but early proved himself a natural, and he would undoubtedly have gone on to a distinguished career in the Faculty of Arts. In 1953, however, surely after much heart and soul searching, he resigned his post and offered himself as a candidate for the ministry of the Church of Scotland. This offer was gladly accepted and the erstwhile lecturer in history returned to his alma mater to embark on a three-year course at New College. To no one's surprise, he graduated BD with Distinction in Ecclesiastical History and was licensed by the Presbytery of Dalkeith in 1956.

Urged by his teachers at New College, he had a further period of post-graduate study in Switzerland and Germany and served

9

for a period as assistant minister at Broughton Place Parish Church, Edinburgh under that redoubtable scholar-minister, Dr George Gunn. He seemed set on a career in the parish ministry for which he was never to lose his respect. It was not to be, however, and after much hesitation on his part and great pressure exerted by others, not least Professor J. H. S. Burleigh, then Principal, in 1958 he joined the staff of New College as lecturer in Ecclesiastical History, with ordination following. In 1964, he succeeded Professor Burleigh in the Chair of Ecclesiastical History. At New College he remained, from 1984 as Principal, until his retirement to Peebles in 1986.

Scholar, teacher, minister. I begin with Alec Cheyne as teacher for two reasons: first because it was in that capacity that he first crossed my path; and second because although the future will remember him as scholar, it was as teacher that he is best known by the present generation and would, I think, himself like best to be remembered. I was lucky enough to be a student at New College when young Mr Cheyne arrived on the scene – he did appear absurdly young then, and his boyish appearance has stayed with him into his eighth decade. There was, though, nothing immature about his lectures. We very soon discovered that for style, orderliness and elegance of presentation he not only matched but excelled his senior and very eminent colleagues. Part of his secret was his eye for the telling quotation. Even though he had a teaching load that would send today's junior lecturers running to the Association of University Teachers to complain, his lectures were without fail meticulously prepared, beautifully structured, and read with energy and enthusiasm. Every now and then he would leave his text and deliver an off-the-cuff comment that would either make the class sit up with its contemporary relevance or bring the house down with its wit. Memorable indeed were the occasions when he would hand back class exams or essays with a pertinent comment to each student, helpful criticism dressed in irony, shrewd, but never unkind. It was no surprise to his students, indeed cause for rejoicing, when he was appointed to the Chair.

At a time of university expansion and when New College was beginning to cater for a much larger and broader constituency than that of candidates for the ministry, Alec Cheyne built up a very lively and efficient department, willing to adopt the latest teaching methods. With a growing band of honours students from Arts as well as Divinity, and with post-graduates, he acquired a just reputation for the helpfulness of his tutorials and for the practical interest he took in his students. One student reflected the experience of many when he remarked that whereas other teachers would enquire after their academic progress and prospects, Professor Cheyne would also enquire about their material welfare – how they were coping with their finances and their accommodation. It is not surprising that over the years he has evoked such affection from former students. Nor is it surprising that so many of his former students have gone on to become teachers in universities and colleges all over the world. Such students' appreciation of his teaching made it inevitable that over the years he should be invited as guest lecturer: USA (including Alaska), Canada (including Newfoundland, where he was awarded an honorary doctorate), Australia, New Zealand, Germany, as well as all over Great Britain. A regular lecturer at St Andrews, both at the St Mary's Summer School and the American Summer Institute of Theology there, his contributions were unfailingly received with enthusiasm. I remember one occasion, a lecture on the Baillies, John and Donald, when his sensitive peroration was greeted not this time with the customary applause but with a moment's silence – with not a few confessing to a lump in the throat or a tear in the eye. A teacher heard gladly, indeed.

Teaching, however, imparts no permanent value unless it incorporates scholarship of the highest level. Ecclesiastical history is a specialist discipline requiring not simply acquisition of scientific historical method coupled with imagination, nor yet simply knowledge of the history of the Church, but a knowledge and appreciation of the theology behind developments in Church history. This means that the practitioner has to be something of a theologian as well as historian, with an ability to relate theology to the historical scene. Alec Cheyne was, I fear, often guilty of denying any theological insight – he would take refuge in the claim of being 'a mere historian'. This was both unfair and unjust. In fact he was a master at detecting and summarising the distinctive theological characteristics of Church leaders and movements. This is abundantly clear for anyone who reads any of his nineteenth-century studies. The social and ecclesiastical

atmosphere leading up to the Disruption of 1843; the tempera-
mental, theological and social emphases of the principal protagonists of the years prior to and following that watershed in
the history of the Church in Scotland, as well as the leaders of
the Oxford Movement in England; the gradual change in the
theology of the main Churches in Scotland from the confident
faith in the Calvinism of the Westminster Confession of Faith of
the earlier years of the century to the more liberal and critical
attitude of the latter years; the reaction and response of the
Churches to the new social and scientific teaching, especially the
evolutionary theory which seemed to pose such a threat to
orthodox Christian belief and biblical authority – all these were
grist to his mill. It is perhaps true that history, like theology, has
to be rewritten in every generation. It is also true that for historians
working in the latter half of the twentieth century, no one had a
better grasp or was better able to analyse and expound these
things than Alec Cheyne. Something of a perfectionist, he was
not one of those scholars who rushed to publish every passing
thought or every routine lecture. Indeed, it is future generations'
loss that he has not published more (though there is more to
come). Nevertheless the study of Thomas Chalmers, *The Practical
and the Pious*, which he introduced and edited, and his account
of Victorian Scotland's religious revolution, *The Transforming
of the Kirk*, with its important 'Postlude' taking the story up to
the mid-twentieth century, will remain required reading for any
serious student of the period as well as a delightful read for the
intelligent general reader. Would that such could be said of more
works of historical and theological scholarship!

John Calvin in his ecclesiology gave a not inconsiderable role
to the Doctors of the Church. It is unfortunately true of some
scholar-ministers that once they become settled in university or
college they get so engrossed in the academic life that they do not
have much time for exercising responsibility in the Church. This
could certainly not be said of Alec Cheyne. Partly because of his
love of the Church and partly because of the high honour in
which he held the parish ministry, he was determined to play his
part. With his polished and eminently listenable style, he is a
preacher of real distinction who rarely refuses an invitation to
preach, however tied up (or down) he might be with his academic
responsibilities. On special historic occasions or just to help out

a former student, he has ever been ready to step in, to the immense satisfaction of the congregation. Indeed, when he retired to Peebles, he preached regularly at Stobo, a most welcome assistant to the minister of Upper Tweeddale. His knowledge of the Church was not confined to its history. His acquaintance with the contemporary Church of Scotland was prodigious. His friends used to tease him that he must have spent too long studying the Church's *Yearbook* ('the Red Book'), for it seemed that he knew not only the exact locations of all the parishes in Scotland but the name of the incumbent in each!

In the courts of the Church he played a full part, whether in the Presbytery of Edinburgh, which, in recognition of his service, in 1987 elected him Moderator, or in the General Assembly. Inclining to a liberal evangelical understanding, he has strong convictions as to the nature and tradition of the Church. Naturally shy, when his hackles were raised (as occasionally they were) he could summon up his courage and be devastatingly effective in demolishing arguments he felt to be defective, or, if he gleaned that the Panel on Doctrine, for example, – of the Panel he was always somewhat suspicious – were in danger of leading the Church astray or when disputed points of doctrine appeared to be being imposed on the Church. Yet for all that, possibly his most telling contribution to the life of the Church has been the quiet and helpful guidance he has so willingly given to the many individual parish ministers (not only former students) who would come to him with their problems and never go away unattended. A convinced Presbyterian, he would nevertheless himself have made an excellent bishop! As it was, as Principal of New College, he had special responsibility for Church of Scotland candidates for the ministry, a role to which he was admirably suited and which he fulfilled with distinction.

Possibly what made him such an attractive teacher is the fact that he is a genuine man of culture. Exceptionally well read in the classics of English literature, he particularly knows and loves Wordsworth and Coleridge. The nineteenth-century novelists, too, were dear to him, and surely contributed to the elegance of his own English style. Music, though, is his great love, as his vast library of LPs and CDs testifies and I am sure he would acknowledge the hours and hours of solace and inspiration it has given him. Gifted with an exceptional musical ear, he can identify almost anything from the classical repertoire from the first few bars – the classical repertoire, please note, for he has not many kind words for contemporary offerings! It is this general cultural interest in addition to his wit, his encyclopaedic historical knowledge and his ability to make fun of himself that makes him such an engaging conversationalist.

This is thankfully not an obituary, and the final word cannot yet be said of his gifts and contribution. For now, however, the closing word must be to acknowledge Alec's extraordinary gift of friendship. Wherever his journey has taken him – at school, as a student, in the Army, as lecturer, professor, churchman or neighbour; in the study, at the table, walking in the hills – he has made friends. Most of us, when we make friends and drift apart, we lose them. Alec doesn't: he keeps them. And that is surely why they value his friendship so highly. So, as one of these, I count it a peculiar honour to introduce this volume as a grateful tribute to A. C. Cheyne: teacher, scholar, churchman, man of culture – and friend.

Part I

FAITH AND DOUBT

Chapter 1

Carlyle and the Secession

Ian Campbell

THOMAS Carlyle was acclaimed throughout the greater part of his writing career, and by many after his death, as a religious force of paramount importance. He preached earnestness, submission, the gospels of work and of silence; many overlooked the contradictions in what he said and wrote, many accepted glaring inconsistencies and were glad to acknowledge that by example and incessant preaching Carlyle awoke in the nineteenth century a consciousness which to many was tantamount to religious awakening. This essay seeks to focus attention on the earliest religious community Carlyle knew, the Seceder congregation of his parents in Ecclefechan, to describe the congregation and if possible assess some of its effects on Carlyle himself. The materials are exceptional: Carlyle's own *Reminiscences* are of his father on James Carlyle's death in 1832, and then cover his own early life and friendships in extraordinary detail when he came to write the bulk of them on Jane Welsh Carlyle's death in 1866. Few have left an autobiography so vivid. Fewer still have left a corpus of surviving letters as brilliant as those of the Carlyles. As these words are completed, volume 28 of the Duke–Edinburgh edition of *The Collected Letters of Thomas and Jane Welsh Carlyle* is at press, taking the series through 1853, well over half-way through the surviving thousands of letters. Carlyle's religion is revealed, as the series unrolls, in its waywardness, its contradictions: in his relations with Thomas Chalmers and with John Sterling, and with his mother whose death on Christmas Day 1853 powerfully took him back to his early roots in Ecclefechan, growing up with his deeply pious parents in the Burgher Secession Church, and it is there that we turn for some understanding of his early life.

*

Ecclefechan, when Carlyle was growing up in the closing decade of the eighteenth century and the first of the nineteenth, was a small but active town, a stage on the Glasgow to London coach route, the centre of regular and important agricultural fairs and markets, and a focus of service industries for a rich farming area. Despite the agricultural emphasis there was considerable industry in the village, with 'trade and manufacture' including the manufacture of linen goods, ginghams and straw hats.[1] A well-developed system of local carriers ensured the distribution of goods to neighbouring England.

Ecclefechan, then, was no sleepy hollow, but rather a moderately industrial busy town, enjoying the through traffic which modern progress has removed from it. A considerable number of bright young men left it to make their careers in the world of commerce, or to study at the University of Edinburgh. At home, the cultural life of the village centred very much on its two churches. One, the Established Church, was at Hoddam, one mile from Ecclefechan village. The other was a Secession charge, based in Ecclefechan itself, in a succession of premises that increased in capacity as the size of the congregation grew. Details of these premises, with illustrations, can be found in John Sloan's *The Carlyle Country* (London, 1904), and silently but tellingly in the churchyard at Ecclefechan where Carlyle himself is buried, along with many of those who attended worship with him in those early years.

The Seceders were in the minority, but it was a flourishing minority. One thousand and seventy-nine of the parish population of 1,198 were members of the Established Church in 1791, while 119 were Seceders.[2] The congregation was proud of being separate and, although poor, could maintain a minister and a meeting-house. The area was vulnerable to change and depression, and the

[1] These details come from *The Statistical Account of Scotland* (Edinburgh, 1792), and *The New Statistical Account of Scotland* (Edinburgh and London, 1845), under 'Hoddam'. Carlyle helped foster local industry: see *Essays and Transactions of the Highland Society*, VII (1829), 290–1.

[2] J. Yorstoun, in *The Statistical Account of Scotland*, iii, 353.

frequent poor harvests in Carlyle's younger years caused scarcity.[3] As Henry Hamilton has noted, 'the standard of living of the mass of Scots people was particularly vulnerable to harvest fluctuations, since the bulk of the country's food was home-grown. . . . A bad harvest could thus send prices soaring and bring great hardship to the labouring population.'[4] Carlyle's father remembered these times vividly, and 'he had noticed the labourers (I have heard him tell) retire each separately to a brook, and there *drink* instead of dining, – without complaint; anxious only to hide it'.[5] James Dawson Burn, a poor boy who lived through this period, recalled the hard winter of 1813–14 when the corn was fit only to feed cattle, after lying unharvested till December. He had the misfortune to see poverty at close quarters, for in Moffat Jail he was almost eaten alive by the rats that infested the place.[6]

It was an area, then, where conditions were not easy. In Ecclefechan itself there was a healthy diversity of industry, but any congregation working in such conditions must have had to cope with fluctuating congregational income and little money for unexpected expenditure. The Seceders of Ecclefechan, as a minority group, suffered these disadvantages to the full; yet casual visitors to Ecclefechan noticed how loyal people were to old, sober, industrious traditions,[7] and the story of the Secession Church in Ecclefechan is just such a story.[8]

In 1747 the Secession Church was split over the administration of the Burgess Oath,[9] and the two resulting branches (Burgher

---

[3] See J. A. Symon, *Scottish Farming, Past and Present* (Edinburgh and London, 1959), 157.

[4] H. Hamilton, *An Economic History of Scotland in the Eighteenth Century* (Oxford, 1963), 375.

[5] T. Carlyle, *Reminiscences*, ed. K. J. Fielding and I. Campbell (Oxford, 1997), 35.

[6] [J. D. Burn], *The Autobiography of a Beggar Boy* (London, 1855), 29, 66, 3.

[7] I. Lettice, *Letters on a Tour Extending Through Parts of Scotland in the Year 1792* (London, 1794), 17–19.

[8] Most of the details of the growth of the Ecclefechan congregations are found in A. Steele, *The Story of a Hundred and Fifty Years* (Annan [1910]), but it is also necessary to consult W. McKelvie, *Annals and Statistics of the United Presbyterian Church* (Edinburgh, 1873), particularly pp. 65–7.

[9] See D. Scott, *Annals and Statistics of the Original Secession Church* (Edinburgh [1886]), and D. M. Forrester, 'Adam Gib, the AntiBurgher', *Records of the Scottish Church History Society*, VII (1941), 141–69.

and Antiburgher) separated according to their willingness or un-willingness to accept the oath. Till 1820, and the United Secession Church, the Secession Church was split in this way, and the two branches were themselves split after the turn of the century; research suggests that the Ecclefechan congregation was a New Light congregation of the Burgher branch – arguably the least extreme of the possible permutations, neither rejecting the Burgess Oath nor clinging to the less flexible dogma of the Old Light body. D. Scott's *Annals and Statistics of the Original Secession Church* lists fully the causes of acrimony between Burgher and Antiburgher, Old Light and New; he lists the Old Light secession charges, and neither 'Hoddam' nor 'Ecclefechan' appears.[10] The exceptionally independent nature of the Carlyles as religious thinkers tallies well with this deduction, as they found their Burgher Church a comfortable one to which they could fully adhere; had they had compulsion brought to bear on them, they would have reacted by simply walking out.[11]

The characteristics of the Secession Church have been described as three: the growth of the evangelical and missionary spirit, the aggressive attitude to the Established Church, and the rapid growth of their congregations in Scotland. In 1747, when the Burgess Oath caused a rift in the Secession Church, there were 32 congregations; in 1820, when they reunited, there were 262.[12] Energy characterises all this description, intellectual and physical energy. The Ecclefechan congregation had its share of this. In 1738 they had first petitioned the Associate Presbytery of Annandale for sermon, and when Ralph Erskine preached to them a crowd of 10,000 is said to have been present.[13] Much of the

---

[10] See chapter viii of Scott's *Annals and Statistics*; also p. 41. I take it that the acrimony was such that congregations would belong completely either to one or the other of the 'Old Light' or 'New Light' persuasions; as we know that Hoddam was a Burgher charge, the absence of its name among the Old Light charges indicates that they were New Light Burghers, 'disowning all compulsory measures in religion'.

[11] Compare James Carlyle's condemnation of bad preaching in T. Carlyle, *Reminiscences*, 15. James Carlyle did in fact walk out of the congregation over one dispute.

[12] A. Thomson, *Historical Sketch of the Origin of the Secession Church* (Edinburgh and London, 1848), 151–2.

[13] Numbers on this scale were not to be seen again till the 1820s, when Edward Irving made a triumphant preaching tour of Annandale.

enthusiasm that sustained the Ecclefechan congregation may have followed from this occasion. From this time onwards sermon was occasionally preached, sometimes in Lockerbie, sometimes in Ecclefechan. It was the only Secession congregation in Annandale, and in 1744 it acquired its own minister. The church which was erected was sited, after bitter controversy, in Lockerbie; when the Church was split in 1747 the Burghers quickly separated from the Lockerbie congregation and petitioned for a minister of their own in Ecclefechan. The Presbytery was in favour, but in the succeeding decade preaching was scarce as ministers were few. In 1757 there was a complaint that there had been no sermon for nine months, such was the scarcity.

The Burghers' congregation grew slowly and occupied temporary premises in Ecclefechan and in 1761 presented a call to John Johnston of West Linton. The Call is preserved today in the vestry of the former Hoddam Free Kirk, now Ecclefechan West Kirk; forty-eight names appear, and one of the elders and three other signatories are Carlyles. Mr Johnston accepted and was inducted in April 1761. From this point onwards the growth of the Church was continuous and remarkable.

Johnston's annual stipend reflected the poor conditions of the parish, being well below £50 in the years before 1780. Nevertheless, in 1766 the congregation managed to acquire bigger and better premises, with accommodation for 600. This might seem excessive for a congregation of some 120, but the Sunday services were beginning to attract attention, and people walked to Ecclefechan to attend this worship from Annan, from surrounding Dumfriesshire parishes – even from England.[14] Johnston himself was the really remarkable feature of the ministry over these years. Although a learned man,[15] and one who could have held high office in the Burgher Church's Divinity Hall, he was content to develop his congregation, to help occasionally a young man prepare himself for university study.[16] In 1766 he was Moderator of the

[14] Carlyle, *Reminiscences*, 209.

[15] Dr Lawson, Professor of the Burgher Church Divinity Hall, regretted Johnston's refusal of that office, as Johnston was 'the best qualified man in our body for that office'. A. Steele, The *Story of a Hundred and Fifty Years*, 17.

[16] Both Johnston and his son saved Carlyle at a crucial period in his schooling, when the local master's Latin proved inadequate and the pupil was in danger of faltering in his progress to high school, and university, as a result.

Associate Burgher Synod. In the early decades of the nineteenth century his efforts were rewarded by the establishment of separate congregations for the offshoots of his morning visitors, at Annan, Chapelknowe, Lochmaben, Rigg of Gretna and Moffat. The geographical distribution of these locations suggests the width of Johnston's fame and sphere of influence. Johnston died in 1812 and the congregation paid him the compliment of a large and handsome (and expensive) memorial. His church and its services were a major influence on the early Carlyle. 'Rude, rustic, bare, no Temple in the world was more so; – but there were sacred lambencies, tongues of authentic flame from Heaven, which kindled what was best in one, what has not yet gone out.'[17]

*

What sort of people formed the congregation which so powerfully affected Carlyle? Carlyle himself gives part of the answer in his *Reminiscences*:

> Annandale was not an irreligious country, – though Annan itself (owing to a drunken Clergyman, and the logical habits they cultivated) was more given to sceptical freethinking than other places; – the greatly prevailing fashion was, a decent form of devoutness, and pious theoretically anxious regard for things sacred.[18]

An interesting illumination of this remark is to be found in one of Carlyle's letters to a student contemporary. Writing from Annan, Carlyle reports that

> there are in Middlebie sundry cunning workmen – some skilled in the intricacies of the loom – some acquainted with the operations of the lapstone – who are notable deists – nay several aspire to taste the sublime delights of *Atheism*! Now when creatures, superior in so few respects (inferior in so many) to the cow that browses on their hills, begin to tread upon the heels of the wise ones of the earth – the hue and cry about freedom from popular errors – defiance of vulgar prejudices – glory of daring to follow truth, tho' alone &c &c &c is annihilated – and – 'all the rest is leather and prunella'.

[17] Carlyle, *Reminiscences,* 210.
[18] Ibid., 176.

Underneath the snobbishness of this remark lies a genuine awareness of the strength of local feeling, the move away from orthodox churchgoing religion.

In these circumstances secession became more than just a doctrinal matter, it often became the only way in which the worshipper could attend church and still maintain his self-respect. Yet local feeling went against this. The worshipper might seek to escape from this unsatisfactory Established Church position, but 'It was ungenteel for him to attend the Meeting-house.' Yet people found it altogether salutory, and 'A man who awoke to the belief that he actually had a soul to be saved', wrote Carlyle (no unbiased judge, of course) '. . . was apt to be found among the Dissenting people, and to have given up attendance on the Kirk.' This was not merely local gossip and rumour (for the minister of Annan had succeeded his father, who had been excellent, and so the people were loyal to the son of such a father). 'This was the case', recorded Carlyle, '. . . as I had remarked for myself, nobody teaching me, at an early period of my investigations into men and things. I concluded it would be generally so over Scotland; but found when I went north, to Edinburgh, Glasgow, Fife, etc., that it was not, or by no means so perceptibly was.'[19] Carlyle went to church very early in his life, trained his memory by repeating the gist of sermons afterwards. He has a pencil note in a book which he read recalling one James Fisher, a blind poet of Dumfriesshire.

He lived in Annan, about 1804; & had died, or gone quite across to England (died, I rather think), before 1806. I remember well once sitting *beside* him in the Ecclefechan meeting-house through a sermon, and gazing with terror *& fascination* at his hideously protrusive blind eyes, or the one of them next me. Poor old soul, he was listening so seriously.[20]

The note is meant to contradict the impression given by the book that Fisher was in Dumfriesshire in 1806; Carlyle supposes

---

[19] Thomas Carlyle to Robert Mitchell, 14 June 1815, quoted from *The Collected Letters of Thomas and Jane Welsh Carlyle* [hereafter *Letters*], ed. C. R. Sanders, K. J. Fielding, *et al.* (Durham, NC, 1970), i, 51; *Reminiscences*, 208.

[20] Carlyle's pencil note to J. Paterson, *Contemporaries of Burns and the More Recent Poets of Ayrshire* ([n.p.] 1840), 141, copy preserved in the Ewart Library, Dumfries.

that he was there in 1804. This would suggest that 1804 is about the time Carlyle saw him in church, from which one can deduce Carlyle attended sermon (and sat through very long services) at the age of eight or nine. The Secession meeting-house was therefore part of his life very early.[21]

From his youth Carlyle felt a part of this congregation, he felt he belonged, certainly as his family belonged to a congregation which respected them;[22] his father may even have been an elder. His own clear definition of the Church, as he saw it, was one which was closer to the truths of Christian religion than the Established Church at the time – in 1867 he was to define it as 'Free Kirk making no noise' – that is, a refusal on the part of those members concerned to belong to a decayed Established Church, carried out without the tumult of the later Disruption of 1843. Everything in Carlyle's Seceder Church was discreet, based on personal conviction unshaking in its adherence to truth. It devoted itself to 'preaching to the people what of the best and sacredest it could'. If it had a fault, it was in excessive severity,

a lean-minded controversial spirit among certain brethren, (mostly of the laity, I think); 'narrow-nebs' as the outsiders called them; of flowerage, or free harmonious beauty, there could not well be much in this system: but really, except on stated occasions (annual fast-day, for instance, when you were reminded that 'a testimony had been lifted up', which you were now the bearers of), there was little, almost no talk, especially no preaching at all about 'patronage', or secular controversy, but all turned on the weightier and universal matters of the Law, and was considerably entitled to say for itself, 'Hear, all men'. Very venerable are those old Seceder Clergy to me, now when I look back on them. Most of the chief figures among them . . . were hoary old men. Men so like what one might call antique 'Evangelists in modern vesture, and Poor Scholars and Gentlemen of Christ', I have nowhere met with in Monasteries or Churches, among Protestant or Papal Clergy, in any country of the world. – All this is altered utterly at present, I grieve to say; and gone to as good as nothing or worse.

[21] Much of the district's social life revolved round the church, including the verbal jousting which the Carlyle family enjoyed. See *Homes and Haunts of Thomas Carlyle* (London, 1895), 8.

[22] The inference is from Frederick Martin's rare biographical article on Carlyle, published in 1877 in the sole number of the *Biographical Magazine* to appear under Martin's editorship.

Written from the perspective of fifty years on, this sums up what remained in Carlyle's mind as the value of his early Church. The value lay in personalities with whom to mingle, with the preaching of the word by life and example. People like Johnston of Ecclefechan, and his own father, lived in his memories as semi-sacred examples of Christian life in an age which had gone to another extreme. He quoted with approval the case of one Burgher Seceder who refused to interrupt family worship in order to save his entire crop, threatened by a sudden whirlwind. 'Wind? Wind canna get ae straw that has been appointed mine; sit down, and let us worship God.' From the vantage point of 1867, this seemed to Carlyle wholly admirable.

> There is a kind of citizen which Britain used to have; very different from the millionaire Hebrews, Rothschild money-changers, Demosthenic Disraelis, and inspired young Göschens, and their 'unexampled prosperity'. Weep, Britain, if these latter are among the honourable you now have! [23]

The minister and congregation of the Ecclefechan Secession Church stood out in Carlyle's memory as near-perfect types of this ideal Christian. One characteristic was individualism – which, as one historian remarks, 'might be expected in those who, though but a small minority in the Christian community, believed the cause of God was in their hands'.[24] Carlyle himself testifies how little the New Light Burghers harped on this theme in their preaching,[25] how much the individuality was expressed in self-education, in the Law, in the shaping of the individual life to make it conform to the highest ideal. So much was this the case in Ecclefechan that even the Established Church assistant minister (who wrote the article on Hoddam Parish in the Statistical Account of 1843) noted respectfully that 'this is one of the oldest dissenting congregations in the south of Scotland, and some of its members are very respectable in their station, and easy in their circumstances'.[26] This information in itself adds little (for we know from Carlyle that people had been driven to the dissenters despite social criticism of their desertion of the Established, 'respectable' Church)

[23] Carlyle, *Reminiscences*, 206–7.
[24] Scott, *Annals and Statistics*, 591.
[25] Carlyle, *Reminiscences*, 208.
[26] *New Statistical Account*, 295.

but the tone and the fact that it finds a place in the *Statistical Account*, shows how much the Seceders of Ecclefechan were held in respect as pious individuals.

Carlyle mentions several cases of this. One is the poor peasant who refused to take time off from worship for mere worldly ends. One is Adam Hope, a man who taught Carlyle in Annan and earned his intense respect. 'He was a man humanely contemptuous of the world; . . . I should judge, an extremely proud man. For the rest, an inexorable logician; a Calvinist at all points, and Burgher Scotch Seceder to the backbone.' Proud, independent, judging for himself what is right. Another such is James Carlyle. 'He was among the last of the true men which Scotland (on the old system) produced, or can produce; a man healthy in body and mind; fearing God, and diligently working in God's Earth with contentment, hope and unwearied resolution.' His greatest maxim was 'That man was created to work, not to speculate, or feel, or dream', and accordingly he set to working with all his heart. 'Though from the heart and practically even more than in words an independent man, he was by no means an insubordinate one,' and he knew (and kept) his social place without showing the least servility. 'The more I reflect on it', concludes Carlyle, 'the more must I admire how completely Nature had taught him; how completely he was devoted to his work, to the Task of his Life; and content to let *all* pass by unheeded that had no relation to this.' Whatever did not interest him (including poetry, fiction, most of the literature which so fascinated his son) he ignored; he sought to live his life by his own lights, and his proud independence fascinated his son who clearly envied it, even if he did not envy the restricted upbringing which had brought about the strength. 'My Father's education was altogether of the worst and most limited,' wrote Carlyle, but then education was not what counted in this case. The Church to which he belonged had educated him in his world-philosophy, a proud and independent one, and so he was in Carlyle's sight a fine and admirable product of the old system – a product perhaps the last of his kind. Unconsciously, unreasoningly, he was religious.

> He was Religious with the consent of his whole faculties: without Reason he would have been nothing; indeed his habit of intellect was thoroughly free and even incredulous, and strongly enough did the daily example of this work afterwards on me. 'Putting out the natural eye of his mind to see better with a telescope': this was no scheme for

him. But he was in Annandale, and it was above 50 years ago; and a Gospel was still preached there to the heart of a man, in the tones of a man. Religion was the Pole-star for my Father: rude and uncultivated as he otherwise was, it made him and kept him 'in all points a man'.[27]

Independence, strict attention to duty, to work, to life, rigorous attention to the preaching of the Word, these characterised Carlyle's father. In this he was true to the Seceders' character, described by one historian thus: 'In attending to their own interests [the Seceders] have acquired that habit of exercising individual judgment, which stands closely connected with the continuance of ecclesiastical and civil liberty.'[28] In the case of the Burghers, this led to a conservative position on theological matters. 'Strictly orthodox', wrote one divine, describing the Burghers, 'and specially called forth, as they conceived, to contend for the faith once delivered to the saints, they could hardly bear a deviation from the accustomed expressions which were wont to be used by sound divines in treating of certain doctrines.'[29] We have seen that the 'special calling' was not overplayed in the case of the Ecclefechan congregation, but their worship certainly did not admit much change. When paraphrases were first introduced to the form of worship, to add variety to the singing of the metre psalms, there was intense opposition,[30] in which the Carlyle family shared. Carlyle himself, now living in Edinburgh, replied to news of this that paraphrases would inevitably 'come in', and they eventually did.[31] The form of worship was sacred; Thomas Somerville recorded that in the eighteenth century Seceders had 'held it sinful in any individual who professed to be a member of their community ever on any occasion to attend public worship in any of the parish churches' – on pain of expulsion.[32] Individual judgment, and freedom of choice, were thus only selectively to be

[27] Carlyle, *Reminiscences*, 7–13, 205.

[28] Thomson, *Historical Sketch*, 164.

[29] Quoted from the unpublished notebook of Dr John Mitchell of Glasgow by Scott, *Annals and Statistics*, 16.

[30] Alexander Carlyle to Thomas Carlyle, 25 March 1819, National Library of Scotland, MS. 1763, fol. 28.

[31] E. W. Marrs, Jr., *The Letters of Thomas Carlyle to his Brother Alexander, with Related Family Letters* (Cambridge, MA, 1968), 27.

[32] T. Somerville, *My Own Life and Times, 1741–1814* (Edinburgh, 1861), 375–6.

exercised. Tradition was strong – Carlyle's father allowed little innovation in his reading – 'Old John Owen, of the seventeenth century, was his favourite author'.[33] Carlyle described his father as 'a serious man who gave his spare time to reading John Owen and other religious writers of that order'.[34] James Carlyle's other literary interests were very restricted, and he forbade his family to read fiction. The theatre, of course, was unthought of, and Carlyle first came in contact with the major literary influence of his life, Shakespeare, only after leaving Ecclefechan and going to live in Annan. This was the debit side to the strenuously upright lives which have been described.

A more open-minded approach would have made room for literary pursuits, for the arts, but one historian of the time saw such an approach as being at too great a price to pay. The Moderates, wrote John Mitchell, cultivated themselves only by 'declining the active and energetic discharge of the duties of their spiritual and evangelical function'. Instead 'they cultivated connection with the upper classes of society in their parishes, declining intercourse with those of low degree to whom the Gospel is preached'.[35] One particularly extreme caricature of the Moderates, as men who discount 'the pungency of sin, the doctrine of salvation by grace, and joy in the atonement', to whom 'justification, adoption and sanctification were rude scholastic terms' while 'learned allusions, and flights of fancy clothed in a kind of half-poetic dress, occupied the place of a simple, grave, scriptural, and experimental preaching such as Scotland in her best days had been accustomed to hear . . .'[36] is by Struthers, who in his *History of the Relief Church* does not spare the Moderates' dereliction of the evangelical duties so dear to the secession. To them 'religion was no longer a thing of deep earnestness'. The phrase could be Carlyle's. But Carlyle was more moderate than

---

[33] M. Conway, *Autobiography* (London, 1904), ii, 88.

[34] I. Campbell, 'Portrait of Carlyle', *The Weekend Scotsman,* 12, viii, 1967, 3; see also my 'Irving, Carlyle and the Stage', *Studies in Scottish Literature,* viii (January 1971), 166–73 for further details of Ecclefechan attitudes to art.

[35] J. Mitchell, 'Memories of Ayrshire', *Miscellany of the Scottish History Society,* vi (1939), 302, quoted from T. C. Smout, *A History of the Scottish People, 1560–1830* (London, 1969), 238.

[36] C. Struthers, *The History of the Relief Church* (Edinburgh and London, 1848), 190.

this – in the wider sense. Like the historian, T. C. Smout, he might have given the Moderates credit for having been a valuable part of Enlightenment Edinburgh, where 'the warm sociability of the eighteenth century town must have formed the ideal environment for the cross-fertilisation of minds'.[37] This is perhaps evident in the most clear-cut tribute he paid to the Church in a letter to John Stuart Mill of 1832. 'The History of the Scotch Presbyterian Church is noteworthy for this reason, that above all Protestant Churches it for some times was a real Church; had brought home in authentic symbols, to the bosoms of the lowest, that *summary* and concentration of whatever is highest in the Ideas of Man; the Idea unutterable in words; and opened thereby (in scientific strictness, it may be said) a free communication between Earth and the Heaven whence Earth has its being.'[38]

What then can be said of the Ecclefechan Secession Church from which Carlyle came? It was an unusually strong congregation, it had its share of strong individual characters, it struck the youthful Carlyle very much, both because his parents adhered to it (and his respect for his parents was very great), and because it was the first church he knew; his teachers at school, his friends, his most intimate acquaintance in his twenties (Edward Irving) attended. It was not extreme, but a well-balanced independent body, stressing the evangelical function, the preaching of the Word, and the regulation of life according to the law, and the performance of the duties of work and submission in an essentially Calvinist universe. Carlyle sprang from such religious roots.

*

The severing of these roots is common knowledge, especially among those who succumb to the temptation of interpreting *Sartor Resartus* as literal autobiography, something Carlyle warned future generations not to do. Teufelsdröckh goes through spiritual agonies before, during and after his conversion enshrined in the 'Everlasting NO', the 'Centre of Indifference' and the 'Everlasting YEA'. These are given artistic form in *Sartor*, with all the artistic neatness of

[37] Smout, *A History of the Scottish People*, 508.
[38] Thomas Carlyle to John Stuart Mill, 19 November 1832, quoted from *Letters of Thomas Carlyle to John Stuart Mill, John Sterling and Robert Browning*, ed. A. Carlyle (London, 1923), 26.

hindsight, for the struggles belong to the 1820s, while *Sartor* was conceived in the early 1830s. What actually lay at the root of the agonies, as the letters make clear, was the separation from the religious community of the Ecclefechan Seceders. First his parents found out about his reluctance to accept the tenets of their faith unquestioningly, especially before he learned to guard his tongue. Innocent questions concerning the miracles met with shock and horror and a sense of family guilt rather like that felt by Robert Louis Stevenson when his freethinking caused a major quarrel with his parents. There was, fortunately, no major quarrel in the case of the Carlyles. After Carlyle's public decision not to enter the ministry,

> I told my Father and they [his parents] were much grieved; it must have been a sore distress to them, but they bore it nobly – and my Father said to me that notwithstanding, his house would always be a home to me and that no one in that house should ever speak or act with severity towards me on account of what I had done.[39]

This was a major decision so far as Carlyle's religious thinking was concerned. Carlyle had rapidly weakened in his religious studies as his reading corroded his simple faith,[40] and as he came into contact with a professoriate who were, in general, successful Moderate city ministers and, in the strongest possible contrast to the saintlike Johnston of Ecclefechan, worldly successful men, and, unfortunately, poor teachers. This had the double effect of repelling Carlyle from the university's Divinity Hall and from the Moderates. Divinity Hall held absolutely no interest for him, as letters home show.

> I have not been within its walls for many months – & I know not whether I shall ever return, but all accounts agree in, representing it as one of the most melancholy & unprofitable corporations, that has appeared in these parts for a great while. . . It may safely be asserted that tho' the Drs Ritchie junior and senior [41] with Dr Meiklejohn, Dr Brunton & Dr Brown were to continue in their chairs, dosing in their

---

[39] Campbell, 'Portrait of Carlyle'.
[40] I have tried to illustrate this process briefly in 'Carlyle's Borrowings from the Theological Library of Edinburgh University', *The Bibliotheck*, 5, 5 (1969), 165–8.
[41] That is, Professors of Logic and Divinity respectively.

present fashion, for a century, all the knowledge which they could discover, would be an imperceptible quantity – if indeed it sign [sic] were not negative.[42]

Soon afterwards, when he called to enrol for another year's divinity study, the professor happened to be out and 'my instant feeling was, "Very good, then, very good; let this be finis in the matter." And it really was.'[43] One small detail has never been noticed: Carlyle could have attended the Burgher Divinity Hall, but instead went to the Edinburgh one of the Established Church. There is no obvious reason for this, but an indirect piece of evidence might be that Burgher entrants were expected to have passed not only a full arts curriculum, 'but . . . to possess a competent knowledge of Hebrew',[44] Carlyle did not do then, or ever – certainly in Annandale only one man spoke Hebrew at this time to Carlyle's knowledge, and that was Johnston in Ecclefechan.[45]

*

The break with Divinity Hall was final, but fortunately there was no family break. Carlyle's most intimate friend at the time was Edward Irving, himself a parishioner of Johnston, whom he had walked from Annan to hear every Sunday. Irving at this time was teaching, preparing for his licensing and ordination; he took Carlyle to church frequently, and the two talked freely and easily on religious matters; one day, 'just as the sun was sinking, [Irving] actually drew from me by degrees, in the softest manner, the confession that I did *not* think as he of the Christian Religion, and that it was vain for me to expect I ever could or should. This, if this were so, he had pre-engaged to take *well* of me, – like an elder brother, if I would be frank with him; – and right loyally he did so, and to the end of his life we needed no concealments on that head.'[46] Both his family and Irving showed extraordinary good

---

[42] Thomas Carlyle to Robert Murray, 31 March 1817, manuscript in Arched House, Ecclefechan, published in *Collected Letters*, i, 98.

[43] Quoted from a conversation between Thomas Carlyle and David Masson, in D. Masson, *Edinburgh Sketches and Memories* (Edinburgh, 1892), 262.

[44] Scott, *Annals of the Secession Church*, 604.

[45] This fact is explicitly noted by Carlyle in his commentary to Althaus' 1866 biographical article, 'Thomas Carlyle', in *Unsere Zeit*, Leipzig, 1866, preserved in the National Library of Scotland, MS. 1799.

[46] Carlyle, *Reminiscences*, 261.

sense and good principle in their treatment of Carlyle's lapse from childhood faith; he retained a warm affection for their Church, and also an important respect for its values. Years later he could listen to the sound of the bell of Hoddam Kirk and find it 'strangely touching – like the departing voice of eighteen hundred years'. The result was that all his life Carlyle retained respect for the Scottish Church in all its branches as well as for those members who still attended a form of worship that he personally could not accept. The scorn he liberally poured on the 'Hebrew Old Clothes' in his later writings was never directed at the Seceder Church, rarely indeed even at the Established Church of Scotland. Generations of diarists and autobiographers testify to Carlyle's warm tributes to the peasantry of his childhood religious community, and the strength (and value) of their Church and its principles. He retained the strong anti-Prelatic prejudice of the Seceders,[47] the strong conviction that a reinfusion of the Holy Spirit into the Church was necessary, which the Ecclefechan congregation certainly believed as a central tenet.[48] Carlyle followed the fortunes of the Seceders with interest; in May 1821, after their union, he wrote to his mother that he rejoiced to see 'so many worthy characters – casting off the old man – laying down their miserable squabbles – and uniting in the good cause with all their heart'.[49] He joined heartily in their theological conservatism, protesting against modernising translations of the Bible, the 'grand old Book, crammed full of all manner of practical wisdom and sublimity – a veritable and articulately divine message for the Heavenward guidance of man'. He could not accept the idea of a new version, '... his whole *feeling* went sorely against the altering of a single word or phrase, for he liked to use the very words his mother had taught him; and that dear old association should be undisturbed'.[50] The people behind the legend, equally,

[47] Carlyle admitted this in 1852: see C. and F. Brookfield, *Mrs Brookfield and her Circle* (London, 1906), 387.

[48] Edward Irving had given this impression strongly to Coleridge; this is reported in T. Brash, *Thomas Carlyle's Double-Goer, and his Connection with the Parish of Row* (Helensburgh [1904]).

[49] Thomas Carlyle to Margaret Aitken Carlyle, [?] 4 May 1821, *Collected Letters*, i, 357.

[50] A. J. Symington, *Some Personal Reminiscences of Carlyle* (London, 1886), 32.

were to be remembered intact, not modernised. One hearer heard Carlyle tirade against universities, parliaments, 'orthodox theologies, railroads and free trade – ', all dismissed as 'sham'; 'while Oliver Cromwell and his Ironsides and the Old Covenanters who sang psalms and handled pikes on Dunse Moor, were held up to admiration as the only heroes in this country for the last two hundred years'.[51]

In this Carlyle is completely in agreement with Irving; it is quite possible that his feelings date from early discussions between the two men. 'No man bred in towns', wrote Irving, 'can comprehend the nature of a Scottish peasant's prayer, and the martyr-wildness of their psalmody.' Nothing, Irving went on to assert, he had heard in churches and cathedrals (and he must have heard Chalmers many times in Glasgow, while he was his assistant), came near to the prayers of the simple in their 'smoky cottages'.[52] Elsewhere, too, Irving said he would prefer these to the 'learned of the land'.[53] Irving liked in his preaching to 'strike a chord in the hearts of his hearers by touchingly alluding to covenanting times'.[54] Hazlitt tried to mock Irving, saying he wished to 'reduce the British metropolis to a Scottish heath, with a few miserable hovels upon it, where they may worship God according to the *root of the Matter*'.[55] But Irving was serious, and so was Carlyle. This, to him, was what the age required, a reassertion of the humble religious values of the Secession Church he had known in his youth.

*

The break with organised religious teaching, then, did not signalise a break with the Secession. Carlyle had the good fortune to remain in the community of the Church. He also had the friendship of Irving. His personal faith, however, as critics have made clear,

[51] A. M. Stodart, *John Stuart Blackie: A Biography* (Edinburgh and London, 1895), i, 242.

[52] E. Irving, *Collected Writings*, ed. G. Carlyle (London, 1865), iii, 223.

[53] E. Irving, *Babylon and Infidelity Foredoomed of God: A Discourse on the Prophecies of Daniel and the Apocalypse* (Glasgow, 1826), ii, 383.

[54] J. Dodds, *Personal Reminiscences and Biographical Sketches* (Edinburgh, 1888), 40. Irving's enthusiasm for the Covenanters is illustrated by his having contributed 'A Tale of the Martyrs' to the *Dumfries Literary Gleaner* (Dumfries, 1830), 328–35.

[55] W. Hazlitt, *The Spirit of the Age: or Contemporary Portraits* (London, 1825), 91.

was a complex amalgam of Scottish and German sources,[56] very different from the faith he lost in 1816 onwards. By *Sartor Resartus*, in the early 1830s, Carlyle had compounded a new faith, the 'Everlasting YEA', from Goethe's writings, from many other Germans, from some still half-held tenets of belief from the Seceders, notably the duty to work, to accept the place allotted to the Universe. But they had become half unrecognisable in a tapestry woven from many complex foreign strands.

Carlyle revisted Ecclefechan many times;[57] he often spoke with gratitude of its religious education, and with admiration of its religious people. Yet in later life he never moved back to its Church. The Secession belongs to Carlyle's early life; his mature faith belongs to a much wider world of experience and incorporates elements widely divergent from the relatively simple (and unforced) beliefs of Ecclefechan. The early admiration, we have seen, consisted largely of an admiration for figures – family, pastor, schoolteacher – even Irving. Irving, as the 1820s progressed, became alienated from Carlyle, who finally gave him up for mad after a serious attempt to talk him out of the two heresies which were to lead to his expulsion from the Scotch Church in London – his heretical beliefs concerning the human form and fallibility of Christ, and his wholehearted support of the 'Gift of Tongues'. Although Carlyle tried hard to reason him out of this,[58] and wrote an eloquent tribute to him after Irving died,[59] this was *finis* to any possible

---

[56] There is much relevant material in G. B. Tennyson, *SARTOR called RESARTUS* (Princeton, 1965). See also 'Carlyle's Religion: The Scottish Sources', in *Carlyle and his Contemporaries: Essays in Honor of Charles Richard Sanders*, ed. J. Clubbe (Durham, NC, 1976), 3–20 and 'The Scottishness of Carlyle', *Carlyle Studies Annual*, Special Issue, 17 (Normal, IL, 1997), 73–82. For a larger discussion of Carlyle's life and thought, see I. Campbell, *Thomas Carlyle* (London, 1974; rev. edn, Edinburgh, 1993).

[57] See, for instance, '"A Mass of Memorandums": Carlyle's Last Visit to Scotland Recorded', *Carlyle Newsletter*, 5 (1984), 42–5.

[58] Carlyle, *Reminiscences*, 340.

[59] 'Death of Edward Irving', in Carlyle's *Critical and Miscellanies Essays* (London, 1857), iii, 297–300. An interesting recent find is an unfinished passage of fiction by Carlyle plainly based on his experiences with Irving, particularly those relating to their spiritual discussions and Carlyle's own religious doubts: see the published version of the manuscript (now in the National Library of Scotland) as '*Peter Lithgow*: New Fiction by Thomas Carlyle', *Studies in Scottish Literature*, xxix (1996), 1–13.

reconnection with the Secession via Irving. Although, obviously, both men had many ideas in common, they were poles apart in their total world-view. Irving was a dedicated minister of the Church, Carlyle a lone individualist who tried to preach to others a doctrine involving self-education and self-perfection, whereas Irving sought to reanimate a national Church to make this possible. Irving did not call Carlyle back to the Seceders, and the other figures largely died off. The Moderates no more attracted Carlyle – particularly in the *Burns* essay Carlyle expresses a contempt for moderatism in any form, but above all in religious matters. The Seceders, as Professor Henderson has noted, 'represented a type that was particularly unhappy and impatient in the company of the Moderates',[60] and Carlyle was no exception. 'Hushing new voices of the Church', writes another historian of the Moderates, 'they fed the secessions and, fearing ecclesiastical innovations, they fell behind the times.'[61] Precisely – this is what Carlyle disliked and attacked in the Moderates. They had fallen behind the times, they belonged to an eighteenth century of enlightenment which, generally speaking, Carlyle detested for its deadening effect on men's spiritual development – to Carlyle the Age of Enlightenment was an age of stultifying scepticism and doubt. Hence his attack in the *Burns* essay on the Moderate clergy of Edinburgh and Ayrshire, who taught Burns more than he needed to know – taught him to mingle religious austerity with artistic pleasure and so destroyed his simple faith. Carlyle disliked this, and disliked the Moderate clergy of the Established Church he met in Edinburgh. Deprived of a living tradition which Irving might have represented, and repelled from a Moderate tradition he considered dying or dead, Carlyle turned to the memory of the Seceders of Ecclefechan, and in a world of change, religious, social and political, he preached to a respectful (but unresponsive) world the necessity of a revival to such standards of life and behaviour. It was a glowing ideal, but one the world of Victorian Britain did not accept. And so, as the century progressed, Carlyle saw the Secession Church more and more in a historical view, as remote but wonderful, belonging to a golden age to which there is no return. After recalling the

---

[60] G. D. Henderson, *The Church of Scotland* (Edinburgh, 1939), 106.
[61] J. T. McNeill, *The History and Character of Calvinism* (New York, 1954), 358.

Church of his youth in the *Reminiscences,* he notes sadly that 'all this is altered utterly at present, I grieve to say; and gone to as good as nothing or worse'.

It began to alter just about that period, on the death of those old hoary Heads; and has gone on with increasing velocity ever since. Irving and I were probably among the last products it delivered before gliding off, and then rushing off, into self-consciousness, arrogancy, insincerity, jangle and vulgarity, which I fear are now very much the definition of it.

Between them and him, a gulf was fixed. Across the gulf, ineffacably, stood the memory of his father.

He was never visited with Doubt; the old Theorem of the Universe was sufficient for him, and he worked well in it, and in all senses successfully and wisely as few now can do; so quick is the motion of Transition becoming: the new generation almost to a man must make 'their Belly their God', and alas even find that an empty one. Thus curiously enough, and blessedly, *he* stood a true man on the verge of the Old; while his son stands here lovingly surveying him on the verge of the New, and sees the possibility of also being true there. God make the possibility, blessed possibility, into a reality![62]

However much he yearned for his father's stable faith and quiet confidence – and obviously he did yearn – he saw that it was not possible for him in the new century. And so his father's memory, and that of the Seceders of Ecclefechan, remains as a sort of backdrop to Carlyle's teaching, not, as many critics would have it, as the 'inherited Calvinism' of his boyhood, but as a distant ideal, separated from real present-day life by an impassable gulf. Carlyle sees both the ideal and the gulf; his religious teaching to the nineteenth century might be in part defined as recommending the ideal and seeking to bridge the gulf.[63]

---

[62] Carlyle, *Reminiscences,* 7, 208–9.

[63] This is a revised and updated version of a paper first published as 'Carlyle and the Secession', *Records of the Scottish Church History Society,* 18, 1 (1972), 48–64. The original paper could not have happened without the encouragement and help of the late A. Ian Dunlop. And for interest, friendship, guidance and critical encouragement, no thanks to Alec Cheyne could be too many.

Chapter 2

A Carlylean Elegy in Auchtertool Kirkyard

Kenneth J. Fielding

A problem in writing about Carlyle and his beliefs is that everyone knows what they were. He was 'a Calvinist'.[1] He may have practically never attended a church, believed Christ to be no more than a man, made many pungent remarks about Christianity and its ministers, and have been the butt of his friends who asked what the devil his religion was. Yet there were those who really knew better. One of them was the rationalist historian William Lecky, who had long talks with him in his old age, and said that he was perfectly clear. Though once 'fully orthodox' Carlyle believed that Christ was 'most authentically human . . . a poor & noble teacher but nothing more'. Christianity 'as to revelation "vanished" as he said "into thin air"'. Gibbon's *Decline and Fall*, which he had read at Kirkcaldy in 1817, had sent 'a burning arrow through' his heart. No doubt all this is true. Yet

---

[1] This over-simplifies a common assumption or implication, but see, for example, C. H. Harrold, 'The Nature of Carlyle's Calvinism', *Studies in Philology*, 33 (1936), 475–86, or A. A. Ikeler, *Puritan Temper and Transcendental Faith, Carlyle's Literary Vision* (Columbus, OH, 1972). Carlyle's contemporaries often had a clearer grasp; see especially, John Tulloch, *Movements of Religious Thought in Britain in the Nineteenth Century*, 1885, republished with an introduction by A. C. Cheyne, Victorian Library, Leicester University Press, 1971. With all his admiration for Carlyle, Tulloch is clear that Carlyle respected Calvinism not because 'it was a great intellectual or theological phenomenon, with a continuous historical life of its own', but as 'the faith of his father and mother' (1971, p. 201), and that he was evidently not a Christian.

37

there are various aspects to Carlyle, to be found at different times, in other places, and in different moods. Lecky himself found this as well as he talked his way on walks round London with his friend; and while he could persuade Carlyle in old age to read the Old Testament he could not get him to look at the New, though 'a religious mind, life, or character he valued beyond all others'.[2] Men and women sought Carlyle out because they saw his sincerity and felt his unexpectedness.

Two or three aspects which help to account for his representativeness at his time have recently struck me in editing the *Carlyle Letters*, all from more-or-less fresh sources. One was Lecky's extensive and largely unused notes of their conversation, which have been left untouched since his widow, Elizabeth, drew on them for her memoir of her husband. The second comes from paying a visit to Auchtertool Kirk in Fife, so easy to reach and seemingly remote in the past.[3] This was the charge held for forty-seven years by Jane Carlyle's nephew, the unmarried Rev. Walter Welsh, occupying its enormous and attractive Tudor-style manse, which his aunt and her husband often visited, and where they found something they felt they had lost in London. The third was the discovery of an entirely unknown and unrecognised tribute to the agnostic Carlyle paid by his friend Thackeray. It appeared anonymously in a review of Carlyle's *The Life of John Sterling* which had been published in October 1851 in the weekly *Leader*. It has not only been completely unknown until now, but in its place an entirely different, savagely back-biting, bitter, and hypocritical review in *The Times* had been confidently said to be Thackeray's on the foolish passing word of his daughter Lady Ritchie. I have written at some length about this elsewhere, pointing out how it highlights Carlyle's sceptical independence, and how widely this was shared by many others at the time. Yet though this is unlikely

---

[2] W. H. Lecky's notes are mixed up with much else among his largely unindexed papers in Trinity College Library, Dublin, to the authorities of which thanks are due for permission to consult and quote.

[3] I am grateful to the Rev. George Cowie, the present minister, for being able to see the church, for kind help from Mrs MacDonald and am greatly indebted in the article, to William Stevenson, *The Kirk and Parish of Auchtertool* (Kirkcaldy, 1909); there are thanks due to others for whom, as Carlyle writes, 'we went to Aberdour in Fife'. See also the *Reminiscences* (1997), 195–6.

to be read by any but the purest Carlyleans and Thackerayans, the details can be skipped over lightly.[4]

The point of bringing the three aspects together is to suggest that as well as there still being much to discover about the major Victorians, we might almost agree with Nietzsche that Carlyle was in fact an 'atheist' without being willing, or with the courage, to admit it.[5] Yet this is where his influence lay. He was able to reconcile the wish to believe in the divine while rejecting what was plainly incredible; and, by the mid-century, he came to it without sheltering in the fantasy of *Sartor* or a certain double talk in other works. At the same time, he rightly reckoned himself a man of piety. Certainly the setting of the church at Auchtertool is evocative. It is to be found across the Forth Bridge from Edinburgh, almost three miles from Kirkcaldy, and three-quarters of a mile from the village. The kirk is approached by little more than a long lane, set back, hidden by tall beeches and elms, with a commanding view from the crest of a hill looking east to the Firth, the Isle of May, the Bass Rock and North Berwick Law; and legend even once had it that part of *The French Revolution* was anachronistically written at the manse because it mentions a little hilltop kirk, with the dead 'slumbering round it under their memorial stones'. In fact all that we may authentically rediscover of Carlyle is, first, a path in the manse garden once called Carlyle's Walk, then there is an actual if unlikely tale that he once took a child by the hand and gently led her round the garden; and another story about a somewhat unspecified dinner-table quarrel with a local clergyman. But, lastly, there is a more characteristic anecdote of his behaviour in the little church. He is said to have once slowly wandered in to hear the sermon, sat down in the manse pew, listened to the sense of it, and left perhaps reasonably enough before the service was over, – without waiting for the collection.[6] It probably happened later in life: an improvement on his

---

[4] Forthcoming in *Victorian Literature and Culture* as 'Thackeray and "The Great Master of Craigenputtoch": A New Review of *The Life of John Sterling* – and a New Understanding'. The review appeared in the weekly *Leader*, 8 November 1851; the wrongly-ascribed piece in *The Times* was 1 November.

[5] 'Basically Carlyle is an English atheist who makes it a point of honour not to be one', *Gotzen-Dammerung* (Turin, 1888).

[6] Stevenson, *The Kirk and Parish of Auchtertool*, 114.

behaviour as he groaned aloud throughout the sermon, when Froude tried to enliven him in London by taking him to Westminster Abbey.[7]

The surroundings of the kirk are quietly impressive: the kirkyard with its ponderous old seventeenth-century table tombstones (for 'the rude forefathers of the hamlet'), with behind it the splendid former manse and large garden laid out 'according to the idea' of Jane's uncle, John Welsh, and now in private hands.[8] In the distance is Kirkcaldy, where Carlyle had been a schoolteacher in 1816–1818 following Edward Irving, and Humbie Farm is a little to the east, where he and Jane escaped in the summer of 1858.[9] They meant to 'bathe and loiter in the woods', Jane sauntering on a horse or donkey led by the bridle, and Carlyle galloping through the district on his favourite Fritz. He told his brother Alexander in Canada that he had ridden up Kirk Wynd in Kirkcaldy to look again at where they had both once stayed, and how he had called on the corpulent provost Peter Swan, once 'a little black-eyed boy', and found the town 'all new paved, old Jail quite swept away; screaming with railways etc'. He wrote to a friend John Forster wishing for his company 'among the silent Hills and Valleys, by the shore of the beautifullest sea in the world'; and he told another how Fritz was

astonished beyond measure at the new phenomena of nature here, the sea waves, the precipitous stony paths, the *cows* almost most of all. It is one of the finest *scenes* I ever saw in the world: woody airy Hills (mostly made of trap rock, & very well cultivated); ours is a Farm House mounted on a Knoll of its own, and looking far over the Forth and its Islands (Inch-Colm has a monastery on it) and its steamers & ships special and miscellaneous, with Edinb. 10 miles off on the other side ... 'like a scene in the theatre', varying in its aspect from hour to hour; truly I question whether the Bay of Naples is prettier on a fine day.... I try to be solitary.... But

---

[7] See Froude, (1882), 4:451; the visit came after a more successful one to St Paul's, when Carlyle could not follow the service so easily and enjoyed the music without the preaching.

[8] Stevenson, *The Kirk and Parish of Auchtertool*, 109.

[9] The Carlyles stayed at Humbie on the upper floor of the farmhouse, 'a rough uncomfortable place', for six weeks, five more at Auchtertool House, a 'big vacant mansion' (now occupied), and perhaps for a while at the manse, fifteen minutes walk away (Marrs, 732–3).

the ground itself is eloquent to me, with memories of 40 years back and more; I find old friendly faces still extant too, tho in small number.

Yet the close connection with Fife has never been counted as part of *The Carlyle Country* (as J. M. Sloan's book has it),[10] though often visited over this period, and with many other associations.[11]

On this visit they stayed close to Auchtertool Manse and Church where they had often been before. There do not now seem to be any available family papers, but we can see that the Rev. Walter Welsh's long ministry there may well have come from his and his father's strong desire to resettle in Scotland, not unlike Jane Carlyle's deep feeling for her birthplace in Haddington. For Jane's most memorable piece of writing, 'Much Ado about Nothing', is her account of her return after about thirty years to Haddington and scenes of her childhood;[12] and there was her profound emotion about Templand where her mother had died, so strong that when she revisited, her friend Mrs Russell would not give her a bedroom with a view of the old home. It was hardly weaker with Thomas, who speaks of Scotland as like Hades, peopled by shadows of memory. Each was accordingly to select an appropriate burial-place or memorial: Jane with her father in Haddington, her mother with her family at Crawford, her uncle John Welsh with his family in Liverpool though memorialised at Auchtertool, and Thomas rejecting the prospect of Westminster Abbey to be buried with his kin at Ecclefechan. For, whatever else they professed, they all showed that their religion was rooted in place, family, and familiar ways, and so almost necessarily connected with their final resting-places and their church and its rituals in birth, marriage, and particularly death.

In a corner of the Auchtertool Kirkyard lie graves of some of Jane's family: Walter Welsh, and presumably his sister Helen, and

[10] J. Sloan, *The Carlyle Country* (London, 1904).

[11] Carlyle maintained his connections through John Fergus and his family at Kirkcaldy, including their close friend, his sister Elizabeth, Countess Pepoli; John was the local MP. He kept in touch with other friends, and through 'Kirkcaldy Helen', the witty, loved, innocent-hearted, alcoholic, suicidal servant they recruited after they were in London when they must have felt that Kirkcaldy almost colonised Cheyne Row. She was with them 1837–49, with a short break. Carlyle wrote that her death was 'like a thing of fate'.

[12] *Collected Letters*, 24:159–71, and much reprinted.

the monument to their father, Jane's beloved uncle John Welsh. There they are crowded 'as near to the manse as it was possible to lay them', 'their graves still covered in spring' with snowdrops.[13] Walter's heavy gravestone is twinned with another like it, that has fallen face down; and this is presumably the one spoken of as erected in memory of his father probably also recording the burial of his daughter (Walter's sister) Helen. They were Jane's family rather than her husband's, but the tale of the connection as told in the Carlyles' letters, and the remote setting in time and place, evoke both their own and other aspects of Victorian religious life. We may easily recall Gray's *Elegy*, an echo of it quoted in Carlyle's *Reminiscences* (the 'short and simple annals'), or its occupants casting 'one longing ling'ring look behind', and even Carlyle's elegiac *Life of John Sterling*. As with Sterling's biography, Gray's poem, Carlyle's memories, and even the two Carlyles' endless letters, we may think of them as bound up with a religion of affection and piety rooted in place, family and conduct.

Walter Welsh is remembered by a tablet in the church, which says that it is sacred to the memory of:

THE REVEREND WALTER WELSH
ORDAINED MINISTER OF THIS PARISH
AND AT HIS DEATH
FATHER OF THE PRESBYTERY
A LEARNED DIVINE
A WISE COUNSELLOR
LOVED AND REVERED BY HIS FRIENDS,
A GENIAL AND INSTRUCTIVE COMPANION,
AND ALL EXEMPLARY IN HIS LIFE;
HE LIVED IN HONOUR AMONGST MEN,
AND DIED LAMENTED
ON THE 17TH DAY OF DECEMBER 1879
AGED 64 YEARS.

It is perhaps too involved to trace the family connections in detail. What it comes to is that the Rev. Walter Welsh was Jane Carlyle's cousin because he was the son of her mother's brother Uncle John. Their father had been Walter Welsh of Templand, near Thornhill, Dumfriesshire, vividly described in Thomas Carlyle's *Reminiscences*. Early in life, as one of a large family,

[13] Stevenson, *The Kirk and Parish of Auchtertool*, 142.

John Welsh had set out for a business career in Liverpool, where he made, lost and remade a considerable living in brass and copper founding. But his eldest of several sons, the physically lamed Walter, was enlisted in the church, licensed to preach at Penpont (near the family's old home) and in 1842 somehow came to be presented by the Earl of Moray as assistant and designated successor to the Rev. David Guild at Auchtertool.

Obviously this had his father's backing, and no doubt he helped with what Jane Carlyle was to call Walter's 'poor little stipend', of just over £200 a year, which would otherwise have been 'dreadfully perplexed to meet all the demands his munificent spirit' was to make on it. For 'dusty, sooty, ever noisy Liverpool', as Carlyle wrote, had not been John Welsh's 'element, few men's less, . . . but his heart and all his pleasant memories and thoughts were in the breezy Hills of Moffatdale'. All this he had greatly suppressed except for once bursting 'into brief fiery recognition . . . in his own drawingroom . . . with memorable emphasis and fury'.[14] Hence his delight in helping his son in his new home, which he was able to visit until he died there in 1853, and thus his association with the church where he is remembered by the memorial in the kirkyard though buried, with other members of the family, in Liverpool at the Old Street Church of Scotland.

It was Jane Carlyle's deep affection for her uncle as well as her liking for Walter that drew her to Auchtertool. He had called on them at Cheyne Row soon after his appointment as assistant, when Jane wrote to his sister Jeannie 'Do you know I find him far more intelligent and agreeable away from all you young ones.' Though staying late, he had not bored them: 'And Carlyle too thinks him "*not* at all a bad fellow! *not* at all without sense" which means in his dialect what Pepoli in *his* would call "*un angelo di bonta*" – and "PIENO PIENO *d'ingegno*"', – or an angel of goodness, full of intelligence.[15] The attachment stood the strain of family differences, so that she could write to Thomas in 1862, 'After all I have no kinder relative or friend than poor Walter. Every summer, when invitations were not so plenty, his house and all that is his,

[14] T. Carlyle, *Reminiscences, A New and Complete Edition*, ed. K. J. Fielding and I. Campbell (Oxford, 1997), 132–3.

[15] T. Carlyle and J. Welsh Carlyle, *Collected Letters of Thomas and Jane Welsh Carlyle*, ed. C. R. Sanders, C. Ryals, K. J. Fielding, I. Campbell, A. Christianson and others, 27 vols., ongoing (Durham, NC 1970–), 16:12.

have been placed at my disposal. It is the only house where I could go, without an invitation, at any time that suited myself.' Just as in 1856, after both Carlyles had been there, she was ready to have 'never done thanking heaven for the freshness and cleanness, and quietness into which I have been plumped down; and for my astonishingly comfortable bed, and the astonishing kindness and good humour that wrap me about like an eider-down quilt! . . . Of course I am sad at times, at all times sad as death, but that I am used to, and don't mind.'[16]

Yet at first Jane had kept away from Scotland because it reminded her of the devastating loss of her mother in 1842; so that it was not until August 1849 that she accepted an invitation to the manse after first paying the 'Much Ado' visit to Haddington entirely on her own. Even then she hardly felt up to staying at the same time as other summer visitors, sisters, various in-laws, and nieces and nephews: 'Breakfast at ten – dinner nearer seven than six – "dandering Individuals" constantly dropping in – *dressings* and undressings world without end! all that is so wholly out of place in a Scotch manse! – and then the chitter-chatter!' – not helped by trying to understand her uncle when he had lost his teeth.[17]

She does not mention church-going, usually refused in spite of her uncle's disapproval, but describes the marriage of a collier, caught because Walter conducted it in his study when she happened to be present. The 'girl had one *very* large inflamed eye', and her partner 'a glass too much to keep his heart up'. Walter married them '*very well indeed*, and his affecting words, together with the Bridegroom's pale excited face and the Bride's *ugliness*, and the "poverty needcessity and want" imprinted on the whole business – and above all fellow-feeling with the poor wretches there rushing on their fate – all so overcame me that I fell a-crying as desperately as if I had been getting married to the Collier myself'. She shook hands with them, presented them with the snuff-box she had meant to give Walter, and so infected her cousin with her generosity that he gave the bride a new Bible. Jane Carlyle's love for her neighbour comes out in this 'fellow feeling', and as she notes in the grateful collier's cry, '"May ye hae mair comfort and

---

[16] J. Welsh Carlyle, *Letters and Memorials of Jane Welsh Carlyle*, 3 vols (London, 1883), iii, 120; ii, 280.
[17] *Collected Letters*, 24:178.

pleasure in your life than ever you have had yet"! Which might easily be! – '.[18]

If one is merely thinking of 'the Carlyle Country', there is much more in the associations of the Carlyles with the manse, the district, and the kingdom of Fife to dwell on. Little is to be found in most accounts of their later lives, which sail past almost everything but the Edinburgh Rectorship; but Jane Carlyle's letters about her visits in the 1850s and 1860s give a detailed account or references to her bathing at Kirkcaldy, shopping in Aberdour, an interest in the manse garden, vivid family interchanges, catering in the hot summer, and encounters with old Kirkcaldy friends such as Provost William Swan. She met him at Auchtertool House, she told Thomas, and made him 'a pretty little speech about your enduring remembrance of his father's and mother's kindness to you, on which account I begged to shake hands with him, which had the greatest success'. He had to be dined at the manse, and given the 'treasure' of her husband's photograph, though, 'So fat a man one rarely sees.' He was followed by another member of his family, Peter, also dutifully dined. Yet they remind us how Carlyle's connections went back to his first venture into life outside Dumfriesshire and Edinburgh, and to his 'first love' for the 'poorish proud and well-bred' Margaret Gordon of Kirkcaldy, who was to be transformed into Blumine of Sartor. She was 'the cleverest and brightest' of those he then knew of 'the Kirkcaldy population, . . . a pleasant honest kind of fellow-mortals . . . of good old Scotch in their works and ways; more *vernacular*, peaceably fixed, and almost genial in their mode of life than I had been used to in the Border home-land. Fife generally we liked', and 'We, I in particular, always rather liked the people.'[19] They were happy to return.

Yet, Jane cannot have been an easy guest at the manse. On later summer holidays she would arrive at Auchtertool, taut nerves fluttering in ribbons, anxious to enjoy its peace, though her female cousins strained to dine, dress up, and entertain, and – if they were not resisted – to fuss. She was thrust into the silent conflict between the ideals of the manse and those of ordinary country society. Walter might be exempt from this and allowed to follow

[18] Ibid., 24:178.
[19] *Reminiscences*, 238–40.

his calling; but one sister (Maggie) had to exert herself to run the manse, while another (Jeannie) was so outrageous as to arrive with a baby and two six-foot nursemaids; and, as members of a large and increasing family, perhaps none of them had the time – if the disposition – to mourn their father, her uncle, mainly remembered in his kirkyard corner, nor their elder sister Helen who lay beside him.

For it had been to Helen that she had written in 1853 on the death of her

> beloved uncle, all that remained to me of my mother, a braver, more upright, more generous-hearted man never lived. . . . It was well he should die thus, gently and beautifully, with all his loving kindness fresh as a young man's; his enjoyment of life not wearied out; all our love for him as warm as ever; and well he should die in his own dear Scotland, amid quiet kindly things. . . . To know that kind, good uncle was in the world for me, to care about me . . . was a sweetness in my lonely life, which can be ill-spared.[20]

Helen died a few months later.

Thomas was affected by the news of John Welsh's death, reporting to his sister:

> Last night we got a sad shock, by the evening Postman; which fell heaviest on my poor Jane, and might as readily on me: the Death of her Uncle at Auchtertool! He seems to have grown ill on Sabbath last, being very weak and lame before; he grew rapidly worse; gave them all his blessing and farewell about 3 in the afternoon; and sank after the . . . kind of sleep, which at 10 had deepened into death. Of course they are all in deep distress, some of them in Liverpool, some on visits elsewhere: poor Helen writes without *dating*. As to Jane here, she has *spoken* little since; and is very sad and low indeed, poor soul; sitting down stairs, making up mournings I can see; refusing to go out any whither. He was a good, brave, and honest and kindhearted man, this Uncle that is gone; the last of all her kindred too, in some measure: so that it is as if the old things had come up upon her again. What can we do? What can we do? Nothing, – except, as it is said, 'Kiss the rod'; and confess that One is sovereign over us, and that His Will is our law. Oh dear, Oh dear![21]

---

[20] *Letters and Memorials of Jane Welsh Carlyle*, ii, 234.

[21] National Library of Scotland MS.: 515.54, 12 October 1853, with grateful acknowledgement for access and assistance. Walter's death certificate confirms that he died in the manse on the morning of 17 December, son of 'John Welsh

Years later, writing from Auchtertool to Mary Russell (8 September 1862), just after the tribute to Walter's kindness, Jane speaks of her cousins'

> naturally hospitable and kindly natures . . . still I miss that congeniality which comes of having mutually suffered, and taken one's suffering to heart! I feel here as if I were 'playing' with nice, pretty, well-behaved children! I almost envy them their light-hearted capacity of being engrossed with trifles! And yet, not that! There is a deeper joy in one's own sorrowful memories surely, than this gaiety that comes of 'never minding'! Would I, would you, cease to regret the dear ones we have lost if we could? . . . Oh no! better ever such grief for the lost, than never to have loved anyone enough to have one's equanimity disturbed by the loss![22]

In its way this is little different from the *Worship of Sorrow* expounded in *Sartor Resartus*, in 'The Everlasting Yea' (Book II, chapter 9), which derived from Goethe's *Wilhelm Meister*, which is said to look back to 'blessed are they that mourn'. And more might be made of this conjunction of elegiac sorrow in the face of death, and its power to awaken a sense of eternity, the passage of time, of love, regret, and the irretrievability of the past. We can see from later letters and Carlyle's *Reminiscences* how sharply yet tenderly he was aware of this on Jane Carlyle's death. Soon after it he realised how, on many of her visits to Scotland, she had made a special point of calling to see her old widowed nurse, Betty Braid, in Edinburgh. No doubt at first for Jane's sake, their friend Thomas Erskine of Linlathen, the curious and saintly theologian and confidant of upper-class families in Scotland, went on calling on Betty, and wrote to Carlyle that instead of wanting to be anyone like his 'weary Fritz' (or Frederick the Great) 'I would much rather be honest Mrs. Braid selling flour and bacon, and lovingly bearing the burden of her bedrid son.' Carlyle wrote Erskine his sincere thanks:

> The world has not many shrines to a devout man at present, and perhaps in our own section of it there are few objects holding more authentically of Heaven. . . . The love of human creatures, one to

---

Copper Merchant and Mary Welsh m.s. Robertson'; with grateful acknowledgement to Mrs Diana Howden.

[22] *Letters and Memorials of Jane Welsh Carlyle*, iii, 121–2.

another, where it is true and unchangeable, often strikes me as a strange fact in their poor history, a kind of perpetual Gospel, revealing itself in them . . . the heart and mother of all that can in any way enoble their otherwise mean and contemptible existence in this world.

It is a side of Carlyle that we are not often allowed to see. Carlyle called on old Betty himself later in the year, 'his only other visit in Scotland', apart from consulting the famous surgeon Professor James Syme. She seemed well enough, but, if otherwise, Erskine was gently told, he should know that further 'help . . . would be a sacred duty to me'. That is to say that Carlyle himself was a man of tender compassion, by no means to be characterised solely by his vehemence and worship of power. Such affections were sacred to him in human terms, as such intimate friends as Robert Browning or Thomas Erskine recognised.

For Thomas Erskine was closely drawn to his great friend Thomas Carlyle, saying of him, 'I love the man . . . he has a real belief in the invisible, which, in these railroad and steam-engine days, is a great matter.' They agreed in believing, as Erskine wrote, that 'the inward revelation in conscience makes us independent of the outward revelation', and that 'outward' belief must be learned from inward.[23] This is at the heart of their agreement. One recalls the evangelistic Prussian ambassador C. J. K. Bunsen's pride in the completion or restoration of Cologne Cathedral, and Carlyle's dismissive 'It is a very fine pagoda, if ye could get any sort of God to put in it.'[24] In return, as John Tulloch says, Carlyle 'might well love Erskine', for he had a warm place always 'in Erskine's heart, who mourned for his unhappiness as if he had been a brother'.[25]

Yet Erskine was probably disturbed by the misgivings of his influential friend and fellow-theologian, Dr John McLeod Campbell. Campbell was usually another Carlylean admirer, still more widely known (and remembered today) for questioning certain aspects of Scottish Calvinistic theology and his

[23] H. M. Henderson, *Erskine of Linlathen, Selections and a Biography* (Edinburgh and London, 1899), 22–3.
[24] D. A. Wilson, *Carlyle to Threescore-and-Ten (1853–1865)*, 6 vols (London, 1929), v, 429.
[25] J. Tulloch, *Movements of Religious Thought in the Nineteenth Century*, ed. A. C. Cheyne (Leicester, 1971), 133.

consequent ejection from the Church of Scotland. For though he liked Carlyle's *Life of John Sterling* because it made Carlyle known to him 'as a *brother* man', he was dismayed at what seemed to be its self-congratulatory tone and triumph at seeing Sterling voluntarily leave his Church: 'His joy over Sterling is a most painful . . . contrast to Paul's joy over Timothy.'[26] The main point of noting Campbell's and Erskine's liking for Carlyle is that both were known as non-Calvinist, both in some ways at least theologically liberal, and that while one was disturbed by the life of Sterling, the other (Erskine) seems to have accepted it together with everything else he agreed on with Carlyle. These were the clergy that usually approved of Carlyle, and with whom he kept on the friendliest terms.

To return to Thackeray's review of the *Life of John Sterling*: he also makes explicit the distinction between loving one's God and one's neighbour. Thackeray's anonymity allowed him to be precise and yet make a general expression of his inability to accept the Church's dogmatic teaching. He writes

> To all orthodox minds, Carlyle must now unhesitatingly stand confessed as not of them. Hitherto he has written on religious subjects as if he hated Cant and Shams; but, somehow, by the very ambiguity of his language, he has always seemed *to have a Bishop in tow*. Now he has fairly cut the cables. . . . Carlyle is working by his powerful denunciations against the *make-believe* which reigns at the present day. For it is in the want of due recognition of free thought that so much hypocrisy lives; men pretend to believe what they do not believe.

Thackeray makes clear his extreme dislike of the close control that apparent orthodoxy had over public opinion, and allied himself with the admirably earnest Professor Francis W. Newman's call, from within the church, for a rational discussion of belief. For Francis Newman, John Henry's brother, was arguing with some success in his *Phases of Faith* (1850) and other persuasive works, for much greater openness and honesty. And here there is a loop into the Carlyle connection. For, as well as Newman's being referred to in Thackeray's novel *Pendennis* (1850), he was praised in Carlyle's biography, and had been chosen by Sterling as guardian

---

[26] D. Campbell (ed.), *Memorials of John McLeod Campbell* 2 vols (London, 1877), ii, 238–40.

for his eldest son. We are also told that the altercation with the clergyman over dinner at the manse about 1851, took place when the Rev. George Gilfillan of Dundee was attacking Carlyle in a peculiarly bitter review of *Life of Sterling* , which had set off the argument.[27] Yet in his unknown review Thackeray had also written of the biography as 'inexpressibly charming', with 'traits of gentle tenderness' and beauty of portraiture, which expressed 'a noble soul'. He knew Carlyle well, and we should not miss the fact that Carlyle's affection for Sterling was one with his love for Erskine, who came to teach universal atonement and 'the essential character of the Gospel as a Revelation of Divine Love'.[28] Certainly Carlyle was paradoxical, but it is not at all clear that Carlyle's 'idea of the Divine', as John Tulloch says, readily and almost exclusively 'sank back into the idea of a Supreme Force'.[29] Carlyle had a deep sympathy for humanity. He and Jane were negative about dogma but positive to much in Christian moral teaching, even when seeming to deny it. He was not, of course, an atheist, any more than he was a Calvinist, a curmudgeon, confined to Prussian history, nor cut off at Chelsea from his Scottish origins.

I touch on the question of Calvinism with an inexpert hand, though so far as Carlyle is concerned maybe no more inexpertly than some who have written about him. It deserves more enlightened investigation, and a willingness to consider his attitudes as more nationally than intellectually 'Calvinistic'. We might also see his apparently detached appraisal of the sermon at Auchtertool as like his response in Westminster Abbey where Froude had taken him to hear Dean Stanley, only to encounter a popular preacher.

Stanley, Froude, Carlyle, and many in their immediate circle were desperately engaged in trying to arrange their ideas in response

---

[27] Wilson, *Carlyle to Threescore-and-Ten*, v, 354; George Gilfillan (1813–78), popular preacher, writer, and united presbyterian minister of School-Wynd Church, Dundee; he, at first, admired and praised Carlyle, who was wary of him because, as he told Emerson, his 'position as a Preacher of bare old Calvinism under penalty of death sometimes makes me tremble for him' (*Collected Letters*, 17:255, 31 January 1844). In the bitter disputes about the *Life of John Sterling*, Gilfillan had reviewed it for the *Eclectic Magazine*, starting favourably, and then (after reading *The Times* review) adding a savagely hostile postscript (*Collected Letters*, 26:273).

[28] Tulloch, *Movements of Religious Thought*, 140.

[29] Ibid., 204–5.

to dramatically changing conceptions of belief in the mid-century;[30] and they sometimes advanced at a different pace from each other, or felt divided within themselves. For, as we have been reminded, as Rector of St Andrews University, Froude assured its students how deplorable it was that Calvinism had 'come to be regarded by liberal thinkers as a system of belief incredible in itself, dishonouring in its object, and as intolerable as it has been intolerant'. He could not believe in it; but he wanted to live by 'Calvinism without the theology', which he thought of as Carlyle's creed. It may be truer to think of Carlyle as having helped to release his own generation from an over-literal acceptance of past teaching; and who yet found himself in a state of tension as his life extended and his beliefs were stretched with it. They stretched until sometimes they snapped back. He was a remarkable mixture of liberalism and illiberalism, and it is a pity that some of Carlyle's biographers, such as Froude, have been happiest when they thought they found him reverting to type – or their idea of his type.

To return to Auchtertool, its interest is that the atmosphere of its evocative setting, the kirk, the kirkyard, and their memorials to Jane Carlyle's nearest relatives, can set us thinking specifically about the actual past, which seems close enough to reach out and affect us. It makes the demand that if we are to know what the Carlyles meant we should avoid generalisation and look for verification in their actions and writing, the world they wrote about, and the actual beliefs they professed, challenged, and evaded.

---

[30] See J. A. Froude, 'Calvinism', *Short Studies in Great Subjects*, 2nd series (1871); cited in A. C. Cheyne, 'Diversity and Development in Scottish Presbyterianism', *Studies in Scottish Church History*, 29 (Edinburgh, 1999), which reconsiders change in this mid-century period.

Chapter 3

Christian Faith and Unbelief in Modern Scotland

William Ferguson

THE question of Christian faith and unbelief, apparently so simple and direct, is actually one of great complexity whose parameters have fluctuated from age to age. From earliest times Christians have stigmatised those of other religions as pagans, infidels or heathens, and no examples need be given here of such a well-known and deep-rooted form of intolerance. In fairness, however, it has to be pointed out that often, as for instance with Islam, this was a matter of mutual intolerance.

The subject of the present essay, however, is not Christian intolerance of other faiths. Rather the concern here is with West European deviations from basic standards of Christian orthodoxy, which, of course, after the Reformation was fragmented, the fragmentations spawning 'heresies' on every hand. Thus at the height of the Reformation turmoil deviations from the dominant creed of a country could lead to persecution, whether at the hands of the Inquisition in Roman Catholic countries or of the state in Protestant ones, though in each case both Church and state would be involved. The career of the great Scottish humanist and reformer, George Buchanan, furnishes a telling example. In 1539, in order to avoid persecution in Scotland, Buchanan fled to London, where, however, he found the Henrician Reformation too dangerous; for Henry VIII, glorying in the plenitude of power conferred on him by caesaro-papistry, executed Catholics and Protestants alike.[1] Later, in 1550–2, after two years of

---

[1] I. D. McFarlane, *Buchanan* (London, 1981), 75.

investigation, Buchanan only narrowly escaped from the clutches of the Portuguese Inquisition.[2]

Heresy appearing in a myriad of guises is one thing; but atheism is something else again. Atheism as a defined creed emerged only in fits and starts. When for the first time atheism was censured it was often as a vague concomitant of another charge which usually involved some form of diabolism. Thus in the sixteenth and seventeenth centuries necromancy was viewed with a kind of fascinated suspicion, tolerated if it could masquerade as science and pay lip service to Christianity. It could, however, go too far and rouse the wrath of the godly. Thus the famous Elizabethan polymath, John Dee (who was astronomer, astrologer, alchemist, mathematician and deep scholar of the occult) could never quite shake off accusations that he dabbled in magic.[3] To turn lead into gold appealed to human nature; but to question any of the tenets of Christianity, or, worse, to sneer at certain aspects of Christian belief, such as its supernatural elements, was to invite serious trouble. Witchcraft, too, which was not as some mistakenly suppose invented at the Reformation, was seen as a form of diabolism and punished according to the biblical text 'Thou shalt not suffer a witch to live.'[4] To those who took the Bible literally this was a categorical imperative, and one furthermore that was backed up by statute law. The famous case of the North Berwick witches, which was supposedly an attempt to raise a storm at sea in order to encompass King James VI's death by ship-wreck, seems to exemplify this, although the case can also be interpreted as James VI hitting out at his troublesome madcap cousin, Francis Stewart, Earl of Bothwell.[5]

[2] See J. M. Aitken, *The Trial of George Buchanan before the Inquisition* (Edinburgh, 1939) and I. D. McFarlane, *Buchanan*, 122–58.

[3] See R. Deacon, *John Dee: Scientist, Geographer, Astrologer and Secret Agent to Elizabeth I* (London, 1968).

[4] Exodus 22:18. There is a huge literature on witchcraft, for which see H. C. Lea (ed.), A. C. Howland, *Materials Toward a History of Witchcraft Collected by Charles Lea* (3 vols, New York, 1957). For Scotland, see C. Larner, *Enemies of God: the Witch Hunt in Scotland* (London, 1981); and for England, J. Sharpe, *Instruments of Darkness: Witchcraft in England 1550–1750* (London, 1997).

[5] Lea (ed.), Howland, iii, 1331–3; C. Larner (ed.), A. Macfarlane, *Witchcraft and Religion* (Oxford, 1984), 9, found the evidence inconclusive: whether there was a genuine conspiracy to kill the King, a ploy that boomeranged or a government plot to incriminate the Earl of Bothwell – it is now impossible to say.

Whatever King James's true feelings about witchcraft (and after all he wrote a tract on that theme in his *Daemonologie*, 1597),[6] there is no doubt that belief in witchcraft and communion with Satan became as widespread in late sixteenth- and seventeenth-century Scotland as it was elsewhere at the time. Nor was that belief confined to the ignorant and ill-educated. Sir George Mackenzie of Rosehaugh, the 'Bluidy Advocate' of covenanting lore, is sometimes represented as expressing rational doubts about the reality of witchcraft.[7] This may not be quite so. Mackenzie did not expressly abjure belief in witchcraft, but he was worried by the way that communal hysteria was apt to prevent fair trials and lead to abuse of judicial procedures.[8] A contemporary of Rosehaugh's, and like him a well-educated man of intellect, George Sinclair, sometime professor of philosophy and mathematics in the University of Glasgow, published in 1685 *Satan's Invisible World Discovered*, incidentally one year before the first book of Newton's *Principia Mathematica* appeared. Sinclair was a Presbyterian who was dismissed from his university post in 1666 for non-conformity. His book, which became very popular, condemned witchcraft as the devil's work and an assault on Christianity. Disbelief in 'Devils, Witches, and Apparitions' was, Sinclair felt, spreading, aided by the doctrines of Hobbes, Spinoza and Descartes. This rising tide of unbelief, he claimed, was practically atheism.[9] These sentiments were not new, for in England Joseph Glanvill in the 1668 first edition of his *Saducismus Triumphatus* had warned of the dangers of denying the reality of witchcraft. He argued that belief in witchcraft was essential to Christianity, and that wanting such belief 'all religion comes to nothing'.[10] As it was, by the early eighteenth century belief in witchcraft began to wane, at least in legal circles, though in the

[6] *Daemonologie* (reprinted Edinburgh, 1966). Larner, *Witchcraft and Religion*, 15–16, regards *Daemonologie* as being slight and derivative, designed to impress public opinion in England with James's importance, and at the same time to refute Reginald Scott, an Englishman, who in his *Discovery of Witchcraft* (1584) had attacked the witch craze.

[7] A. Lang, *Sir George Mackenzie, King's Advocate of Rosehaugh. His Life and Times 1636(?)–1691* (London, 1909), 39–47.

[8] Lea (ed.), Howland, iii, 1339–43. See *Works of Sir George Mackenzie of Rosehaugh*, 2 vols (Edinburgh, 1716–22), ii (1722), 84–95.

[9] Lea (ed.), Howland, iii, 1325.

[10] Sharpe, *Instruments of Darkness*, 246 and n. 18 on 336–7.

popular mind a considerable residue lingered on.[11] As Dr Larner noted, 'Scottish seventeenth-century theological disputes and witch beliefs were deflated partly by technological progress, partly by economic aspirations and political settlements, but most effectively by the eighteenth-century political dethronement of God.'[12]

Other anti-social behaviour could give rise to charges of atheism. Blasphemy, profanity and swearing, if persisted in, could be regarded as atheistical. Such charges had a long history. Before the Reformation the Church courts would deal with those matters under canon law. The earliest Scottish statute against blasphemy was passed by parliament in 1551, laying down penalties according to the rank of the offenders for cursing and for 'blasphemation of the name of God'.[13] Further legislation followed in 1581.[14] But that these laws were not very effective is suggested by re-enactments in 1639, 1645 and 1649, the last making the offence capital for those 'not distracted in their wits'. The major statutes, however, were those of 1661 and 1695, which confirmed capital sentences on those who, not being fatuous, persisted in such practices.[15] In the popular mind those acts could easily give rise to the grapeshot charge of atheism, and modern research has shown that charges of atheism were often loosely bandied about where the philosophy of atheism was absent.[16] Indeed, much of the 'atheism' encountered in the early modern period would today be more correctly described as blasphemy or profanity. Thus Roger Ascham in *The Scholemaster* railed against Machiavellian, Italianate Englishmen who were 'Epicures in living, and atheist in doctrine'.[17] Unguarded words after too much wine at dinner

---

[11] See B. Levack, *The Witch-Hunt in Early Modern Europe* (London, 1987), chapter 3. As late as 1830, witchcraft was said to have been practised in the parish of Resolis in the Black Isle; see M. Shortland (ed.), *Hugh Miller's Memoir: from Stonemason to Geologist*, Introduction by H. Hanham and M. Shortland, 38–9.

[12] Larner, *Enemies of God*, 14.

[13] *Acts of the Parliaments of Scotland* [hereafter APS], ii, 485.

[14] APS, iii, 212.

[15] APS, vii, 202–3 (1661); and APS, ix, 386 (1695).

[16] M. Hunter, 'The Problem of "Atheism" in Early Modern England', in *Transactions of the Royal Historical Society*, 5th ser., 35 (London, 1985), 135–57.

[17] Ibid., quoted 140; and on p. 155 Hunter describes Machiavelli as being central to the 'atheist' stereotype.

could easily lead to charges of atheism or blasphemy. Indeed, there came to be something like a litany of such rash vaunts – denouncing Christ as an impostor and mountebank magician, Moses as a necromancer, the Gospel as a mere tale, and the Law as a fable.

Such matters figured in the best known blasphemy case in Scotland, that of Thomas Aikenhead in 1696–7. Aikenhead was a young divinity student at Edinburgh University, who, on flimsy evidence, was found by the High Court to be guilty as charged of the list of blasphemous utterances given above, and on 8 January 1697 was executed.[18] There was much more to this notorious case, however, than is sometimes made to appear. It is often represented simply as an example of the blood lust of fanatical Presbyterian ministers. This was undoubtedly a factor but by no means the only one. The presbytery of Edinburgh, like the Church of Scotland as a whole, feared that the establishment was in danger, and consequently was in no mood to show leniency to Aikenhead. That he was a divinity student and should harbour such views told against him. He looked too much like the enemy within at a time when the recently re-established Presbyterian system of church government was under threat from political and ecclesiastical opponents. Jacobitism and its supporters, who were mostly Episcopalians though a minority were Roman Catholic, seemed poised to undermine, if not to overthrow, the Revolution Settlement.

But as well as the threat from Jacobitism, new ideas were flooding into Scotland, and these seem to have caught the eighteen-year-old Aikenhead in a deadly snare. At first he made out that the blasphemous statements attributed to him were merely quotations from atheistical books he had been loaned, which he had uttered only to refute; but latterly he admitted that he had been influenced by those pernicious publications. Their ideas, deistical largely, seemed to strike at the root of Calvinist orthodoxy, just as George Sinclair had earlier feared that they might.[19] Apart from his blasphemous railing against God, Christ, the Trinity and the Gospel, Aikenhead was apparently a materialist who denied the

---

[18] T. B. Howell, *A Complete Collection of State Trials* (London, 1812), xiii, cols. 918–39.

[19] Hunter, 'The Problem of "Atheism"', 156, notes that in the late seventeenth and eighteenth centuries, deism tended to become equated with 'atheism'.

existence of spirit and 'maintained that God, the world, and nature, are but one thing ... and that the world was from eternity'.[20] Novel trends in philosophy, such as Cartesianism with its rationalist content, Spinoza's pantheism, and Locke's defence of reason, were all felt to be subversive of the faith. To add to the Church of Scotland's alarm, mysticism had also gained entry to the country, and danger was apprehended from such cults as those of Antoinette Bourignon and Madame Guyon.[21] Bourignonism, a strange pantheistic melange, was condemned by the General Assembly in 1701, and ten years later it was added to the list of heresies that ordinands were required to abjure.

There were, however, few state trials for blasphemy in Scotland, and the significance of Aikenhead's case has often been greatly exaggerated. His execution was a disgrace. Still, he had continued obdurate to near the end, and his recantation came too late to save him. Admission of guilt and timely repentance would in all probability have saved him from hanging. Trials for blasphemy, however, seldom went to such extremes. The outcry against Aikenhead's trial and execution, which John Locke and many others found execrable, may well have affected the decision in the case of Patrick Kinnynmount which arose shortly thereafter. In December 1697 Kinnynmount, a notorious malefactor with a violent past, was tried for blasphemy and adultery. The blasphemies that he was alleged to have uttered followed the usual lines. He gave in an elaborate defence denying everything and pointing to the weakness of the hearsay evidence brought against him. He condemned the alleged blasphemies, but finally conceded that if such impious utterances had been made by him,

> the same hes certainly bein when the pannal hes bein excessively drunk; and it is weel knawen that men in drink and after cups are mad and furious, and the pannall humbly conceaves that if any such villanous expressiones when he was so madly drunk have escaped him (which he absolutely denyes, detastes and abhorres) yet the same can never be sustained to infer against the pannal the paines libelled.[22]

The act of 1661, he pointed out, specifically exculpated people distracted in their wits. On this plea the case folded, and the

---

[20] Howell, *State Trials*, col. 919.
[21] See G. D. Henderson, *Mystics of the North East* (Aberdeen, 1934).
[22] Howell, *State Trials*, xiii, cols 1281–2.

question of adultery was not gone into but probably left to the Kirk Session. Indeed, most cases concerning blasphemy or adultery, and moral questions in general, were dealt with at that level.

What today would be regarded as real atheism, the denying of the existence of God, which seems to have been virtually unknown in the Middle Ages, appeared flickeringly in the period of Renaissance and Reformation. It stemmed from the rise of rationalism, and something of its essence can be found in the career of Giordano Bruno, who embraced the Copernican theory and was tried for heresy and burnt at Rome in 1600. Niccolo Machiavelli, too, in drawing up his advice to princes had challenged Christian morality, and in the sixteenth and seventeenth centuries he was regarded as an atheistical monster. The judgement was too severe; but his influence on the statesmen of the period of Renaissance and Reformation was marked, even among those who paraded their piety. Thus such an essentially secular statesman as William Maitland of Lethington, who as Secretary played a prominent part in the troubled career of Mary, Queen of Scots, was regarded as an atheist. He had, it was said, been heard to declare that God was only 'ane Bogill of the nursery'.[23] Indeed from the outset of their association Knox and Lethington had been at odds. When Knox preached to the Reformation parliament of 1560 he took his text from Haggai, vehemently stressing the need to build the House of God. The cynical Maitland mocked that 'We must now forget ourselves, and bear the barrow to build the houses of God.' 'God be merciful to the speaker', commented Knox in his *History*.[24] Knox and his allies came to regard Lethington as the father of all mischief. Maitland vigorously denied Knox's accusations that he was an atheist and enemy to all religion who scornfully declared that there was neither heaven nor hell, and 'that these are things devised to mak barnes affrayed'. Maitland denied all such accusations, and attributed them to Knox's vanity

[23] J. A. Froude, *The Reign of Elizabeth* (London, Everyman edn), iii, 158. J. Skelton, *Maitland of Lethington and the Scotland of Mary Stuart, a History*, 2 vols (Edinburgh, 1887–8), ii, 395–6, notes the accusation but dismisses it as unsubstantiated. More recent writers have followed Skelton's line and seek to rehabilitate Maitland as a patriotic moderate who opposed the zealotry of Knox and his friends. But none of these revisionist studies is entirely convincing.

[24] *John Knox's History of the Reformation in Scotland*, ed. W. Croft Dickinson, 2 vols (London, 1949), i, 335.

and malice.[25] However this might be, the Lethington who in 1560 caused the First Book of Discipline to be thrust aside as 'devout imagination' was obviously of the school of 'Michel Wylie', as Machiavelli was dubbed in Scotland. Indeed, William Bannatyne called Maitland 'Michel Wylie'; while to another former ally, George Buchanan, Maitland, because of his twists of allegiance, became notorious as the Chameleon. Devious and ruthless, though much talented, he undoubtedly was, and he seems to have used religion simply as a pawn in the complicated game of high politics. But, though strongly suspected of atheism, the correct verdict on him in this respect would seem to be 'not proven'.

Atheism as a reasoned and complete alternative to orthodox theism made its first tentative appearance in the late seventeenth century in the shape of deism raised to a much sharper profile than hitherto. But as a great nineteenth-century expert has observed, 'It is only by slow degrees that the philosopher can hope to disperse the existing prejudices, and extend the borders of his intellectual cosmos over the ancient realms of chaos.'[26] What chaos may be is a matter of opinion, but this dictum about the slow acceptance of novel ideas certainly holds true, and is particularly true perhaps of theological change. Traces of deistical thought can be found in the early seventeenth century. In 1624 Lord Herbert of Cherbury published his *De Veritate* in which he outlined a scheme of natural religion. Charles Blount, who was much influenced by Herbert, in 1680 published *Great is Diana of the Ephesians*, a fierce tract against priestcraft. Deistical ideas were clearly in the air. The essence of the deist position is to be found in Spinoza's pantheistic *Tractatus Theologico-Politicus*; and Hobbes's materialism also rested on deistical principles. Reason and observation in advanced thinkers began to challenge traditional authority, and prescription was no longer a sufficient warrant for belief. René Descartes was a mathematician who sought to impose mathematical proofs on philosophy, and these had tangential effects on theology. In order to do so he posited the theory of innate ideas. Though attacked by John Locke in favour of mind as a *tabula rasa* on which only sensory experience

[25] *The History of the Kirk of Scotland by David Calderwood*, ed. T. Thomson (Edinburgh, 1843) iii, 230–2.
[26] L. Stephen, *History of English Thought in the Eighteenth Century*, 2 vols (Harbinger edn, 1962), i, 5 (1st edn, London, 1876).

could register, nonetheless elements of Cartesianism can be detected in the rationalising school in the eighteenth century. It is of some significance, too, that Cartesian ideas played some part in the tragedy of Thomas Aikenhead.

To sum up so far, by the end of the seventeenth century in the mindset of those in authority in Church and State belief in magic and in witchcraft was on the wane. The imputation of atheism, therefore, had to be sought elsewhere. It was found in the flurry of deistical writings occasioned by the great Deist Controversy that was sparked off by the anonymous publication in 1696 of *Christianity not Mysterious.*[27] Through his own vanity the author of this controversial tract was soon discovered to be John Toland, a wandering Irish scholar who had studied at the universities of Glasgow and Edinburgh, and subsequently in Holland and Oxford. Toland crudely extended the arguments that John Locke the year previously had advanced in his *Reasonableness of Christianity.* Locke's position was in the main orthodox, and his aim was to prove that if human reason, the gift of God, were properly applied it would support the Christian faith, supernatural elements and all. Toland, however, went the whole hog and boldly argued for the primacy of reason. What was contrary to human reason must, he claimed, be false. Locke, alarmed by this, assailed Toland, as, indeed, did many others. *Christianity not Mysterious* was, for example, condemned by the Irish parliament and burnt by the public hangman. Toland became a denizen of Grub Street, and latterly he was forced to seek patronage as far afield as Hanover where he gained the friendship of the great German polymath, Leibnitz.

Like Charles Blount earlier, Toland was fiercely anti-clerical and became a pioneer freethinker. In 1719 he published an odd philosophical work, *Pantheisticon: or the Form of Celebrating the Socratic Society.* Here he adopted the pantheist position, contending that God or Mind is the soul of the universe. His views were incompatible with the Mosaic version of Creation, and seemed to hint, if hazily, at a notion of evolution. He contended that natural laws govern the universe and that 'right reason is the

---

[27] Hunter, 'The Problem of "Atheism"', 156; as early as 1596 deism was identified as atheism, but such an identification was not common before the eighteenth century.

only true Law, a Law befitting nature, extended to all, consistent with itself, and everlasting'.[28] The influence of Newton here is palpable. Newton held that 'hypotheses are not to be regarded in experimental philosophy';[29] and this dictum could be extended to cover theology and so discountenance miracle. In his *Pantheisticon* Toland led the way for the later deists and followers of the Newtonian philosophy, who, whilst professing belief in rational Christianity, nonetheless, in Carl Becker's memorable phrase, 'denatured God and deified Nature'.[30] There is no need to attempt to summarise here the main trends in Enlightened eighteenth-century thought, the principal thrust of which was to separate philosophy and natural science from revealed religion. The works of David Hume advocated scepticism, and not just in matters metaphysical. But amid the furore that greeted his sceptical philosophy few noticed that Hume had also disposed of deism. At all events to the Enlightened philosophers of the eighteenth century theology was no longer regarded as the Queen of the Sciences, but rather as an embarrassing encumbrance from the past. The Moderate Party in the Church of Scotland in the eighteenth century contributed substantially to the Enlightenment.[31] Its members, however, rarely touched upon theology. As has been well said, 'Moderatism was primarily an intellectual movement.'[32] Most Moderates would have agreed with Adam Smith that 'Science is the great antidote to the poison of enthusiasm and superstition.'[33]

But the Moderates did not have everything their own way. Many people in eighteenth-century Scotland held by the traditional

---

[28] J. Toland, *Pantheisticon* (Garland reprint edn, 1976), 85. For Toland, see R. E. Sullivan, *John Toland and the Deist Controversy: a Study in Adaptation* (Cambridge, MA, 1982); and S. H. Daniel, *John Toland, His Methods, Manners and Mind* (Kingston and Montreal, 1984).

[29] J. Rendall, *Origins of the Scottish Enlightenment* (London, 1978), 20, citing Newton's *Opticks*.

[30] C. Becker, *The Heavenly City of the Eighteenth-Century Philosophers* (New Haven, 1932), 63.

[31] See I. D. L. Clark, 'From Protest to Reaction: The Moderate Regime in the Church of Scotland, 1752–1805', in N. T. Phillipson and R. Mitchison (eds), *Scotland in the Age of Improvement* (Edinburgh, 1970), 200–24.

[32] G. R. Cragg, *The Church and the Age of Reason (1648–1789)* (Harmondsworth, 1960), 89.

[33] Adam Smith, *An Inquiry into the Nature and Causes of the Wealth of Nations* (Everyman edn, n.d.), ii, 278.

theology, miracles and all. Necessary reading on this is John Macleod's *Scottish Theology*, which is the clearest exposition of the anti-deistical evangelical tradition in eighteenth-century Scotland, not in the sense that Professor Macleod's book refutes the deists but rather because it illustrates the continuing strength of what its author called 'Old School Reformed Theology'.[34]

Something strange needs to be pointed out here. Much has been written about the great advances made by philosophy and science in the eighteenth century. Undoubtedly great discoveries were made, and new theories proliferated in philosophy, science, medicine, and nearly every branch of knowledge.[35] And yet the Book of Genesis still dominated in a crucial subject, that of cosmology, whose great concern was the universe and how it came to be. The deists might to the orthodox be 'atheists' by imputation, but genuine atheism still could not convincingly replace the account of Creation given in Genesis. This, one of the prime facts about eighteenth-century thought, is too often overlooked or ignored. That it was, however, a massive stumbling block in the path of the Enlightened is only too evident to those who look at eighteenth-century thought in the round. Here two examples of this must suffice.

Firstly, how old was the earth? This was a fundamental question, for chronology is essential – not just to the historian but to any human activity. Try gardening without any heed paid to time, and the truth of this contention becomes dolefully apparent. The odd fact is that, in spite of the advances made by natural science in the course of the eighteenth century, at the end of that period a minor luminary of the Scottish Enlightenment could still state in his book on general history that, 'The chronology observed in this View of Universal History, is that of Archbishop Ussher, which is founded on the Hebrew Text of the Sacred Writings.'[36] That system of chronology, which put the year of Creation at 4004 BC,

[34] J. Macleod, *Scottish Theology in Relation to Church History since the Reformation* (Edinburgh, 1943), 215.

[35] Good introductions are G. Bryson, *Man and Society: the Scottish Inquiry of the Eighteenth Century* (Princeton, NJ, 1945); and Rendall, *Origins of the Scottish Enlightenment*.

[36] Alexander Fraser Tytler, *Elements of General History, Ancient and Modern, To which are added a Table of Chronology, and a Comparative View of Ancient and Modern Geography*, 2 vols (Edinburgh, 1801), i, 6.

still governed Western thinking.[37] But advances in knowledge, especially in the new science of geology, led in the early nineteenth century to slight extensions of the globe's lifespan. Of the fact of Creation, however, few expressed any doubts. Ussher's reckoning of the earth's age might need to be stretched a little, but it still had to serve as the basis of any acceptable estimate of the duration of earth history.

Secondly, another major topic that still called for recourse to the Bible was the origin of language, and specifically of the languages of Europe. The study of philology intrigued eighteenth-century intellectuals. This preoccupation led to a marked increase in the number of dictionaries, such as Samuel Johnson's *Dictionary of the English Language* (1755), and John Jamieson's *Etymological Dictionary of the Scottish Language* (1809–10). But philology was then more a speculation than a science, and any attempt to explain the origin of the chief languages of Europe, past or present, usually ended up in the Tower of Babel, where according to Scripture all the languages of man were born.[38] Such arguments on this theme were, of course, very Eurocentric, and were increasingly troubled by encounters with languages across the globe which seemed to have no relevance to the Bible narrative. All sorts of efforts were made to force those awkward items under the rubric of Genesis 11. Ingenious though some of these arguments were, however, they could carry little conviction. The breakthrough that was in time to produce scientific philology came in the closing decades of the eighteenth century. In 1786–7 the father of modern philology, Sir William Jones, a distinguished judge in British India, mentioned in one of his letters a new theory that he had hit upon.[39] That theory was destined in time to revolutionise linguistic studies, and as A. D. White long ago noted in a book first published in 1896, Babel took 'its place quietly among the sacred myths'.[40] For Jones's study of Sanscrit led him to believe that the chief

[37] James Ussher, *Annals of the World, deduced from the Origin of Time, and continued to the beginning of the Emperor Vespasian's Reign, and the total Destruction of the Temple and Commonwealth of the Jews* (London, 1658).

[38] Genesis 11.

[39] G. Cannon (ed.), *Letters of Sir William Jones*, 2 vols (Oxford, 1970), ii, 769.

[40] A. D. White, *A History of the Warfare of Science with Christendom*, 2 vols (New York, 1960), ii, 204.

languages of Europe shared a common source with Sanskrit, and this vital piece of knowledge was without any reference to the Bible and the Tower of Babel.[41] Not until the early to mid nineteenth century, however, was the theory firmly established, but when thus modernised the science of philology was to play a crucially important role in nineteenth-century Western culture.[42] It would be hard to exaggerate the importance of this seminal advance which helped to clarify thought and led to a new and more realistic rhetoric.

Another theory first raised in the 1780s was to tick away like a time bomb, and in the end its detonation destroyed the old cosmology based on the Bible. Its originator was James Hutton, an Edinburgh doctor whose study of the rocks around Edinburgh and in Berwickshire and elsewhere led him to conclude that the earth's history was much older and more complex than the Bible made out. No single act of creation, he argued, could account for the earth's crust. In a famous lecture delivered before the newly chartered Royal Society of Edinburgh in 1785 he stated that 'we find no vestige of a beginning, – no prospect of an end'.[43] The challenge to Genesis was implicit in that statement, and that challenge was even more obvious in Hutton's insistence through-out on scientific method unfettered by theological preconceptions. Hutton, indeed, was not of orthodox religious belief. He rejected all mystery in religion, was anti-clerical, and his very vague and ill-defined deism probably merited the title of atheism in the modern and precise sense of that term. In thus speaking out so boldly, well aware as he was of the hostile reception his views might encounter, Hutton showed great intellectual integrity and considerable courage. He was one of the greatest thinkers of the

[41] See Sir William Jones's discourse as president of the Bengal Asiatic Society, in *Asiatic Researches, or Transactions of the Society Instituted in Bengal for inquiring into the History and Antiquities, and Arts, Sciences and Literature of Asia* (London, 1786), 422–3.

[42] For subsequent developments of Sir William Jones's linguistic theory, see W. B. Lockhart, *Indo-European Philology, Historical and Comparative* (London, 1971).

[43] James Hutton, *Theory of the Earth, from the Transactions of the Royal Society of Edinburgh* (Edinburgh, 1788), 96; also in facsimile in G. W. White (ed.), *James Hutton's System of the Earth* (Darien, CN, 1970), 304. An Abstract of 1785, also in White (p. 28), concludes that 'this world has neither a beginning nor an end'.

Scottish Enlightenment, and his work was in the end to exert worldwide influence and transform human thought.

As it was, however, Hutton's work published in 1795, entitled *Theory of the Earth*, was to give rise to much controversy. He was one of those savants who spoke well but wrote poorly. His book was ill arranged and his arguments at times incoherent. Only his conclusion was clear, and that was that the earth's crust had been formed and shaped by natural forces, and that the biblical Flood was an irrelevance. Hutton's supporters were derided as 'Vulcanists' by those of an opposite school who followed the line taken by a distinguished German mineralogist, Abraham Gottlob Werner. The Wernerians were dubbed 'Neptunists' because they believed that the Noachian Flood and its consequent precipitation of salts were the main agents of change in producing the earth's crust. Christian opinion, for obvious reasons, tended to favour the Neptunists, and this enabled the Wernerians to struggle on in the face of steadily mounting evidence for the Huttonian theory. John Playfair's *Illustrations of the Huttonian theory of the Earth* (1802) clarified much that was obscure in Hutton's *Theory of the Earth*. The science of geology rapidly developed, and the discovery of more and more fossil remains also tended to support Hutton's views. Hutton had been well aware of fossils, but he was mainly interested in mineralogy and rock formations. Biology, however, was also progressing, and what exactly fossils were was another matter of controversy that was keenly disputed after Baron Cuvier's report of 1812 on his finds in the Paris Basin. To this accumulation of new facts the Neptunists could offer no satisfactory explanation, and as a result doubts about the literal acceptance of the biblical account of Creation steadily grew. By the end of the first half of the nineteenth century such doubts were widespread though seldom openly expressed. They were held in check largely because of an outburst of evangelical fervour which the alarms raised by the first French Revolution had done so much to produce.[44]

[44] The best accounts of these developments are C. C. Gillispie, *Genesis and Geology: The Impact of Scientific Discoveries upon Religious Beliefs in the Decades before Darwin* (New York, 1959; 1st edn, Cambridge, MA, 1951); and L. Eisely, *Darwin's Century: Evolution and the Men who discovered it* (London, 1959).

As far as Scotland was concerned the writings of an eminent Scottish historian played a significant part here. Thomas McCrie, a distinguished Secession minister, wrote two learned biographies, that of John Knox (1811) and that of Andrew Melville (1819), which were admiringly regarded as the Iliad and the Odyssey of Scottish Presbyterianism. Extremely influential, they fired the enthusiasm of the generation that waged the bitter nonintrusionist battles against lay patronage. The resulting Disruption of 1843 at first strengthened the traditional theology and so reinforced acceptance of the biblical account of Creation.

The question, however, was beginning to press. Could the new science be reconciled with religious faith? Could religious faith accept the new science? If so, what exactly would that faith be? Some interesting and important work bearing on those issues was produced by Scots. At first theologians sympathetic to science saw it as the handmaiden of theology supplying ever more conclusive proofs of Paley's Natural Theology. In the early nineteenth century, for instance, Thomas Dick, an Antiburgher minister turned schoolmaster, was keen on science, and his natural theology has been described as 'a theology of creative immanence'. In 1823 he published *The Christian Philosopher* in which he claimed that scientific fact should be welcomed as a revelation from God as well as the declaration of his Word. Dick opposed theologians who scoffed at science and nature, and who 'deprecated the wonderful works of Jehovah'. His natural theology had many affinities with the work of Paley, particularly in stressing that the study of nature proved the existence of an Infinite Intelligence. As a result of the popularity of his works, at home and abroad, Dick became known as 'the Christian Philosopher'.[45] The great Thomas Chalmers also wrote on astronomy, and his *Astronomical Discourses* (1817) were immensely popular. They were intended to refute any idea of antagonism between science and religion. The famous English critic William Hazlitt found them fascinating, and wrote that 'they ran like wildfire through the country, were

---

[45] For Thomas Dick, see *DNB*, xv, 18; H. Macpherson, 'Thomas Dick: "the Christian Philosopher"', in *Records of the Scottish Church History Society*, 11 (Edinburgh, 1955); Gillispie, *Genesis and Geology*, 203, 293; and *Dictionary of Scottish Church History*, ed. N. M. de S. Cameron (Edinburgh, 1993), 242–3.

the darlings of watering places, were laid in the windows of inns'; and he described how he picked up the volume in an orchard at Burford Bridge near Boxhill and spent a delightful morning reading it 'without quitting the shade of an apple tree'.[46]

But contemplation of the sky at night did not assure everyone of the truth of Christianity. The poet Shelley opted for science and atheism. The immense void opened up by astronomy he could only see as

> this interminable wilderness
> Of worlds at whose immensity
> Even soaring fancy staggers.[47]

In this juvenile poem, 'Queen Mab' , which was privately printed in 1813, Shelley argued that Religion, which with Kingship, he regarded as the sources of all evil, should be superseded by the Spirit of Nature. The poet hated the world's imperfections and looked forward to a future perfect state. 'There is no God', Queen Mab cries triumphantly; and as a result there is to be universal harmony. Shelley never lost his youthful credo.[48] Just nine days before his death in 1822 he wrote to a friend

> that things have now arrived at such a crisis as requires every man to utter his sentiments on the inefficacy of the existing religious, no less than political systems for restraining and guiding mankind. Let us see the truth, whatever that may be. The destiny of man can scarcely be so degraded that he was born only to die – and if such should be the case, delusions, especially the gross and preposterous ones of the existing religion, can scarcely be supposed to exalt it. If every man said what he thought, it could not subsist a day. But all, more or less, subdue themselves to the element that surrounds them, and contribute to the evils they lament by the hypocrisy that springs from them.[49]

[46] W. Hazlitt, *The Spirit of the Age or Contemporary Portraits*, 4th edn, ed. W. Carew Hazlitt (London, 1894), 73 and note.

[47] From 'Queen Mab', in *The Complete Works of Percy Bysshe Shelley*, eds R. Ingpen and W. E. Peck, *Poems*, i (London, 1965), 74.

[48] On this, see G. McNeice, *Shelley and the Revolutionary Idea* (Cambridge, MA, 1969). Shelley hated tyranny but advocated gradual rational reforms. As Professor McNeice remarks, Shelley deserves praise for his 'quality of heroic persistence in a good cause in a bad time'.

[49] D. H. Reiman, *Shelley's 'The Triumph of Life', a Critical Study* (Urbana, 1965), 114–15, citing Shelley's letter to Horace Smith of 29 June 1822; the full letter is in *Complete Works of Shelley*, eds Ingpen and Peck, x, 409–10.

Though much frowned upon in Shelley's lifetime, clearly unbelief was stirring; and, indeed, Charles Darwin in his brief period of study at Edinburgh University met up with it in the student high jinks in the Plinian Society.

A decade or so later the question of the relationship between science and religion became more pressingly addressed. Sir Charles Lyell' s *Principles of Geology*, published in three volumes in 1830–3, opened up new vistas that were not to be found in Paley. Accepting Hutton's theories and arguing with the skill of a trained barrister, Lyell, a Scot, attempted a new cosmogony. His uniformitarian views obviously ran counter to Genesis and just stopped short of enunciating a theory of evolution, though his work obliquely hinted at some such. The fact seems to be that Lyell, well aware of the hostile reception that would greet an open challenge to Christian orthodoxy, did his best not to give offence. Nonetheless, he disposed of Neptunism, and he obviously influenced the anonymous author of a famous, but to many notorious, bestseller that was published in 1844.

The author of this work, who went to a lot of trouble to remain anonymous, was in fact the well-known Scottish publisher, Robert Chambers, and his *Vestiges of Creation*, although weak and sometimes even ludicrous in many of its details, undoubtedly popularised the concept of evolution.[50] It went beyond earlier vague speculations about the transmutation of species. It accepted Lamarck's work on acquired characteristics and argued the case for organic as well as cosmic evolution. In spite of its faults *Vestiges* put clearly before the public an impressive case for evolution as against static Scriptural Creationism. But, predictably, though selling well, *Vestiges* ran into a storm of criticism.[51] Scientists, on the whole, excoriated it as wild and amateurish, as indeed it was in many respects, and none was more scathing in his criticisms than T. H. Huxley, who later became an ardent evolutionist and gloried in the nickname of 'Darwin's bull-dog'. The religious also anathematised *Vestiges*, including Chambers's acquaintance Hugh

---

[50] Reprinted as R. Chambers, *Vestiges of the Natural History of Creation* (Leicester, 1969), with an Introduction by Sir G. de Beer. The authorship of *Vestiges* was not revealed until the edition of 1884, three years after Chambers' death.

[51] For good accounts of *Vestiges*, see Eiseley, *Darwin's Century*, 132–40; and de Beer's introduction to the 1969 reprint of *Vestiges*.

Miller, who was blithely unaware of his friend's authorship of the detested work. And yet Chambers had tried hard to temper his views to theological dogmas. Indeed, strong elements of deism can be detected in *Vestiges*, and it contained a specific rejection of atheism. But, without arguing the point, it disposed of the biblical account of Creation, whilst still cautiously adhering to the idea of the Flood. It gives the story of geological development over long, if indeterminate, periods of time, and concludes that the result of all this 'must be allowed to exalt the dignity of science, as a product of man's industry and his reason'.[52] Later he considers the formation of species by 'the Divine Author', and finds the Mosaic account of Creation to be ill-interpreted in that it speaks of the will of the Deity, not of his actual acts. He concludes, 'I freely own that I do not think it right to adduce the Mosaic record, either in objection to or in support of any natural hypothesis', since 'there is not the least appearance of an intention in that book to give philosophically exact views of nature'.[53]

Although rejected by scientists and condemned by churchmen, the *Vestiges* was an extremely influential book. It became a best-seller, went through numerous editions and was much discussed. In spite of its faults it appealed to a mass readership which was evidently becoming confused about the reigning orthodoxy and the authority of Scripture. Its influence, albeit in the shape of *angst*, is clearly reflected in the literature of the mid nineteenth century, most notably in the poetry of Tennyson and Matthew Arnold.[54] That *angst* intensified in the second half of the nineteenth century and provided the theme of Mrs Humphrey Ward's acclaimed novel, *Robert Elsmere* (1882). The author, incidentally, was the niece of Matthew Arnold and held the same religious doubts as her famous uncle.

In the mid nineteenth century another Scot, and this time one of strict Calvinist orthodoxy, wrestled with these problems. Hugh Miller was a brilliant autodidact, who from being a stonemason in his native Cromarty became an accomplished geologist. He was also an outstanding writer, and because of his literary flair

[52] *Vestiges* (1969), 145–6.
[53] Ibid., 156.
[54] This is particularly apparent in Tennyson's 'In Memoriam', and Arnold's 'Dover Beach'.

he was made editor of *The Witness*, a newspaper founded to support the non-intrusionists and latterly the Free Church of Scotland. Miller played a prominent part in the controversies that led to the Disruption in 1843. At the same time he pursued his geological studies, kept well abreast of current issues in geology and palaeontology, and published popular works such as *The Old Red Sandstone* (1841), *Footprints of the Creator* (1847), which was a riposte to *Vestiges of Creation*, and *The Testimony of the Rocks* (1857). He became obsessed and perturbed by the fossil record that was being unfolded, and tried hard to reconcile it with the biblical account of Creation. Miller's science, though self-taught, was sound, and he never dreamed of perverting it. No more could he tamper with his religious beliefs. He found it increasingly difficult to accept both geological facts and biblical texts. The result for Hugh Miller was intellectual torment, and possibly in the end mental derangement. His last book might almost be said to have killed him, and a strange, brilliant and fascinating book it was, and is.[55] In 1856 he was working on the proofs of this volume when he committed suicide. Years of over-work undoubtedly contributed to his breakdown, but it seems likely that depression caused by difficulties of reconciling his scientific learning with his religious faith played some part in his tragic end. This was hinted at by a contemporary, William Honyman Gillespie, an Edinburgh lawyer, who wrote shortly after Miller's death that he had been crushed between the testimony of the rocks and the claims of the Westminster Confession.[56] *The*

[55] H. Miller, *The Testimony of the Rocks, or Geology and its Bearing on the Two Theologies, Natural and Revealed* (Edinburgh, 1857).

[56] W. Gillespie, *The Theology of Geologists, as exemplified in the cases of the late Hugh Miller and others* (Edinburgh, 1859), 23; and on 30, writing of Miller's horror at the savage world revealed by the fossil record, Gillespie contends that 'Such views as those entertained by Hugh Miller must have told on any mind and organism. It is impossible to say what were the effects on a deeply pondering mind which was oppressed by the belief of such fearful secrets touching the moral order of the universe to which man is related.' G. Rosie, *Hugh Miller: Outrage and Order* (Edinburgh, 1981), 78–9, rather skirts round the problem, and N. Ascherson in the Introduction, 10, rather discounts Rosie's speculation that Miller at the time of his suicide may have been suffering from tertiary syphilis. Ascherson believes that it was mental tension brought on by the clash between religious faith and scientific knowledge that destroyed Miller. Shortland (ed.), *Hugh Miller's Memoir*, Introduction by Hanham and Shortland,

Testimony of the Rocks certainly had something to do with Miller's death. In this learned and fascinating book, developed from a series of lectures, Miller admitted that his beliefs had been altered by the onward march of science, but still he strove desperately to bring scientific fact into some kind of harmony with his religious faith. He found he could not do it. As he honestly wrote, 'no student of natural science is entitled to have recourse, in order to extricate himself out of a difficulty, to supposititious, unrecorded miracle'.[57] But, asked the pertinent Gillespie in his *Theology of Geologists*, how could Miller, genius though he was, manage this feat? How, indeed?

Yet, Hugh Miller came so near to a solution. His keen intelligence saw a possible answer, but his mindset rejected it. He appreciated that literal acceptance of the biblical account could not solve the problem, and he castigated those who attacked the geologists. He concluded that the biblical account was, as he put it, 'poetical'. But he was unable to take the next logical step and interpret the Bible in terms of myth, which is a possible modern solution to the problem. Instead, he noted that 'science has its field, and theology has its field'.[58] However, shortly before making this statement he has a revealing confession to make:

> In looking abroad on that great history of life of which the latter portions are recorded in the pages of revelation, and the earlier in the rocks, I feel my grasp of a doctrine taught me by our Calvinistic Catechism at my mother's knee, tightening instead of relaxing. 'The decrees of God are his eternal purposes,' I was told, 'according to the counsel of his will for his own glory He hath fore-ordained whatsoever comes to pass.' And what I was told early I still believe. The programme of Creation and providence, in all its successive periods, is of God, not of man.[59]

And in 1856 when he committed suicide he may have sensed that evolutionary theory, which he had furiously rejected when offered

---

72–4, suggests that Miller may have been a repressed homosexual, only to conclude that pressure of work and conflict between science and religion may have caused his suicide.

[57] Miller, *Testimony of the Rocks* (1869 edn), 121–2.

[58] Ibid., 241.

[59] Ibid., 222–3.

in *Vestiges*, was about to receive an enormous boost. After all, he had corresponded with Charles Darwin, who was to publish in 1859 his epoch-making *Origin of Species*.

Hugh Miller was by no means alone in his agonising quandary. Another who was torn between the claims of science and those of Christianity was Philip Henry Gosse, a distinguished English zoologist who was also a devout member of the Plymouth Brethren. He, too, became increasingly disturbed by the fear that scientific fact might clash with biblical truth. In 1857 Philip Gosse sought to fend off the impending crisis by publishing *Omphalos*, a strange book that appeared in the same year as Miller's posthumous *Testimony of the Rocks*. In the summer of that year Gosse had been sounded out by Sir Joseph Hooker and Darwin for his views on the gist of the latter's thesis. He rejected evolution with horror and hastily composed *Omphalos*, which he believed everyone would find a satisfactory solution to the problem.[60] The first part of the book gives a knowledgable and fair summary of the progress of geology to date, but later Gosse introduces some bizarre notions in an effort to stave off any likely clash between science and religion. The argument is based on the theory of 'prochronism' whereby God at the Creation pre-empted and anticipated all future time. This was simply Calvin's Eternal Decrees again at work. Gosse cites the omphalos or umbilicus to support his contentions. It had long been a puzzle whether Adam and Eve, divinely created and not born of woman, could have had navels. Medieval scholastics had debated the issue. Michelangelo had to confront it when he painted the Sistine Chapel, and in the event gave Adam a large and very prominent navel. Gosse believed that his solution to the problem of science versus faith would be accepted by all parties, and he was mortified when it was greeted with derision by scientists and churchmen alike. Nonetheless, he persevered with his scientific work (at which he excelled) and resolutely clung to his fundamentalist religious faith. His travails are recorded in his son Edmund's *Father and Son*.[61]

[60] P. H. Gosse, *Omphalos: An Attempt to Untie the Geological Knot* (London, 1857).

[61] E. Gosse, *Father and Son: A Study of Two Temperaments*, ed. with introduction by J. Hepburn (London, 1974). This, the best of Sir Edmund Gosse's numerous works and a landmark in the development of biography, was first published in 1907.

A recent book by W. J. Dempster shows how the work of a significant Scottish scientist has been unjustly disregarded. This was Patrick Matthew, a Perthshire small laird.[62] Matthew was educated at Edinburgh University where he studied science and medicine. But in 1808 after the death of his father, he left university without graduating. Thereafter he managed his mother's estate at Gourdiehill in the parish of Errol where he developed a large orchard and closely studied forestry and plant breeding. In 1831 Matthew published a book on *Naval Timber* in which he argued for the need to improve native forests as a source of supply for the navy. In an appendix to this work he clearly enunciated the principle of natural selection.[63] He was not, as has been supposed, a Catastrophist.[64] His views were uniformitarian before Lyell popularised that term, and his brief appendix eschewed the idea of Creation as given in Genesis and argued in purely materialist and naturalistic terms. But his theory was not just lucky guesswork. It rested on a solid foundation of knowledge acquired in many years' experience of plant breeding. He later remonstrated with Darwin, whom he sincerely admired, for his failure to recognise the contribution he had made to the subject of species formation. Darwin was forced to acknowledge that Matthew had indeed introduced the principle of selection in 1831, but at the same time he seems to have been put out by Matthew's pertinacity.[65]

Matthew had undoubtedly conceived the idea of natural selection, but in 1831 the time was not ripe for it. His book in fact was banned by the public library in Perth, and Matthew, perhaps discouraged by this slight, developed new interests, particularly in political and social problems. His interests and standards of value changed a great deal. In 1831 when his book was published Matthew, who on his mother's side was related to Admiral Duncan of Camperdown fame, had been a militarist, an imperialist and a racist who believed in Teutonic superiority, his racism possibly

[62] W. J. Dempster, *Patrick Matthew and Natural Selection* (Edinburgh, 1983).

[63] P. Matthew, *On Naval Timber and Arboriculture; with critical notes on authors who have recently treated the subject of planting* (London, 1831); Appendix, 381–8, for his notes on natural selection and his doubts about the immutability of species.

[64] Eiseley, *Darwin's Century*, 127, mistakes Matthew for a Catastrophist; refuted by Dempster, *Patrick Matthew*, 25–6.

[65] Dempster, *Patrick Matthew*, 29–31.

influenced by John Pinkerton and Thomas Carlyle. He later supported, for example, Bismarck's ruthless assault on Denmark in 1864 and the Prussian seizure of Schleswig-Holstein; and in 1870, pretty much following the line taken by Carlyle, Matthew also condemned France as the aggressor who had forced on the Franco-Prussian War. But by then his views were mellowing as he became more socially aware and radical in sentiment. He was much distressed by the terrible social effects of industrialisation in Dundee, 'where every year hundreds of little children, like hecatombs of cattle, are sacrificed'.[66] As an expert on breeding Matthew evidently felt that the country's basic asset, its people, was deteriorating and that if this degeneration were to continue unchecked it could in the end lead to a national disaster. Patrick Matthew remains an important and intriguing enigma with whom history has dealt unjustly, though of late W. J. Dempster has redressed the balance.

In the wake of Darwin's *Origin of Species* the new science-based cosmology and man's place in it was advanced by such ardent propagandists as Thomas Henry Huxley in Britain and Ernst Heinrich Haeckel in Germany.[67] Both were dedicated Darwinians, and they became staunch allies in the evolutionary cause. They distinguished themselves in many branches of biology, but their real importance was as first-rate popularisers. Both were anti-clerical and keen to make science the basis of state-controlled education. As for religion, Huxley was an agnostic, a word that he had coined after making a close study of David Hume's philosophy. Haeckel argued for monism, a system of philosophy that regarded all things as material and subject to the laws of science. Monism could be regarded as an extension of Auguste Comte's positivist philosophy which enjoyed a great vogue in the mid nineteenth century.[68] Haeckel strongly opposed

[66] Ibid., 147.

[67] The first phase of the Darwinian controversy is covered in W. Irvine, *Apes, Angels and Victorians: a Joint Biography of Darwin and Huxley* (London, 1956).

[68] G. H. Lewes, *Biographical History of Philosophy* (London edn, 1893), concludes by holding, 645, that 'We have no hesitation in recording our conviction that the *Cours de Philosophie Positive*, [by Comte] is the greatest work of our century, and will form one of the mighty landmarks in the history of opinion.'

Christianity and was particularly bitter about the Roman Catholic Church, which he regarded as an outdated tyranny bitterly hostile to science. His anti-clericalism and fierce scorn for revealed religion of any sort was aggressive and at times highly offensive. He sneered, for example, 'that orthodox Christianity made of God a kind of gaseous vertebrate'.[69] Sometimes his arguments were so venomously expressed as to embarrass the pacific Darwin, and even the fiery Huxley. To understand Haeckel's rage it is necessary to glance at the attitudes adopted by the Roman Catholic Church to intellectual developments in the nineteenth century.

Of the major Christian denominations the Roman Catholic Church was the most implacably opposed to the secular trends of the nineteenth century. This was so because the papacy was ultra-conservative, and was committed to the maintenance of its temporal power as well as to traditional Catholic theology and practice. Thus in 1832 in the bull *Mirari Vos* Pope Gregory XVI condemned liberalism. After 1848–9 and the shortlived Roman Republic headed by Mazzini and defended by Garibaldi, Pope Pius IX became an unbending ultra-conservative. Ultramontanism thereafter became the papal answer to every perceived threat. The *Syllabus Errorum* of 1864, which condemned a long list of topics which were felt to be hostile to the faith and authority of the Church of Rome, practically declared war on the science and philosophy of the nineteenth century. Catholic control of education was extolled and toleration condemned as an evil. Thereafter in many countries battle was joined between liberal Catholicism and Ultramontanism, but by some adroit manoeuvring the liberals were routed at the Vatican Council of 1870, and the victory of the Ultramontanists was underlined by the controversial Infallibility Decree.[70] The opposition to papal claims was particularly strong in the new German Empire that was set up in 1871, where Bismarck initiated the attack on Ultramontanism that became known as the *Kulturkampf*. Haeckel, a Prussian born at Potsdam, supported the Iron Chancellor in his struggle with the Catholic Church, and advocated a secular system of education

---

[69] E. Haeckel, *The Riddle of the Universe*, tr. J. McCabe (London, 1913), 235.

[70] For these developments, see N. Sykes in *New Cambridge Modern History*, x, *The Zenith of European Power, 1830–70* (Cambridge, 1960), 76–103.

run by the State and based on science and rational thinking. The ferocity of Haeckel's rhetoric on religion derived from this epic struggle.

Whatever his theme Haeckel wrote with great force, wit and acerbity, and his best known book, *The Riddle of the Universe*, which was translated into many languages, long remained a secularist Bible.[71] Haeckel's English translator, Joseph McCabe, a former Roman Catholic priest and professor, also helped to promote rationalist secularism in numerous learned books, tracts and public lectures. He was bitterly anti-Catholic but also actively undermined religious faith in general.[72] In fact McCabe was one of the founders of the Rationalist Press Association which was set up in 1899 to advance the cause of rationalism. The RPA, with atheism as its core belief, was to produce many volumes, some of them works of distinguished scholarship, supporting the rationalist movement. In 1902, for example, it published a revised edition of a weighty volume entitled *Supernatural Religion*, a scholarly work which examined the Bible, patristic writings and the findings of the Higher Criticism in order to refute all claims to miracle and supernatural power.[73] It concludes that 'There is nothing in the history and achievements of Christianity which can be considered characteristic of a religion divinely revealed for the salvation of mankind'; and that 'The great transformation of Christianity was effected by men who had never seen Jesus, and who were only acquainted with his teaching after it had become transmuted by great tradition.'[74] Perusal of this tome serves to explain the rigid opposition of the Catholic Church to rationalism and all its works. A later volume put out by Watts and Co., London, who were the RPA's publishers, shows that this strain of strong anti-Catholicism continued throughout the first half of the twentieth century. This book contended that in the 1930s and 1940s the

[71] The work first appeared in German in 1899, in English in 1900, and it is still a good read.

[72] For Joseph Martin McCabe (1867–1955), see *Dictionary of National Biography 1951–60* (Oxford, 1971), 661–2.

[73] [W. R. Cassels], *Supernatural Religion, An Inquiry into the Reality of Divine Revelation* (London, 1902) (first published, 1874). For the RPA, see F. J. Gould, *The Pioneers of Johnson Court: a History of the R.P.A.* (London, 1929).

[74] [Cassels], *Supernatural Religion*, 908–9.

papacy co-operated with fascist regimes in order to mount a crusade against rationalism conveniently bracketed with atheistic Bolshevism. This work by Avro Manhattan was highly polemical, but at the same time it presented a good deal of hard evidence, though it overstrained its thesis of papal attempts at world domination.[75] It should be noted, however, that Protestant fundamentalism was also very hostile to the rationalist onslaught.

On the whole the Roman Catholic Church in Britain escaped the anti-clerical strife that raged in the late nineteenth century and the early part of the twentieth in the Catholic countries of Europe. The Church accepted the Ultramontanist position, but could not implement its tenets in practice. There was no powerful Liberal Catholic movement to cause internal discord, and, besides, as a minority and unpopular faith, Catholicism in Britain had no wish to rouse further ill will. In Scotland throughout the nineteenth century the Catholic Church concentrated its limited resources on the work of expansion and consolidation that was made necessary by large-scale Irish Catholic settlement.[76]

By the end of the nineteenth century most of the large Protestant churches were also alarmed by the onward march of science and its ally rationalism. Alfred Russel Wallace hailed the nineteenth century as the great age of science, though latterly he turned to spiritualism, as some prominent scientists did in the following century. Nonetheless, he was right about the nineteenth century being the great age of science. The progress of science in that century was phenomenal, and it produced what really amounted to a new civilisation, whose heirs we are to this day. But it was not without its disturbing features and jarring notes. By the early 1900s most scientists no longer accepted all the tenets of Christianity, and theology could no longer claim to be 'the Queen of the Sciences'.

---

[75] A. Manhattan, *The Catholic Church against the Twentieth Century* (London, 1950). This book was translated into many languages, notably in Eastern Bloc countries, where it suited the aims of communist regimes. Nonetheless, it also sold well in Britain and the USA, indicating the progress made by rationalist doctrines.

[76] See J. F. McCaffrey, 'Roman Catholicism in Scotland in the 19th and 20th Centuries', in *Records of the Scottish Church History Society*, xxi (Edinburgh, 1983), 275–300; see, too, B. Aspinwall, 'Popery in Scotland: Image and Reality, 1820–1920', in ibid., xxii (1986), 235–57.

Before examining the ways in which some Scottish Presbyterian theologians reacted to the advance of science, however, it should be noted that some leading Scots scientists, and those of the first rank, retained their Christian faith. In the first half of the nineteenth century Sir David Brewster, a noted physicist, was a devout evangelical Presbyterian and Free Churchman; and in the second half of the century James Clerk Maxwell, a very great physicist, was a Christian who believed that men of science as well as other men needed to learn from Christ. His distinguished contemporary, Lord Kelvin, was also a Christian who queried evolutionism. The physicists, busy exploring the nature of matter, were not, it would seem, so much given to materialism as were the biologists. Indeed, two prominent Scottish physicists (P. G. Tait, Professor of Natural Philosophy in Edinburgh University and Balfour Stewart, who was latterly Professor of Physics in Owens College, Manchester) in 1875 published anonymously a book entitled *The Unseen Universe* or *Physical Speculations on a Future State*. The stated aim of the book was to prove from theological postulates and scientific doctrines the existence of soul and of a transcendental universe. The book ran through numerous editions and roused a good deal of interest. Inevitably, it encountered opposition from both theologians and scientists who like their potions to be taken neat and undiluted. The authors anticipated antagonism and took issue with their critics. As an indication of how hostile was the reception of the book in some quarters, it was not until the fourth edition appeared in April 1876 that the authors put their names to it. Tait had an international reputation as a physicist, and though religious he was not as devout in the faith as his collaborator, Balfour Stewart. Stewart later became interested in psychical research and latterly in spiritualism. He was one of the founders of the Society for Psychical Research and its president from 1885 until his death two years later. The main thrust of *The Unseen Universe* was that science, properly understood, was not antagonistic to the claims of Christianity. It is a very interesting work but not entirely convincing, relying so much as it did on speculation. In any event, the eminent Christian men of science just mentioned, including the greatest of them all, Clerk Maxwell, were exceptions, for by the end of the nineteenth century more and more scientists and lay people in general were either rejecting Christianity, querying its doctrines, or becoming Laodicean in its observance.

Anyway, the problem of the relationship between science and religion did not abate. When the alarms and disorders of the Age of Reform had ceased the conflict between science and religion noticeably intensified, and especially in the wake of Charles Darwin's bombshell in 1859. It is not possible here to go into details of the Darwinian impact on Scotland but some leading reactions to it need to be noted. The best selling, but certainly not the best, contribution was made by Henry Drummond, a Free Church evangelical, who in 1884 published a book called *Natural Law in the Spiritual World*. This volume stemmed from a series of lectures to workingmen which aimed at reconciling science and religion, but which did little credit to either. Drummond, influenced by R. W. Emerson's transcendental thought and by Stewart and Tait's *Unseen Universe*, had only a smattering of science and his book, though hailed at the time, was verbose and unconvincing. Without properly defining his terms, he elevated 'law' as a scientific concept into a mystical force, his grand contention being that Natural Law and Spiritual Law (he had a passion for capitals) were, as manifestations of God, one and the same. The following passage is typical of Drummond's work: 'After all the true greatness of Law lies in its vision of the Unseen. Law in the visible is the Invisible in the visible. And to speak of Laws as Natural is to define them in their application to a part of the universe, a sense-part, whereas a wider survey would lead us to regard all Law as essentially Spiritual.'[77] The book is stuffed with such gnomic riddles which preclude any real argument. Other similar works issued from Drummond's facile but flawed pen. His *Ascent of Man* (1894), an obvious attempt to rebut Darwin's *Descent of Man*, was a little less cloudy but was still a clear failure and did not rouse the interest his first book had enjoyed. The fact is that as a scientist and as a writer Henry Drummond was not in the same class that Hugh Miller had been.

Of an altogether superior order was the work of Professor Robert Flint of the Church of Scotland who also wrestled with the problem of evolution and its bearing on theology. In Flint's work the easy optimism of the earlier nineteenth century was muted. By the late nineteenth century too many enemies of the

---

[77] H. Drummond, *Natural Law in the Spiritual World* (London, 29th edn, 1890), 55.

old orthodoxy were actively at work, and accommodation on so many fronts was not feasible. Literal scripturalism was under attack and German idealism had wrecked the Scottish philosophy of Thomas Reid which could encompass the existence of God. Flint opposed the Hegelian idealism that was so popular in the second half of the nineteenth century and which could substitute for God almost any earthly concept so long as it was called Absolute. Evidently hankering after eighteenth-century tradition Flint tried to breathe new life into natural theology. Thus, he accepted Darwinism, arguing that it confirmed Paley's great work on creation from design. This was a *non sequitur*, but it still had a certain integrity. Flint, unlike John Caird and so many of his contemporaries, did not give up the fight and seek refuge in German philosophy.[78]

The curious fact is that in Scotland the conflict between science and religion did not rage as bitterly as it did elsewhere. Evidence for this emerges in Principal Rainy's address to the General Assembly of the United Free Church in 1902 in which he spoke up for the Reverend George Adam Smith whose book on *Modern Criticism* had offended many. Rainy argued that facts had to be respected even though they might at first seem distasteful, and it was no good simply denouncing 'infidel science'.[79] Earlier, Rainy had shown some sympathy for the new criticism but his attempts at mediation in the Robertson Smith case had been ruined by Smith's obstinacy.[80] In England the contention raged more fiercely partly because in that country the two great universities of Oxford and Cambridge were strongly clerical and long continued to uphold the Anglican ascendancy. Until 1871 most of the college fellows were in orders, and if they hoped for preferment in the Church of England, it behoved them not to impugn its doctrines.[81] Few had the courage of Benjamin Jowett, an advocate of university reform, who in 1860 roundly stated that a theology divorced from scholarship and scientific progress would be useless. As he

---

[78] See A. P. F. Sell, *Defending and Declaring the Faith: Some Scottish Examples 1860–1920* (Exeter, 1987), 39–63.

[79] P. C. Simpson, *The Life of Principal Rainy*, 2 vols (London, 1910), ii, 269–75.

[80] Ibid., i, chapters xii and xiii.

[81] See T. W. Heyck, *The Transformation of Intellectual Life in Victorian England* (London, 1982), chapter 6.

stringently put it, 'the time has come when it is no longer possible to ignore the results of criticism'.[82] The Oxford Movement in its efforts to stave off reform in the 1840s had tried to do that and had failed, with disastrous results for the Church of England.

But in Scotland no one denomination or institution sought to monopolise learning. Diversity of views was possible, indeed inevitable, given the divisions of Scottish Presbyterianism that then existed.[83] It is noticeable, for instance, that new standards of biblical criticism and theological study came from the Free Church and the United Presbyterian Church in spite of opposition from the traditionalists who sought to cling to the Westminster Standards. Another factor that helps to explain differing attitudes in England and Scotland was the wide range of courses needed for the Scottish university degree. This enabled many Scots theologians to be more appreciative of the work of the scientists than was the case with many of their counterparts in England. Scottish churchmen were also aware of the Scottish contributions to the new science. Thus Darwin's bombshell did not have quite the same devastating effect in Scotland that it had elsewhere. James Iverach, for example, a minister of the Free Church, who had studied mathematics and physics, attempted to work out a *modus vivendi* between science and religion in such works as *The Ethics of Evolution Examined* (1894) and *Theism in the Light of Present Science and Philosophy* (1900). Iverach accepted Darwin's theory of natural selection as a useful working hypothesis whilst rejecting 'the evolutionary Pantheism of Spencer and Haeckel'.[84] A rather similar position was adopted by James Orr of the United Presbyterian and latterly the United Free Church who gave some countenance to Darwin's theory as a hypothesis

---

[82] Jowett's 'On the Interpretation of Scripture', in *Essays and Reviews* (London, 1860), 374. Those famous, and to many at the time infamous, *Essays* raised a storm of vituperation, and Jowett, then Professor of Greek at Oxford and later a great Master of Balliol College, was at the receiving end of much of the *odium theologicum*. Jowett is best remembered today as a Greek scholar, but in his own time he was a considerable theologian whose scholarship was leavened by sound good sense. See *Theological Essays of the late Benjamin Jowett*, ed. with Introduction by L. Campbell (London, 1906).

[83] For some brief remarks on the church situation in nineteenth-century Scotland, see Christina Larner's Gifford Lectures for 1982, printed in *Witchcraft and Religion*, 103–11.

[84] Sell, *Defending and Declaring the Faith*, 118–36.

but contended that Darwinism could not explain origins and was also unable to cover moral questions.[85] Something of this also appears in the work of David William Forrest, also United Presbyterian and then United Free Church, who feared in particular the Hegelian tendency towards pantheism.[86]

An interesting minor figure in those debates was the Rev. George Matheson, Church of Scotland minister of Innellan. He too confronted Darwinism, but unfortunately he was too much influenced by the work of Henry Drummond. He tried at first to build a faith on the acceptance of evolution by examining the points where revelation appears to come in contact with evolution. He held that 'no amount of scientific discovery in the field of Natural Evolution can dispense with the necessity for a Presence and a Power which evolves'.[87] His overuse of capitals showed the influence of Drummond. He draws sharper distinctions than Drummond and uses more direct language, but, like Drummond, his arguments are rigged in favour of theism. He concludes that the old faith can live with the new, and that:

> we must pronounce the religion of Christ the most persistent of all the forces which have yet been manifested to man; nor does there seem to be any reason in the nature of things why it should cease to persist in the future. One thing at least is clear, that this persistence will not be destroyed by the establishment of the doctrine of evolution, for the doctrine of evolution itself will add but another voice to these many testimonies which have indicated for Christianity a place in the light and life of men.[88]

As dogma this pious hope did not have much to recommend it, and latterly Matheson came to regard evolution as mistaken. Nonetheless, his *Can the Old Faith Live with the New?* is an interesting book in spite of its niggling logic-chopping, for it brings out very clearly the nature of the crisis facing Christianity in the late nineteenth century. Matheson was handicapped by very poor eyesight, and this may to some extent account for the superficiality of his work. But for all that, he is interesting because he struggled

---

[85] Ibid., 137–71.

[86] Ibid., 172–94.

[87] G. Matheson, *Can the Old Faith Live with the New? Or the Problem of Evolution and Revelation* (Edinburgh, 1885), 19.

[88] Ibid., 391.

out of the rigid Calvinism of his upbringing, and tried to justify a new system of Christian belief.

By the early twentieth century, however, it was becoming ominously clear that the Church could not halt the triumph of the Zeitgeist. Paul Tillich describes the resistance put up by the Churches against scientific materialism as being 'like an army retreating in face of an advancing army', in which 'With every new breakthrough of the advancing army, in this case, modern science, Christian theology would attempt to protect the Christian tradition which still remained intact.'[89] The resistance was all in vain, however, and the hold of Christianity on the masses steadily weakened. Tillich sought to end the wasteful conflict between science and religion by dismissing it as a mistaken encounter, and concluded that 'the witness of science is the witness to God'.[90] As a QED this falls short of being a proof. But other theologians, most notably T. F. Torrance, an Edinburgh professor, have developed this theme and regard science and religion as compatible. The proof of this, however, is elusive, and possibly illusory. The old orthodoxy has gone and most denominations are left crying 'Ichabod'.

Gone with the old orthodoxy too is a whole world of thought. James Hastings, a United Free Church minister, was one of those who in the early twentieth century became alarmed to find among educated people an increasing scepticism about the Christian faith. He attributed this loss of faith chiefly to the fact that the authority of the Bible had been eroded by the Higher Criticism. This problem had already been diagnosed by Thomas Carlyle, who at the time of the Robertson Smith case in the late 1870s had snorted to Dr James Begg, who was orthodox of the orthodox – 'Have my countrymen's heads become turnips when they think that they can hold the premisses of German unbelief and draw the conclusions of Scottish Evangelical Orthodoxy?'[91] As Carlyle had noted then, and as Hastings later agreed, the contradiction was inevitably debilitating. Hastings tried to arrest

---

[89] P. Tillich, *Perspectives on Nineteenth and Twentieth Century Protestant Theology*, ed. C. E. Braaten (London, 1967), 159ff.

[90] Ibid., 162.

[91] Carlyle is quoted in J. Macleod, *Scottish Theology in Relation to Church History since the Reformation*, 2nd edn (Edinburgh, 1964, reprinted 1974), 310.

the continuing decline of faith by undertaking extensive editorial work for T&T Clark, the well-known Edinburgh publishers of theological literature. The thrust of his argument was that moderate criticism of the sources strengthened the Christian faith and that it was only a misinterpretation of modern scholarship which saw it as undermining faith.[92] The drift towards Modernism, indifference and even atheism could not be halted, however, strengthened as that drift was by the traumatic effects of two world wars. That God should be prayed to aid the belligerent nations in their careers of mass murder undermined faith in religion. Sir John Squire sardonically dealt with this question on the outbreak of the Great War in 1914:

> To God the embattled nations sing and shout,
> 'Gott strafe England' and 'God Save the King'.
> God this, God that and God the other thing.
> 'Good God', said God, 'I've got my work cut out.'

Sixty years earlier, at the outbreak of the senseless war in the Crimea, such irreverent verse could hardly have been put before the public – a telling indication of the great change that had befallen religion in Britain. As it was, midway through the Great War to end all wars, the satirical, the jaunty and the *'Dulce et decorum est'* views of warfare gave way to the bitter elegiac and accusatory poetry of the Western Front, as in Wilfred Owen's 'Anthem for Doomed Youth':

> What passing bells for those who die as cattle?
> Only the monstrous anger of the guns.

Those who survived the carnage carried with them the black nihilism of those five years that ushered in a century of horrors, and which reached a crescendo in 1939–45. It is perhaps too soon to attempt to assess the effects of those terrible conflicts on the human psyche and its attitude to God. Some may have found their Christian faith strengthened by such trials. But what of the many who did not? Leslie Mitchell, writing as Lewis Grassic Gibbon, has the minister in his novel *Sunset Song*, in opening the local war memorial, say that it was 'the sunset of an age and an epoch'.

[92] For James Hastings and his labours, see *Dictionary of Scottish Church History*, ed. Cameron, 394–5.

This chapter has been concerned with the extrinsic factors which helped to change the religious background in a country once noted for its Christian faith, though its Christian witness cannot be idealised into a state of perfection. The perfect Christian nation, or community, is perhaps more aspiration than reality. However that may be, this chapter has dealt mainly with philosophical and scientific developments which increasingly called in question the old fundamentalist and literalist theology built up in Scotland since the Reformation. Not all of those developments, of course, were peculiar to Scotland. There was a strong international sweep to them, but in time they all made a sizable impact on Scotland. The Scottish contribution to the rise of modern science, however, was very considerable. Indeed, the chief names here make up a remarkable galaxy – Hutton, Lyell, Murchison, Kelvin and Clerk Maxwell are still great stars in the firmament of science.

True, in this chapter, more might have been made of social and economic change in Scotland, but these important topics involve complex issues that would require separate consideration. Of outstanding importance here would be the rise of industrialism and the gradual decline of the small and largely self-contained rural communities on which, with their clachans and kirktons, the older pattern of kirk life had depended. One of the great silent revolutions was the resulting redistribution of population in Scotland whereby numbers in the Highlands and Islands fell dramatically and the industrial towns of the Lowlands steadily expanded.[93] The changeover to a predominantly urban environment brought in its train many problems. Quite apart from the inherent difficulties of spreading the Gospel message in teeming and often squalid cities and towns, the sheer magnitude of the needed operation was daunting. Nor was it easy to maintain the old-style church discipline in such densely populated areas amid a fluctuating and often transient population. That so much was achieved by the ministers and priests of that time is the real cause for wonder, bearing in mind that in the crucial stages of this social transformation the state was paralysed by *laissez-faire* ideas.

---

[93] For these developments, see J. G. Kyd, *Scottish Population Statistics*, Scottish History Society, 3rd series (Edinburgh, 1952); and D. F. Macdonald, *Scotland's Shifting Population 1770–1850* (Glasgow, 1937).

But, of course, intrinsic factors also played an important part in making the silent revolution which church life in Scotland underwent in the course of the nineteenth century. Far more than in any previous period change came pell mell and at an increasingly relentless pace. Overwhelmed by these pressures, as bastion after bastion fell, the old ecclesiasticism all but foundered. The main movements that led to theological, confessional and liturgical change have been expertly treated by Professor Alec Cheyne.[94] It should be remembered, however, that, while Protestantism in Scotland was weakened in the course of the nineteenth century, the Roman Catholic Church, in spite of serious obstacles that had to be overcome, made great headway.[95]

So, stands Scotland where it did in matters of religion? Will Christianity in that old country survive the end of the second millennium? Has God, as so often is alleged to be the case today, been given his *congé*? One writer on the situation of the churches in Scotland today, George Rosie, describes God's Scotland as a shadow of its former self, and concludes, with considerable justification, that 'the ancient conceit that the Scots are among God' s "elect" peoples is very hard to maintain'.[96] Other writers on this same subject more or less agree with this verdict. Callum Brown reaches the conclusion that in Scotland 'organized religion appears at present to be on the path towards the margins of social significance'.[97] That the plight of the churches is not altogether new is made clear by D. J. Withrington in a closely argued paper on non-church-going, 1880–1920.[98] The facts that have led to

[94] A. C. Cheyne, *The Transforming of the Kirk: Victorian Scotland's Religious Revolution* (Edinburgh, 1983).
[95] For a detailed account, see McCaffrey, 'Roman Catholicism in Scotland in the 19th and 20th Centuries'.
[96] G. Rosie, 'Religion', in M. Linklater and R. Dennison (eds), *Anatomy of Scotland* (Edinburgh, 1992), 96.
[97] C. G. Brown, *The Social History of Religion in Scotland since 1730* (London, 1987), 209–56, quotation on 256.
[98] D. J. Withrington, 'Non-church-going, church organisation and "crisis in the church", *c.*1880–1920', *Records of the Scottish Church History Society*, xxiv (1992), 199–236; see, too, a brilliant brief conspectus of the problem in Cheyne, *Transforming of the Kirk*, 130–6; Brown, *Social History of Religion in Scotland*, 209–56; and some interesting information in J. Highet, *The Scottish Churches, a View of their State 400 Years after the Reformation* (London, 1960), and J. Highet, *The Churches in Scotland Today* (Glasgow, 1950).

these conclusions can hardly be gainsaid: church attendances and church membership have fallen; churches have closed and are now used for a variety of secular purposes; traditional morality has slumped; entertainment is now preferred to edification; and Sunday shopping attracts more people than Sunday worship does. This is not to say that there are no God-fearing Christian worshippers left in Scotland, but simply to note that their ranks have been depleted.

Does this mean that atheism has triumphed? That is a very difficult question to answer. It is too easy to see in the cumulative effect of the changes outlined in this essay the overthrow of the Christian faith by science-based infidelity. That has, undoubtedly, wrought some changes. True, evolutionary theory, pursuant to its essence, has continued to evolve and will probably go on doing so. But each new synthesis has only served to strengthen Charles Darwin's claim to be a great scientist and a major thinker of the modern age.[99] As John Passmore puts it, 'all of us, not only scientists but everybody except a few reactionary dissentients, see the world and man's place in it in a Darwinian way'.[100] Not only was Darwin a great scientist, but he was also a great trans-former of human culture. Few historians would deny this. But does that necessarily make the case for atheism? Antony Flew, a distinguished philosopher, believes that it does, and he has published closely argued works to justify his beliefs.[101] Recent writers have been more dogmatic on this point. An article by Jan Van der Veken begins by asking, 'Why is it that a "theism" [i.e. atheism] which started as a minority problem in the seventeenth or eighteenth century, has taken over almost completely the intellectual scene . . . How and why is it that the christian [sic] God understood theistically has become incredible?'[102] There is some point to this question-cum-statement, but at the same time it is far too sweeping. It refers specifically to 'the intellectual scene',

---

[99] A. Flew, *Darwinian Evolution* (London, 1984).

[100] Cited in D. S. Bendall (ed.), *Evolution from Molecules to Men* (Cambridge, 1985), 569.

[101] A. Flew, 'The Presumption of Atheism', in J. Houston (ed.), *Is it Reasonable to believe in God?* (Edinburgh, 1984), 12–30.

[102] J. Van der Veken in S. Andersen (ed.), *Traditional Theism and its Modern Alternatives* (Acta Jutlandica lxxx; 1, Theology Series 18, Aarhus University Press, 1994), 44.

not to people in general. It is not necessary to have a PhD in science or philosophy in order to hear and heed the Gospel message.

The problem, of course, is that not everyone is, or wishes to be, an intellectual, whether theologian, scientist or philosopher. The present writer, for example, does not regard himself as an intellectual. What is taken to be the intellectual position does not necessarily settle the matter at issue. The question of non-church-going, for instance, is not to be so easily solved. The number of committed, dedicated Christian believers whose conduct is shaped by the teachings of Christ has probably always been limited, and it is a fallacy to jump to the conclusion that 'the Ages of Faith', wherever suspended in time, were one hundred per cent Christian in belief and conduct, free of sin, vice and all manner of evil. The historical record shows quite clearly that this is not, and never has been, the case. Granted, the rise of science and the theory of evolution have tended to undermine traditional Christian belief, but for many lapsed 'Christians' this is probably not the result of conviction or any intellectual search for truth, but comes simply as a good excuse for doing what they want to do in any case, and what many of their ancestors would have done if freed from the constraints of their time. The kirk session records of the past can furnish some testimony to this effect.

These are all debatable matters which cannot be answered in a nutshell. But, finally, a curious circumstance has to be noted. At the end of the nineteenth century the weaknesses of organised Christianity were being exposed, and undoubtedly in the end this led to declining congregations. But now it is the secular Nirvana that is beset with problems. The religion of science, if one can call it that, has notoriously produced forces that could unleash Armageddon and inflict fearful and possibly terminal damage on humanity. Science can evidently create, but equally evidently cannot solve such problems. Thus over a host of related problems – warfare, abortion, euthanasia, cloning – the morality and ethics of science are causing great concern. When all is said and done, it is more and more becoming apparent that, for Western man at any rate, the best ethical and moral precepts are still to be found in the Gospels.

Chapter 4

Old Testament Criticism and the Education of Victorian Children

Barbara J. MacHaffie

IN her recent book on *The Bible for Children*, Ruth Bottigheimer makes the observation that for many modern scholars religious, devotional and quasi-biblical literature for children is an 'obscure and unknown field'.[1] This is at least partly due to the reluctance of intellectual and Church historians on both sides of the Atlantic to treat the history of religious education as a serious research topic. While there has been substantial scholarly interest in the evolution of state education and even the growth of the secular curriculum, religious education needs to be studied more extensively and thoroughly.[2] One area in particular which has been neglected is the effort in late Victorian Britain to convey to children knowledge of the Bible based on the results of historical criticism and source criticism (referred to in the nineteenth century as literary criticism).[3] Bottigheimer does acknowledge that some school Bibles for 'older pupils' prepared by 'theologians and officers of the Church of England' did incorporate critical scholarship[4] and Philip Cliff, in his study of Sunday Schools in England, documents discussions held by the Sunday School Union on finding a place for the 'assured results' of Old Testament criticism in Sunday

---

[1] R. Bottigheimer, *The Bible for Children* (New Haven, 1996), 8.
[2] See, for example, H. Archibald, 'History of Religious Education 1850–1950: A Documentary Trail', *Religious Education*, 82 (Summer 1987), 405–14.
[3] S. L. McKenzie and S. R. Haynes, *To Each Its Own Meaning: An Introduction to Biblical Criticisms and Their Application* (Louisville, 1993).
[4] Bottigheimer, *The Bible for Children*, 45.

School teaching.[5] Yet the volume and variety of critical literature for children, which illuminates an important phase in the development of religious education, remains unrecognised and unexplored.

A search which is not exhaustive yields over fifty such titles published in Britain between 1870 and the First World War. Some were written by Church of England leaders but many authors were Nonconformists, a couple were Unitarians and one of the most popular was a Jew – Claude Goldsmid Montefiore. The books and articles were written to be used with and by a wide variety of ages, from very young children to young adolescents, and they were intended to improve Bible instruction in elementary, secondary and Sunday schools as well as in the home. The authors were clergymen, educators and concerned lay people, many of whom were women. Also, like the authors of the children's Bibles analysed by Ruth Bottigheimer, most of them are now forgotten.[6]

This dimension of Victorian education is explored in the following chapter. The chapter begins by considering the environment out of which such literature grew and looks particularly at the lively interest in reforming Bible teaching, the flourishing publishing industry of the late nineteenth century and the comfort many late Victorians felt in accepting what they perceived as the 'assured results' of biblical criticism, embraced by 'believing critics' such as George Adam Smith and Samuel Rolles Driver. It then analyses the literature itself by looking at the dominant themes of progressive revelation, historical and edifying truth, the role of the prophets and composite authorship. The concluding section looks at the significance of the material in terms of the role women played in popularising biblical scholarship, the theological and educational issues raised by the texts and the impact of these attempts to reform Bible education.

Although it had been going on for much of the century, discussion on appropriate provision for educating the children of Britain reached a new level of intensity in the 1860s and 1870s. Major issues included what role the State should play, what kind of curriculum would best train the newly-enfranchised men of Britain and how much education should be offered to women. No

---

[5] P. B. Cliff, *The Rise and Development of the Sunday School Movement in England 1780–1980* (Birmingham, 1986), 227–8.

[6] Bottigheimer, *The Bible for Children*, xii.

less passionately debated was what was identified as 'the religious difficulty': what kind of religious instruction should be given to children in England and Scotland, especially in schools supported by the rates?[7]

It was in fact the Education Act of 1870 in England and the 1872 Act in Scotland which fuelled the most intensive debates over religious education. The bill in England originally allowed school boards complete freedom on the issue, but the fear that boards could choose denominational instruction at the ratepayer's expense led to the passage of the Cowper–Temple Clause. Religious instruction was not compulsory in the board schools, but if it was given, the clause had to be respected and 'no religious catechism or religious formulary distinctive of any particular denomination' was to be taught.[8] Most school boards in England followed the example of London, which resolved that the Bible should be read and teachers should give 'such explanation and such instruction therefrom in the principles of morality and religion as are suited to the capacities of children'.[9] At the same time the Sunday schools, freed from the need to teach reading and arithmetic, increasingly focused on the conversion of children and the narrative of salvation history found in the biblical text.[10] Thus the Bible, which had always been important in schools of all types, assumed an exaggerated importance after 1870. And the more Bible teaching was emphasised, the more apparent were its shortcomings.

In 1907 an examiner for the London School Board called Bible instruction 'the greatest delusion outside of bedlam'.[11] Cries of condemnation in fact came from many quarters: educators, secularists who wanted no religious teaching, Church leaders who wanted catechetical teaching and a chorus of writers influenced by biblical criticism who saw Bible teaching as one of the most

[7] J. Gray, 'The Religious Difficulty', *New College Bulletin*, 7 (February 1973), 10.

[8] C. M. Jones, *The Development of Religious Education in the State Schools of England and Wales* (London, 1958), 7.

[9] M. Cruikshank, *Church and State in English Education: 1870 to the Present Day* (London, 1964), 43.

[10] Cliff, *The Rise and Development of the Sunday School Movement*, 78, 141.

[11] F. Hayward, *The Reform of Moral and Biblical Education along the Lines of Herbartianism* (London, 1902), 31.

pressing issues of the day.[12] What could provoke such a strong reaction? The Bible earlier in the century had been used primarily to teach reading and arithmetic. Children in National Society schools, for example, were acquainted with the text primarily in the form of questions such as, 'Of Jacob's four wives, Leah had six sons, Rachel had two, Billah had two, and Zillah also had two. How many sons had Jacob?'[13] Gradually, however, the content of the Bible was studied in its own right as textbooks for reading and arithmetic became available.[14] But children were learning little about the Christian faith or the godly life and the reasons seemed obvious. They were required to memorise facts unrelated either to each other or to the lives of the children. Charles Marson expressed his frustration with this kind of 'unassimilated fact-lore'[15] by pointing out that:

> These children can tell you who Huppim, Muppim and Ard were; they know the latitude of Beersheba, Kirioth, and Beth-Gamul; . . . they can name the destructive miracles, the parables peculiar to St. Luke, and above all, they have a masterly knowledge of St. Paul's second missionary journey. They are well-loaded and ballasted with chronicles of Baasha and Zimri, Methuselah and Alexander the coppersmith. This may be valuable as historical, geographical or memorial education, but it can hardly be called religious education . . .[16]

Bible teaching was also poorly done because it was widely believed that the words of the Bible had a magically efficacious quality apart from the comprehension of the reader. Thus, in many classrooms, the Word of God had to be memorised. And whether it was whole Bible passages or 'fact-lore' which children were learning by heart, unfortunate choices were made in terms of which parts of the Old Testament were emphasised. Too much was made

---

[12] A. Mitchell, *How to Teach the Bible, being suggestions as to the best way of teaching the Bible in view of modern knowledge of the Bible and of the child mind*, 2nd edn (London, 1906), 10.

[13] 'Explanations on Education', *Westminster Review*, 55 (July 1851), 463.

[14] A. Ellis, *A History of Children's Reading and Literature* (New York, [1968]), 89–99.

[15] E. Tylee, 'The Bible in the Schoolroom', *The Journal of Education* (June 1896), 358.

[16] C. L. Marson, *Huppim and Muppim: A Few Words upon the Sore Need of Religious Education* (Oxford, 1903), 7–8.

of the Pentateuch, Judges and the books of Samuel – of the plagues and Joseph and Elisha and the bears – and not enough of the psalms and prophets.[17]

Some of these complaints had been expressed earlier in the century but a new concern with Bible teaching was provoked by the expanding secular curriculum. By the 1880s the lower standards in schools were adding geography, history and grammar while the upper standards were adding science and languages.[18] Many educators and churchmen and women were concerned that children would discover information in other classes which contradicted their Bible teaching.[19] And while teaching methods in these other subjects were more cognizant of advances in educational theory, Bible classes continued to stress rote learning:

> Bible study is either carried on in the same antiquated method it shared with most branches of education fifty years ago, or has degenerated into a harmful process of 'cramming'. In almost every other study there has been considerable advance. The teaching of science and modern languages, especially, has been revolutionized; yet a glance at the textbooks employed and the examination papers set in Bible history will prove that those discredited phantoms – learning by rote and unassimilated fact-lore – have found a refuge in the Bible class.[20]

Yet while Bible teaching was in a deplorable state, education in the late nineteenth century also held the promise of change. While the voluntary schools after 1870 experienced a temporary surge of expansion, the board schools by 1900 had established themselves as places of quality education by providing expanded facilities, curricular innovation and well-prepared teachers. The Education Act of 1902 allowed for the use of rates to support secondary education and it was religious education in the state schools that seemed most amenable to improvement. In addition Cowper–Temple had created a genuine interest in the Bible as the repository of those fundamental religious and moral truths on which all

[17] E.g., N. P. Wood, 'The Present State of Scripture Teaching in Secondary Schools' in N. P. Wood (ed.), *Scripture Teaching in Secondary Schools* (Cambridge, 1913), 76.

[18] Ellis, *History of Children's Reading and Literature*, 91.

[19] E.g., T. Raymont, *The Use of the Bible in the Education of the Young* (London, 1911), 19.

[20] Tylee, 'The Bible in the Schoolroom', 358.

Protestants agreed and on which British civilisation was based.[21] This was coupled with a consensus among parents and teachers that children must be guarded against the prevailing winds of religious scepticism. In all cases, a critical approach to the Bible seemed an attractive alternative.

Simon Eliot highlights another feature of the late-Victorian environment relevant to the growth of critical literature for children: 'print products didn't just surround the nineteenth century, they penetrated and pervaded it, became so ubiquitous and so commonplace as to be taken for granted'.[22] Britain led the world in book production in the nineteenth century and especially after the 1840s, when a rapid increase in titles published and tons of paper consumed is especially evident. Behind this growth was the introduction or quick adoption of a whole variety of technological innovations involving printing, paper production and book illustration. Mass production led to the emergence of cheap and moderately priced books, cheap books selling for less than three shillings and moderately priced books for between three shillings and ten shillings each.[23] Books were thus within the reach of middle class and better-off working class families.

The material considered in this chapter is part of this publishing phenomenon in that almost all of the books fell into the moderate price range and many went through several editions and printings. The publications, however, are also part of something else: the development of a market for children's books. Sunday schools and the Education Act by the end of the century had created a young reading public and publishers responded by applying the new techniques in printing and illustration to children's books.[24] Many of the publications such as Robert Gillie's *God's Lantern Bearers*[25] and Cyril Bickersteth's *Letters to a*

[21] H. H. Henson, *Religion in the Schools: Addresses on Fundamental Christianity* (London, 1906), 18–19.
[22] 'Some Trends in British Book Production 1800–1919', in J. O. Jordan and R. L. Patten (eds), *Literature in the Marketplace: Nineteenth-Century British Publishing and Reading Practices* (Cambridge, 1995), 19.
[23] Ibid., 39–41.
[24] C. S. Hannabuss, 'Nineteenth-century Religious Periodicals for Children', *British Journal of Religious Education*, 6 (Autumn 1983), 21.
[25] *God's Lantern Bearers: The Story of the Prophets of Israel Retold for Young People* (London, 1908).

Godson[26] were part of this publishing trend as they were clearly intended to convey the results of critical scholarship directly to children.

Willis Glover in his classic work *Evangelical Nonconformity and the Higher Criticism* explores another important dimension of late-Victorian religious culture essential to understanding the literature on critical Bible teaching.[27] He observes that clergy and lay people began to accept the methods and conclusions of historical and literary criticism in any numbers only in the 1880s. He argues that this transition was made possible because Victorians concluded that criticism left evangelical Protestantism, for the most part, intact, and in some instances strengthened its presuppositions. Scholars such as William Robertson Smith became known for their insistence that the heart of the Christian faith was not an infallible text but the claim that 'God in Jesus Christ has made himself personally known to us, has entered into personal relations with us'.[28] This was 'believing criticism' for the Victorian public and it was in this atmosphere that literature aimed at conveying a critical approach to the Bible for children appeared.

Helena Powell, for example, author of a paper on 'Religious Teaching in Schools', pointed out that many biblical scholars were 'pillars of faith'[29] and John Paterson Smyth's *Bible for the Young* told children that there were 'good and holy scholars' who believed that the Creation story was a 'parable'.[30] But it was not simply the reconciliation of evangelical beliefs and higher criticism that made a difference to these authors; they also noted that scholarly critics could remain devoted servants of the Church and models of Christian conduct. Authors especially recommended Samuel Rolles Driver and George Adam Smith to parents and teachers. Driver, who was regius professor of Hebrew at Oxford from 1882 until his death in 1914 and the author of a celebrated *Introduction to the Literature of the Old Testament*, was remembered

[26] *Letters to a Godson: How to Read the Old Testament in Light of the New*, 2nd edn (Oxford, 1905).

[27] (London, 1954).

[28] W. Robertson Smith, *Lectures and Essays*, ed. J. S. Black and G. Chrystal (London, 1912), 123.

[29] *Religious Teaching in Schools, a Paper read before the Cambridge District Association of Managers and Teachers* (Cambridge, 1905), 2–3.

[30] *Genesis* (London, 1901), vii.

as teaching criticism to the faithful far beyond the Anglican communion in England. Those he taught were assured that:

> Criticism in the hands of Christian scholars does not banish or destroy the inspiration of the Old Testament; it *presupposes* it; it seeks only to determine the conditions under which it operates, and the literary forms through which it manifests itself; and it thus helps us to frame truer conceptions of the methods in which it has pleased God to employ in revealing Himself to His ancient people of Israel and in preparing the way for the fuller manifestation of Himself in Jesus Christ.[31]

George Adam Smith served as professor of Old Testament language, literature and theology at the Free Church College, Glasgow, and later as principal of Aberdeen University. He was widely known for his belief that higher criticism had positive effects on the Old Testament as a resource book for the preacher. In the first of his Beecher Lectures given at Yale in 1899, Smith argued that the critical enterprise was thoroughly evangelical, 'concerned with faith, and the assistance of souls in darkness, and the equipment of the Church of Christ for her ministry of God's Word'.[32] Nowhere was this more true than when the preacher confronted the prophetic material: scholars had rescued the prophets from the role of soothsayer and placed them as critics of the social and civic circumstances in which they lived. Their message was particularly relevant to the social turmoil of late Victorian Britain.[33]

Among believers sympathetic to biblical criticism, Driver and Smith had reputations as sober and careful critics. Some English scholars found Driver's caution irritating[34] but for many such as Rev. G. A. Cooke, it was comforting: 'We can be sure that he [Driver] does not speak until he has carefully weighed every point and given it its full value.'[35] The authors of critical material for children were able to speak, therefore, with confidence. They

---

[31] S. Driver, *Introduction to the Literature of the Old Testament*, 4th edn (Edinburgh, 1892), xx.

[32] *Modern Criticism and the Preaching of the Old Testament* (London, 1901), 28.

[33] Ibid., 215–83.

[34] 'Samuel Rolles Driver', *Dictionary of National Biography: 1912–1921* (Oxford [1927]), 163.

[35] *Expository Times* (September 1898), 536.

emphasise over and over again that they are teaching the 'assured results' of scholarship.[36] Parents and teachers could be comforted that they were not being asked to swallow the fantasies of a few radical scholars; rather, they were being given the conclusions reached by the 'whole intellectual world' which included careful men such as Driver and Smith.[37] And what were the 'assured results' of historical and literary criticism that the popular material presented? In the literature for children they included the claims that:

(1) The Old Testament documents were compiled in their present form at a late date.

(2) The Law has been built up over centuries from various strata.

(3) There was a primitive and later history of Israel, the latter being coloured by the priestly circle.

(4) The main source of information before the ninth century B.C. was oral tradition. The solid ground of written material was not reached until the time of David.

(5) The religion of Israel before the appearance of the literary prophets was closer to that of kindred nations than previously supposed.[38]

This was the environment in which literature concerned with the biblical education of children from a critical perspective appeared in such volume. The books and articles tend to fall into one of several categories: there are works setting out general principles for the transformation of Bible teaching; general Old Testament histories; Bibles for children in which the material is retold or reorganised and commented upon; Bibles which distinguish one literary form from another, and books on special topics such as the prophets or the literary history of the Bible. Although this material differed in format, it is unified in terms of stated purpose and in terms of the ways in which it demonstrates the value of biblical criticism.

---

[36] E.g., A. S. Peake, *Reform in Sunday School Teaching* (London, 1906), 14, and G. C. Bell, *Religious Teaching in Secondary Schools* (London, 1897), 35–6.

[37] Tylee, 'The Bible in the Schoolroom', 359.

[38] F. Foakes-Jackson, 'Is the Old Testament Worth Presenting to the Young?', in N. P. Wood (ed.), *Scripture Teaching in Secondary Schools* (Cambridge, 1912), 22.

Almost all the authors try to engage the attention and approval of the public by presenting their work as a righteous cause. The old orthodoxy might be fine for very young children, as headmaster Henry Craddock-Watson claimed, but this was a 'flabby credulity' which soon foundered as children grew older and discovered historical and moral problems in the biblical text.[39] Too often the tragic result was scepticism. Parents and educators therefore had a duty to teach critical views as a way of maintaining biblical authority on religion and morals.[40] Children would learn, for example, why there are two very different Creation stories and thus their faith would be safeguarded when unbelievers paraded such inconsistencies before them.[41] Arthur Peake borrowed a powerful image from medical science:

> It is our privilege to place our young people at the right point of view, and preserve a faith which shall not be incompatible with intelligent integrity. We must vaccinate them with criticism to save them from the smallpox of skepticism.[42]

There is a remarkable degree of consensus among the writers of this literature as to what children before the age of twelve or thirteen needed to know in order to be properly 'vaccinated' against scepticism. By the time they reached adolescence children should have learned that:

(1) God has gradually taught humanity about himself. Humanity's response to this teaching has also been gradual.

(2) The Bible contains mistakes in history and science but not in religious truth.

(3) The prophets were spokesmen for God to their own day.

(4) The Bible is a compilation of many different books written at different times. Some individual books are also the work of more than one author.

Since these four topics – progressive revelation, truth of edification, a new role for the prophets and composite authorship – are

[39] H. Craddock-Watson, 'The Teaching of the Miraculous in the School Lesson', in Wood (ed.), *Scripture Teaching in Secondary Schools*, 19.

[40] Mitchell, *How To Teach the Bible*, 6.

[41] R. H. Kennett, 'The Teaching of the Old Testament', in Wood (ed.), *Scripture Teaching in Secondary Schools*, 38–9.

[42] A. S. Peake in F. W. Farrar (ed.), *The Bible and the Child: The Higher Criticism and the Teaching of the Young* (London, 1897), 55.

recurring themes in the literature, they can provide a basis for analysing it. They also lead us to ask what such writers believed should happen in Bible education with children beyond the age of twelve and it is at this stage that the specific theories of literary criticism are discussed.

Pre-critical Bible teaching was based on the assumption that all the material in the text was of equal value and contained the same divine message. As Craddock-Watson put it, everything in the Bible was presented by teachers as being 'on the same plane of truth'.[43] The inconsistencies were only apparent and could be sorted out by the devout reader. A critical view of the Bible, however, accepted that there was enormous variety in the material both in terms of literary genre but also in terms of moral and religious concepts. By carefully scrutinising the biblical text the critics had revealed that the human grasp of divine truth was not only a developing process but also a progressive one. Many of the writers of educational literature agreed with Mary Bramston that revelation had a 'dawn' and reached its highest point in Jesus.[44] This was an important strategy for the popularisers of higher criticism: they tried to convince parents, children and teachers that the chief value of the Old Testament was as a means to a glorious end – the full revelation of God in Jesus Christ. Teachers and parents did not have to defend the religious and moral teaching of some parts of the Old Testament because it was neither infallible nor final.[45] Nor did they have to fear that criticism would touch the revelation of the New Testament. The New Testament was on 'solid ground' historically because it was written so soon after the events it describes whereas the Old Testament was 'full of difficulties'.[46]

But the work of the critics not only allowed Jesus to stand out in more majesty; it also revealed some parts of the Old Testament to be closer to Christian truth than others. Moral and religious truth reached its highest levels in the writings of the prophets and some of the post-exilic texts. Parts of the Old Testament which

[43] H. Craddock-Watson, 'Opening Address', in Wood (ed.), *Scripture Teaching in Secondary Schools*, 3.

[44] *The Dawn of Revelation: Old Testament Lessons for Teachers in Secondary Schools*, 2nd edn. (London, 1899).

[45] F. Foakes-Jackson, 'Is the Old Testament Worth Presenting to the Young?', 16.

[46] Ibid., 17.

had been excluded from Bible teaching (such as the prophets and the Wisdom literature) needed to be restored. Differences in concepts of God and morality in regularly taught material also had to be highlighted, as Philip Wicksteed does when he has children compare and contrast the two Creation stories: 'This second account is really hundreds of years older than the first. See whether you can perceive that it is more child-like and primitive in its ideas; less thoughtful, less scientific.'[47]

What was significant about this intense focus on progressive revelation was its harmony with changes in educational theories in the late nineteenth century, particularly those of German educators Johann Herbart and Friedrich Froebel. By the end of the nineteenth century Froebel's work had become widely known through the Froebel Societies established in London and Manchester in the 1890s and Herbart had been given international recognition through Tuiskon Zeller's book, *Foundation of the Doctrine of Educative Instruction*. Both educators are associated with many principles, such as the need to demonstrate the harmony and interconnectedness of all studies, which were accommodated by the critically-informed teaching of the Bible. Most significant for teaching biblical criticism was their emphasis on the idea that religious education should be sensitive to the development of a child as he or she progressed toward maturity. Zeller, Herbart's disciple, claimed that each individual recapitulated the progress of the human race from sense perception to imagination to reason, and curricula therefore should be designed according to the age of the children being taught.[48] It is not difficult to see how the theories of developmental education influenced religious education and how the Bible, as a record of progressive revelation, was identified as the perfect resource for home and classroom teaching. Parts of the Old Testament were, argued Louisa Houghton, the product of a child-nation and could thus be effective with very young children.[49] But the Old Testament also reflected God's progressive revelation that corresponded to the development of

---

[47] *The Sunday School Helper*, 1 (1885), 158.

[48] F. Schweitzer, 'Developmental Views of the Religion of the Child: Historical Antecedents', in J. Fowler, *et al.* (eds), *Stages of Faith and Religious Development* (New York, 1991), 78.

[49] *Telling Bible Stories* (London, 1906), 4.

the child into a young adult.[50] On this basis reformers of Bible education drew up a host of lesson plans for teaching children and adolescents which, while differing in detail, attempted to put into practice the same assumptions about education and the Bible. They also contend with the same issues.

There is general agreement that the Genesis or 'morning' stories of the race – the Jahwist's account of Creation, the Tower of Babel, the Flood – were appropriate for teaching very young children. Many authors agreed with Walter Adeney that the stories should be presented in their 'quaint old world simplicity'.[51] In the same collection of essays F. C. Porter urged, 'Let the children read them as they are, but see that they seize upon their spirit so that if questions of fact afterward arise, they may feel that their treasure in the story does not depend upon the answer.'[52]

The authors, however, faced more complex and controversial issues when they began to outline lessons for children between the ages of six and ten. This was a developmental stage when, it was believed, stories were still important, but now they were to be drawn from a much wider part of the biblical narrative. Stories therefore set from the time of Abraham to the division of Solomon's kingdom became 'a marvellous storehouse of material singularly suitable for the instruction of the young'.[53] For Robert Horton, the Bible was the supreme children's story-book. Its stories of heroism and adventure fired the imagination of the six to ten-year-olds and could be supplemented by more detailed studies of the early origins stories in Genesis.[54]

Teachers and parents were warned, however, that at this stage they would have to deal with morally dubious stories and also the issue of historicity, growing out of a childish craving to know, 'Is it true?' The morally questionable tales gave rise to the lesser of the two dilemmas. Some authors, such as Montefiore, wanted these stories to be omitted altogether. In his *Bible* Elisha and the bears

---

[50] Craddock-Watson, 'Opening Address', 2; M. Glazebrook, *Notes and Outline Lessons for Teachers on Bible Lessons for the Young* (London, 1907), vi.

[51] *The Bible and the Child*, 87.

[52] Ibid., 135.

[53] Raymont, *The Use of the Bible in the Education of the Young*, 49.

[54] 'The Religious Training of Children in the Free Churches', in *The Child and Religion* (London, 1905), 265.

are omitted although the story was a favourite in the school syllabi.[55] Other writers believed children at this stage could be introduced to the idea of progressive revelation. On the behaviour of Jael, Bickersteth wrote to his young nephew, 'We cannot remind ourselves too often that the Bible records the gradual education of the children of Israel, and the morality of the Old Testament is a very different thing from that of the Sermon on the Mount.'[56]

There was overwhelming agreement, however, on how the issue of historical accuracy should be handled. The attention of children should be deflected away from the 'facts' to the 'purpose' of the story, its moral and spiritual lesson or 'truth of edification'. Regardless of what the historian or scientist said of the biblical record, these truths stood as universal, eternal and fundamental.[57] They comprised what most of these authors identified as 'revelation': ideas communicated by God to the biblical writers and then given a historically-conditioned setting. The authors were willing to concede that very young children could not move beyond the facts of the tale; children at this second stage, however, could begin to deal with abstract truth. One of the major functions of the literature of reformed Bible teaching, therefore, was to provide teachers and parents with guidance regarding the lessons to be drawn from the stories. Glazebrook's *Notes* for teachers using his *Bible Lessons for the Young* is just one of several such tools. Lesson XXXVI, 'The Quails', for example, drew from Numbers 11 the lesson that, 'Most children know what are the consequences of being allowed to eat as much as they like of some dainty. That experience should be taken as a type of other indulgences. All through life we desire what is bad for us, and the granting of our wishes brings satiety and disappointment.'[58] Bennett and Adeney's *Bible Story Re-Told for Young People* identify as the religious truth of Genesis 'that God ... was the God of the whole world, and made men and women and all things'.[59]

---

[55] *The Bible for Home Reading*, First part, 2nd edn, Second part (London, 1897, 1899).

[56] *Letters to a Godson*, 177–8.

[57] E.g., Horton, *The Child and Religion*, 275.

[58] *Notes and Outline Lessons for Teachers on Bible Lessons for the Young*, 106.

[59] W. H. Bennett and W. F. Adeney, *The Bible Story Re-Told for Young People* (London, 1897), 180.

It was recognised in some of the literature that older children in this category will still want their question, 'Is it true?' answered. Parents and teachers were encouraged not to eschew the matter of historicity. Children should be told frankly when scholars have questioned the veracity of the details of a particular story and such stories should not be accompanied by the use of maps and illustrations that could reinforce debatable details.[60] Parents and teachers should keep stressing that the 'local' setting of a story could be separated from its 'universal truth'; the former could be dispensed with while the latter remained unharmed.[61] Such was the case with the biblical numbers, for example, which did not reflect historical truth but rather were a device to aid in story-telling, similar to memory aids which children themselves use.[62] In the end the numbers were not important but rather what was learned about God and the duty of humanity to God.

Teachers of the Bible did not have to become too anxious about the number of men in an army or the age of a patriarch when he died, but what about the miracles reported in the text? To question miracles seemed to strike at the very heart of belief that God was active in the world. The literature suggested that such events in the Old Testament narrative should be given minimal attention. If children insisted on raising the issue, they could be told that such events do happen but they are rare.[63] Many of the Old Testament stories represented either natural occurrences which were misunderstood or were the product of primitive imaginations. One thing, however, was certain: the New Testament miracles were reliable because they were described in writing so soon after they occurred.[64]

This emphasis on the spiritual and moral truth of stories gave teachers a strategy for discussing the uniqueness of the Old Testament narrative. Children would be more than likely to observe

[60] W. F. Adeney in Farrar (ed.), *The Bible and the Child*, 81.

[61] M. Spencer, 'The Case Against Scripture Teaching in Schools', *The Journal of Education* (August 1896), 466; Bickersteth, *Letters to a Godson*, 292.

[62] Kennett, 'The Teaching of the Old Testament', 39.

[63] See Bickersteth's treatment of a variety of miracle stories, including Balaam, in his *Letters to a Godson*.

[64] Craddock-Watson, 'The Teaching of the Miraculous in the School Lesson', 16; Foakes-Jackson, 'Is the Old Testament Worth Presenting to the Young?', 17.

similarities between what they read in the Old Testament and the stories they heard from other cultures in the ancient world. They were to be told that all peoples tell stories and the Hebrews borrowed some of their tales from their neighbours. What was important to understand was that the people of Israel changed what they borrowed to make it 'better' so that the material could teach uplifting truths.[65] In their introduction to stories told in ancient Israel, Walter Adeney and William Bennett told their young readers that:

> Next I want to tell you some of the stories through which the Israelites were taught many useful lessons ... They are often thought to be rather poems or parables than history. The Babylonians had stories very much like these Israelite stories, only the Babylonian stories do not teach true and helpful lessons like those of the Bible.[66]

Another major change growing out of the developmental perspective on religious education was the regular inclusion of a study of the prophets with 'older children' around the age of twelve or thirteen. In the past the prophets had either been excluded from the curriculum or treated as a body of enigmatic predictions of future events. But in the scheme of progressive revelation the prophets occupied an exalted position as the forerunners of Christ. Also, their connection to world politics and their focus on the social issues of their times gave them a special relevancy to a society trying to teach civic duty to young men after the extension of the franchise.[67] Alexander Wilson's *The Prophets and Prophecy to the Close of the Eighth Century* was intended to 'interest children and young people in the prophets as brave men who lived in communion with God and did not hesitate to point out the evils of their time'.[68] Rose Selfe's *The Work of the Prophets*, in the *Simple Guides to Christian Knowledge Series*, had a similar purpose and was written to be placed in the hands of children themselves.[69] Both authors overturned the conventional

---

[65] E. Nixon and H. R. Steel, *The Bible Reader*, Part I (London, 1907), 1; Montefiore, *The Bible for Home Reading*, First part, 556–7.

[66] Bennett and Adeney, *The Bible Story Retold for Young People*, 180.

[67] Mitchell, *How to Teach the Bible*, 103.

[68] Review of A. Wilson, *The Prophets and Prophecy to the Close of the Eighth Century* (Edinburgh, 1903) in *Life & Work* (July 1903), 158–9.

[69] (London, 1904).

understanding of the prophetic role and then went on to devote separate chapters to the lives and messages of individual prophets. In so doing, Wilson fell back upon a definition of the word 'prophet' for children to memorise:

> God speaks to the prophet, then the prophet explains or interprets to the people what God says. Predicting the future is not necessarily a part of a prophet's work. A prophet was a forth-teller, not a fore-teller – one who told forth to the world what God had revealed or told to himself. The prophet makes clear to the world the truths of righteousness which God had implanted in the prophet's own heart.[70]

Selfe explained to her readers that the prophets were men who lived in close contact with God and saw events going on around them through his eyes. It was a common mistake to think that a prophet told people what was going to happen in the future. The prophets very often did foretell future events but this was only natural since they were taught by God to understand the meaning of their present situation; they were thus more likely to know what the future would bring forth and they demonstrated great courage in pointing out the sins of the society around them.[71]

But a new casting of the prophetic role by Selfe and Wilson and others was based on the conclusions of biblical critics regarding the dating of books such as Daniel and Isaiah. Such endeavours confronted writers for children with a question: how far should children be acquainted with the technicalities of critical scholarship such as Wellhausen's documentary hypothesis?

The response among educators and clergy and parents was that it depended upon the age and development of the children. Although sympathetic to biblical modernism, Canon R. H. Kennett asserted that, 'To hear Js and Es and Ps and Ds dropping from the lips of those who are spiritually mere babes . . . is to me almost as painful as it would be to hear an infant school debate the divorce laws.'[72] No one favoured teaching children under twelve to see the Bible as a 'jigsaw puzzle'; rather, teaching at this early stage had to give children full possession of the contents of the Bible and the spiritual and moral truths therein. Yet it was recognised that parents and teachers themselves should always be mindful of

---

[70] Wilson, *The Prophets and Prophecy*, 141.
[71] Selfe, *The Work of the Prophets*, 3–4.
[72] Kennett, 'The Teaching of the Old Testament', 38.

the assured results of criticism and might even introduce children to these conclusions while minimising the processes by which those conclusions were reached: 'We may not be able to explain Kepler's laws to young children, but that is no excuse for doggedly persisting in representing to them that sun, moon and stars all revolve around the earth.'[73] The genre most favoured for teaching the generally accepted results of biblical scholarship was the edited Bible for children and young people.

The edited Bibles, some of which were a retelling of Bible narratives along with commentary and some of which were a re-arrangement of the actual biblical text with commentary, introduced children in subtle ways to conclusions on the authorship and dating of the Old Testament material. Nixon and Steel's *The Bible Reader* drew the attention of children to the fact that there are two different Creation and Flood stories by using titles such as 'The Creation Story No. 1' and 'The Creation Story No. 2' for lessons. Burnside's *Old Testament History for Schools* divided the legal material of the Pentateuch into three strata – Mosaic, Deuteronomic and Priestly – and associated each with a different historical context. The First Part of Montefiore's *Bible for Home Reading* actually presented and discussed Genesis 1–11 in the chapters on Israel after the Exile.

Even children below the age of twelve were sometimes acquainted with the evidence used by scholars in determining the dating and authorship of the Old Testament books. Robert Gillie's book on the prophets, *God's Lantern Bearers*, was praised in the press as providing children with the benefits of higher criticism without mentioning it.[74] Gillie made it clear that much of Isaiah was the work of 'The Prophet of Comfort During the Exile' but he goes on to tell children some reasons why scholars drew this conclusion: 'God always moved the prophets to speak in such a way as to be of immediate use to their listeners, and it is not easy to see how these chapters could have greatly helped Isaiah's hearers.'[75] In order to help children understand how the critics did their work, Eugene Stock asked them to imagine how the editor of a book worked to collect old and new pieces of writing and put

[73] Adeney in *The Bible and the Child*, 75.
[74] *Life & Work*, 31 (January 1909), 19.
[75] *God's Lantern Bearers*, 358.

them together for a particular audience: 'Now learned men who have examined the Book of Genesis very closely tell us that it had an editor, perhaps one editor after another. It was not written or put together all at once.'[76]

By the time a child had reached early adolescence, a few of the authors of this literature were comfortable revealing details about authorship; the assumption was, however, that the child would have already come to appreciate the divine truth embedded in the text. N. P. Wood, an assistant master at Bishop's Stortford College, laid out one of the most explicit lesson plans 'to tackle critical questions directly'.[77] Students were to be asked to examine the Creation stories in Genesis 1 and Genesis 2 and note differences. On this basis, they were introduced to the symbols 'P' and 'J' and eventually to the rest of Wellhausen's hypothesis. Those who recommended such a course of teaching were convinced that a good teacher could help young people 'cross-examine' the documents and come up with much the same evidence for composite authorship as the biblical scholars.[78] One of the most imaginative attempts to introduce older children to the documents of the Pentateuch was a series of lessons in *The Sunday School Helper* by the Unitarian minister Philip Wicksteed.[79] Wicksteed began by introducing young people to a short history of early England made up of statements from many historians strung together. They were encouraged to think about the criteria for distinguishing the authors and when they might have lived. They were then encouraged to move on to an analysis of some of the Genesis stories and were familiarised with the Jahwist, Elohist and Priestly sources. Thus, even a young adolescent could begin to understand the way in which biblical critics did their work.

What can the historian say about the significance of this material? First, it is remarkable that this material was written and published at all. Traditional views of the Bible as a harmonious text dictated by God and infallible in every way still held the

---

[76] *The Story of the Bible* (London, 1906), 16.

[77] N. P. Wood, 'Prolegomena to the Study of the Bible. More Especially the Old Testament', in Wood (ed.), *Scripture Teaching in Secondary Schools*, 64.

[78] F. C. Burkitt, 'Preface', in Wood (ed.), *Scripture Teaching in Secondary Schools*, xi.

[79] *The Sunday School Helper*, 1 (1885), 57–60, 156–8, 250–3.

allegiance of many people and they launched a formidable attack on biblical criticism in books and periodicals. Yet the writers explored in this chapter did not play it safe, willingly challenging the pre-critical perspective. They did so in ways which would be applauded by late twentieth-century scholars who condemn biblical critics for their absorption in sterile academic debates or who struggle with effective ways of presenting the Bible to children: the authors examined here were at pains to show the positive results of critical scholarship for the believer, to make certain that the past became alive and illumined the present with 'new possibilities for personal and social transformation'.[80]

A reader of the critical literature for children cannot help but notice the presence of women in significant numbers among the authors. They represent a variety of occupations and interests – Bramston was a freelance writer and daughter of a Dean of Winchester; Soulsby, Powell, Edna Nixon and H. R. Steel were all teachers or headmistresses and Violet Stuart-Wortley was a socialite – and women, as mothers and teachers, were also clearly a part of the audience to which the material by both male and female authors was directed. Louise Houghton and Elizabeth Barker in fact targeted mothers as the primary consumers of their works.[81]

It is useful to see this literature against a background of turmoil as appropriate roles for women and their status in Church and society were debated. The ideal woman in middle-class Victorian Britain was believed destined by God and physiology to inhabit a sphere very different from that of man.[82] She was to manage a domestic haven, teach good conduct to her children and perform works of charity. Yet these fixed notions about women were being challenged as the new century dawned. A movement for the higher education of women was making strides, suffrage for women loomed on the horizon and evangelical groups such as the Salvation Army offered women a place as preachers. The critical literature

[80] W. Wink, *The Bible in Human Transformation* (Philadelphia, 1973), 1–15; M. C. Boys, 'Religious Education and Contemporary Biblical Scholarship', *Religious Education*, 74 (March–April 1979), 185–7.

[81] Houghton, *Telling Bible Stories*; E. Barker, *The Religious Instruction of Children at Home* (London, 1903).

[82] J. N. Burstyn, *Victorian Education and the Ideal of Womanhood* (New Brunswick, New Jersey, 1984).

on the biblical education of children reflected these developments, revealing an interesting ambivalence as it tried to hold tradition and change together.

This literature required women both as authors and consumers to engage in a scholarly study of the Bible at a level few women in the past had achieved. It assumed that women could understand critical views of the Bible, summarise them and present them to their children, their pupils or the public. Such an assumption was a challenge to the prevailing notions that women who used their intellects would endanger their reproductive functions and that their cognitive skills were not as highly developed as their intuitive.

Yet the pull of tradition is also felt in this body of material. The fact that mothers and female authors were simply acting as conduits of scholarship produced by men was compatible with the popular Victorian idea that women were not capable of great intellectual breakthroughs on their own; they were consigned to passing along the achievements of male academics.[83] But even acting as scholarly go-betweens may have been too risky. The historian cannot help but raise the question of whether women who wrote on biblical scholarship would have been acceptable to publishers and readers if they had not been doing so for children, considered to be their special responsibility. Female authors are noticeably absent from the body of writers of books popularising biblical criticism among adults.

Although biographical information about these women is difficult to locate, there is some indication from Lucy Soulsby and Mary Bramston that learning in the area of biblical studies was seen as compatible with the Victorian ideal of womanhood.[84] By learning something about composite authorship and progressive revelation, women were preparing themselves to do what they did most competently – teach morality to their children and be thoughtful companions to their spouses. The movement advocating the higher education of women, to which some of these authors were attached, was, in the minds of many supporters, a strategy for providing married women with the requisite skills to carry out

---

[83] Ibid., 73.

[84] Bramston, in *The Dawn of Revelation*, argues that it was a divine command that woman give up a will of her own; see also L. Soulsby, *The Victorian Woman* (London, 1914).

their traditional duties as well as providing unmarried women with respectable employment. Thus Lucy Soulsby, who wrote *Bible Reading in the Present Day*, could argue that women should not be content with 'little' devotional books and 'baby knowledge' but rather follow the educated thought of the day on Bible study. This, however, was to make them more competent in their own sphere.[85]

Finally, as far as the sources allow us, we can make the observation that female authors of the literature under consideration never make the transition into what would currently be identified as a 'feminist' perspective on the Bible. Their concern for historical context could have led them to identify the patriarchal character of the ancient world and question the appropriateness of transferring such time-bound values to the modern world. They had models for such a perspective in the *Woman's Bible* and the writing of Catherine Booth, yet there is no evidence that they ever made this transition.[86]

The content of this critical literature for children also highlights some of the difficulties inherent in mediating between the world of biblical scholarship and lay audiences, particularly juvenile ones. Emphasis on progressive revelation helped teachers deal with primitive thought and morality, but the reader can detect an almost agnostic tendency to demean the value of the Old Testament, which is constantly seen as a necessary but inferior prelude to the fullness of revelation in Jesus. By describing the Old Testament as 'dubious' and the New Testament as 'higher and deeper', the texts leave little doubt as to what was being conveyed to pupils.[87] In addition, the authors' use of progressive revelation obscures the complexity of the Old Testament material. There is little recognition that the simplistic model of the upward-sloping line does not represent adequately the religious life of ancient Israel. The texts present the prophets as the high point of Old Testament faith and link them to the life and work of Jesus; the formalism and legalism of the post-exilic period is rarely dealt with.

[85] *The Religious Education of Women* (privately printed and circulated pamphlet), 16.

[86] *The Woman's Bible*, Part I, II (New York, 1895, 1898); C. Booth, *Female Ministry: or, Woman's Right to Preach the Gospel* (London, 1859).

[87] Bell, *Religious Teaching in Secondary Schools*, 45; Horton in *The Bible and the Child*, 49.

The attention paid to 'truth of edification' in this material raises other issues. In order to help children deal with myth, legend and historical mis-reporting in the biblical text, authors exaggerate the importance of 'truth of edification' over 'truth of fact'. Children could easily get the idea that the actual occurrence of Old Testament events was a matter of indifference, while they were asked to accept unquestioningly the historicity of the New Testament. The writers of this literature also encouraged parents and teachers to announce the 'truth' embedded in the texts with great confidence because such truth was derived from a context-conscious approach to the Bible. Historical and literary criticism, they believed, could 'distil the true word of God out of the Scriptures' and avoid the pitfalls of subjectivity because they were scientific methods.[88] Yet the truths which were selected or extracted from the Old Testament were frequently coloured by the theological and cultural perspectives of these late-Victorian writers. Many of them, for example, betray a liberal evangelical persuasion by emphasising the 'brotherhood of man' as a fundamental Old Testament truth and spiritual transformation as the goal of Old Testament study.[89] Victorian middle-class morality is also evident. Glazebrook's lesson on 'Saul's Jealousy' in 1 Samuel 18 concludes with the truth, 'Friendship is best between equals'[90] and 'Aunt Amy' or Marian Pritchard asks her young readers, after thinking about the story of Joseph in Egypt, if they would have been as brave or done their duty 'so manfully' if they had been in his place.[91]

What of the significance of this literature for religious education between 1870 and 1914? Historians have an abundance of resources to reveal what people thought should happen in schools and Sunday schools but nothing is harder to document than what actually occurred.[92] This quest is made more difficult since board

[88] P. T. Forsyth, 'Sunday Schools and Modern Theology', *Christian World Pulpit* (23 February 1887), 127; Peake in *The Bible and the Child*, 58.

[89] Bramston, *The Dawn of Revelation*, 5–6; M. Wolseley-Lewis, 'Methods of Religious Teaching in Secondary Schools for Girls', in *Methods of Religious Teaching* (London, 1908), 7.

[90] Glazebrook, *Notes and Outline Lessons for Teachers on Bible Lessons*, 192.

[91] M. Pritchard, *Book of Beginnings or Stories on Genesis and How to Teach Them* (London, 1896), 92.

[92] Archibald, 'History of Religious Education: a Documentary Trail', 412.

schools were not required by the government to examine or inspect religious education, and syllabi from voluntary schools were often not preserved. One way to probe this question of influence is to look at the publishing details for the critical texts – who published them, how often and at what price? A list of relevant publishers demonstrates that most of the major publishing houses of the late nineteenth century are represented. Between 1870 and 1890 the market was dominated by Longmans and Macmillan, publishers of a number of the volumes considered here. Methuen, Hodder & Stoughton and Sampson, Low & Marston had made names for themselves publishing the works of major British literary figures. A&C Black and Edward Arnold had become well-known because of their general reference works and textbooks.[93] But it was not just the fact that major publishers produced the critical works. It is interesting to see that at least a third went through two or more editions, with Burnside's *Old Testament History*, Bickersteth's *Letters to a Godson* and Montefiore's *Bible for Home Reading* leading the rest in terms of popularity. As mentioned above, *Bookseller's* analysis of late-Victorian book prices includes a category of prices designated as 'medium range' (between 3s 7d and 10s) which accounted for about thirty per cent of books sold. It is into this medium range that the critical literature for children fell and most of the books were at the lower end of the range, with prices averaging around three shillings per volume.[94] While still priced too high for most working-class families, the Victorian middle classes could have easily afforded to purchase such publications.

The practicalities of publication generally were, therefore, in favour of a wide circulation and consumption of this critical literature; in addition, the books considered here were regularly reviewed in popular periodicals with large circulations such as the *British Weekly*, the *Guardian* and *The Sunday School Chronicle*.[95] The

[93] For histories of particular publishing houses see F. A. Mumby, *Publishing and Bookselling: a History from Earliest Times to the Present Day* (London, [1954]) and Ellis, *A History of Children's Reading and Literature*.

[94] Book prices are taken from the *English Catalogue of Books* (London: seriatum).

[95] The *Guardian*, for example, reviewed Burnside's *Old Testament History for Schools* (29 June 1904), Mitchell's *How To Teach the Bible* (6 June 1906) and Smyth's *Bible for the Young* (18 March 1903); *The Sunday School Chronicle*,

authors interested in promoting critical Bible teaching recommended each other's works in their own publications, particularly commending the publications by Bell, Glazebrook and Bickersteth. Seven of the titles were on a reading list for teachers on the place and form of religious education drawn up by the Board of Education in England.[96]

Yet these practical circumstances have to be seen over against others which could have functioned to undermine the wide consumption of the literature. Maura Ives in 'A Bibliographical Approach to Victorian Publishing' discusses the physical analysis of printed texts and claims that the physical formats through which works met the public contributed to ways in which the readers perceived the works and the authors themselves.[97] Noticeable about these books is the absence of illustrations and the use of plain covers despite the rich illustrations and ornamental typeface that were found in abundance in secular children's books at the turn of the century. Children's books generally had cloth covers inlaid with gold and bindings with highly decorative lettering and they included sophisticated illustrations prepared with new or revived techniques in wood engraving and photography. The texts we have been considering, however, tended to be bound in dark, dull colours (Smyth's *Bible* was dark green) with black lettering. The typeface in the books was often, though not always, dense and only a small number contained illustrations of any kind. They were in stark contrast to the conservative texts intended to promote verbal inspiration which were replete with engravings and photographs illustrating the customs, flora and fauna and archaeological sites of Palestine.[98]

Another factor mitigating against the absorption of a critical perspective in the classroom was the sheer weight of tradition.

---

in addition to Mitchell (19 April 1906), reviewed *Telling Bible Stories* by Houghton (15 November 1906) and the *Bible for Home and School* by Bartlett and Peters (9 December 1897); see also the reviews of the *Bible for Home Reading* by Montefiore (27 July 1899) and Selfe's *The Work of the Prophets* (23 March 1905) in the *British Weekly*.

[96] 'Books and Papers on Religious Instruction in Schools', *Parliamentary Papers* 1906 [Cd 3208] XC., pp. 291ff.

[97] Jordan and Patten (eds), *Literature in the Marketplace*, 269.

[98] E.g., T. Nicol, *Recent Explorations in Bible Lands* (Edinburgh, 1892) and E. Ranyard, *A Bible Portfolio for Sunday Afternoon Leisure* (London, 1887).

Many voices claimed that biblical criticism would help to reform and reinvigorate Bible teaching, but there was also an outcry against teaching children such dangerous views. The London School Board member James Allenson Picton in 1907 described the reaction of parents to critical Bible teaching: 'We pay our rates and taxes . . . to have the Bible taught in its simplicity as the Word of God. It would be an outrage on our conscience if teachers were allowed to teach it as a human book.'[99] The proliferation of popular books refuting higher criticism such as Alfred Cave's *The Battle of the Standpoints* and Robert Anderson's *Daniel in the Critics' Den* were in part motivated by the realisation that criticism was 'passing to the populace' and influencing the home and school.[100]

The obstacles which parents and teachers faced in conveying a new perspective on the Bible were formidable and were likely also to have contributed to the persistence of a traditional curriculum. The preface to a report on a conference on scripture teaching held in 1912 was candid enough to admit that, 'Much depends on the teacher now.'[101] Numerous authors we have been considering recognise and sometimes lament that such mediation between the world of scholarship and the world of children required diligent study and special knowledge. Spencer was concerned about where teachers would get the books they needed to master biblical scholarship and Powell and Tylee complained that teachers quickly abandoned their scholarly studies because the material was too difficult to teach.[102] This was especially true of the moral and religious lessons teachers had to convey and examine.[103] An added complication was that teachers were expected to bring to their jobs piety and moral earnestness to help children see that higher criticism did not threaten faith.[104]

Those who observed religious education in Britain between the wars made it plain that a critical perspective on the Bible generally had not been absorbed into biblical instruction in the State and

[99] *The Bible in School* (London, 1907), 5.
[100] *The Battle of the Standpoints: The Old Testament and the Higher Criticism* (London, 1890); *Daniel in the Critics' Den*, 3rd edn (London, 1909).
[101] Burkitt, 'Preface', xi.
[102] Spencer, 'The Case Against Scripture Teaching', 466; Powell, *Religious Teaching in Schools*, 2–3; Tylee, 'The Bible in the Schoolroom', 359.
[103] Bell, *Religious Teaching in Secondary Schools*, 54.
[104] Craddock-Watson, 'Opening Address', 6.

Church schools. The 1912 conference referred to above was called because of the poor state of scripture teaching; the new publications did not seem to be making much of an impact. Although he was sent to schools to inspect subjects other than religion, A. W. Newton in 1919 was discouraged by the fact that in the Board and denominational schools all biblical material was presented to children on an equal historical footing and teachers seemed to choose material in an almost random manner.[105] 'Religious education' consisted almost entirely of teachers' summaries of sections from the Bible. In 1925 an instructor at Aberdeen Provincial Training Centre observed that religious education was handicapped by a failure of teachers to understand the concept of progressive revelation.[106] Several years later both the chaplain and the principal of Bede College, Durham, declared that the Bible was the 'worst taught subject' in the British schools. They had to remind their readers that a critical and historical approach to the Bible, and not simply an acquaintance with its factual material, could both interest children and conform to state regulations.[107] The consensus among educational leaders of this period was that teachers were not equipped in their training to teach the Bible in a scholarly manner.[108]

The picture is not much different in the Sunday schools of Britain. The Sunday School Union, which held a Conference of Experts and Biblical Scholars in 1906, was divided on how much modern biblical scholarship should be introduced to children. Frank Johnson and Peake argued vigorously for the teaching of biblical criticism but most participants were reluctant and no manifesto on the subject was ever issued.[109] Philip Cliff's history of the Sunday school in England indicates that biblical scholarship did not make much of an impact before the late 1930s.

[105] *The English Elementary School: Some Elementary Facts About It* (London, 1919), 180.

[106] F. J. Rae, *How To Teach the Old Testament* (London, 1925), 9ff.

[107] E. F. Braley and M. C. Petitpierre, *The State and Religious Education* (London, 1934), 66, 94.

[108] E.g., G. Mack, 'The Teaching of Religious Knowledge in the Sixth Form', *Journal of Education*, 67 (June 1935), 367; and Braley and Petitpierre, *The State and Religious Education*, 64.

[109] F. Johnson (ed.), *Bible Teaching by Modern Methods* (London, 1907), 161–5.

Teachers may have found the material simply too difficult to teach and the Sunday school movement seems, at least early in this period, to have been preoccupied with its discussions of graded material as opposed to the uniform lesson plans. Also, as Cliff suggests, the First World War brought an older generation of teachers who embraced verbal inspiration back into the Sunday school classrooms.[110]

A hundred years after Glazebrook and Houghton and Montefiore published their works, the proper use of the Bible with children of all ages remains an unresolved issue. New life was breathed into this debate with the Education Act of 1944, which made religious instruction a requirement in state schools, and with the work of Ronald Goldman in the 1960s.[111] Whether and how to make the riches of biblical scholarship accessible to non-specialist lay people including children continues to be part of this debate and remains an unfinished task of the Church and the educator.[112] Although we may be discomfited by the confidence revealed in these works or readily identify the flaws, we cannot help but admire their authors' commitment to the ideal that an intelligent use of the Bible needs to be cultivated from the earliest years.

[110] Cliff, *Rise and Development of the Sunday School Movement*, 226–31.
[111] R. Goldman, *Readiness for Religion: a Basis for Developmental Religious Education* (London, 1965) and *Religious Thinking from Childhood to Adolescence* (London, 1964).
[112] Boys, 'Religious Education and Contemporary Biblical Scholarship', 182–3.

Chapter 5

Transforming the Creed

Peter Matheson

THE 'Transforming of the Kirk' was a world-wide phenomenon in the second half of the nineteenth century. In far-flung New Zealand, as well as in Scotland, Sabbatarianism was challenged, hymns and choirs introduced, and the rigid certainties of the past challenged, as minds were opened up to the new science and the *via rhetorica* of poet, novelist, and historian. Ministers who read George Eliot preached different sermons. Young Women's Literary Societies drank deep at the well of Romantic poetry. The Subordinate Standards were weighed in the balance and found wanting.

A pioneer society, or rather a consolidating colonial one, such as that of New Zealand, did more than mirror the changes taking place 'back home'. Otago, in New Zealand's Deep South, was demographically a young society, quite direct, if not abrasive, in style. Its dreams remained more idealistic, but paradoxically its people more down to earth than those in contemporary Scotland. The Gold Rush had pulled the plug on the pious hopes of a Presbyterian utopia. Intra-Presbyterian disputes had almost no resonance at all in a thinly peopled landscape which was proud of having no religious establishment. The Anglican 'Little Enemy', and worse still, Irish Catholics, had to be reckoned with.

Above all, this was a lay person's patch. Would-be clerical autocrats were given short shrift. The fierce hunger for education, progress, enlightenment swept all before it. Protestant evangelicals saw themselves in the van of this progress, as 'liberals', as advocates of a new civilised age, of which missionary expansion was a key element. A minister such as James Copland, with his experience in the gold-fields and North Dunedin, was as much a banner-carrier of such optimism as those who could not share his authoritarian view of Scripture, or his implacable opposition to Darwin.[1] Evolution, with its gospel of progressive development, was a cruelly difficult and seductive theory for such evangelicals to resist. They felt torn apart, and indeed the ferocity of the controversies generated reflects this pain. It was not only a matter of how Scripture was to be read, or the natural world understood. Personal and community identities were at stake. Who was at the sharp edge of progress? Who had the right to be adjudged 'liberal'? Terms such as 'liberal', 'conservative', 'evangelical' all have to be saddled with riders.

In the bustling small town of Dunedin, with its 33,000 inhabitants, new infrastructures emerged to facilitate this debate, to take it beyond the laboratory and field-trip and the ministerial study. Certainly the professionals, clerical or scientific, took a leading role. Undoubtedly, something of a turf war was involved. Who was qualified to speak and lead and guide the community? Who were the experts about literature which was also Holy Writ and about a world for which Christ, it was believed, had died? Who were the high-priests of the progress, of which every one felt part? But beyond such demarcation issues were much greater ones. A lively Press, a steady flow of pamphlets, and a remarkable number of public meetings ensured that the whole community engaged with the real issues. It was a struggle for the soul of the community as well as for that of individuals.

Mechanics' Institutes were very effective as resource centres and cradles of new thinking. The impressive Otago Institute provided a scholarly forum for debates on evolution between believing scientists, and scientifically literate ministers. It was a semi-public forum for intelligent debate, the rules of the game apparently impartial. Rival opinion-leaders were on trial. One is reminded of the role played by civic disputations in the Reformation period. One particular meeting in the spring of 1876 (September!) proved crucial. It convinced many leading clergy to modify their positions. Sermons were another semi-public forum. Ministers

---

[1] Cf. J. Stenhouse, 'The Rev Dr James Copland and the Mind of New Zealand "Fundamentalism"', *Journal of Religious History*, 17 (1993), 475–97.

such as Dr Thomas Roseby, the Dunedin Congregationalist, the Methodist A. R. Fitchett, and the Presbyterian Charles Fraser in Christchurch coaxed their congregations to accept a theistic understanding of evolution. The Evolution debate, moreover, was in the context of wider debates about the new biblical criticism, about Christology, about the Atonement. Public meetings on matters theological were often crowded out. Especially when William Salmond spoke.

The son of a grocer and wine merchant in Edinburgh, William Salmond was the first professor of the new Theological Hall of the Synod of Otago and Southland. He arrived in 1876, at the age of forty-one, 'a spare-built man, of diminutive stature. His hands clasp the desk, the left shoulder being slightly raised above the right (suggesting) a sickly constitution.'[2] Like so many others, including his self-appointed Inquisitor-General, the Rev. James McGregor, of Oamaru, lately professor of New College, Edinburgh, he had come out to the new colony for his health.

Salmond was a United Presbyterian; his wife Jane, whom he married in 1861, was the daughter of another UP minister, James Young, a strong teetotaller. He studied in Edinburgh and then in Germany. His seventeen-year ministry at North Shields, near Newcastle, saw him win a reputation for moral courage. He had no time for rigid sabbatarianism[3] and introduced his parishioners to all the lively controversies of the time; the relationship of free will and providence, the challenge of new geological and biological discoveries. By 1871 he was informing his flock of his doubts as to whether those unconverted to the Christian faith in this life were necessarily doomed. In 1873 he argued for more liberty in the interpretation of the Westminster Confession.[4] He spoke well, wrote memorably, and was well liked as a pastor.[5]

---

[2] Letter by J. G. S. Grant, *Saturday Advertiser*, 18 March 1976; a monograph on him is lacking; cf. the good account in S. Swain-Ingham, 'William Salmond: Hero or Heretic?' Otago University, BTh dissertation, 1993.

[3] W. Salmond, *Sabbath Observance under the New Testament: A Lecture* (North Shields, 1866).

[4] W. Salmond, *The Limits of Comprehension within the Church. An address delivered at a meeting of the English United Presbyterian Synod* (Edinburgh, 1873).

[5] G. Angus, *The Square 1779–1929. Being the History of the Congregation of Northumberland Square Presbyterian Church, North Shields* (Newcastle, 1929).

His dashing pen, gift for presenting complex issues in digestible and popular form, and his crusading zeal to spread enlightenment led to his instant lionisation by the Presbyterians of Otago. He addressed the YMCA on rationality as the basis of all moral excellence, a common enough topos among Otago Presbyterians, but the qualities of mind recommended are more than a little reminiscent of a good eighteenth-century Moderate such as 'Jupiter' Carlyle: 'candour, discretion, magnanimity, thoughtfulness, geniality, tolerance, a questing mind'.[6] He made a name for himself as an apologist for the reasonableness of Christian faith. His evening lectures on the inspiration of Scripture and on the person of Christ, fully reported in the local papers, were models of lucid and broad scholarship.[7] He was a successful editor of the *New Zealand Presbyterian*. This was a scholar with a popular touch. Within a decade, however, he was to be hauled up on an accusation of heresy. His case is of interest far beyond the little world of Dunedin. The double DDs from Glasgow and Edinburgh, awarded before the great controversy for which he is now remembered, are an indication of his standing.

On a personal level, the livid reaction to his main writing, the *Reign of Grace* of 1888, appears to have so traumatised him that he was never again to write on theological matters. Those who are opinion-makers, or opinion-breakers, can pay a high emotional cost.

Secondly, the quality of his rhetoric, like that of his main opponent, James McGregor, gives one pause. His communication skills, his ability to arouse feeling as well as convey information and ideas, remind one of the Reformation pamphleteers at their most effective. Salmond's generation, of course, inherited the pamphleteering traditions of the Disruption, but his language certainly repays attention. Although he was no populist, he could reach the nub of the matter in a moment, and express in pregnant phrases what many were too confused or timorous to think. His material is arranged logically enough, but the power of the writings lies in their emotional integrity and what one might call their unguarded polemic. He was an orator. He seized on pivotal ideas

---

[6] *Otago Daily Times*, 6 May 1878.
[7] *Otago Witness*, 8,15, 22, 29 June 1878; 6, 27 July 1878 ; 3, 10, 17 August 1878.

and gave them a popular twist. He was by no means alone in this, but one of a team of genial religious opinion-breakers in Dunedin: Fitchett, Waddell, Gibb, Nevill, Dutton. They took theology out of the study into the market-place, in an interesting parallel to the very highly developed communication skills of New Zealand scientists at the same time, such as F. W. Hutton. The educated lay public, assisted by a lively and critical journalistic world, was trusted to be the judge.

Thirdly, all these preachers, lecturers, and publicists propagated and themselves epitomised an extraordinary shift in the basic metaphors through which the scientific universe, the moral universe, and indeed, and above all, God came to be seen. The paradigm shift in any one of these 'worlds' involved all the others with which it was interlocked. The challenge to a scientific orthodoxy, as so often before in church history, appeared to destabilise biblical and confessional orthodoxy. Quite apart from the intellectual challenge, it took considerable courage to review such dearly held opinions, to accept the emotional risks involved, and to allow one's moral imagination full play.

Shortly after his arrival in Dunedin, Salmond had his North Shields lectures on prayer and the laws of nature republished. They illustrate well the imaginative revolution required of thinkers and believers at the time, the threat posed by scientific determinism to Christianity's personalist understanding of the universe. We inhabit an 'iron-bound world'. The predictability of natural events such as the return of a comet, due to the 'remorseless sweep of law', is freely acknowledged. Prayer cannot halt fire or stop water from drowning people. Creation, after all, is the orderly product of a deliberating intelligence. On the other hand, to make prayer something purely subjective would be to entomb it in the heart. The world is not a machine, but has mystery at its core. Nature is 'tender, subtle, yielding, variable to an incredible extent', it is a magazine of wondrous forces, 'Every time you plant your foot upon the ground you send an echo through the universe.' God himself 'plays Creation like a harpist'.

The musical analogy is intriguing. Salmond's God was not crudely interventionist, and did not violate the laws of reason and causality, despite 'suffering incredible drains upon his resources from our ceaseless perversities'. The world of matter and that of spirit, he suggests, may well be foreordained to dovetail into one another. The labour of Science and the intuition of the Hebrew are one.[8] Matter dissolves into energy, and so has kinship to prayer.

Despite this poetic, and remarkably modern-sounding understanding of science and God, Salmond initially adopted a gladiatorial stance against Darwinism. His arguments in 1876 were interesting. All thought and literature is pervaded by the ideas of evolution; our nature, however, is radically conservative and slow to accept new ideas especially when they invade the 'most awful and sacred treasure' of one's religious persuasions. He does not presume to pronounce on the truth of evolution, and agrees that it is not necessarily atheistic; he flirts with the possibility of it being restricted to animal and vegetable life. His concerns are spiritual: that it is irreconcilable with essential Christian beliefs about human nature, the divinity of Christ, and the doctrine of immortality. We must be more, surely, than 'an improved and metamorphosed gorilla'.[9] He was soon to revise such views.

In his evening lectures on Christology in First Church in 1878 he fought a two-front battle. On the one hand, Christianity cannot be reduced to a mere moralism. On the other, theology must be open to constant revision, and the propositions of the seventeenth century cannot be absolutised. This leads only to wretched sectarianism.[10] The controversies about Christology in the Early Church showed a shameful ferocity, a failure to realise that we are dealing with 'inscrutable mysteries'.[11] Theology is not the Gospel.[12] This is a distinction that will be taken up in a fruitful way a generation later, by John Dickie, the real midwife of the 'New Theology' for New Zealand Presbyterianism.[13]

Faith requires room if it is to flourish. Luther pointed out that Christ's first disciples moved progressively from a recognition of his humanity, to his Lordship, and only then to his divinity. We

[8] W. Salmond, *The Christian Doctrine of Providence and Prayer and the Reign of Law. Three lectures* (North Shields, 1875; also Dunedin, 1876).

[9] 'The Doctrine of Evolution and Christianity', *The New Zealand Magazine*, 1 (January 1876), 271.

[10] *Otago Witness*, 8 June 1878.

[11] Ibid., 10 August 1878.

[12] Ibid., 17 August 1878.

[13] Cf. G. S. King, 'Organising Christian truth: an investigation of the life and work of John Dickie', Otago University, PhD thesis, 1998.

must not downplay Christ's humanity. He was truly tempted, and his incarnation points to the value of our emotions and our bodies.[14] Yet he was also truly divine, a mystery we cannot explain away. If we water that down we deny our sin and need for redemption, and the whole earnestness of faith is lost.[15]

Meanwhile, in an address to Dunedin Presbytery, apparently 'of considerable length', he spoke about the theological training required for candidates in a new country. A one-sided intellectual conception of Christianity and the ministry was inappropriate, and 'scholarship and the gift of sermon making were by no means absolute necessities in a minister in a country like this; what was wanted was men of large hearts and practical attainments and sympathies'.[16]

Salmond's most important writing was *The Reign of Grace*. Like all his works, it is a pamphlet (one shilling), rather than a book. It appeared in 1888. Two years earlier Salmond had left the tiny Theological Hall for the more prestigious post of Professor of Mental and Moral Philosophy at the infant Otago University. As the full title suggests, the pamphlet dealt with the question of Universalism, and argued for a second chance for salvation after the grave, a Protestant variant of Purgatory, as it were. The whole work is very much a period piece. It reflects the more optimistic anthropology of the era and a gentler understanding of God as Father, rather than as King and Judge. McLeod Campbell's understanding of the Atonement was an important influence. Maurice, Farrar, Plumptre, Norman MacLeod, Thomas Erskine are also mentioned approvingly. It could hardly be described as a considered work of scholarship, although it rests on wide reading. As a piece of demolition, however, it was quite magnificent. It shattered the tottering edifice of high Calvinist thought in Otago for ever.

The main thrust of Salmond's writing was directed against an exclusive view of Gospel and Church, against the apparent predestination of the vast majority of humanity to eternal damnation, including unbaptised infants, the ungodly, the mad and the bad, together with the untold masses of 'heathen' overseas. Salmond's solution was to reject the view that this short life on earth represents

[14] *Otago Witness*, 15 June 1878.
[15] Ibid., 6, 27 July 1878.
[16] *Otago Daily Times*, 2 May 1878.

the only opportunity to embrace the redemption of Christ. Death has not this monstrous, 'gorgonising' power to petrify one for all eternity. This image of Gorgo or Medusa was important for him.

For it is clear that the pamphlet was written under compulsion. Salmond was aware of the division and controversy within the Church that it would excite. He shrank from the 'appalling spectacle' of furious theological animosity, which had always caused him to 'shudder'. He knew that he would be reproached with cowardice for keeping silent so long about his doubts about the Westminster Confession, as a teacher of the Church sworn to uphold it, and with waiting until he could speak out with impunity as a professor at the University. However, 'there is a point of luminous conviction which brings with it a summons to open confession'. His privileged position enabled and compelled him to speak out against the 'intellectual terrorism' which intimidated others, and sought to stem the spirit of the times. He felt he could no longer help himself.

We have, he argued, to face the reality that our inherited creed is 'hanging about us in shreds and tatters', demoralising the Church in New Zealand as secularisation advances on all sides. Such intellectual stagnation is leading the Church which is a 'living organism', and must always be ready to evolve and change, to fall behind 'the living thought of our age'. His hope was that his writing would appeal to those who have wrestled with the issues, and who have learned, through the scars of their own internal conflict, 'the gentleness of intellectual pity', itself a memorable phrase.[17]

Salmond was not an absolute universalist. Hell, though much spiritualised, remains a necessary hypothesis, as does the doctrine of original sin. The wicked, it appears, deserve their doom. What he denies is that the 'day of grace', or the 'day of mercy', is necessarily limited to this life. This truncates the reign of grace, and provides a 'selfish, sensuous and narrow' motivation for evangelisation. It also suggests an 'appalling' view of human life, and a hell packed to suffocation. 'My brain reels, and a horror of great darkness comes down on my heart as I try to realise what these centuries of human history signify.'[18] For the sake of a few elect

[17] W. Salmond, *The Reign of Grace. A discussion of the question of the possibility of salvation for all men in this life or in the life to come* (Dunedin, 1888), 3–6.
[18] Ibid., 16f.

souls most of humanity are to be treated as dung. It is far too easy to avoid this horror by glib talk of the mysteries of Divine Providence.

Theological logic (Salmond almost always uses 'theology' pejoratively in this writing) condemns all unregenerate infants on the basis of original sin. Folk religion, on the other hand, seeks to avoid this by declaring all dead children angels, which is quite illogical. Surely there must be an alternative. How can we condemn the myriads upon myriads of unregenerate heathen to an eternity in hell? Again, Salmond talks of his 'shivering horror' (the word 'shiver', and its cognates occurs again and again) at such a contradiction to 'our belief in the infinite worth of souls and the Fatherhood of God'.[19]

Death, however, need not be seen as this ultimate and absolute barrier. It is but a new form of self-consciousness. For many a soul, indeed, it would be an emancipation from a crushing material struggle, from illness, or even madness. If there is a moral government of the universe, if in the 'full blaze of Self-consciousness' every soul can recognise its infinite dignity and value why should the future life only figure as a retributive judgement? After all, most of those so condemned are already disadvantaged in this life.[20] God, the Father of our spirits, cannot possibly treat his children worse than the most depraved parents.

Salmond then develops his view of the progressive preparation of humanity for the Gospel, which he regards as an evolutionary process. A false supernaturalism ignores the cultural preconditions for the reception of the Gospel. In saying this Salmond is aware that he is closer to a 'Roman' than to a Protestant doctrine of justification. The regenerated, he suggests, however, are the first fruits of humanity, but the mighty purpose of grace encompasses all. Thus 'the extension of human probation into the future life is an inevitable inference from the universal Fatherhood of God as manifested in the universal death of Christ'.[21] The traditional teaching of predestination, on the other hand, is 'a poisonous error and a parasitical growth, the enwrapping of the mouldering garments of a superstition'.[22]

---

[19] Ibid., 21.
[20] Ibid., 24.
[21] Ibid., 34.
[22] Ibid., 36.

Dealing with the objections to his views, above all that they are novel and unscriptural, Salmond argues that the overwhelming drift of opinion in the German, American, and some of the British Churches, including the Established Church of Scotland, leans towards his view. Scripture may be far from unanimous. It was, after all, 'composed under practical exigencies to meet current situations'.[23] But its central message is of God's love and of the magnificence of God's gracious purpose.

There would appear to be a Platonic tinge to much of this, but we come closest to Salmond's own concerns, perhaps, when he cites a pastoral encounter with the aged widow of a fisherman whose three sons had also perished at sea. How could he fail to assure her of God's mercy to them? 'Oh, men and brethren! by the mercy of God, by the love of truth, and by the sorrows of Christ, let us tell no more lies. Oh hard, relentless Orthodoxy! have pity . . . !'[24] He becomes quite lyrical about a positive evangelism that draws people out of their wretchedness to a vision of their own moral personality and of the glory and pathos of the eternal mercy of God.

Clearly his pamphlet touched a nerve. It speedily reached five editions, and sold six thousand copies, quite remarkable for a young colony. Of the many outraged ripostes the most imaginative and substantial was James McGregor's, who lampooned Salmond's 'curiously ferocious humanitarianism'.[25] In Scotland McGregor had already crossed swords with Norman Macleod, accusing him of breaking his oath by his anti-Sabbatarian views. Salmond now comes under the same accusation for this 'flimsy performance' of his.[26] He makes Jehovah a double-tongued Apollo, imputes insincerity not only to professing Christian believers but to Christ himself. Real salvation is replaced with a paper sovereignty. Salmond's real problem is recognised, as he warms to his task, to be a moral one; he is a degenerate, and his pamphlet will encourage ungodliness.

[23] Ibid., 41.
[24] Ibid., 56.
[25] J. McGregor, *The Day of Salvation Obscured in a recent pamphlet on 'The Reign of Grace'* (Dunedin, 1888) 4; another more stolid response was by the layman, Adam D. Johnson, in *The Two-edged Sword: Being an examination of Professor Salmond's 'Reign of Grace' in the light of Scripture* (Dunedin, 1888).
[26] Ibid., 11.

Such sentimental Moderatism, reminiscent of William Robertson, was no substitute for the tradition of our fathers, which stretches back through the Puritans and Calvin, to Augustine and Nicaea. After all, the Westminster Confession is 'the noblest symbolical representative of the Golden Age of evangelical theology'.[27] Salmond's penny-whistle will hardly silence the trumpet of Sinai. He understands neither Scripture nor the Atonement, abandoning the rationality of Scripture for the sake of the 'feeling' of the modern world. God's distinctive moral qualities: holiness, justice, and veracity, cede to a sort of Mahommedan paradise. His 'shrieking eloquence' endangers the nation as well as individual souls, for those who undo the terror of a future life will have to answer for it.[28] There is no doubt that MacGregor makes many shrewd points, but as far as the wider community was concerned, Salmond's views carried the day.

Within the Church, however, a massive polarisation took place. Salmond's 'penny-whistle' was in fact mightily effective. The hegemony of the Westminster Confession in New Zealand Presbyterianism was soon to be toppled for ever, and its defence henceforth become the rear-guard battle of a minority. *The Reign of Grace* itself was as much symptom as cause of that collapse. Salmond, as already noted, was only the most notorious member of a militant, campaigning minority. The cost, however, was high. From an extraordinarily early period dialogue between 'liberal' and 'orthodox' broke down within New Zealand Presbyterianism. Instead of recognising the pain and evangelical passion which underlaid Salmond's intemperate words, an immediate attempt was made to silence and discredit him. Dialogue, and a burgeoning popular interest in theology, was replaced by bitter controversy and a succession of heresy trials which were to culminate with that of Lloyd Geering in the 1960s. There has never been much room for respectful, differentiated debate within Presbyterianism since, and – perhaps more important – little priority has been given to the type of apologetic that Salmond had sought to initiate. It is

---

[27] Ibid., 17.

[28] Cf. also McGregor's elegant, if somewhat disingenuous, defence of the Westminster Confession: *Freedom in the Truth. Under Shield of a Constitution, of Government and of Doctrine, in accordance with the Word of God* (Oamaru, 1888). McGregor was a considerable scholar of the old Calvinist mould, with a well-stocked, subtle mind.

arguable that the outcome of this controversy was to accentuate the drift of the Churches towards increasingly sectarian, and individualist solutions, whether revivalist or liberal, and to confirm a growing section in society in their dismissive rejection of the Churches as a locus for intelligent debate.[29]

On a personal level, too, the results were dramatic. Salmond had functioned for a decade as a genial apologist for a self-transforming Presbyterianism. His swingeing polemic, and the equally trenchant retorts to it, forfeited him that role, and from now on he was effectively marginalised. His views were pronounced heretical by Dunedin Presbytery, one of the many meetings devoted to the subject lasting seven hours. The confident young group of 'liberals', such as James Gibb, Rutherford Waddell, and the layman Keith Ramsay, could only convince their colleagues there and in the Synod of Otago and Southland that further action against him would achieve nothing and bring them into public contempt.[30] Salmond, after all, as a university teacher, was beyond their jurisdiction.

He retreated into his role as a professor of philosophy, where he was much loved and respected for his wit, clarity and humanity.[31] The only other occasion on which he took up a public stance was interesting, because it was directed against prohibition, which was fast becoming a hallmark of New Zealand Presbyterianism. His *Prohibition: a Blunder*, which appeared in 1911, and went into five editions, boasted some splendidly barbed diction and is a rather fine plea for the rights of the individual against 'vicious moral coddling'.[32] He died in 1917, being survived by his wife, four sons and four daughters.

Salmond's case reminds us of the infirmity of our labels. His language, as in his 1880 public lecture, 'What is Christianity?',

[29] I have argued this case elsewhere: *'A Time of Sifting': Evangelicals and Liberals at the Genesis of New Zealand Theology* (Dunedin, 1991); cf. also P. Matheson (ed.), *The Farthest Jerusalem. Four Lectures on the Origins of Christianity in Otago* (Dunedin, 1993); P. Matheson, *The Finger of God in the Disruption* (Dunedin, 1993).

[30] Minutes of Dunedin Presbytery, 2 May, 6 June, 4 July, 1 August, 15 September 1888; cf. also proceedings of the Synod of Otago and Southland, October and November 1888, 23, 109–16.

[31] Cf. the moving appreciation of his twenty-eight-year term by Professor Gilray, *Otago University Review*, xxv, 11/4 (1913), 14ff.

[32] W. Salmond, *Prohibition: a Blunder* (Dunedin, 1911), 46.

while rejecting an infallible bible or creed, could have a strongly evangelical ring. He testifies that 'the blessing which Christ gave us has been beyond all comparison the best thing in all our life's experience, and that it has been the light of our light, the joy of our joy, the secret root and spring of all the good of our existence on this earth; bringing with its wondrous presence a prophecy of eternal life and of a hidden source of good immeasurable as God'.[33] Faith, for Salmond, was always less an intellectual act than 'entrance into sympathy with Christ's thoughts and aims by a moral act of heart and will'.[34] His own imaginative leaps were to cost him dear. He was, perhaps, an opinion-breaker rather than an opinion-maker, as far as the evolution of theology and church life in New Zealand was concerned. However, as far as the transforming of the Kirk was concerned, his penny-whistle pamphlets pointed the way to the future far more effectively than the trumpeting tomes of his weightier opponents. There is, after all, something to be said for a jig!

[33] The lecture was held in the Queen's Theatre on Sunday, 13 June 1880; New Zealand Presbyterian (1 July 1880), 9; again John Dickie will use very similar language about blessing as prior to theologising.

[34] From his lecture in the same theatre on 16 May 1880: 'Did Christ Indeed Rise From the Dead?', New Zealand Presbyterian (1 June 1880), 233.

Chapter 6

John Baillie and Friends, in Germany and at War

George Newlands

I

THE First World War brought to Europe the deaths of young men on an apocalyptic scale. The war was to change many things, not least theology and Church. It is sometimes thought that the liberal theology of the nineteenth century succumbed to a myopic nationalism, and was entirely discredited, only to be rescued by Karl Barth. The situation is more complex. This chapter looks at the period of the First World War in the light of some unpublished letters by the Scottish theologian, John Baillie, and his friends. Baillie would become one of the most celebrated theologians of the twentieth century, a distinguished scholar-teacher who held posts in North America and Scotland, and a Church leader who played a leading role in the ecumenical movement and the founding of the World Council of Churches. Alec Cheyne has already shed much light on John Baillie and his brother Donald in a number of elegant essays. The aim of this chapter is to explore the role of his experiences in the Great War in the formation of John Baillie as a Church leader and theologian. The chapter draws heavily on the recently rediscovered, and as yet uncatalogued private papers, diaries and correspondence of John Baillie, which have been gifted to New College Library of the University of Edinburgh.[1]

---

[1] As these papers have not yet been grouped and catalogued, it has not been possible to provide references for the many quotations from the diaries and correspondence included in this chapter.

'War is God's judgement on our sins of militarism', asserted John Baillie in a sermon delivered on 13 June 1915, at Waterbeck, Scotland, 'the lust for power, the desire for material and military supremacy, international jealousy. There are lessons here for us all.' John Baillie's sermons on the general theme of Christianity and Patriotism from the period 1914–15 refused to indulge in simple denigration of the Germans, and instead offered a critique of excessive nationalism and militarism. Baillie's correspondence with his friends – including J. H. Oldham, already a pacificist, R. H. Husband, C. S. Simpson and A. J. Young – indicate that attitudes to the war were the subject of critical debate through-out the period to 1918. But the correspondence also revealed hope for a post-war future. It becomes clear that the failure of the peace after 1919, following so much carnage, rather than the war itself, was a major cause of despair. Although some versions of liberal theology were vulnerable to charges of lack of realism, this was not always the case. For many young theologians the war reinforced the best of liberal values, and would be the spur to developments over the next half-century. The magnitude of the slaughter in the war came as a huge shock to all European culture. The aftermath called for new beginnings, and would doubtless have done so even if the prevailing theology had been closer to Barth than to Herrmann.

From the amalgam of Calvinist piety and humanist culture at Inverness Royal Academy in Scotland, followed by Arts and Divinity at Edinburgh University, there graduated a remarkable group of young men who were to have considerable influence on theological education – John and Donald Baillie, John A. Mackay, J. Y. Campbell (who was Alec Cheyne's uncle) and John Dow. Many of these friends, including Cecil Simpson and Ross Husband, were to be killed in the war, leaving the survivors to reflect in letters and in poetry on the meaning of the disaster. Andrew Young wrote of 'the hope we have that partly mends, Life's broken purpose, but is not enough to satisfy the deep desire of Love, Or pay the heavy mortgage held upon the dead'.[2]

This sense of 'life's broken purpose' was to affect the survivors' complex attitudes to the next war, as they sought peace but

---

[2] C. B. *Simpson Memorial* volume, ed. A. Young and D. M. Baillie (Edinburgh, 1918).

prepared for war. Awareness of the diversity of responses among its victims to the First World War made the survivors critical of all global solutions to theological problems. It led them to notions of paradox and constructive tension, which would lead to the development of 'critical realism' in the 1930s and might still have things to say to theology in the future. The tension created by the Great War was especially poignant for the Baillies and their circle, as they had many German friends, the result of idyllic summer semesters spent in the Universities of Heidelberg, Jena and Marburg, amply documented in their letters. Indeed, the Baillies' theological education had been in large part a deliberate and successful combination of Evangelical piety with German theology.

John Baillie was intensively involved with theology all his life. But neither he nor his brother Donald saw theology as divorced from concern with social issues. The 1942 report of the Church of Scotland Committee which he chaired on 'The Interpretation of God's Will in the Present Crisis', noted that Goebbels had said 'Churchmen dabbling in politics should take note that their only task is to prepare for the world hereafter', leaving the affairs of this world to the totalitarian state. The report then noted that 'It is impossible to read the Bible without realising that there are many issues in our public life which belong to God too.' It had after all been public values, like loyalty, friendship and courage, which had appeared to him to have been significant when doctrines had failed. This he had noted in his reflections on the attitudes of the troops in the trenches of the First World War in *The Interpretation of Religion*.[3]

Many, indeed most, of John's and Donald's closest and most brilliant student friends died at an early age in the First World War. These were shattering experiences. John and Donald were, in that sense, brands plucked from the burning, and life for them was not something to be taken for granted, but to be lived with a high sense of purpose. Behind John's frequently mordant humour and caustic wit, and Donald's light-hearted frivolity, there was a deep seriousness, the Calvinist tradition renewed and re-imagined. It was not perhaps surprising that they were given to reflection on the future life, where so many of their nearest and dearest had already gone.

---

[3] J. Baillie, *The Interpretation of Religion* (Edinburgh, 1929), 301.

The Baillies' contemporaries included other men of real distinction, in theology and not only in theology. There is a quite remarkable portrayal of an idyllic lost world, almost, in the volume entitled *Charlotte Barbour* and published in 1935 by her son, G. F. Barbour. Charlotte Barbour was a Liberal in politics. She was deeply affected by the war and the deaths of Robert Whyte, her nephew, and so many others. On 30 December 1917, she wrote in her *Journal*:

> All through this year the terrible war has gone on. Amid all the suffering and cruelty there is the sense that in every country many are looking to God with yearning faith and believe that he reigns supreme and over-rules. The best men seem to cherish a living hope that out of the darkness of this Great War a brighter day will dawn for many nations.

After the war she took a keen interest in the newly founded League of Nations. Most of these bright young men were to have no part in the society of the 1920s. They were killed in the war, a war which the Church successively extolled, regarded as the wages of sin, and then tried to forget because of embarrassment at its own uncertain gospel.

John and Donald came into a Church conscious of a long scholarly and widely civilised tradition, handed down faithfully from one generation to another. It was increasingly a critical tradition, not disposed to unthinking dogmatism. New College was much more liberal around 1890–1910 in theology than one might imagine. A striking testimony of this open atmosphere is provided in a letter home to New York by Henry Sloane Coffin, age twenty, to his parents in October 1897. 'If I am not a deep dyed higher critic, it will be no fault of New College, for you get it everywhere in most attractive form and I must say that whatever more conservative ideas I had have been rudely blown away.' Slightly later he added: 'Do not worry about the heresy of New College. The Scotch Church seems to stand it and preach better sermons than the bluest Princetonians.'[4]

---

[4] M. P. Noyes, *Henry Sloane Coffin: The Man and his Ministry* (New York, 1964), 42.

II

New College had links with America. But it also had links, crucially, with Germany. Scottish theological education traditionally involved for the most able students summer semesters spent in Germany, which generated considerable correspondence. This exposure to the German academic scene would almost inevitably introduce Scots students to a much broader range of culture and experience, producing in many ministers an interesting combination of the perspectives of Scottish village life and German thought. But the Scots by no means regarded everything new as better, as we see from some of John's reflections at the time and later.

The German experience was of seminal importance for both John and Donald. We have letters exchanged between the members of the family and their friends from Heidelberg, Jena and Marburg, and these illuminate a whole culture in remarkable detail. There are letters in 1908 from Cecil Simpson and Ross Husband, a 1908 letter from John Laird in Heidelberg in German, letters from Peter from 1909, from John to his mother in 1911. In 1909 John spent the summer in Jena. We have John's lecture notes from Jena in 1909 and also his account of the Halle Conference of the German Student Movement in 1909: 'The most telling, as they were the most eagerly expected, addresses, were those by Mr Mott.'[5]

John wrote many letters to his mother from Jena in 1909. A letter that he wrote while en route in Belgium, ends: 'a considerable quantum of love to everybody'. He wrote to Donald on 9 May 1909 from Jena as follows: 'Denney's *Death of Christ* I also rather wearied of. If you really want the best book on the subject, you should read McLeod Campbell's *Atonement*. He was put out of the Church of England for writing it [*sic*!].' There are bills preserved from Jena for Baillie and J. H. Oldham. John paid Fraulein Zeiss for the period 22 June to 22 July 1909 (116DM, 17Pf). This includes washing done by Frau Elstermann, 20Pf for stamps and 40Pf for a broken lamp mantle.

From the visits to Germany there are lecture notes, for example, on Juelicher on 1 Corinthians 10–13 in German, extensive notes on Herrmann's lectures in German, and on Cohen's *Logik* (from

---

[5] *The Student Movement* (June 1909), 204ff.

an address at Friedricksplatz 11, Marburg). There are short pieces on 'An Alpine Holiday' (from Marburg 1909), on the Franco-Prussian War, and, on a related theme but from 1916, on the Dardanelles campaign. There are surviving essays on a large number of themes, from Stout's view of conation (8 June 1906) to the Vision of Immortality (February 1909) and the general definition of religion. There is a highly critical essay on Subliminal Consciousness of 11 October 1910 (later published) and a critique of Weinel of Jena on Jesus. From Gartenstr.3, Jena, John attended Eucken's lectures and made full notes:

> Mit Kant beginnt das geistliche Problem der Menschheit. Der Deutscher Volk aus den Tiefsten, kann man sagen, hat gesprochen. Und besonders Jena, hier hat Fichte seinen maechtige Worter gesprochen. Und Hegel, Schopenhauer, Hebart sind damit verbunden.[6]

In July 1911, John was in Marburg. 'I have to preach here on the 23rd.' He had dinner with three sorts of wine. He was considering the possibility of a DPhil on Kant's ethics – a project that was to continue. Around this period John wrote a lecture on 'German Student Life', which included the following accounts:

> Although I am fond of Germany beyond all other continental countries which I have seen, and though I admire many things German, I certainly do not admire German Student Life. But German educational system is the most highly developed in the world. The boy who leaves the German school is usually a shy and retiring youth with a badly-developed figure – but he knows as much as many a Scotch student knows when he is capped Master of Arts . . . He has hardly played a game, or had a spare moment to himself. As sure as he worked hard before, he now ceases to do a stroke of work.
>
> Student clubs. The Corps are very aristocratic and very expensive. Then the Burschenschafte, then the Verbindungen. Corps life. Very little sport as such. Much student debt. Despite the fact that all German students drink beer, and that all German students drink too much beer, there is really no drink problem in Germany. Very elaborate and rigid system of etiquette.

---

[6] 'The problem of the human spirit begins with Kant. One may say that the German people has spoken out of the depths. And especially here in Jena, Fichte uttered his powerful words. With this are associated Hegel, Schopenhauer and Hebart.'

Duels. Students take lessons in fencing Spirit of militarism. In Germany every man is a soldier. Pride in scars.

I remember how surprised I was, when I first went to Germany to study theology, to discover that my professor of practical theology had an enormous scar across his cheek, telling very clearly the tale of his student life.

Duels 6 am Saturday.

I remember the first time I went was on a beautiful morning in May. The combatants must stand absolutely still on a fixed spot. An Englishman feels queer for the rest of the day, and may even be disturbed in his dreams at night. But in Germany one often see ladies attend and look on calmly, even though the floor may be covered with blood.

The Kneipe. Fasspartie. Foundation Day, Jena 1909.

The ushering in of Summer on last day of April at Midnight. Marburg. Bonfires. Standing on one height one can look across the broad valley and see half a dozen tongues of yellow flame leap suddenly out of the darkness from the other side. All the students join in the magnificent chorus, 'Der Mai ist gekommen'.

He described Midsummer Eve, with its torchlight processions and the singing of 'Gaudeamus', and suggested hidden delights, such as Maibowle.

Annie Baillie's letters to John in 1911 show her detailed concern for her two sons in a strange land. John and Donald portrayed their impressions of lectures, ideas and customs in German university towns. There had been Scots students in Heidelberg since 1618. Donald's descriptions of Heidelberg and Marburg, and John's of Jena, echoed the accounts of David Cairns and others fifty years earlier. Donald wrote to John from the Heidelberg suburb of Rohrbach, and to their fellow student, Peter Ross Husband, from Heidelberg on 16 July 1912. In 1912, John, Donald and Cecil Simpson made another visit to the Continent, this time on a barge from Rotterdam to Antwerp. John was given a copy of Peploe's poems, *Roses in Return*, published in Edinburgh in 1912. On 12 December 1912, Peter Ross Husband wrote from Dundee: 'I admire your pluck in tackling the Glaubenslehre in the midst of your other duties. Goethe is my latest enthusiasm.'

The diaries for the period 1909–14 are not very informative but indicate the sorts of things John was doing. On 4 January

1909, for example, he addressed the Lads' Club and on 23 January was involved in the Pleasance Concert – both of these were part of New College's missionary work project. On 16 January and 3 March he went for a walk with J. H. Oldham. On Friday, 5 March, at 8 pm he went to a Theological Society Valedictory address (his own was to be later). On Friday, 23 April, he recorded simply 'go to Jena' and then there is nothing till 23 October, though he appears to have stayed en route with Pastor Branlegt, 3 Wanningstraat, Amsterdam.

Andrew Young was a talented member of the circle of friends of John and Donald from Arts and Divinity. He went to France with Donald in 1917 to serve with the YMCA. Donald was invalided home, but Young stayed, and wrote later that this experience made him a pacifist.[7] Young was born in Elgin on 29 April 1885, but moved to Edinburgh as a child and attended the Royal High School. He studied Arts for five years at Edinburgh University, graduating MA in 1908. In 1910 he published a collection of poems, *Songs of Night*, but published no more till *Winter Harvest* in 1933. Proceeding to New College, he became a minister of the United Free Church in 1912 at the age of twenty-seven. He was an assistant minister at Berwick-on-Tweed, then minister of the Presbyterian Church at Hove, Sussex, drawn to England, he says, by a love of Gothic architecture. He married Janet Green, a lecturer in English literature, with whom he had two children. He developed an interest in liturgy and mysticism (St John of the Cross), became an Anglican in 1938, was Vicar of Stonegate in Sussex from 1941 to 1959, was a Canon of Chichester from 1948, received an Hon. LLD from Edinburgh in 1951 and the Queen's Gold Medal for Poetry.[8]

Like Robert Frost, another Scots poet residing outside Scotland, Young eventually published many books of poems, often on nature themes, though also on nature and death, as well as books on British flowers. He loved the countryside, and especially that of Shropshire. One critic wrote that his flower poems had an under-current of guilt and mental disturbance.[9] An homage volume

---

[7] A. Young, *Remembrance and Homage*, ed. Leslie Norris (Cranberry Isles, Maine, 1978); L. Clark, *Andrew Young* (1964); article on Andrew Young, *World Authors, 1950–70*, ed. J. Wakeman (New York, 1975).

[8] Entry in *Who Was Who, 1971–80*.

[9] Entry in *Who's Who in Literature*.

included poems by Christopher Hassall, the biographer of Rupert Brooke, John Arlot the cricket commentator, and one by Richard Church, which included this memorable stanza:

> Dour old Scot from Edinburgh
> Whose theology was thorough
> From Presbyterian first stage
> Then gentle in a vicarage.

If Church had known Donald Baillie, he might perhaps have realised that there were gentle Presbyterians too. Andrew Young lived in retirement, till he died on 25 November 1971, in an old house in Church Lane, Yapton, about eight miles from Chichester, on his own for a few years after the death of his wife.

W. W. Peploe (1869–1933) was another of John's close friends and correspondents.[10] He produced several collections of poems, including *The Heart of a Dancer* in 1910. He also made drawings, showing the influence of the Vorticists and Aubrey Beardsley – there are two large abstract colour sketches produced in 1919. His professional career was as a bank manager with the Commercial Bank of Scotland, Stockbridge, where John Baillie banked, and John probably consulted him on investments. W. W. was a brother of the much better known S. Peploe, an artist who exhibited between 1910 and 1940, was an RSA and died in Edinburgh. The brothers painted in Barra from 1894.

John Baillie's diary entries for 1910 included mentions of dinner with Professor Kennedy on 24 January and with Dr Whyte on 20 February, two meetings in February with Newlands, the speech training adviser (no relation of the author!), a meeting in March with Professor Seth, a Hebrew examination, a visit to St Mary's to hear passion music and a sermon delivered at the North Parish Church in Paisley. He borrowed Caird's *Hegel*, and works by Macdougall and Green from the University library, and he went off by boat from Greenock to Skipness on 30 April, while Don sailed for Hamburg on 27 April. John was at the Scots Philosophical Club in Aberdeen on 20 May and on 14 June he dined with Seth. On 20 August he reached Bruxelles Nord, and John, Donald and Peter met up that day in Brussels. On 11

---

[10] P. J. M. McEwan (ed.), *Dictionary of Scottish Painting and Architecture* (Suffolk, 1994).

October at the West End Clock, he met Oldham at 2.45 pm, and on Friday, 25 November, at 7.30 pm, he was at a debate at Coates Hall. On 23 December, at 8 pm, he enjoyed Carols. The end notes of the diary mention Herr Cocker, Ferienkursen-sekretaer, Marburg, the *Hibbert Journal* editor, L. P. Jacks, 28 Holywell, Oxford, and one James Macalaster, Muirholm, Paisley. All his life, too, no doubt as a result of his frugal upbringing, John kept careful accounts, and there is a characteristic list of costs:

> Milk 2d, Sponge cake 2d, Key 9d, Razor 4d, bananas 2d etc. Skipness Salary for May £4.5.0. In Germany Bier 20, Kafee 60 etc.

In about 1910, John wrote a fictionalised account of a journey on a steamboat from Rotterdam to Antwerp for *The Magazine*, in which he supposedly travelled with a single companion, a Mr W, born in Germany but educated at Oxford University. 'I am ready to swear that it was the smallest boat that was ever worked by steam, and which wasn't called either a tug or a launch.' There was cheese and coffee for breakfast. On approaching Dordrecht, John reported: 'the most amazing thing about the landscape was the absolute flatness and lowness of the country. Nowhere was the land a foot above the level of the water.'

A few of John Baillie's sermons from this early period have survived. For example, there is a sermon on 'Onesimus the Slave', delivered on 3 December 1910, a sermon on 'St Polycarp – one of the earliest Christian martyrs', given at the South Morningside Fellowship Association, December 1910: a sermon on 'the Serpent in the Garden – Genesis, Exodus', delivered to the East Hawick Bible Class. He employed the theme of the Burning Bush, in Exodus 3.14, no fewer than sixteen times between 1913 and 1915. He was back in the United Kingdom in January and April 1915, when he preached at Waterbeck and St John's United Free Church, Bathgate. Other sermons included 'Of Such is the Kingdom of God', delivered at Skipness on 15 May 1910, at Hope Park, St Andrews, on 2 October 1910, and at Blair Atholl on 1 October 1911.

The pre-war letters are interesting. On 21 September 1909, J. A. K. McClure, an American student who was at New College and at Jena with John, wrote from Liverpool, commending another American named Hall, son of Cuthbert Hall of New York, who was coming to New College. In 1910, along with his literary interests, John was beginning to develop a taste in art, purchasing etchings and porcelain, in which he was to become something of an expert collector. In 1913, Peter's letters from the Mildmay Missionary Hospital in East London documented the preparation of a missionary doctor and described the scope for the practice in surgery in this rather poor area.

III

August 1914 brought war to a Church unprepared for such devastation and in general naively optimistic about a speedy victory and God's blessing. Friends of the Baillies volunteered, or from 1916 were conscripted, and died, especially the students who became junior officers, in increasingly huge numbers. The loss was felt as catastrophic. John and Donald would remember those lost friends throughout their lives. A decade after the war's end, for example, John would dedicate *The Interpretation of Religion* (1928) to the 'memory of Peter Ross Husband, Cecil Barclay Simpson and Peter Baillie'.

Peter Ross Husband had been one of John and Donald's closest friends. Born on 7 February 1886 in Dundee and educated at Dundee High School, Ross Husband had later studied theology with the Baillies at New College. In the summer of 1910 he had been in Marburg, listening to Herrmann, Juelicher and Budde, and had been much taken with Germany and German culture. After completing his studies at New College, he had returned in the spring of 1912 to Heidelberg, with his sister Marjory and Donald Baillie, and he was much impressed by J. Weiss and Ernst Troeltsch. Donald recalled that 'the people we stayed with took us, I remember, to a public garden-party in support of the German Navy League'. Returning to Scotland, Ross Husband became assistant to P. D. Thomson, a later Moderator, at Kelvinside United Free Church, Glasgow, then in 1914 he was assistant to R. S. Simpson at the United Free High Church, Edinburgh. His reaction to the outbreak of war had been one of profound shock. Enlisting as a combatant, he was commissioned, and sent to France in 1916. He landed at Boulogne on 5 September, and was attached to a battalion of the Black Watch. Three weeks later, on 26 September, he was killed.

The selections from Ross Husband's sermons in D. M. Ross, *A Scottish Minister and Soldier* (London, 1917) reveal a spirit more of sorrow than of anger, though including anger too.

> Sermon on 'Love your enemies': 'Extremes of passion are sowing the seeds of future trouble. There is more than fighting with bayonets to be done . . . the more magnanimous and large-hearted we can be, the better will it be for generations yet unborn.' (45)

> Sermon from 1915: 'A year or two ago we could talk glibly about the progress of mankind . . . Such dreams have been most rudely dashed to the ground. In many an ardent heart hope has been quenched.' (48)

> Sermon on 'Courage' from 1915: 'To be afraid and yet to go on – there you have the truest courage.'

> Sermon on 'The Seeming Waste of Young Lives' preached in the High Church, Edinburgh, in Autumn 1915: 'It may be that those whose lives seem broken and wasted will have the larger part in the making of the future. When we have all passed away, the memory of these dead boys will still be a living force in the world. It is a high destiny God Almighty has appointed them . . . There will be a sacred tradition to hand down from father to son, from generation to generation. The influence will spread far and wide: it may touch young lives.' (120, 118)

Ross Husband's sermons suggest that the theology of the period did not fail its adherents during the war as much as has been suggested, and that there was a hope that Britain would be rewarded for its fortitude with the emergence of a more just and righteous post-war society. On Ross Husband's death, John wrote:

> I have never known a more loveable man than Ross, nor have I heard the word loveable applied so often to any man by his friends. I have never known so remarkable gifts to be allied with such great humility. Everybody liked him, and everybody who knew him well loved him.

Donald recalled of Ross Husband: 'he was indeed a noble fellow with a pure, unselfish, simple nature . . . His death in action is just the final self-sacrifice of one who was always unselfish.' Similarly, W. M. Christie, MA, 2nd Lieutenant 2/7 Royal Scots, observed that Ross Husband 'was gentle by nature, but in that gentleness there was no trace of weakness. He was strong and fearless in doing the right'.

Neither John nor Donald Baillie volunteered for the trenches. Warm memories of German friends meant that not all Scottish ministers embraced the shrill anti-German sentiment which engulfed the Scottish Churches in 1914. Both Baillies applied instead to go to France with the YMCA. John was always very close in his attitudes to pacifism, and may well have sympathised with J. H. Oldham's pain over the break-down of international and ecumenical commitments, and his conception of 'positive neutrality'.[11] Donald, meanwhile, soon became seriously ill in France, and was invalided back home. John remained in France, giving lectures on education, architecture and military history to the troops. In Scotland, his friends missed him. W. W. Peploe sent John poems. John also remained in contact with some German friends, the Wickerts, from Marburg. Elli Wickert had by now emigrated to South Africa, and on 8 September 1914, she wrote to John, 'Warum musste dieses grosses Elend in die Welt kommen?' On 6 December 1914, she wrote that her brother, Werner, had been wounded. Because of problems with the censors, she sent letters to her fiancé and her mother in Hannover through John.

John kept a diary in France during late 1914 and during 1915. He described the difficulty of fitting in with his colleagues, and his lack of hatred for the Germans (though curiously there is almost no reference to the wounded – or to German prisoners, with whom he would have been able easily to converse). Surviving diary entries for 1915 include the following:

24 Sept. We have two orderlies. One is 'Jack' Russell, who was gassed on Hill 60. His eyes are still. Half-closed, and his digestion is so much upset in the mornings that he is unable to eat any breakfast.

Sept 25th. Willis, the Boulogne leader, told me that he had preached in Havre to 1400 English soldiers who were kept in a prison there. Their crimes were rape and looting. That number from the little British army, and not on enemies' soil, but in their allies' country.

27th. Soldier shot for escaping from gaol. Soldier who got wounded intentionally shot. 'Jack's opinion is that vast numbers of soldiers would desert from their trenches in sheer terror, if they were not kept in their places by fear of their officers' revolvers.' Macdonald said 'There's no glory in scientific murder.'

[11] K. Clements, *Faith on the Frontier: A Life of J. H. Oldham* (Edinburgh, 1999), 121–47.

7 Oct. I heard that my cousin Evan Baillie was killed, and also Dr Whyte's son.

10 Oct. One Gordon, who had been in the recent advance, said, 'We took no prisoners, that is the Gordon motto. We believe in finishing them, wounded and all. One hears many things that do not make good telling.'

John returned to Scotland during his periods of leave. The sermons he preached in 1914–15 in Scotland were anything but belligerent in their tone, and as a result may not have been universally popular. In his sermon, 'The Lesson of the War', preached on 13 June 1915 at Waterbeck, he proclaimed boldly that 'War is God's judgement on our sins – the sins of militarism, the lust for power, the desire for material and military supremacy, international jealousy – there are lessons for us all.' (It is interesting that he took a similar theological view even in the Second World War, when he was clear about the evil of the Nazis. Writing on *The Theology of the War*, he reflected: 'We believe that we must do no other than fight as bravely as we can to defend the world against the Nazi menace, and we believe that God is with us as we fight. Dare we say that God is on our side? That can hardly be the right way of putting it. It is doubtful whether we should ever speak of God taking sides in human conflicts. It is for us to be on His side rather than for Him to be on ours.')

On 15 January 1915, James Black wrote to John to say that he was pleased to hear that John intended to try to publish articles. 'After all', he observed, 'that is the only way in which a man's worth can be known in these rushing days of ours.' Elsa Gallant, a close friend of the Baillie family, was also in France as a nurse. On 30 June 1917, she confided to her diary: 'today John, Don and I met and we had lunch together. It was so funny meeting in Boulogne and we went to Boulogne Cathedral, which is a magnificent building.'

John would work with the YMCA in France until 1919. For him these were important years. Life with the army was a broadening experience, suggesting values and perspectives beyond the Scottish ecclesiastical scene. He was committed to his work among the men. In 1917 a soldier named Fred Hilsey asked John to 'always think of me as one who says that the YMCA has no kinder man in France than you'. It is true that John and Donald had been in Germany as students, and this experience, to be sure, was a traditional source of wider perspectives for Scottish ministers. It is also the case that some ministers found that their experience with the army confirmed them in the rightness of an extremely conservative theological stance. But for John the war accelerated the broadening process which had developed for him at University.

In France John lectured on 'The growth of Christian Architecture as exemplified in some French Cathedrals'. In *The McGilliken* (from the Canadian General Hospital – McGill) published in France on 15 February 1916, he wrote about the strategy in the battle of the Marne. In *The Music Student* for 17 September 1916 he contributed a piece on 'Soldiers' Concerts – a Plea for Good Music', in which he called for concerts that would seek 'to educate the Tommy musically, not just to amuse'. In *The Expositor* he wrote on 'Belief as an Element of Religion'. In a Supplement to *The Red Triangle* for June 1918, he contributed a piece on 'The YMCA and Social Reconstruction', in which he asserted that the future YMCA 'must avoid theological narrowness. It must stand for the education of taste. It must keep the ideas of self-sacrifice and Christian social service at the forefront of its message.' As is clear from John's comments in the report after the war on the state of religion in the forces, John saw this as a time of turning to the basic moral virtues, not to the high doctrines of traditional dogmatics.

IV

The end of 1916 brought a momentous change for John, as an encounter with Miss Florence Fowler, a volunteer with the British Expeditionary Force, led to a friendship that developed swiftly into romantic passion. Letters began to flow back and forward. There are delightful early letters from 'Jewel' (Florence) to John, expressing her sadness after they had decided to separate themselves from each other for a period, because of the local gossip! They became engaged, after some resistance from her father, who objected to John's lack of financial prospects. On 17 January 1918, Annie Baillie wrote, upon receiving a photo of Jewel, 'I like her face and am ready to love her if she is your choice.'

In 1917 John decided to submit the Edinburgh DPhil thesis, completed in haste in France. The external examiner, his namesake

Professor J. B. Baillie of London, did not like it. Professor J. Seth sent Baillie's critique to John on 13 December 1917. He then wrote a long letter to John on 5 February 1918, explaining that the thesis would have to be revised and re-submitted.

On leave (now with Miss Fowler) in London, he bought two tickets for the performance of 'Professor's Love Story' on Saturday, 7 April 1917. On 14 May, he had dinner at the Hotel du Pont with Jewel and on 16 May he is again at the cinema. In September, he was on leave in Sutton, and on 6 November, he sent in his revised DPhil thesis. On 12 April 1917, John wrote to Jewel from YMCA APO3: 'I think I must put into permanent form for you the new Beatitudes we composed together in the Moorish Lounge. They are the philosophy of life of people we don't like. Let me have a try.'

> And he opened his mouth and taught them, saying,
> Blessed are all ladies and gentlemen, for they will know how to behave in heaven
> Blessed are all who have over three thousand a year, for everybody likes money
> Blessed are the brainy, for they know a thing or two
> Blessed are the good-looking: for nobody would have the heart to damn them
> Blessed are they who hunger and thirst after noisy things: for some day they will be fed up.

Baillie the 'Highland minister' becomes perhaps more relaxed in his mock YMCA Logic Paper, which he drafted in March 1917:

> 1. Discuss the question whether the darning of Stockings is to be understood in a literal, or in a metaphorical and spiritual sense.
>
> 9. How would you compare the historical importance of the Battle of Waterloo, with that of a little talk in moonlight and mist?
>
> 10. Estimate, a, the nutritive value
> b, the romantic properties, of the tongue sandwich.

This period saw the first stage of what was to be an almost daily correspondence between John and Jewel. These are very private letters, full of the routine stuff of everyday life, sometimes passionate, often poetic. As such they constitute a remarkable evocation of a fascinating slice of the culture of the period, especially as seen through the eyes of faith. Coming from very different backgrounds in Scotland and the South of England, the two found common ground in the world of the YMCA. Their romance blossomed in classic style, and they were to forge a rich and solid relationship which was to last for more than forty years. This relationship was not without tensions, occasionally deep strains and potentially disastrous disagreement. But the long-term balance was one of great happiness for both parties.

Their letters reflect a world long since vanished. They may not reach the highly sophisticated levels of the contemporary Bloomsbury correspondence. But John was highly intelligent and Jewel was far from dim. Between them they unconsciously recorded the hopes and anxieties of their generation. On 23 January 1918, John wrote to Jewel:

> You were as pretty as a witch when with your hair hung over your shoulders and your eyes and cheeks, ablaze, you leaned back and I leaned over you and looked at you . . . It's not a witch but a gipsy that you are. And I am not so much bewitched as kidnapped.

Writing to Jewel on 18 August 1918 from his posting in France, John rhapsodised on their future:

> I wonder what you and I will be doing on a Sunday morning in five years time? Will I be preaching in some ivy-clad country church in Scotland and you be sitting demurely in the 'Manse pew'? Shall we be going to church together in some colonial University town? What a sealed book the future is. And how we mortals have to live from hand to mouth, trusting in God!

He even wrote her poetry, such as his poem, 'Laughter', from 1919:

> How often on the old brown walls
> that memory endears
> I laugh with you from evenfall
> Till the white morn appears!
> You bid me tell the cause thereof?
> Sometimes it is to hide my love
> Sometimes to stay my tears.

During the last year of the war, John continued to give lectures to the men. He delivered, for example, four lectures on poetry, divided as follows: (1) poets of half a generation ago; (2) poets known before the war; (3) the Irish poets; and (4) the war poets, including Sassoon, Brooke, Wilfred Owen and Robert Graves.

The war years were crucial to John's development from Edinburgh student to professor of theology. Donald had shared with his brother the cultural revolution of moving from Inverness to Edinburgh, but he did not share to the same extent John's experiences of war on the Western Front, experiences which made John in some ways much more a man of the world. Later John would become immersed again in a church-centred culture, but the influence of a different social world that he had experienced during the war was to remain.

The end of the war saw John as an Assistant Director of Education for the YMCA, but otherwise without gainful employment. His war-time work had attracted praise. He retained the friendship of Z. F. Willis, the General Secretary of the YMCA, throughout his life, and also of Sir Graham Balfour, who had held leadership roles in the YMCA and would later become Vice-Chancellor of the University of Sheffield. The friendships and experience of the YMCA years lent a breadth to John's character and interests, which his subsequent teaching career in North America was to reinforce, and the Church in Scotland in some ways to restrain.

In 1919 Baillie got some temporary work as a tutor with the YMCA at its Mildmay training hostel, and he entertained the possibility of a philosophy post at Dalhousie in Canada. On 10 April 1919, John and Jewel were married in Erdington Parish Church, with a number of their YMCA friends present. There was a notice in the *Warwickshire Standard* for 11 April, which reported that Baillie had been Assistant Director of Education for the YMCA in France. Andrew Young sent the new couple a collection of poems by war poets, while Willie Peploe sent 'the valuable old Lille box [that] was one of his most treasured possessions'.

Baillie and his bride, however, were soon to be drawn far way from the world of post-war Britain, of austerity and disillusionment and loss, and of the Youngs and the Peploes. On 14 January 1919, an offer had come to Baillie through H. R. Mackintosh, an offer of a temporary lectureship in theology at Auburn Theological Seminary in New York State. 'You would find the atmosphere of this Seminary' Mackintosh assured him, 'most congenial . . . I spent a week there in 1913 and found the staff excessively pleasant . . . I could quote Denney's private remarks to me about your work, so that even though dead his voice would tell.' But the Baillies were not certain about Auburn. There was the possibility of the parish of Macduff; there was also talk of a chair in Winnipeg. On 30 March, John wrote to Jewel, 'I have not yet heard any more about the American business. I had a talk last night with Prof Macafee who holds the same chair in Chicago Theological Seminary, and who knows Auburn well.' There was caution on both sides. A member of the staff at Auburn confided to John on 18 June that 'we are not prepared at present to elect any one to this vacant chair as its permanent occupant'. H. R. Mackintosh wrote on 1 July to say that he expected they would offer Baillie the chair in time. 'The tone of the place', Mackintosh enthused, 'is an enlightened evangelical spirit – you would feel altogether at home. I can't help feeling that Auburn is your true line, not YMCA. The prospects in the YMCA are necessarily vague.' Baillie finally accepted the post, for a period from the end of September to April 1920. With typical confidence and astuteness, he also informed the staff at Auburn that he had had two other offers, but he also admitted that he was 'just back from France, where for four years I was entirely cut off from my books, and from any connection with my former work'. Mackintosh was delighted when he heard that Baillie had decided to accept the post. 'My dear Baillie,' he wrote on 17 July, 'I am very glad that you have decided to go to Auburn. I do not begin to imagine that you will regret it.'

By 27 August Baillie had booked cabin D 20 on the *Mauritania*, and on 20 September, he and Jewel sailed for America and a new future.

V

It has been particularly pleasing to write about John Baillie and his circle within the context of a volume in honour of Alec Cheyne. Alec has long been an admirer of both John and Donald Baillie and their contributions to theology and Church. There have also been connections between Cheyne and the Baillie circle. For example, Alec Cheyne's mother, 'Poppy' Young, was a sister of J. Y. Campbell, and lived in Inverness. On 6 April 1905 John's Diary records, 'P [John's Inverness friend, Percy] and Poppy called and we had a nice time'. In 1927 Alec's father, the Rev. Alex Cheyne of Errol (where Alec was born in 1924), was one of the signatories to the testimonial for the Chair of Practical Theology in New College for Donald. On 8 August 1930, Donald wrote to John, 'Yesterday morning we went to Munlochy, where Poppy and her husband and children are staying for the month in the manse. Both Jack's children and the Cheyne children are very jolly.' On 26 November 1947, Donald wrote again to John, 'I spent last weekend with the Cheynes at Kirkcaldy, preaching at the Bi-centenary of Dunnikier Church. What a nice bright girl Mona is! I don't think I ever met her at your house. And her brother Alec is an extraordinarily able fellow – First Class Honours in History, and now lecturing in the Army Education service.' Later John would entertain Alec, by now a lecturer in History at the University of Glasgow, to tea in the New Club, to discuss the possibility of his coming to New College and entering the ministry.

Perhaps not surprisingly, the student who delivered a most moving and eloquent address to John on his retirement in May 1956 was Alec Cheyne. His address included the following:

> All of us here today are conscious that we stand at the close not only of a session but of an epoch in the history of our college. We have always been proud of you, and of being your students . . . And our pride is mingled with gratitude for all that you have done for us. We think of your books. We think of your lectures – and what lectures they were! . . . They were never shrill, never unnecessarily contentious, never vindictive, never obscure, often inspiring, not seldom sublime. We recall Newman's description of the gentleman: 'He may be right or wrong, but he is too clear-headed to be unjust.' We think too of the gracious hospitality of your home. And – perhaps above all – we think of your conduct of worship in the Martin Hall. You have never ministered in a parish, but you have made of this college and university your parish, and we thank you for your ministry. And now, as we recall all that you have done for us we ask ourselves what we can do for you. We would therefore assure you of our determination to strive in some measure to serve the Church as you have served her, to follow truth as you have followed it, and to lead our people in worship as you have led us. That, I think, is what you would wish us to do. . . .

No less could be said of Alec Cheyne.

Part II

CHURCH, STATE AND SOCIETY

Chapter 7

Reactions in Scotland
to the Irish Famine

John F. McCaffrey

IN spite of the growing number of studies on nineteenth-century
Irish migrants in Scotland published over the last thirty years,
there has been little dealing specifically with the one event which
confirmed the Irish presence as a major element in modern Scottish
life – the Great Famine of 1845–52. With one or two exceptions
which deal with some related consequences of that event[1] there is
still only James E. Handley's book for historians to turn to with
grateful thanks for any extensive and specific investigation of the
topic.[2] And even in that pioneering study (now over fifty years
old), it was only part of a much wider picture being constructed
of these Irish migrants and their descendants in Scottish society
extending to the 1940s. Yet the Irish Famine in its consequences

---

[1] Such as, for instance, Brenda Collins' study of 'Irish Emigration to Dundee
and Paisley during the First Half of the Nineteenth Century', in J. M. Goldstrom
and L. A. Clarkson (eds), *Irish Population, Economy, and Society: Essays in
Honour of the late K. H. Connell* (Oxford, 1981) esp. 202–6.

[2] J. E. Handley, *The Irish In Modern Scotland* (Cork, 1947). Some of the
background on the Irish in Scotland at this time is explored by J. F. McCaffrey,
in 'Irish Immigrants and Radical movements in the West of Scotland in the
Early Nineteenth Century', *Innes Review*, xxix (1988) and in 'The Stewardship
of Resources: Financial Strategies of Roman Catholics in the Glasgow District,
1800–70', in W. J. Sheils and D. Wood (eds), *The Church and Wealth: Studies
in Church History*, 24 (Oxford, 1987); by B. Aspinwall, in 'Children of the
Dead End: the Formation of the Archdiocese of Glasgow, 1815–1914', *Innes
Review*, xliii (1992); and the essays by B. Collins, G. Walker and W. Sloan in
T. Devine (ed.), *Irish Immigrants and Scottish Society in the Nineteenth and
Twentieth Centuries* (Edinburgh, 1991).

was one of those major turning points which helped to create the modern Scotland we know today.

Despite the revisionist and post-revisionist arguments over the interpetation of their past by Irish historians, it seems now to be accepted that the Famine was a watershed in Irish history.[3] From a population base of around 8 million in 1841, about a million had died as a result of the Famine and another million had permanently emigrated by 1851.[4] Over 80% of the latter went to North America but many of the rest came to Britain, mainly through the ports of Liverpool, London and Glasgow.[5] Ireland, with its 8 million people just miles away by sea seeking escape from a national disaster, must thus have seemed like a lowering giant threatening to swallow up a Scottish society still very small and self-contained with a population of around 2,800,000 in 1845 and an infra-structure of law, local government and politics only just recently beginning to be modernised to meet the strains and challenges posed by industrialisation and urbanisation. For the potato blight was not a one-off event. There was no knowing when it would end or when relief from the pressure of these new numbers on the cities and towns of the Scottish central belt would finally come. The partial failure of the Irish potato crop in 1845 (which resulted in comparatively few deaths in this first year) was followed by an almost total failure in 1846 and 1848, with consequent horrifying increases in mortality, disease and emigration. In each succeeding year right up to 1852 there were successive failures to varying degrees of the staple food in what was becoming a weaker and more vulnerable society. In addition,

---

[3] See, for instance, C. O Grada, 'Making Irish Famine History in 1995', *History Workshop Journal*, 42 (1996), 99–100, and also C. Kinealy, *A Death-Dealing Famine* (London, 1997), 2–6, 179–180. In 1988 in his *The Great Irish Famine* (Basingstoke, 1989), 41, O Grada had considered 'the dispassionate, sanitized approach to the Great Famine [to be] now dominant in Irish historical scholarship', but already in that year careful writers like K. Theodore Hoppen, in his *Ireland Since 1800: Conflict & Conformity* (London, 1989), 58, were questioning the revisionist concept of pre- and post-1845 continuity and likening the effects of the Famine on Irish society instead as 'something akin to a Big Bang'. R. Foster, *Modern Ireland 1600–1972* (London, 1988) and C. Kinealy, *This Great Calamity* (Dublin, 1994) are representative of the revisionist and post-revisionist stances.

[4] O Grada, *The Great Irish Famine*, 49.

[5] Ibid., 55; Kinealy, *This Great Calamity*, 298–305.

the winters of 1846–7 and 1847–8 were particularly severe and 1848 also saw the return of cholera to British towns. Not only hunger but the associated, and contagious, diseases of typhus and dysentery accompanied those fleeing from Ireland. By the later 1840s, commentators spoke as if living under seige and the threat of being swamped.[6] In 1841 the first-ever census, tracing people by birthplace, showed that Scotland already contained 126,321 Irish-born. Statistically, this represented 4.8% of the total Scottish population of 2.6 million, but in reality it was very much more concentrated in the new Scotland developing in these years in the towns and industrial counties in the south-west and west of the country. By 1851, the total of Irish-born in Scotland, though only accounting for 28.5% of all the Irish-born in Britain, had soared to 207,367 (7.2% of the total Scottish population). Although, in numerical terms, the flood was still mainly to England (where, although only 2.9% of the total population, they constituted 519,959, concentrated in the congested urban areas such as Lancashire, the north-east Tyne/Tees region or London), the already large Irish concentrations in the west of Scotland increased even further (1841 figures given in brackets): to 16.8% in Lanarkshire (13.1%), 16.2% in Wigtownshire (14.7%), 15.9% in Renfrewshire (13.2%), 11.9% in Dunbartonshire (11%), 11% in Ayrshire (7.3%). In addition, they were also now significantly spilling out across Scotland and in many cases doubling their presence – into West Lothian, 9.4% (4.9%), Forfar, 8.5% (3.8%), Stirlingshire, 6.3% (5.2%), Midlothian, 5.9% (3.1%) and Clackmannanshire, 3.2% (0.8%). In cities like Glasgow and Dundee nearly a fifth of all inhabitants were from Ireland, and there were also high local concentrations in smaller towns and mining areas.[7]

Such, indeed, were the scale and effects of the Irish Famine that, of necessity, it was also (a point not always remembered or

[6] E.g. the *Glasgow Herald* of 21 December 1846 declared that 'the city of Glasgow is at present overrun with poor', and the *Edinburgh Medical Journal* for 1848 recorded that 'Many poor, starved, destitute, and diseased creatures were brought and laid down before the doors of the Glasgow infirmary, their relatives, if they had any, not knowing what to do with them, and in numerous instances it was destitution and starvation more than fever which was their chief affliction.' Both quoted in Handley, *Irish in Modern Scotland*, 24, 26.

[7] Even counties where their numbers were low showed the same tendency to sharp increase, such as Fife from 0.6% to 1.7% and Perthshire from 0.5% to 1.8%.

readily acknowledged) a determining moment in those countries where this desperate Irish exodus settled. It is the contention of this essay that it marked an irrevocable change in the nature of Scottish society not only in the obvious numerical changes in the composition and elements making up the country's structure, but more subtly and pervasively in altering the nature of the Scottish psyche and indeed, the whole mental outlook of anyone living in Scotland around and after 1845. People of the old Scotland observing the new world emerging at this time from the focus, say, of an Edinburgh advocate's drawing room in the New Town, or a laird's mansion in Perthshire or a weaver's cottage in Kirriemuir, associated that new world with the west (Glasgow in particular) and with industry and its associated traumas of urban congestion, disease, deprivation and depravity. Inevitably, just at the point when it was realised that this new world was becoming a fixture and the first major perceptions of it were being formed, the old Scotland associated the Irish diaspora from the Famine, as well as the contemporary arguments over what caused that event and how it was handled, with that new world of challenge. For those already inhabiting that new industrial Scotland, the sudden increase in numbers blunted whatever willingness there had been hitherto to absorb the newcomers. From the very outset, therefore, the Irish were associated with the darker side of this new, threatening, unpredictable world emerging from the smoke and clamour of the central belt. Stereotypes of the Irish were formed from the experiences and perceptions of the dark days of the late 1840s and early 1850s which proved particularly long-lasting, many of them vigorously alive and kicking right up to the present day: such as the belief in the general inherent fecklessness of the Irish as a race making them unable to organise any sort of life or culture for themselves or demonstrate any capacity for independent action and progress; that, once here, as a static group they replaced the more adventurous and self-reliant Scots as many of the latter emigrated; and that they diluted the native traditions of radicalism and prevented its true fruition by failing to fall in with the ideals espoused by Scots. The following examples are among many that could be cited. The statement in the *Third Statistical Account* on Cambuslang written in 1952 that: 'In common with all rural areas which have become industrialised, the life of the people has changed and the composition of the population has altered. A large number of people of Irish descent have settled in the district and many members of Cambuslang families have emigrated to the United States and countries of the British Empire.' Or the Church and Nation Committee report, also in 1952, which, commenting on the large Roman Catholic population in the industrial west, stated that: 'There is at least some ground for supposing that this increase is leading to the displacement of the native Scots Protestant population from the industrial areas of the west.' Or the picture so often presented in current analyses of modern Scottish political life of the Irish contribution consisting solely of 'a well organised political machine' or 'machine politics', with scant acknowledgment of the historical struggles to hammer out a philosophy confronting modernisation made by figures like John Ferguson, Michael Davitt, John Wheatley or James Connolly.[8]

Of course, the 1840s was a decade notable for a series of major shocks to long-held certainties and assumptions of which the potato failure in Ireland and the western Highlands was only one. In 1843 the national establishment of religion which had moulded and controlled the country since the Revolution Settlement had broken in two. By 1845 observers were begining to realise that the economic revolution was now becoming permanent, making industry and commerce the dominant elements as textile growth extended into iron, coal and engineering, the whole bound together by railroads such as those connecting Edinburgh and Glasgow in 1842 and the cross-Border routes being constructed via Annandale and Berwick to link Scotland more closely with England. The 1840s had seen heightened public tensions with demonstrations and pressure from Chartists and Free Traders and Irish Repealers. In 1846 the Conservatives, returned with a large majority under Peel just five years before, now found themselves split over Corn Law

---

[8] *The Third Statistical Account of Scotland. The County of Lanark*, ed. G. Thomson (Glasgow, 1960), 257. *Reports to the General Assembly of the Church of Scotland, 1952*, 328. These follow the line, expressed by J. R. Fleming in *A History of the Church in Scotland, 1875–1929* (Edinburgh, 1933), 146, that by 1932 'Considerable areas of a once Protestant character have been occupied, one might say colonised by a race of antagonistic habits and ideals.' For an example of the political generalisation see M. Keating, *The City that Refused to Die* (Aberdeen, 1988), 9–10. For a counterblast to the latter attitude see my 'Irish Issues in the Nineteenth and Twentieth Century: Radicalism in a Scottish Context?', in Devine, *Irish Immigrants and Scottish Society*, 116–37.

Repeal, a sure sign in that measure of further transfers of authority to newer commercial elements and movement away from traditional landed and aristocratic influences, leaving party loyalties and patterns in considerable disarray and flux thereafter. In 1845, Peel, leader of a Protestant nation, had also given the Roman Catholic College of Maynooth in Co. Kildare a permanent endowment, something which had recently been denied to Presbyterian evangelicals and which outraged a principle dear to Dissenting Voluntaries. Coming when it did in 1845, the Irish Famine intertwined with these events to add to and be associated with the public sense of crisis in this decade.

The increasing number of Irish in Scotland was an obvious physical fact. Since the Irish Act of Union in 1801, constitutionally as well as economically this represented just another movement of labour adjusting from the narrowing opportunities in one part of that United Kingdom to areas of growing labour demand in another. Psychologically, however, there was a distinction. Irish labourers in Scotland were not regarded in the same way as Scottish workers going to England or English workers transplanting to Scotland. The first were seen as constituting a problem and exacerbating pressures on already strained local medical, housing and poor relief resources. The easily measurable physical impact of numbers had thus a subtler ideological aspect: of Ireland as a colony and the Irish as a lesser group within the United Kingdom. (The pervasiveness of this almost unconscious assumption is still evident today in the way historians use 'immigrants/immigration' in referring to the Irish within the United Kingdom – a typecasting which can be traced directly from contemporary usage in the 1830s.) It has been well established that the almost universal response to these new Irish numbers was to see them as a threat: to the stability and working of the newly amended Scottish Poor Law of 1845, to job security in the growing extractive industries of coal and iron, and to public morale in creating inner-city housing congestion, disease and encouraging drunkenness.[9] The Famine was often

---

[9] Handley, *Irish in Modern Scotland*, 248 *et seq*. A. B. Campbell, *The Lanarkshire Miners* (Edinburgh, 1979), 180 *et seq*. '. . . This very high proportion of the Irish race in Scotland has undoubtedly produced deleterious results, lowered greatly the moral tone of the lower classes, and greatly increased the necessity for the enforcement of sanitary and police precautions wherever they have settled in numbers', *Census of Scotland 1871*, ii, Report, xxxiv.

portrayed at that time as something suffered inevitably by a race unable to look after itself and, indeed, its punishment for such failure.[10] Did it, therefore, reinforce the teutonic nationalism appearing by the 1840s, as frugal, industrious and commercially successful Scots began to be conscious of their own particular contribution to the growing greatness of Britain, with all that implied in terms of contemporary race theory and the inherent superiority of the Saxon as opposed to Celtic mind?[11] Post-Famine Irish nationalism has been accused of hijacking Irishness to Catholicism; but, did the equation also work the other way in Scotland where, in reacting to the Irish Famine by treating the Irish as Catholic and therefore ineffectual in a modern society, the stereotype of Irish = Catholic = nationalist = a colonial problem was created and reinforced? It is a sign of the complexities behind the issue of the Irish in Scotland that such antagonisms existed not only between Catholic Irish and Protestant Scots (especially in the heightened evangelical temper of the times), but also between Scottish Catholics and their Irish co-religionists. Scottish priests and bishops generally 'cracked down' on anything which smacked of a political or national feeling in their new flocks. It was this fear of political involvement, with its threat to community toleration achieved by a policy of quiet living, which lay behind the growing tensions between the Scottish Roman Catholic authorities and their Irish priests and congregations, tensions which finally spilled over in the *Free Press* affair of the 1860s leading to the re-establishment of a hierarchy in the 1870s.[12] All this raises questions

[10] E.g., *Blackwood's Edinburgh Magazine*, 59 (May, 1846), 576–8, 603.

[11] C. Kidd, 'Teutonist Ethnology and Scottish Nationalist Inhibition, 1780–1880', *Scottish Historical Review*, lxxiv (1995), 47–62.

[12] Consideration of the tensions which developed between the Scottish and Irish Catholics would require a separate chapter. What can be said here is that the former had to cope suddenly with an alarming influx with scant resources in personnel or buildings. Their problem was how far to commit resources to what was a fluctuating population with no guarantee of permanence and support. Records of the time show that Bishop Murdoch in the Western District was as active in everyday pastoral care as any of his curates. One of the latter (Irish, as it happens) recorded of the duties they shared: 'The year 1847 opened with gloomy prospects for Priests and people. . . . The fever scenes were truly awful. I had often to administer the sacraments to the living as they lay . . . a family in an open court in Calton; another under a tree at Partick – and a third in a deserted hut or hole at Hoganfield [*sic*]; and others at the stairfoot of closes.'

regarding varieties of Irishness and Scottish responses in this seminal nineteenth-century period only some of which can be explored here.

At the outset, it has to be acknowledged that these suspicions of Irishness long pre-dated 1845. There are many examples before then of economic fear, religious antagonism and racial attitudes; of contrasting political traditions and of a sense of Ireland being more favourably treated in contrast to a 'loyal' Scotland which was already stimulating a nationalist strand in a society redefining its relationship to the shifting centres of British power. As early as 1819 a writer in the *Glasgow Chronicle* had declared: 'It would doubtless be a galling spectacle to see the room of our sober, religious, industrious, frugal and intelligent countrymen filled with these ignorant, hapless, wandering [Irish] wretches.' The Rev. Robert Buchanan, the Free Church historian, told the *Irish Poor Report* in 1835 that Irish settlers not only drove down wages but corrupted the Scots, 'by the example, which they too often set before our people, of a disregard of religious observances, and of a violation of all the rules which govern a moral and orderly society'.[13] In 1825 Sir John Sinclair was warning government not to make the Scots resent being less favourably treated than their Irish counterparts, contrasting, long before such arguments were being made by Scottish Rights activists in the mid-1850s, the higher payments per head to the Treasury from Scotland with

---

Constant journeys on foot of up to ten or twelve miles were a regular occurence. Scottish bishops at this period were generally reluctant to rely on priests brought in from Ireland. When Bishop Murdoch tried to bring in new priests from Ireland and purchase new buildings he found that, because of the poverty of the new congregations thus formed, his expenditure over 1842–8 increased by 69% but his income by only 16.5%. Glasgow Archdiocesan Archives, Condon Diaries, Miguelide and Hamiltonia volumes, *passim*: and Bishop Murdoch's Diary. For fuller discussion see: McCaffrey, 'Irish Immigrants and Radical Movements in the West of Scotland', 49–53, and 'Roman Catholics in Scotland in the 19th and 20th Centuries', *Records of the Scottish Church History Society*, xxiii (1989), 278–85, and 'The Stewardship of Resources', 359–70. Also, B. Aspinwall, 'Scots and Irish clergy ministering to immigrants, 1830–1870', *Innes Review*, xlvii (1996), 45–56.

[13] *Glasgow Chronicle*, 9 October 1819, quoted in J. E. Handley, *The Irish In Scotland 1798–1845* (Cork, 1945), 147; *Parliamentary Papers. State of the Irish Poor In Great Britain, Appendix G, 1836, 114, 124.*

the greater political representation and government spending given to Ireland.[14] In 1825 the senior priest in Glasgow, the redoubtable Andrew Scott, was trying to prevent some of his flock from supporting O'Connell's Catholic Association because the Town Clerk had hinted to him that such actions might lead to Glasgow manufacturers withdrawing their support from the Glasgow Catholic Schools Society which they largely ran. 'I am fully convinced from experience', he wrote to his bishop in Edinburgh, 'that if such rebellions be not quelled in the bud, it will very soon become impossible to manage such congregations as we have here. This is the most numerous and consequently the most difficult to manage.'[15] However, the many instances, of which the above are but a few, never achieved the sustained, intensively abrasive and racial level which they did in the years after 1845. In the mid-1830s, William Dixon, one of the leaders in the burgeoning Scottish iron industry, expressed a racial preference for north Highlanders (with their supposed more industrious and non-Celtic, 'Norse' characteristics) to either Irish or west Highland labour, but he still found the Irish, 'very useful'. He and others similarly recognised that outright economic competition was limited by job differentiation in which the Scots were trained to expect apprenticeships and artisan skills, whereas the Irish had come from a society in which their contribution was expected to be made in muscle power.[16] Some of his fellow employers, like Joseph Browne, dyeworks proprietor and one of Dr Chalmers's original deacons, thought that 'if the Irish had the same facilities as our countrymen, they would surpass both them and the English in intelligence and usefulness'.[17] Such acknowledgments of the positive aspects of Irish settlement, however, became markedly scarcer in the decade or so after 1845; there was a perceptible edge, something new in the tension creating a mood qualitatively

---

[14] Sir J. Sinclair, *Analysis of the Statistical Account of Scotland* (Edinburgh, 1825), Part I, App., 68–7.

[15] Scott to William Reid, 5 February 1825, Edinburgh, Scottish Catholic Archives, BL5/180/1.

[16] *Parliamentary Papers. State of the Irish Poor*, 107, evidence of J. G. Hamilton, Monteith and Co: 'the Scotch do not show much disposition for labouring work; they would rather go to trades'; and also ibid., 114, the evidence of William Dixon.

[17] Ibid., 112.

different from the patchy responses of the decades before then, a patchiness which reflected perhaps the limits of the modernisation of Scotland's economy up to the 1830s.

A clearer impression of this post-Famine atmosphere can be obtained if one looks at some obvious aspects (by no means exhaustive) such as its effects on population, the changing mood of public opinion, at religious and political attitudes. To start with population first: there is no doubt that in purely numerical terms alone the numbers of Irish arriving in Scotland were bound to have an impact. As noted earlier, the total Irish-born (which did not include children born in Scotland) had jumped from 126,321 in 1841 to 207,367 in 1851, a 64% increase; and although the overall total fell slightly by 1861 to 204,083, this still left a 62% increase over the 1841 numbers. The certainty behind such snapshots, of course, is more apparent than real and gives no indication of the ebb and flow over the period, the removals by deaths or further outward movements or their replacement by further inflows, or whether such movements occurred regularly over the decades or quickened so as to be concentrated and cause extreme pressure in certain years. Nor, since they only date from 1841, do they provide any firm comparison with the effects of Irish in Scotland in the earlier period before the Famine against which to measure just how great the shock of the Famine numbers must have been. *Prima facie*, of course, the greatest inflows must have been in the later 1840s and early 1850s, corresponding to the Famine exodus from Ireland when the numbers leaving there jumped from the 100,000 level to an average of 242,000 annually between 1847 and 1852.[18]

Some comparisons might still be attempted, however, by utilising sources other than the national census. For instance, Glasgow's statistician, James Cleland, compiled a fuller census of the city as part of the 1831 national return which was published locally[19] and which does give a figure for the number of Irish-born in that year – 35,554. Taking that with the comparable figure given for Glasgow in the national census for 1841 – 44,345, and extrapolating backwards gives an increase of 24.7% over the decade.

[18] D. Fitzpatrick, *Irish Emigration 1801–1921* (Dublin, 1984).
[19] J. Cleland, *Enumeration of the Inhabitants of Glasgow for the Census of 1831* (Glasgow, 1832).

That figure, applied to the total Irish-born figure of 1841 – 126,321, would mean the Irish-born in Scotland had totalled around 101,300 in 1831.[20] It next falls to work out the reduction by death over the decade of this base group of 1831. For the purposes of the calculations in this essay an average death rate of 34/35 per 1,000 was chosen. It could be argued that during the cholera of 1832 and the typhus epidemic of 1836 death rates could go as high as 49 per 1,000, especially in the poorer inner city areas likely to be inhabited by Irish newcomers. However, against this it has to be remembered that even the Famine migrants were not the very poorest and weakest – these had perished in Ireland; and that contemporaries generally remarked on the sturdy physique and height of the Irishmen and women fed on the highly nutritional potato diet; nor, because of their age structure, were their ranks so severely thinned by the current high rate of infant and child death.[21] On this basis around 71,000/72,000 of the 1831 total would have survived and, since the Census gives a total of 126,321 in 1841, some 55,000 must, therefore, have entered in the preceding ten years, perhaps from a rate of about 4,000 per annum in the early 1830s to a rate of about 7,000 per annum by the end of the decade, reflecting the worsening conditions in Ireland at this time. When this is placed beside the figures for 1841–51 the contrast becomes evident and explains the sense of shock being generally expressed by the later 1840s and early 1850s at the flood

[20] Given that Glasgow's experience of Irish migration was likely to match that of the rest of modernising Scotland at this time, such an extrapolation seems not unreasonable. The figure it gives, incidentally, is not too out of line with Handley's estimates (*Irish in Scotland*, 91 *et ante*) of the size of the Irish group in Scotland in this decade, if one makes an allowance for the numbers born since arriving in Scotland: nor with the estimate by B. Collins, in her 'Irish Emigration to Dundee and Paisley', 196, or her essay in Devine, *Irish Immigrants and Scottish Society*, 8: or with the figures which can be extracted from the *Royal Commission on Religious Instruction. Scotland. Reports 1837–39*.

[21] M. W. Flinn, *The Report on the Sanitary Condition of the Labouring Population of Great Britain by Edwin Chadwick 1842* (Edinburgh, 1967), Introduction, 13–14, suggests an average of 34.2 per 1,000 for Glasgow in the 1830s and 1840s, although pointing out that much higher rates could prevail in certain years, as does the *1842 Sanitary Inquiry. Local Reports Scotland*, 167. See also R. H. Campbell, *Scotland since 1707* (2nd edn, Edinburgh, 1985), 150. The 1851 Census showed that the proportion of Irish-born under twenty years was 29% compared with 46.7% for the Scottish-born population. *Census of Great Britain 1851*, ii, 1038, 1041.

of poor Irish entering Scotland. Assuming the same average death rate, the base group of 126,321 in 1841 would have been reduced to around 87,000/88,000 by 1850. That means that some 120,000 Irish must have arrived over the 1840s; and, since the bulk obviously came after 1845 (perhaps in the ratio of 1:2 as between 1841–45 and 1846–50), the conclusion must be that 40,000 came in the first half, giving a rate of 8,000 per annum, and 80,000 in the second half, giving a rate of 16,000 per annum, over double the rate experienced in the later 1830s.[22]

Such a sudden jump, coming at a time when the economy was going into a deep recession in 1847, must have given a severe jolt to contemporaries and helps to explain the air of almost panic with which Irish arrivals were greeted and the apparent callousness with which those with no visible means or already ill with fever were so readily and rapidly shipped back to Ireland.[23] No doubt, some of this feeling of being submerged in waves of incoming Irish was exaggerated. Handley, in his usual careful fashion, has shown that the 33,267 Irish reported by the Glasgow Parochial authorities as landing at the Clyde ports in just thirteen weeks between 15 June and 12 September 1847 must have included many temporary Irish harvesters as well as those fleeing the Famine. He has also shown that the figures of 42,680 destitute Irish landing at the Clyde for the four months preceding April 1848 and continuing at a rate of 1,000 a week for a year thereafter, takes no account of how many of these moved on or were again temporary migrants.[24] Nevertheless, they do indicate the mood of crisis which attended the inflow from Ireland. A sudden jump to a rate of 16,000 per annum was by any standards a frightening experience and one

[22] Again, this is in line with Handley's estimate of 115,000, in *Irish in Modern Scotland*, 45, and that in M. W. Flinn, *Scottish Population History* (Cambridge, 1977), 303, 457.

[23] For examples, see Handley, *Irish in Modern Scotland*, 24–32, *passim*.

[24] Ibid., 45. This has not stopped later historians from citing such figures, minus his justified reservations, as proven facts. They were originally quoted by Sir Archibald Alison, Sheriff of Lanarkshire (never a writer to let accuracy spoil a good argument) in *Blackwood's Edinburgh Magazine* as late as the issue of August 1851, vol. 70, 129. Suspicion is aroused by the thought that a rate of 1,000 per week during just this one year, 1848, would have accounted for half of the total of Irish migrants to Scotland estimated by Handley or Professor Flinn as coming to Scotland in the 1840s.

with little need of exaggeration. It represented the addition of a sizeable new industrial town each year in the later 1840s and early 1850s onto a society already struggling to cope with the new levels of social provision demanded after 1845 to sustain temporary claimants for poor relief at a time of economic downturn, plus the demand for emergency medical attention during the cholera of 1848–9.

An earlier example of population figures being used to convey a social and political message occurs in the comparisons made by John Strang, Glasgow's City Chamberlain, of the 1841 Glasgow census totals with those for 1831. He noted that in the old Royalty area comprising the ten parishes of inner Glasgow there were proportionately more Irish than there had been ten years before. He arrived at this conclusion by comparing what the Scottish and Irish numbers would have been had they increased at the same rate as the city population overall. In this way he demonstrated that there were now 5,199 fewer Scots to the total Royalty population compared with 3,495 more Irish than there had been in 1831. What he omitted to say was that if he had taken the numbers for the whole city, which included the Barony districts like Calton and Anderston, as well as Gorbals, the true figures would have shown that there had been a greater increase in Scots than in Irish inhabitants overall. Nevertheless, this allowed him to state that since these figures did not include the children of Irish incomers born in the city

> the real amount of the inhabitants who are imbued with Irish characteristics, habits, feelings and religious sentiments is infinitely greater. Whether or not this vast infusion into our City Population, of a people whose ideas of comfort are so far below the level of this nation, has had the effect of altering, in any degree, the tastes and habits of those with whom they are in daily intercourse, is somewhat problematical, but it cannot be denied that this constant Irish immigration is producing a more densely and closely packed community, and is tending to a less comfortable condition in the dwellings of the labouring classes of our City.[25]

There is more than a hint here of later nativist claims of the Scots being driven out by the Irish; and little acknowledgement that the Irish were also being just as affected by economic challenges in

[25] *Glasgow Herald*, 26 July 1841.

the search for work as their fellow subjects, or that they, too, were part of a fluctuating stream of labour migration drawn along by the same economic currents. After the Famine influx such feelings inevitably became more pronounced and more widely propagated. Typical of a wider range of newspaper comment was an editorial on the burden imposed by the export of paupers from Ireland which declared: 'In addition to the poor rates, the police and prison rates are vastly increased by the lowest class of Irish who pour in upon us unsought, and our own lower orders have been much degraded and demoralised by contact with them.'[26]

Indeed, some of these sharper reactions can be measured most clearly in the desperate efforts made to prevent ill and starving Irish immigrants becoming a permanent charge on the rates. Cities like Glasgow and Liverpool, which had to bear the whole burden of the hordes landing on their streets with no visible means of support, lobbied government hard in this period to get some temporary relief and many were shipped back to the nearest Irish port, often with scant regard for the justice of their claims. In March 1847 the Glasgow Police Board reported that of the 938 beggars brought before it over a six-week period, 163 had been returned to Ireland. Handley quotes an overall figure of 1,000 per month in 1849 being sent back to Ireland from Glasgow, and 6,000 per annum over the whole eight-year period of 1845–53. In this it was not alone. Similarly high figures of removal were also recorded in Liverpool and Cardiff.[27] On the other hand, there were also cases where the parochial authorities did spend time and money in trying to care for the cases of destitution and fever which they had discovered, obviously in an attempt to prevent a local epidemic.[28] Indeed, a variety of attitudes reflecting fluctuations in public mood in which sympathy mingled with rejection can be detected. In 1846, one newspaper was already expressing the view that the wretchedness due to the Famine was mainly confined to the south and west because that area was Celtic, Catholic and thus indolent as compared with the industrious and Protestant,

[26] *Glasgow Herald*, 9 April 1849.
[27] *Glasgow Herald*, 5 March 1847; Handley, *Irish In Modern Scotland*, 31, 260; Kinealy, *This Great Calamity*, 334–9.
[28] *Glasgow Herald*, 25 January 1847, cited in Handley, *Irish in Modern Scotland*, 25.

Saxon north: 'most of this state is due to how the Irish choose to live – in crude mud cabins . . . It is instructive that all this is in the Roman Catholic parts. In the North, which is Protestant, [there is] education, security, little crime.' However, while dreading further emigration from Ireland which would, 'pour her dissolute and degrading population on our shores', the same journal was urging its readers to be generous to their starving fellow beings. Yet another, equally critical, similarly stressed the need for positive, early and extraordinary measures to prevent the present famine 'being the parent of of a worse famine next year'.[29] In general, one might say that the popular attitude as reflected in the local press mingled sympathy for the plight of the starving masses in Ireland with resentment that their localities were having to bear the brunt of that country's exodus. Such attitudes were not confined to the Irish immigrants. Similarly racial attitudes were widespread in Scotland as regards west highlanders currently suffering from successive failures in their potato crops. Articles and letters categorising the Celtic west highlander as inherently idle and inferior to the superior and successful Saxon lowlanders, and linking the present highland destitution to the backwardness of the Gaels, were also common currency in the Scottish press at this time.[30] Generally, it might be said that attitudes, as measured in the popular press, hardened as time went on and the condition of Ireland appeared to become ever more hopeless, and became definitely hostile after the abortive rebellion of the Young Irelanders in late July 1848.

Similar variations can be found amongst the leading opinion-forming journals in Scotland, with an overall bias towards the disapproving. As befitted a radical evangelical, George Troup, editor of *Tait's Edinburgh Magazine*, was inclined to lay the blame for Ireland's problems on the landlords. His solution was close to the social revolution advocated by the Young Irelander, James Finton Lalor (and later by Michael Davitt, especially in his Scottish tours) of reforming the land system and thus improving social

---

[29] *Glasgow Examiner*, 18 April 1847 and 27 November 1847; *Glasgow Herald*, 4 January 1847.

[30] For a comprehensive analysis see K. Fenyo, '"Contempt, Sympathy and Romance". Lowland perceptions of the Highlands and the Clearances during the Famine years 1845–1855' (University of Glasgow, PhD thesis, 1996).

conditions. 'From the soil of Ireland, and from that alone, is there real hope for her people. Emigration can never bring them relief', he wrote.[31] Troup's opposition to mass emigration as a solution and insistence on sympathy for Ireland being shown by direct government intervention remained consistent, but he tended to express a minority view.[32] *Blackwood's*, on the other hand, more usually adopted a brisk and censorious tone with little patience for Irish woes (or, indeed, for Whig government policies during the Famine). Its analysis was that the Famine was largely self-induced because of the incorrigible nature of the Irish, exacerbated by their Catholicism which had the effect 'of checking rather than encouraging any habits of thought or reflection'.[33] In its opinion this made them unfit for self-government, a view which continued to have a long life in Scottish politics.[34] Such views generally came from the pen of regular contributors like Sir Archibald Alison, the historian and Sheriff of Lanarkshire. Some more occasional contributors, like his brother, Professor W. P. Alison, the poor law and health reformer, did, however, categorically reject the idea that there was something inherent in the Celtic character which made the Irish incapable of developing their country. Instead it was 'the absence of skill and capital to give them work . . . which ought chiefly to fix the attention of those who wish to see the resources of the country developed', and what was needed was employment for the poor in order to give them purchasing power.[35] However, by the end of 1848, Alison's argument that the Irish should have the security of a firmly administered poor law was beginning to look rather threadbare given that the cost of maintaining the nearly 2 million who had received relief was now, by government decision, being borne solely by the Irish authorities, including the worst affected Famine areas. He, therefore, now

---

[31] *Tait's Edinburgh Magazine* (December 1847), 794 and (May 1847), 333–8. For Davitt in Scotland see J. Hunter, 'The Gaelic connection: the Highlands, Ireland and nationalism, 1873–1922', *Scottish Historical Review*, liv (1975), 178–88.

[32] E.g. *Tait's Edinburgh Magazine* (February 1847), 120.

[33] *Blackwood's Edinburgh Magazine* (December 1848), 662.

[34] *Blackwood's Edinburgh Magazine* (April 1847), 524. On the latter point see J. F. McCaffrey, *Scotland in the Nineteenth Century* (Basingstoke, 1998), 76–7.

[35] *Blackwood's Edinburgh Magazine* (November 1847), 639.

advocated further relief, partly, through siphoning off some of the population through official and well-supervised emigration schemes, but mainly through government aid and intervention so as to ensure some sort of worthwhile employment for the many more poor who would remain.[36]

Despite his obvious humanity, one wonders if Alison had really grasped the enormity of what had happened in Ireland in 1845, and was only really now beginning to understand what it meant for mainland Britain when the situation had passed beyond the realm of long-term analyses such as he was offering. It is ironic, in view of their former roles in 1840 in the argument over improvement in the poor law, in which Alison is generally lauded as the pragmatist and Thomas Chalmers as the theorist, that these should appear to have been reversed in face of the challenge of the Irish Famine. In the *North British Review*, Chalmers, even more strongly than Alison, rejected any idea that the tragedy was due to any inherent fault in the Irish people.[37] In contrast to Alison's rather discursive and long-term approach, however, Chalmers argued loudly for direct government intervention from the very outset. In times of national crisis normal rules of market economics went out of the window in face of the greater moral claims of suffering humanity, he wrote. Categorising the situation which had led to the famine and its continuance as making Britain a byword in Europe, he wanted government to force a redistribution of the nation's resources via measures such as an income tax so that those starving in Ireland (while most people still ate pretty much as usual just across the Irish sea) should be saved. Normally, he wrote, the Adam Smith analogy of a famine being like a ship which had gone short of supplies prevailed: only by each of the crew receiving less could they all hope to reach port safely. But in this case it was as if those in the hold were starving while those on deck were living in luxury. Little wonder then if they were to revolt. 'Better for all to be on bread and water than for some to have no bread at all.'[38] The people of Ireland, peasants and landowners, should be conciliated, not have abuse heaped upon them. The country had plenty of resources to make good the difference in

---

[36] Ibid. (December 1848), 658–71.
[37] *North British Review* (May 1847), 247–90.
[38] Ibid., 277.

provision. 'Rather than that so much as one of our fellow countrymen should perish of hunger, no expense should be spared to prevent a catastrophe so horrible.'[39] Chalmers saw that the Irish Union meant that this was a national, not merely an Irish problem, and, like Nonconformist opinion in general in Britain by 1847, was critical of the prevailing public policy of *laissez-faire* and of leaving the Irish local authorities to solve the problem of the starving masses themselves. Chalmers's views were expressed in his usual long-winded and roundabout fashion but, also, as usual, contained a kernel of sound common sense as well as an acute awareness of the urgency of the situation.[40]

Some of these various outlooks, with a general bias towards the censorious, can be seen at a more local level in the Dean of Guild reports written by James Pagan for the *Glasgow Herald* between 1848 and 1851. These were, in effect, jeremiads against the deterioration of the old historic buildings in the city centre and, equally bad in his view, the philistinism and utilitarianism of the speculators and councillors who were presiding over the decline – a decline which demanded not only the regulation of buildings but also the regulation and reformation of the debased masses, many of them recent Irish arrivals, who inhabited them. Pagan contrasted the merchant worthies who had inhabited, within living memory, areas such as St Andrew's Square, with its present denizens, 'ragged Irish and dirty Scotch'. 'When once these Milesians (who have imported the principle of "tenant-right") of the lower class make a settlement, we are told it is nearly as difficult to expel them as to hunt rats out of a city drain.' He described wakes held in these plague spots as punctuated by 'varied Celtic howls' from a packed company 'smoking tobacco vigorously, drinking whisky daintily, and discussing earnestly the question of repeal, the wrongs of Ireland, and the cruel persecution of Meagher and Smith O'Brien'. Those who burrowed there, he likened to modern Huns and Vandals who would destroy civilisation unless they were themselves reclaimed by coercive measures. 'Looking at these, and a hundred other instances of the pestiferous influence

---

[39] Ibid., 248; Kinealy, *This Great Calamity*, 198–9.

[40] 'He foresaw that . . . to wait till the cry of actual hunger was heard [meant that] relief would come too late.' W. Hanna, *Memoirs of Dr. Chalmers*, 4 vols (Edinburgh, 1849–52), iv, 235. See also S. J. Brown, *Thomas Chalmers and the Godly Commonwealth* (Oxford, 1982), 367–9.

of these immigrants, we cannot help exclaiming – Repeal the Union.'[41] Nevertheless, by contrast, Pagan never failed to remark favourably on any sign of developing social habits among these new Catholic Irish, such as their efforts to maintain educational ventures or build churches, a dichotomy in attitude still evident in the *Glasgow Herald* in the 1860s and later.[42]

An increasingly popular strategy to incorporate these new numbers into the standards of civic consciousness preached by Pagan was to develop Home Missions. This more aggressive pros-elytising campaign, coming up against the new masses of Catholic Irish in the 1850s, in turn, produced more sectarian tensions as yet another of the traits which the Famine exacerbated in Scotland. Missions to the submerged masses, living in apparent abandon-ment in the city wynds and closes, had existed, of course, ever since the beginning of Chalmers's St John's ministry in 1819. A combination of Catholic Emancipation in 1829, an unease over the failure to get government support for a campaign to rein-vigorate the Reformation tradition nationally which had culmi-nated in the Disruption, the resulting interdenominational rivalry, plus the growing strength of the Catholic community in industrial Scotland due to increased Irish immigration in the 1840s and 1850s, demanded an intensification of such efforts. Because 'the Gallowgate and its neighbourhood seem now largely tenanted by emigrants from the Emerald Isle who, by their ignorance and poverty, tell too plainly they have come from a land under the blighting influence of the Pope',[43] it was evident that they too should be treated as part of the pagan mass existing in the slums requiring salvation. In cities like Edinburgh, the Irish Catholics in such areas as the Cowgate were specifically targeted by such groups.[44] Not surprisingly, such attentions were widely resented, as much for their class bias – such aggressive visiting was never

[41] *Glasgow Past and Present*, 3 vols (Glasgow, 1884), i, 21–174, *passim*.

[42] Ibid., 89, 120, 138, and *Glasgow Herald*, 2 March and 8 August 1868.

[43] *Reformed Presbyterian Magazine* (1 August 1867), quoted in B. Aspinwall, 'Popery in Scotland: Image and Reality', *Records of the Scottish Church History Society*, xxii (1986), 239.

[44] D. Jamie, *John Hope Philanthropist and Reformer* (Edinburgh, 1900), 273 *et seq.*; N. L. Walker, *Chapters from the History of the Free Church of Scotland* (Edinburgh, 1895), 84–5; C. G. Brown, *The Social History of Religion in Scotland since 1730* (London, 1987), 143–8.

directed at middle-class areas – as for their religious message, as the response to one tract distributor shows: 'You missionaries tell us that carters and factory lassies hae souls as weel as ither folk. For my pairt I aye thocht they had, – why is it, man, you canna tell us something we dinna ken? . . . dinna bring your tracts here, for we dinna want them.'[45] Such efforts, identifying poverty with inferiority and lack of success as concomitant with Irishness and Roman Catholicism, could work in the other direction. It helped to give respectable Scottish artisans, in the more expansive economy of the 1850s and 1860s outside of the wynds, a sense of their distinctiveness from the masses below them, reinforcing their feeling that the material skills and the status which went with it came from qualities nurtured by Anglo-Saxon and Reformation values. This is clear from the enthusiastic receptions given in Scotland to those engaged in struggles against the Catholic Habsburgs or the Papal States, like Kossuth, Mazzini and Garibaldi. Ex-Chartists joined with middle-class Liberals to laud such figures as fighters for civil and religious freedoms which they themselves already enjoyed as Britons (freedoms which they were convinced were conspicuously lacking in Famine and post-Famine Ireland). Historical heroes like William Wallace were projected as 'symbols of everyman's struggle for freedom and of the virtues of British Protestantism now being exported abroad'.[46]

Finally, some brief consideration must be given to the immediate political effects of the Irish Famine in Scotland. Coming as it did at the same time as the Maynooth Grant, the Famine exodus must have hardened political attitudes in Scotland and was bound to lead to challenges to the existing political establishment of Scottish MPs supportive of conciliatory Whig (and Peelite Conservative) policy to Ireland. As we have seen, by 1848 there was a growing tide of thought in Scotland which looked on Popery as breeding the qualities which had led to the Famine and the problems it had washed up on their shore. It was something, therefore, which needed to be opposed, not given encouragement and support. It is no surprise, therefore, to find that Scotland was one of the main centres of anti-Maynooth agitation nor that many of its sitting

[45] *Midnight Scenes and Social Photographs: By Shadow* (Glasgow, 1858; reprinted 1976), 14–20.
[46] For background, see McCaffrey, *Scotland in the Nineteenth Century*, 60.

Whig MPs found themselves under increasing threat for their agreement with Peel on this subject. A full exploration of the issues involved is beyond the scope of the present chapter. Suffice to say that opposition to those who supported the Maynooth Grant helped Free Church and Voluntary interests, at a crucial period of changing political allegiances just after 1843, to forge an alliance which both caused Conservative electoral fortunes to sink further and allowed new, middle-class commercial interests to challenge successfully the hitherto accepted leadership of the Whigs in matters of Reform.[47] Although such alliances would change under future fresh challenges, they provided much of the basis for the continuing Liberal hegemony in mid-nineteenth-century Scotland and beyond. Here, as in the other areas discussed above, both the immediate and the longer-term effects of the Irish Famine on Scotland were to reinforce those values finding expression in its new commercial elites of self-confident nationalism, pride in Britain and its material achievements, the whole based on Saxon virtues and Reformation values in sharp contrast to those associated with the Celtic Irish. For the latter, the longer-term effects of the Famine were to reinforce a political outlook in which the inadequacies of the British governmental system and questions of social relationships and property were the main focus.[48]

The appearance of the blight which caused the Irish Famine was quite fortuitous, but it struck, and its desperate survivors poured into its towns just at the point in the short period between the later 1840s and early 1850s when the old Scotland was giving way to the new; just, indeed, when the new industrially based and economically more secure society of the 1850s was still painfully and, to contemporaries, uncertainly emerging. Coming thus at a particularly crucial stage, the Irish Famine did much to form the values and attitudes which came to prevail in Scotland in the nineteenth and twentieth centuries.

[47] G. Millar, 'Maynooth and Scottish Politics: the role of the Maynooth Grant issue, 1845–1857', *Records of the Scottish Church History Society*, 27 (1997), 222. For background, see G. I. T. Machin, *Politics and the Churches in Great Britain 1832 to 1868* (Oxford, 1977), 169 *et seq.*, and I. G. C. Hutchison, *A Political History of Scotland 1832–1924* (Edinburgh, 1986), 62–70.

[48] See, for example, J. F. McCaffrey, 'The Roman Catholic Church in the 1890s: Retrospect and Prospect', *Records of the Scottish Church History Society*, xxv (1995), 436–41.

Chapter 8

The Sacrament at Crathie, 1873

Owen Chadwick

EVERY October and November Queen Victoria stayed at Balmoral. She had been brought up in a loyal Christian and Protestant tradition and she tried not to miss worship every Sunday. It was possible to hold a service in the big house but she regarded that as suitable only in sickness or for some equally urgent cause. The only church near Balmoral was the parish church of the Church of Scotland in the village of Crathie. It was true that she was a member of the Church of England – indeed by the law of the land she could not be the sovereign unless she was a member of the Church of England; and the constitution gave her special rights in the Church of England as, since the reign of Queen Elizabeth 1, its 'Supreme Governor'; especially that she had the final responsibility for approving the choice of its bishops, a work which she regarded as no mere matter of protocol. In summer many upper-class or middle-class English went on holiday into Scotland and most of them were Anglicans and most of them attended the parish church of the Church of Scotland where they were on holiday and did not mind that the Presbyterian form of worship was different from the liturgy of the Book of Common Prayer. The Queen was no different; she was on holiday in Scotland; the parish church of Crathie was Presbyterian. Though she was central to the Church of England she had no hesitation in going each Sunday, if she was well, to say her prayers at the church in Crathie.

For her there were three differences from most of the other English who went on holiday into Scotland. She was not only on holiday, she was the owner of the land and the laird of the district. She had a responsibility to the people of Crathie and the valley which ordinary holidaymakers did not have. By her place as laird she was an heritor of the parish of Crathie, an office which gave her certain responsibilities, especially financial: a part in appointments to the parish, a part in the care of the church and churchyard, a part in ensuring the stipend of the minister. These responsibilities she felt. A laird ought to be encouraging the people to their worship and setting them an example. This was a fundamental reason why the services at Crathie church became so important to her. There was a second reason, more of theory than of practice but not to be overlooked in her attitude. As sovereign she had a constitutional relationship to the established Church of Scotland; very different from her relationship to the Church of England, for in England her place was not only as sovereign but as the key lay member of the Church; in Scotland her place towards the Established Church was, so to speak, from 'outside', by being represented, for example, at the meetings of its General Assembly. And yet it was not wholly from 'outside', because by the Act of Union she was required to take an oath, at her Accession Council, that she would 'inviolably maintain and preserve . . . the government, worship, discipline, rights and privileges' of the Church of Scotland. The third reason was history. Hanoverian of Hanoverians though she might be, she carried in her veins the blood of the Stuarts. She was queen in Great Britain because she stood in the line of descent from the historic Scottish line of kings and queens.

Some of the English who came north refrained from attending the services of the Church of Scotland, or of the Free Church of Scotland, because they wanted an English form of service and knew that they would find it in the Episcopal Church of Scotland; and if they were instructed Anglicans, they knew that the Church of England was in communion with the Episcopal Church and that they might loyally receive the sacrament at its altars.

This attitude was impossible for the Queen. First, there was no Episcopal Chapel near Balmoral. Secondly, she owed a responsibility to the people of the glen, who were Presbyterians. To seek out some distant Anglican church, or hold her own Anglican service inside the castle and neglect the parish, was directly contrary to her sense of duty towards the people. Thirdly, she believed in establishments, one should go to the Established Church of England if one was in England and to the Established Church of Scotland if one was in Scotland.

This last conviction had the corollary that she regarded the Episcopal Church as a disaster for Scotland – as one more way of keeping some of the people of Scotland, and especially the upper class among the people of Scotland, away from their Presbyterian parish church. If it were suggested to her that as the leading Anglican lay person she ought to attend a service of the Anglican Church in Scotland, she would look on the suggestion as an invitation to go into schism and to commit an irresponsibility. No one dared to suggest it to her.

Therefore each Sunday, unless not well, she went to church at Crathie. It was not the church which now stands at Crathie but its predecessor. She was to help its reconstruction near the end of her reign. Every Sunday that she was there she appeared, unless she was poorly, in the front row of the gallery. The church was square and whitewashed, and still traditional in its form of service, with no organ and no hymns but metrical psalms sung unaccompanied. The collection plate was the rattling ladle, into which she always put her money.

Her courtiers were almost all Anglicans and found the services unfamiliar and unexciting and long. She had no such feeling. She felt herself at home in her prayers. She liked the Scots. They were associated with all that she loved about the mountains – the peace, the glory and variety of the scenery, the retreat from crowds, even (sometimes) the retreat from prime ministers, the knowledge that her husband had loved it all. She wanted to worship with her tenants and workers on the estate. She usually liked the form of preaching. And she had a personal reason for valuing ministers of the Church of Scotland. In the traumatic religious crisis of her life, the adjustment to the death of her husband, it was a Scottish Presbyterian minister, Norman MacLeod, who helped her most. And with her strong sense of the sovereign's place in the constitution, she knew that though her constitutional relation with the Church of Scotland was very different from her relation to the Church of England, such a relationship existed. She valued it and wanted to show that she valued it.

On the first or second Sunday in November in each year the church at Crathie held its quarterly communion, a solemn moment of its worshipping year. Since the Queen was at Balmoral on that Sunday she was in church at the start of the service. In November 1870, for the first time in her life, she was present at and witnessed the celebration of the communion at Crathie. The sight raised a scruple of conscience in her mind. Slowly it began to bother her that she did not go forward to receive the sacrament with her tenants and the villagers. *Bother* is too weak a word to describe her feelings. She began to feel that she was not behaving in a Christian way. But when she asked the advice of her favourite religious advisers she was grieved that several of them were decisive – that she should not do it.

Their reasons were of doctrine and of practice. She was a communicant of the Church of England – and the Church of England was not in communion with the Church of Scotland and did not accept that a sacrament celebrated by a minister not ordained by a bishop was in the fullest sense a valid sacrament. Therefore a communicant of the Church of England ought not to receive the sacrament in the Church of Scotland. This doctrinal argument was pleaded by none of her advisers, because they did not believe it. What they did believe was practical – that this doctrinal argument was accepted by enough of the English to cause real trouble in her relation with the Church of England – and therefore in the whole delicate nexus of Church and State – if she did receive the sacrament in the Church of Scotland.

Her Anglican advisers were three: the Archbishop of Canterbury, Tait, who had lost five children within a month in an epidemic of scarlet fever and so won her profound sympathy. He had the merit for these purposes of being a Scot, born in Edinburgh, brought up as a Presbyterian, with Glasgow as his first university, with Campbell as his second name, and with one brother a sheriff in Perthshire and another brother a writer to the signet. Then there was the Dean of Windsor, Gerald Wellesley, nephew of the great Duke of Wellington, and anyone who bore the name of Wellesley commanded her respect, and this Wellesley shared his uncle's gift of laconic utterance full of common sense. Then there was the Dean of Westminster, the biographer of Dr Arnold of Rugby, Arthur Stanley, a man whom she found distant and reserved but who won her esteem when he escorted her son the Prince of Wales on a tour of the Holy Land and who was married to Augusta the daughter of the Earl of Elgin, a lady of whom the Queen was fond;

and when Augusta died, too young, the loss opened the Queen's affection for the widower.

These three shared little charisma between them. Tait and Wellesley were as solid and sane and unexciting as was possible for a member of a Church like the Anglican which made so high a virtue of sanity in religion. Stanley was not solid, was the least solid of the Anglican eminences of the Victorian age, but was clever, and knew a lot though not quite all that he knew was accurate, and loved the Church of Scotland and had close friends among its members; and as he never minded offending people by an action which his conscience decided to be right, and despised prudence as a virtue, he had friendships with Scottish churches so public as to offend stiffer churchmen who surrounded him in London.

In 1872, just when this Crathie dilemma troubled the Queen's conscience, Arthur Stanley published *Lectures on the Church of Scotland*. This book is rare among books about Scotland; such romantic history that the reader cannot help wondering whether it is true; illustrated with delightful and telling anecdotes and an authentic ecstacy at places and monuments; and with a portrait of the Scottish people which fitted how (he imagined) they liked to see themselves – as doughty fighters for independence, always ready to say 'No' on some principle or other, with unyielding conviction, and courage to resist external pressure, their 'devotion of themselves not only to death, but, at times, even to absurdity, for what were deemed the rights of conscience and the sacredness of truth and the glory of Scotland';[1] the tendency on conscientious grounds to make religious mountains out of theological molehills. Therefore its Church – indeed Churches – had 'a contradictious character'. He portrays the Scots as possessed of too hard a logical quality of mind. Yet he asserted that these characteristics were the source of some of the finest and noblest spirits in the Scottish Church. The picture of the past Presbyterian world was very unfavourable while he claimed great exceptions like Rutherford or Leighton or Chalmers – even, surprisingly, Robert Burns – and as himself a Latitudinarian fastened on the eighteenth-century moderate divines as his intellectual heroes. But what mattered to his Scottish hearers was his inference: 'It was a dream to think that the great Scottish

[1] A. P. Stanley, *Lectures on the History of the Church of Scotland delivered in Edinburgh in 1872*, 2nd edn (London, 1879), 65.

nation would be extinguished by incorporation with the civilization of England.'[2]

Queen Victoria had another constitutional adviser in London, perhaps the only one who might think that he had a right to be consulted, the prime minister. At that moment he was Gladstone. She was not likely to ask his opinion on such a matter. Their antipathy had not yet reached the furies of twenty years later when he thought her a tiresome woman and she thought he was mad. But it was already antipathy. He had just disestablished the Church of Ireland and given a boost to Roman Catholicism in part of these islands. In her eyes that disqualified him for giving her advice about her behaviour with regard to the Church of Scotland; she could see that he was patently unsound on any such question.

Her meditations on the difficulty were affected in early September of 1871 by the behaviour of an Anglican bishop. During the first week of that month the Queen was really ill. She had been very ill at Osborne before she came north, and found the journey to Scotland difficult, and after she came to Balmoral a swelling had to be lanced. Norman MacLeod, on holiday in the region, expected to be invited to preach: but wrote in his diary: 'Owing to the severe illness of the Queen I did not preach last Sunday, so I have had a most blessed time.' He meant, that he could enjoy his children, and preach in less formidable surroundings, and play croquet and whist and enjoy dancing and singing.

It is probable that in this weak plight the Queen asked herself how she could receive the comforts of religion in Scotland if she needed them.

Just in that week Samuel Wilberforce, the Bishop of Winchester, came to stay with his friend Mr Ellice, the laird of Glengarry, in high and in those days remote Highland country to the south-west of Fort Augustus. The incumbent of Glengarry was away and Ellice asked Wilberforce if he would conduct the service for them. He agreed. He used Anglican prayers but shortened the service to bring it nearer to the Presbyterian form, and at the end, though he again used Anglican prayers of intercession he spoke the words as if they were extempore.

[2] Ibid., 94.

This piece of piety started a little scandal. Since the word *bishop* carried an oppressive ring by folk-association among some of the Scots, there were those who much minded a bishop leading the prayers in a Presbyterian church. And since there was no unity between the Church of England and the Church of Scotland, there were Anglicans who minded Wilberforce. He was famous from his youth as the son of the slave-emancipator, and was better known to a wide public than his archbishop. His name was justly associated with controversy and unjustly associated with butter and adulation; but his was still the biggest name of any of the English bishops and it was the doubt about his quality as a controversialist which had kept away from him the invitation to be archbishop instead of Tait. He had charisma which Tait had not, but less common sense and less prudence.

Formerly many had admired him as a stout defender of church rights. They were now astonished that such a person with such a record should by his conduct at Glengarry cry aloud of the common Christian faith and worship of the two Established bodies which were not in communion with each other. It was soon put about that this Anglican prelate conducted a Presbyterian service in a Presbyterian manner; a rumour for which Wilberforce's shortening of the service and his apparently extempore prayers gave the vestige of an excuse.

That feelings were roused was proved when two heavy-weights were called in to defend Wilberforce. The Primus of the Episcopal Church of Scotland, Bishop Robert Eden of Moray, Ross and Caithness, wrote to the press a letter of gratitude to Wilberforce for what he had done so that the Sunday congregation could have a service. Since the Scottish Episcopalians were likely to be chief objectors to Wilberforce's unusual forms of worship, this intervention of Bishop Eden had importance. It was more important that Glengarry lay in the diocese of Moray than that Eden was Primus. Eden was the nephew of the former governor-general of India, Lord Auckland, and was personally much respected except by those who were nervous of a bishop telling funny stories. He had the demerit that he was English; but had won the Scottish episcopalians by building Inverness Cathedral. His place as Primus, and his record over Inverness Cathedral, did not endear him to all members of the

Church of Scotland, and with some of them his letter in defence of Wilberforce at Glengarry was more likely to inflame than to pacify.

Next, a fortnight after Wilberforce, none other than the Archbishop of York, William Thomson, came to officiate in Glengarry Church. In the pulpit he did not wear cassock nor surplice. And he freely adapted the litany to what he thought would be most helpful to his Presbyterian hearers. When he came to the prayers he followed the example of Wilberforce, he spoke them as though they were extempore but his memory was less good than Wilberforce's because often he could be seen to steal a glance at the print.

This was not a gain to the Glengarry cause. Southern high churchmen had once venerated Wilberforce, they had never venerated Thomson. They assumed that messing around with forms of service without authority to do so was in harmony with his earlier record. Thomson's parents were Scots but his life had lain in England. It had been the life of an able unexciting practical man with a Liberal point of view.

By mid-September the newspapers dwelt upon what happened. *The Times* even wrote a leading article (25 September) headed 'Prelacy in the Kirk'. Samuel Wilberforce had to defend himself to the press. This does not represent the extent of the scandal nor how it came indirectly to affect the mind of Queen Victoria. The language of critics was very strong – 'the extraordinary coquetting of certain prelates with the Kirk' – 'Thomson's conduct as contemptible as can be imagined' – 'breach of episcopal vows' – 'undignified fraternisation with heretics and schismatics an uncommissioned overture to a hostile body and a very insulting slight put upon an allied communion'.[3] No doubt to the vexation of Bishop Moray, his diocesan synod passed a vote of censure upon the two Glengarry bishops.

The Queen, still poorly, seems to have meditated on these events. If an English bishop could not only join in the worship of the Church of Scotland but even lead it, the commonness of faith was very marked. And more: for a woman who cared about good religion, and valued the Scots, and valued the Church of Scotland

---

[3] *Daily Telegraph*, leader, 16 September 1871; *Church Times*, leader, 22 September 1871.

for what it did for the Scots, the comments of critics on Glengarry could hardly do other than make her heart move in a different direction.

Four days after Wilberforce's service at Glengarry, Queen Victoria raised with her English advisers the question whether it would not be right to make her communion when Crathie church held its sacrament early that coming November.

On 8 September 1871, worrying that she did wrong in not joining her tenants for communion, she formally consulted the Archbishop of Canterbury for the first time. At least, she wrote that day to Dean Wellesley at Windsor, saying that she thought of making her communion at Crathie, asking his advice, and asking him to consult Archbishop Tait.

For Tait the problem was of 'intercommunion'. No one could deny that the Queen was a member of the Church of England. No one could deny that she was the most important non-ordained member of the Church of England and that whatever she did would have influence. If she received the sacrament in a Presbyterian church it would be an act of intercommunion. A large body of Anglicans then thought intercommunion wrong. Their prayer book was understood in its rubric to say that no persons should receive communion unless they were confirmed by the bishop; and this rubric seemed to prevent Scottish Presbyterians from receiving the sacrament in Anglican churches in England. If it were wrong for Presbyterians to receive communion in England, Anglicans should be discouraged from receiving communion in Scotland lest they receive the sacrament as unqualified persons and lest they receive a sacrament from a ministry about which their Church had a doubt.

The Archbishop, while he entertains the sincerest sympathy for the established Church of Scotland, and desires its welfare, considers it his duty to be guided in his own conduct by the principle he has thus laid down, and he ventures to think that Your Majesty's position requires similar caution. He acknowledges indeed the peculiar relation in which Your Majesty stands to the established Church of Scotland, and trusts Your Majesty will use every effort to protect it; but still, looking to the place belonging to Your Majesty by the laws of the Church of England, as its temporal Head, and the great importance of maintaining a ready and loyal acceptance of the Royal Supremacy by the members of our English Church, he thinks that no step such as that indicated in Your Majesty's letter of the 8th to the Dean of Windsor could be taken at present without some danger.[4]

Dean Wellesley wrote to her on 8 October in much the same sense. She was not satisfied. Tait had to write again from Addington Palace on 18 October. He was plagued with the fierceness of the English struggle over ceremonial practices or the use of a pastoral rite like confession. Troubled by his duty to preside over a Church not at peace with itself, he could not want his Supreme Governor to commit an act which would surely offend one of these parties, perhaps to vehemence. He said so to the Queen on 18 October 1871:

> ... best not to shock the feelings of any considerable body in the Church of England or implying any departure from the established principles of the Church. And he therefore cannot advise any action on the part of those in authority which breaking suddenly through established usage in the matter of intercommunion is likely to be repugnant to a large party ...

But it was not only the Anglicans who were concerned. Ministers in the Church of Scotland felt a different kind of reluctance but still were unwilling to encourage her. To receive the sacrament in the Church of Scotland was a very solemn act, only open to full members of the Church. It still needed a ticket. The Queen was not qualified to receive. And even if this were overlooked because she was the Queen with a national duty, would not her example lead other Anglicans, or other persons not Anglicans, to claim a right which it would be undesirable to concede except to exceptions made on clear grounds? The minister of Crathie, Dr Taylor, was of this opinion. The Queen had taken a part in appointing Dr Taylor and as heritor had helped generously with building him a new manse which made it the best manse in all that area of Scotland. She did not think highly of Dr Taylor's preaching but she respected him and in February 1871, as a sign of her respect for him, for his church, and for the Church of Scotland, she gave Crathie new communion plate (flagons and cups and salvers, all silver and inscribed 'Presented by Her Majesty Queen Victoria to the Church of Crathie 1871').

[4] Archbishop Tait to Queen Victoria, 30 September 1871, Tait Papers, Lambeth Palace Library, 89/281–2.

Dr Taylor did not say, in the circumstances could hardly say, to the Queen that he thought it would be better if she did not receive the communion. To meet her religious needs he was willing to use prayers at Crathie which were then not normal, perhaps were even forbidden, in the Church of Scotland. When Gladstone came to stay at Balmoral and went to church he was astonished to hear a prayer for the departed.

More important than the minister of Crathie was Dr Norman MacLeod. He was not only the minister of the Barony parish in Glasgow, he was the 1869 Moderator of the Church of Scotland and the most celebrated minister in all Scotland and the Queen's favourite pastor – 'such a wise man, with such knowledge of human nature', she wrote in her Journal on 25 March 1863. In that great crisis of her private life when Prince Albert died, he was the person who helped her by his persuasion of the future life. Henceforth he was not only her favourite Scottish minister, he was her favourite Christian pastor; and her talks with him were one of the reasons why she preferred the prayers of the Church of Scotland to the prayers of the Church of England.

Because this question arose in the Queen's conscience explicitly during MacLeod's last year of life, it is not clear what he thought or what he said to her. The Anglicans had two views of his influence over her. One was that he took the same view as Dr Taylor of Crathie, that a Queen's communion would cause problems and was better not done or was better postponed; and they had evidence that this was what he thought. The other Anglican opinion was that his views on such a matter were likely to be unsound and that his advice to her might make everything more complicated, but at that time it was the two Anglican bishops at Glengarry who made the matter complex. 'The Dean [of Windsor]', noted Tait in his diary on 22 October 1871, 'naturally thought that the Glengarry proceedings of the Bishop of Winchester and the Archbishop of York made the case more difficult.'[5]

Before the end of October 1871 – that is, only a few days before the communion was to be celebrated at Crathie – the Queen gave up the idea – but only for this year, she would consider it again

⁵ Archbishop Tait's Diary, 22 October 1871, Tait Papers, Lambeth Palace Library, 48.

later. On 27 October 1871, Dean Wellesley, though crippled with gout, wrote to Tait:

> She has given it up – *but* next year will renew the charge but 'sufficient for the day' – Dr Taylor of Crathie himself by no means wishes it and the Kirk has had enough of it with the row of the Archbishop and the Bishop.[6]

Tait and Wellesley heard that she was about to consult Dr Norman MacLeod. Dean Wellesley was still a pessimist:

> if Dr MacLeod gives her good advice, she may be induced to give up communicating in Scotland, but I fear much that this will not be the case remembering the coal which he blew between Her Majesty and the late Archbishop [this was Archbishop Longley, Tait's predecessor at Canterbury] on the occasion of the laying the first stone of the Inverness cathedral. However, it is over for this year, and if she does it next year, she does it on her own responsibility – and against our advice.[7]

On 13 November she went in deep snow to the communion service at Crathie. She abstained from going forward to receive the sacrament. But the service moved her: 'most touching and beautiful, and impressed me more than I can express. I shall never forget it.' And again:

> It would be impossible to say how deeply we were impressed by the grand simplicity of the service. It was all truly earnest, and no description can do justice to the perfect devotion of the whole assemblage. It was most touching, and I longed to join in it. To see all these simple good people in their nice plain dresses (including an old woman in her mutch) so many of whom I knew, and some of whom had walked far, old as they were, in the deep snow, was very striking.[8]

On 20 November 1871, the Queen wrote to Dean Wellesley:

> The Queen saw Dr MacLeod and had some lengthened conversation with him. While being of opinion that it would be wise and desirable

---

[6] Dean Wellesley to Archbishop Tait, 27 October 1871, Tait Papers, Lambeth Palace Library, 194.

[7] Dean Wellesley to Archbishop Tait, 3 November 1871, Tait Papers, Lambeth Palace Library, 295.

[8] *More Leaves from a Journal of a Life in the Highlands, from 1862 to 1882*, 3rd edn (London, 1884), 152, 155.

that the Queen should partake of the Holy Communion in the Presbyterian Church as a *sign* of that union of the Protestant Churches which is unfortunately so little understood and practised. But [*sic*] he also thought it better deferred – as the amount of violence and bigotry on the part of the episcopal clergy is quite dreadful. The harm done by the aristocracy in never going to the Church of the country, but building episcopal chapels which no one but themselves go to is not to be told, and separates the people entirely from them. It does seem quite inconceivable that people do not see this. It will end in doing dreadful mischief.[9]

Dean Wellesley did not like this letter for two reasons. It seemed to him to show Norman MacLeod working behind the scenes to set the Kirk against the Episcopal Church of Scotland. And he thought that the Queen was exaggerating. In answer he told her that the Episcopal chapels were not numerous and they were not so influential as she supposed. He said to her that the Church of England at least had no such feelings against

a sister establishment whose destruction would be followed by her own – that the different mode of administration was a distinctive feature in each – that all establishments have distinctions, as regards the Holy Communion – and that if she confounded them by attending both – she would weaken the arguments on which the Church membership would depend – and that as establishments were now to depend on numerical majorities [he meant, since the 1871 disestablishment of the Church of Ireland on the plea that it was not a majority], the danger of the Kirk was from the Free Kirk as ours was from the Dissenters.

So ended the year 1871. The Anglicans were sure that they were not yet over their difficulty because the Queen had said not only that she was deferrring the matter but that 'she is quite decided to take it on some future day'.[10]

But in June 1872 Norman MacLeod died and Queen Victoria, who wept at the news and wrote a private appreciation of him in her Journal and later gave two windows in Crathie church to his memory, had as yet no other Presbyterian minister who was

---

[9] The Queen to Dean Wellesley, 20 November 1871, Tait Papers, Lambeth Palace Library 312–13.

[10] So H. Ponsonby quoting an 1871 utterance on 10 November 1873, Royal Archives, Add. A/36/682.

intimate with her thoughts. On present evidence she desisted from questioning her advisers on a Crathie communion during this year and abstained as she had abstained, though reluctantly, the year before. That is not quite certain since the debate certainly came up in her entourage during 1872. Henry Ponsonby her secretary fell into an argument with Dean Wellesley. Ponsonby was an Anglican communicant. He told the Dean that there was no reason why he should not receive communion in a Presbyterian church. The Dean said that he ought not to do so.[11] Ponsonby believed that any Protestant could rightly receive communion in any Protestant church. This debate among the courtiers shows that the Queen must have kept the discussion alive even during 1872.

The change to her resolution happened in the early autumn of 1873. There was to be a new minister at Crathie, for whose appointment her approval was sought. Through her secretary Henry Ponsonby she told Norman MacLeod's brother what she wanted:

> What I think the Queen wants is not a very distinguished scholar or eminent theologian but a quiet parish minister who will understand the humble parishioners of the district. The Queen is making enquiries in various quarters.[12]

In September 1873, Campbell was appointed the future minister of Crathie. The Queen was keenly interested. She is likely to have asked him privately for his opinion on the sacrament.

That October the conflict in Germany had an effect in Balmoral. Bismarck was struggling with the Catholic Church in Germany in the ostensible effort to repress its political force in or out of Parliament; and fierce comments passed to and fro between the Pope and the German government. The Queen, despite her principles of tolerance, was on the side of the German government, and had the special interest in that her daughter was married to the Crown Prince. This concern had an effect upon her attitude to the Crathie sacrament. If Catholicism was rampant against the Protestants, the best way was that Protestants should shed their divisions and unite. This effect may be seen in the letter to her daughter written on 24 October 1873, some ten days before the communion was to be celebrated at Crathie:

[11] H. Ponsonby to his wife, Royal Archives, Add. A/36/674.
[12] H. Ponsonby to Donald MacLeod, 4 July 1873, from Windsor.

All over Europe there is an attempt made to resist authority, and to defy it, by the Priesthood, and the ritualists in England are a stepping stone to this – wherefore we should all try and unite the Protestant Churches as much as possible together in order to make a strong front and protest against sacerdotal tyranny – as well as against unbelief.[13]

Her daughter had a little more tolerance than she quite approved.

During that October 1873 it was clear to those close to the subject that little could now stop her from making her communion with the village at the early November sacrament. She did not make up her mind finally till the day before the sacrament, or at least till then she did not say that this was her intention. On 2 November 1873, Henry Ponsonby wrote to his wife: 'The grand excitement here is about tomorrow. It seems that the Queen had for some time meditated taking the sacrament and now intends to do so, Gardner who [sic] I saw for minute at Aberdeen was full of it and when I got here I found a long letter from Bids on the subject.' 'Bids' was Sir Thomas Biddulph, who was in charge of the Queen's finances. He had argued to the Queen that she should do nothing that could produce trouble and as this might cause trouble, she should weigh her desire well and take further advice. 'Late at night Lady Erroll sent for me to her room', Ponsonby continued to his wife,

and discoursed further upon it. . . . Whether politically it is wise I am not sure. I believe Norman MacLeod told the Dean that he hoped she would never take it in the Scotch Church as it might be used to show she belonged to neither [i.e. neither Church of England nor Church of Scotland] and this would be an argument for disestablishment. Bids says she has been persuaded by J.B. [John Brown her Highland servant and favourite] and Lady Erroll is to take it – but Lady Erroll says she has letters to show she [i.e. the Queen] has thought of it for two years . . .'[14]

This remarkable letter proves, first, that Henry Ponsonby, who knew more about the Queen's political affairs than any of her other servants, had no idea till he arrived at Balmoral on

[13] *Darling Child; Private Correspondence of Queen Victoria and the Crown Princess of Prussia, 1871–78*, ed. R. Fulford (London, 1976), 114.

[14] H. Ponsonby to his wife from Balmoral, 2 November 1873, Royal Archives, Add. A/36/674.

2 November 1873 that there was any question of the Queen receiving the sacrament. He had heard nothing at all of the arguments between the Queen and Dean Wellesley and Archbishop Tait. Second, that the lay Presbyterians in the Queen's immediate company and not the Presbyterian ministers like Norman MacLeod, were those who encouraged her to the sacrament. The Countess of Erroll was a Presbyterian. But John Brown is likely to have had more influence because he was an authentic representative of the working Highlander, and was at her side, a man who was like the tenants and villagers in Crathie. Thirdly, that the Queen had scruples even to the twelfth hour because she gave instructions through Lady Erroll that the courtiers were not to talk about the subject, and that after the sacrament the event was not to appear in the Court Circular. Her scruple was also shown because even so late she was asking legal experts about the legality of her proposed action.

Gardner hinted it would be illegal – an opinion which Henry Ponsonby denounced as *bosh*. Forster, who was vice-president of the Council and the cabinet minister residing at Balmoral for that moment, seems to have been alarmed to hear of this notion of Gardner and wondered whether if not against the law of the land it might trespass against canon law. He went to see Taylor, the Crathie minister, about it – but came to the conclusion which Ponsonby had already reached for himself, that it depended on individual feelings and there could be nothing illegal about it. He preferred the Queen not to do it, at least yet, but was persuaded that there was neither law nor canon law to stop her if she felt it right.

Lady Erroll told Henry Ponsonby that the Queen wished him to join with her in receiving his communion:

Lady Erroll: I am going to take it – but then I am a Presbyterian – and Miss Macdonald is going to take it. Do you wish to do so?

Ponsonby: Well, as you ask me I must repeat I would rather not.

Ponsonby was troubled about refusing a request of the Queen. He disliked any suggestion that he was *ordered* to take part in a sacred rite. But he had no objection on principle. He continued to hold that any practising Protestant could receive the sacrament in any Protestant church. Therefore he would be free to do so if he wished (but he did not wish) and the Queen was free to do so if she wished (and she did wish). He consoled himself, 'I think it would be intolerant for anyone to object. It may conduce to the union of the two Churches and the extension of our Establishment on a broader basis.'[15]

So they went to church. The minister's sermon: a hymn: the elders brought the elements to the Table – then the Queen and Lady Erroll and Flora went down to the minister's pew and the others from Balmoral went away. Flora did not find the rite reverent. The cup was full to the brim and the Queen's hands trembled.

It was a big event to the Queen. We should not know that from her Journal. Of course we are not sure that we have all her own words or whether it is the Journal as Princess Beatrice edited it. But the entry is laconic:

> Have rather a tiresome cough. Took a short walk before going to the Kirk, where I took the Holy Communion. Dr Taylor officiated.

Though it did not appear in the Court Circular it was soon known. The reactions were as varied as could be expected. The *Dundee Advertiser* thought it wonderful. Some English high churchmen thought it lamentable. Though the courtiers were not supposed to talk about it in Balmoral Castle, Ponsonby remarked to his wife that theological discussions were prevalent for days. They referred to it by a euphemism, as 'the event of last Sunday'. Lady Erroll talked about it but in an almost inaudible whisper. Batches of letters, of protest or praise, poured in and Ponsonby resented it when he was told to read them, 'dollops of letters'. He skimmed through them, 'very superficially'. He told Lady Erroll that he did not think that what happened had produced much interest.

Dr Taylor, still the Crathie minister, was nervous at the publicity. The Archbishop of Canterbury was against, still more strongly. Tait said that he wanted intercommunion with the Church of Scotland but that the Queen's communion at Crathie might be repugnant to attached members of the Church of England. The Dean of Windsor on the other hand accepted the Queen's decision

---

[15] H. Ponsonby to his wife, Balmoral, 3 November 1873, Royal Archives, Add. A/36/675.

and much pleased her by a consenting though not enthusiastic letter – he saw no harm if it had been a comfort to her.

Even Dean Stanley of Westminster, who of all her English advisers could be expected to back what she did, still had a scruple. He declared that nothing in the coronation oath prevented her from doing what she had done. But what about the law of the Church of Scotland? Does not that law require from each communicant a certificate or token of membership? Dr Taylor of Crathie, consulted on the point, said that ministers are permitted to admit 'strangers' at their discretion. No one asked whether the resident of the Castle and lady laird of the district could reasonably be defined as a 'stranger' to the parish.

Dean Stanley then asked a different question. Suppose that one of her family wishes to receive the sacrament in a Roman Catholic Church or an Eastern Orthodox Church. Will they now claim to be able to do so? The question was put to the Queen. She dismissed it as 'most unlikely'.[16]

Amid the praise or protest came abuse of the Queen. A shaft of the abuse appeared to her intimates gross in its unfairness. It was said that she had a political motive; that the act was nothing to do with her religion; that she so resented English ritualism that she meant to strike a blow at the Church of England. Even Biddulph suggested this as her motive. But those closer to her were sure that this was not true. These included not only Lady Erroll who was a Presbyterian, but Henry Ponsonby who agreed with Disraeli in thinking Presbyterianism not a religion for gentlemen. Ponsonby accepted that she hated ritualists, she thought they hurt and divided the Church of England and were against the truth. But like Lady Erroll, Ponsonby was sure that this was a purely religious act. She went to communion 'for its own sake'. The motive was for the good of her own soul, and to receive the sacrament with her own people.[17]

A wilder charge against the Queen said that in thus weakening church membership she intended to ally herself with 'Secularists' against all religion. Even Ponsonby's wife heard the charge and asked her husband about it, but he dismissed her fears: 'I don't

[16] H. Ponsonby to his wife, 11 November 1873, Royal Archives, Add. A/36/683.

[17] H. Ponsonby to his wife, Royal Archives, Add. A/36/684.

think the Queen makes allies of Secularists as you say. She is very Protestant – and Presbyterianly Protestant.'[18]

The abuse had an effect upon her. That very day, 13 November, she wrote a long letter to Dean Stanley, to say that the English Church needed 'a complete Reformation' and that the Archbishop of Canterbury must be given power to stop all the dressings and bowings and confessions, and to give permission to other Protestant ministers to preach in the churches, and get rid of the *'bigotry* and *self-sufficiency* and *contempt* of all *other Protestant Churches,* of which she had some *incredible* instances the other day . . .'.[19] So all her force was lent to the promoting through Parliament of the disastrous Public Worship Regulation Bill which itself failed to content her.

Henceforth each November the Queen received her communion at Crathie and no one objected. Henceforth the Church of Scotland regarded her as a full member. In 1874 she tried again to persuade Ponsonby to join her but he preferred not. The courtiers tried to turn the minister's wife out of her pew to make room for her but this plan was stoutly resisted in Crathie. The 1874 service had a visiting preacher, Cameron Lees; and the Queen thought his sermon so beautiful that Cameron Lees, bearded and bald, expert on the Highlands by his origins, stepped onto that ladder which was to make him her chief northern pastor in her later life, the successor to the dead Norman MacLeod, and in the end the preacher at her death; though in her later life she also, at last, had an Anglican pastor whom she fully trusted in things of the soul, Randall Davidson, who married Archbishop Tait's daughter and was himself to be Archbishop after her death.

In 1875 there was again trouble over the seating at Crathie, in which John Brown took a part. The Queen tried again to persuade Ponsonby to come and again he would not – unless it were an *order,* distinct, from the Queen. It was not made an order but he came under such pressure from the ladies that at last he gave way. His wife disapproved of his consent but he told her that he read St

---

[18] H. Ponsonby to his wife, 13 November 1873, Royal Archives, Add. A/36/685.
[19] *Queen Victoria's Letters, 2nd series: A selection from H.M.'s Correspondence and Journal between the Years 1862 and 1885* (London, 1926–8) 2, 29.

Paul in 1 Corinthians 10 (presumably verses 1–4: 'All our fathers
. . . were baptized . . . ; and did all eat the same spiritual meat; and
did all drink the same spiritual drink; for they drank of that
Spiritual Rock that followed them; and that Rock was Christ').
The text seemed, he thought, and claimed to his wife, to back
what he did.

At the church he found there were about 500 communicants
that day (in successive services) and thought it all very reverent
and devotional.

In 1876 the Queen did not ask him to go and he did not.

Her Majesty The Queen graciously allowed me to consult and
quote from the Royal Archives. I owe thanks to Oliver Everett
and Pamela Clark for their help with the Royal Archives; to
Melanie Barber for her help with the Lambeth Palace Archives;
and to the archivists at the Archives of Glasgow University.

Chapter 9

'Unrestricted Conference?' Myth and Reality in Scottish Ecumenism

David M. Thompson

I

THE reunion of the Church of Scotland in 1929 has generally been regarded as a positive achievement. It was also more significant in wider British church life than has often been recognised.[1] One reason for this is the quite distinctive balance between issues related to theology and those related to church structure. The history of ecumenism has been dominated by attempts to resolve differences of view over Christian doctrine, the sacraments and the ministry of the Church. Issues other than these have sometimes been regarded as 'non-theological factors' in the division of the Church.[2] Yet they often reflect more fundamental questions about the relation of the Church to the wider society than those on the conventional ecumenical agenda.

At first glance Scottish reunion did not depend on the resolution of many theological differences. Lord Sands, one of its chief

---

[1] Cf. D. M. Thompson, 'Scottish Influence on the English Churches in the Nineteenth Century', *Journal of the United Reformed Church History Society*, ii (October 1978), especially 43–5.

[2] The term 'non-theological factors' was first used in an American report to the Second World Faith and Order Conference in 1937; it was picked up by C. H. Dodd in a letter of 1949 on 'unavowed motives in ecumenical discussions', which led to a discussion at the Third World Faith and Order Conference in 1952 and a subsequent study programme on institutionalism and church unity: see L. Hodgson (ed.), *Second World Conference on Faith and Order* (London, 1938), 258–9; O. S. Tomkins (ed.), *Third World Conference on Faith and Order* (London, 1953), 174–203.

architects, confidently asserted in 1925 that 'as regards "faith and order", there has never been any divergence among Scottish Presbyterians'.[3] The question of doctrine was actually more subtle than Sands implied; and reunion did depend on agreement about the use of the Church's endowments, the Church's spiritual freedom and the national recognition of religion.

Seventy years after union some of the issues may be seen in a broader perspective. Ecumenical theologians have always felt a tension between affirming the fundamental articles of Christian faith and acknowledging the changed theological climate of modern times. This is particularly acute for those committed to the Reformed tradition. In an early article, Alec Cheyne asked whether the Declaratory Acts adopted by the three main pre-union Scottish Churches in order to loosen the terms of subscription to the Westminster Confession reconciled 'the irreconcilable'. According to the Declaratory Acts, ministers had only to affirm that the Confession contained the 'fundamental doctrines' of the faith, but those 'fundamental doctrines' were undefined.[4] Cheyne wondered whether the Church should be content with such a situation, or whether it might look to the ecumenical movement for possible lines of advance. The answer to that question is still unclear.

The pattern for the national recognition of religion worked out between 1912 and 1921 gained a consensus, though not a unanimous one, among Scottish Presbyterians. But the dominant position of the reunited Church of Scotland among the non-Roman Catholic churches in Scotland arguably made subsequent ecumenical progress more difficult. Was the national religion to be understood as essentially Presbyterian? Such issues remain on the ecumenical agenda at the end of the twentieth century.

Detailed attention to the Established Church's endowments came late in the process. The solution achieved in the 1925 Church of Scotland (Property and Endowments) Act was a compromise between principle and economic realism. But how should endowments entrusted to an undivided national Church be handled in

---

[3] Lord Sands, 'Church Union in Scotland', *Review of the Churches*, n.s. ii (October 1925), 563.

[4] A. C. Cheyne, 'The Westminster Standards: a Century of Re-appraisal', *Records of the Scottish Church History Society*, xiv (1962), 214.

an age when the national Church represented only part of the nation? That is another version of the question about the nature of national religion, which is not sufficiently answered by saying that the Church's endowments were church property, not national property.

This chapter explores and explains some of these themes, since the issues only partially resolved in 1929 are still relevant to the wider ecumenical discussion today.[5] The immediate issues had emerged from the layers of nineteenth-century Scottish Church history. The Disruption of 1843 raised the question of the relationship between the jurisdiction of the State and the Church; but disestablishment did not become a real possibility in Scotland until after 1874. There was a separate debate about the terms of subscription to the Westminster Confession, which was partially resolved by Declaratory Acts in the United Presbyterian Church in 1879 and the Free Church in 1892.[6] Finally, the issues raised by the continuing Free Church's successful legal challenge to the recently formed United Free Church over the latter's title to the property of the former made it necessary to rethink the independence of the Church.

II

Ironically the formation of the Free Church in 1843 provided the impetus for the disestablishment movement. As recently as 1838, Thomas Chalmers had defended the principle of Church establishments in a famous series of lectures in London. Chalmers hoped to press the Whig government to supplement the endowments of the Church of Scotland for the purposes of his Church Extension scheme.[7] He failed, and the series of legal judgements by the Court of Session, supported by the House of Lords, against the General Assembly of the Church of Scotland from 1838 onwards led the Evangelicals to regard the burden of establishment under existing

---

[5] In the standard history of the Ecumenical Movement Bishop Neill did not explain why some opposed reunion: R. Rouse and S. C. Neill, *A History of the Ecumenical Movement, 1517–1948* (London, 1954), 449–51.

[6] A. L. Drummond and J. Bulloch, *The Church in Late Victorian Scotland* (Edinburgh, 1978), 36–9, 267–72.

[7] S. J. Brown, *Thomas Chalmers and the Godly Commonwealth* (Oxford, 1982), 269–71.

conditions as intolerable. Nevertheless Chalmers told the first Assembly of the Free Church of Scotland, 'We quit a vitiated Establishment, but would rejoice in returning to a pure one. To express it otherwise – we are the advocates for a national recognition and national support of religion – and we are not Voluntaries.'[8] Although he moderated these words in the following October, they were often quoted later, and especially by the Law Lords in the Free Church case of 1903–4.[9]

In England, the conjunction of the Disruption and the Wesleyan Methodist Conference's opposition to the education clauses in Sir James Graham's Factories Bill encouraged the radical nonconformist, Edward Miall, to propose an alliance of nonconformist radicals, whigs and tories against the principle of an established church. This led to the formation of the Anti-State Church Association in 1844.[10] It also inspired a more positive conception of non-established churches than that denoted by traditional titles of 'dissenter' or 'nonconformist'. The Free Church of Scotland could not at first decide how to describe itself. It claimed to be the continuing Church of Scotland, but the terms 'Protesting Church', 'Free Protesting Church', and 'Free Presbyterian Church' were all used in its inaugural Assembly. No formal decision was taken then, but by the autumn of 1843 the title 'Free Church' was increasingly used.[11] The English nonconformist bodies, gradually copied this by describing themselves as 'free churches'.[12]

---

[8] W. Hanna, *Memoirs of the Life and Writings of Thomas Chalmers* (4 vols, Edinburgh, 1854), ii, 647.

[9] Mr Johnston's speech, R. L. Orr (ed.), *The Free Church of Scotland Appeals, 1903–4* (Edinburgh, 1904), 225–6; the Lord Chancellor regarded this as decisive, ibid., 567; Lord MacNaghten did not, ibid., 575–6; cf. K. R. Ross, *Church and Creed in Scotland* (Edinburgh, 1988), 57–8.

[10] D. M. Thompson, 'The Liberation Society, 1844–1868', in P. Hollis (ed.), *Pressure from Without in Early Victorian England* (London, 1974), 213–17.

[11] A. L. Drummond and J. Bulloch, *The Church in Victorian Scotland* (Edinburgh, 1975), 13; cf. Chalmers's letter of 6 November 1843 to Hugh Tennant, cited in Hanna, *Memoirs of Chalmers*, ii, 655.

[12] E.g. H. S. Skeats, *History of the Free Churches of England* (London, 1868) (subsequent editions expanded by C. S. Miall). Skeats was Edward Miall's son-in-law. The 'Free Church Congress' (1890–5), so-called by analogy with the Anglican Church Congress, was the genesis of the 'National Council of Evangelical Free Churches' in 1896.

But how free was 'free'? The House of Lords' judgement in the Free Church of Scotland case in 1904 exposed significant limitations to the freedom of non-established churches under British law. The fact that the practical effects of that judgement were dealt with by the Churches (Scotland) Act of 1905 highlighted the fact that no church could escape statute law. 'Are there any free churches?' asked the English nonconformist journalist, W. T. Stead, following the judgement.[13]

In this context the rapid development of a movement for union between the Church of Scotland and the United Free Church after 1906 was very odd. To be sure, Queen Victoria had noted in 1869 that since 'there is no difference of form or doctrine, . . . the Free Church and United Presbyterians, [if combined] with the present Established Church, would become one very strong Protestant body', but Taylor Innes (who was the main legal adviser of the Free Church) was probably being mischievous in using this to imply royal support for such a development.[14] The United Free Church Assembly reaffirmed its belief in disestablishment in 1906 and also the right of the Church to change its doctrinal standards. The Church of Scotland was firmly committed to establishment and only cautiously moved to take advantage of the power given by the 1905 Act to change the form of subscription to its doctrinal standards.[15] Perhaps even more remarkable was the Church of Scotland General Assembly's decision to accept the proposal for 'unrestricted conference', that is, without ruling out a reconsideration of establishment, in 1909, at a time when the United Free Church was still passing motions about disestablishment. Why then did the union discussions begin?

[13] A. T. Innes, 'The Creed Crisis in Scotland', *Hibbert Journal*, iii (January 1905), 231.

[14] [Queen Victoria], *More Leaves from the Journal of a Life in the Highlands* (London, 1884), 221; quoted (without reference) in A. T. Innes, *Studies in Scottish History* (London, 1892), 331. The context was a conversation between the Queen and Dr Norman MacLeod (Moderator of the General Assembly) at Balmoral, 3 October 1869, in which MacLeod expressed great alarm for the establishment. As Moderator he had spoken of the dependence of the Church of Scotland on the confidence of the nation, D. MacLeod, *Memoir of Norman MacLeod* (2 vols, London, 1876), ii, 300, 306–7.

[15] The change was made in 1910; Lord Sands, *Dr Archibald Scott of St George's Edinburgh and His Times* (Edinburgh, 1919), 162–72.

One reason might be that disestablishment was a dead horse by the first decade of the twentieth century, despite ritual motions to the contrary. Alec Cheyne has argued that the turning point against disestablishment came in 1885. In that year Principal Tulloch successfully defended establishment on the same grounds that were winning favour in England, namely that the voluntary system failed to provide an adequate ministry to the poor. Only a territorial parochial system supported by endowments could guarantee pastoral care in areas where people could not pay for it themselves. Tulloch, like Chalmers in 1838, combined an appeal to usefulness with an affirmation of God's intention for the civil order which went beyond pure utilitarianism.[16] In a memorable speech in the Free Church Assembly Hall in Edinburgh on 11 November 1885, Gladstone, despite private anxieties, said that 'if the Church question is not to be a test question in England, it ought not to be in Scotland'; he was not prepared to risk the unity of the Liberal party by backing disestablishment in Scotland at a time when it would be divisive to do so in England.[17]

But whatever the importance of the events of 1885, it was not clear to contemporaries that disestablishment was a dead cause in the early twentieth century. The return of a Liberal government

[16] A. C. Cheyne, 'Church Reform and Church Defence: The Contribution of John Tulloch (1823–86)', *Records of the Scottish Church History Society*, xxiii (1989), reprinted in *Studies in Scottish Church History* (Edinburgh, 1999), 150–64; Brown, *Chalmers and the Godly Commonwealth*, 148–9, 269–71. Innes noted that Tulloch, 'a convinced State churchman', stopped unfettered conference between the Churches in 1869, A. T. Innes, *Chapters of Reminiscence* (London, 1913), 109–10.

[17] P. Carnegie Simpson, *The Life of Principal Rainy* (2 vols, London, 1909), ii, 37; cf. H. C. G. Matthew, *The Gladstone Diaries*, xi (Oxford, 1990), 427, where Gladstone noted in his diary that 'the present agitation does not strengthen in my mind the principle of Establishment'; quoted in J. Morley, *The Life of William Ewart Gladstone* (3 vols, London, 1903), iii, 248. For the support offered by Hartington and Gladstone to disestablishment in the late 1870s, see Innes, *Studies in Scottish History*, 333–5. Innes recorded that Gladstone did not wish the breadth of his views on disestablishment to be known in 1868, and it was not mentioned in the biographies of Gladstone or Rainy, *Chapters of Reminiscence*, 81–106, 116–20, 123–32. This source seems to have been missed by many, e.g. I. Machin, 'Voluntaryism and Reunion, 1874–1929', in N. MacDougall (ed.), *Church, Politics and Society: Scotland, 1408–1929* (Edinburgh, 1983), 226–7.

in 1906 led immediately to a two-year political conflict over education in England, with three unsuccessful attempts to remove the privileged position given to the Church of England by the 1902 Education Act. A Royal Commission was set up to consider the church situation in Wales, and eventually a Bill to disestablish the Church of England in Wales received the royal assent under the Parliament Act in 1914. One Church of Scotland minister wrote in 1909 that 'No one knows what a general election may bring forth'; though another said that the disestablishment agitation had '*practically* passed out of Scottish ecclesiastical politics'.[18] Nevertheless leading figures in the Church of Scotland were clearly concerned about disestablishment. In 1910 Lord Balfour of Burleigh feared that the voluntaries in the United Free Church, even though they did not represent the majority of the laity, could wreck any arrangement which did not please them, in 'alliance with English political dissenters'.[19] As late as May 1914, John White, minister of the Barony Church, Glasgow and Clerk to the Church of Scotland's Committee on Union, was anxious that any pause in the progress towards union would bring dis-establishment back on to the political agenda at the forthcoming General Election.[20]

The proposal for talks about union was something of a pre-emptive strike by leaders in the Church of Scotland. In 1906 Principal Rainy of New College, Edinburgh, died. He had been the acknowledged leader of the Free Church and then the United Free Church for a generation. At his funeral, Archibald Scott of the Church of Scotland said to his United Free Church friend, Ross Taylor, 'If we don't move, they [the supporters of

[18] D. Frew, 'The Scottish Establishment from an Inside Point of View', *Hibbert Journal*, vii (July 1909), 883; D. MacMillan, 'The Ecclesiastical Situation in Scotland', *Hibbert Journal*, ix (January 1911), 402 (italics mine). J. A. Paterson's reply to MacMillan noted that the overwhelming majority of Scottish Liberals were pledged to vote for disestablishment and disendowment, 'The Ecclesiastical Situation in Scotland: Another Point of View', *Hibbert Journal*, x (January 1912), 425.

[19] Notes by Lord Balfour on Mr Johnston's paper of preliminary proposi-tions with reference to a scheme of union, 19 October 1910, John White Papers, New College Library, Edinburgh, Box 2/6.

[20] A. Muir, *John White* (London, 1958), 171.

disestablishment] will take it out of our hands.'[21] Scott gave notice of a motion in the Edinburgh Presbytery in March 1907 for an overture to the General Assembly: 'the boat is on the move', he said, 'if we do not steer, we shall assuredly drift'.[22] There were other reasons: some thought that a move for co-operation and possible unity would reinvigorate church attendance.[23] But it was not plain sailing. Lord Balfour of Burleigh, for instance, was not keen on reunion as an objective in April 1907, though he was reluctant to oppose it publicly. He had already bluntly told William Mair, who was writing a series of articles on reunion, that he disapproved of his policy.[24]

The Church of Scotland Assembly in 1908 invited the United Free Church Assembly to 'confer in a friendly and generous spirit on the present ecclesiastical situation', laying special emphasis on fuller co-operation, 'consistently with the continuance of the national recognition of religion'.[25] The United Free Church requested 'unrestricted conference', and this was accepted by the Church of Scotland in 1909.[26] Each Church appointed a committee of about a hundred to take the matter further. The Joint Reports of 1910 and 1911 were largely statements of the positions of the two sides, though there was some convergence on the question of spiritual freedom. The position was decisively changed by what became known as 'The Memorandum', prepared by C. N. Johnston (later Lord Sands), Procurator (chief legal officer) of the Church of Scotland, outlining a process by which the Established Church would prepare a new constitution, on the basis of which union

---

[21] W. Mair, *My Life* (London, 1911), 336; cf. J. R. Fleming, *A History of the Church in Scotland, 1875–1929* (Edinburgh, 1933), 82 (which mistakes the page reference).

[22] Sands, *Archibald Scott*, 211. This interpretation of Scott's motivation was known before Sands's biography was published; see D. MacMillan, *Hibbert Journal*, ix (January 1911), 404.

[23] Sands, *Archibald Scott*, 215–16. Sands's detailed account of Scott's correspondence at this time does not refer to Mair's story.

[24] Sands, *Archibald Scott*, 219, 226, 232, 235; Mair, *My Life*, 320–3, 329–46 (Balfour's comment is on p. 330); R. Sjölinder, *Presbyterian Reunion in Scotland, 1907–1921* (Edinburgh, [1962]), 117–22. Mair wanted an emphasis on union and also a private conference, rather than an Assembly overture.

[25] D. Cairns, *Life and Times of Alexander Robertson MacEwen* (London, 1925), 251; Sjölinder, *Presbyterian Reunion*, 146.

[26] Muir, *John White*, 113–15; Sjölinder, *Presbyterian Reunion*, 146–51.

could take place. Statutory recognition of this constitution would be secured from Parliament, and the question of the ancient endowments addressed. This procedure was accepted by the United Free Church, though progress was then delayed by the war. The Church of Scotland Act of 1921[27] changed the relationship between Church and State substantially, and after the endowments question was resolved by the Act of 1925, reunion took place in 1929.

The reunited Church of Scotland had a different relationship to the State and a different relationship to its doctrinal standards. Part of the achievement of union was to separate two issues, which previously had been regarded by many as intertwined. In the reports of the Joint Conference the issues of establishment and doctrine were discussed under the headings of 'the national recognition of religion' and 'spiritual independence (or freedom)'. That redefinition of the issues was itself significant. Supporters of establishment believed that the legal backing of the State for the Church was not only desirable in itself, but also ensured that the Church's doctrinal basis could not easily be changed. Establishment was also supported on the grounds that it was unfriendly to dogmatism in the church, and friendly to progressive thought in the classical Moderate tradition. 'Comprehensiveness, not exclusiveness, must be the characteristic note of a national Church.'[28] Opponents of establishment, on the other hand, also saw close links between the two questions. For them, however, the legal backing of the State for the Church was not only of questionable value, but could also restrict the Church's ability to take account of intellectual developments.[29] It was important for the Church to be able to move with the times, and the need to secure parliamentary approval for changes would be a restriction.

---

[27] 11 & 12 George V, ch. 29.

[28] A. J. Campbell, 'The Church of Scotland and its Formula', *Hibbert Journal*, vi (July 1908), 872–5. Campbell thought the new Formula inadequate. The Church of Scotland had, however, been sceptical about Dean Stanley's 'broad church' defence of the Church's dependence on parliament in 1872: Innes, *Studies in Scottish History*, 278–80.

[29] This was a constant theme of Taylor Innes: e.g. his discussion of the Church of Scotland General Assembly's debate on the formula of subscription in 1901, A. T. Innes, *The Law of Creeds in Scotland*, 2nd edn (Edinburgh, 1902), 126–49, 187–202.

The analysis which follows first considers the discussion about the new Church–State relationship, crystallised in the Memorandum of 1912, then reflects on the doctrinal issues, as exemplified by the formulation of the Articles Declaratory of the Constitution of the Church of Scotland in Matters Spiritual, and concludes with some reflections on the outstanding issues related to establishment in the final years of the reunion process.

III

The relation between Church and State was bound to be a central issue. Over the years so many issues had become entangled under the slogan 'disestablishment and disendowment' that one important task was to disentangle them. The main hope lay in the possibility of drawing together the significant majorities in both Churches that no longer took extreme positions. Professor A. R. MacEwen (who became a member of the United Free Church Committee for conference with the Church of Scotland), in describing the discussions which led to the Articles of Agreement submitted to the Assemblies of the Free Church of Scotland and the United Presbyterian Church in 1864 (but not at that stage approved), said that they showed

> that, on the one hand, advocates of disestablishment and disendowment may ascribe Christian duties to communities and rulers, and that, on the other, those who maintain that in some circumstances the establishment and endowment of the Church by the State are permissible and even beneficial may hold that this does not imply the title of the State to prescribe a creed and form of worship or to deal with affairs specifically religious.[30]

His hope that these discussions gave the Civil Magistrate 'his final dismissal from Presbyterian debate' was still optimistic in 1895; but it indicated a possible basis for compromise.[31]

[30] A. R. MacEwen, *Life and Letters of John Cairns*, 4th edn (London, 1898), 513–14. Although the discussions between the Free Church and the United Presbyterians were broken off in 1873 because of the establishment question, they did lead to the coming together of the congregations of the two Churches in England with the formation of the Presbyterian Church of England in 1876.

[31] This is virtually a summary of the United Presbyterian statement (drafted by MacEwen) on the issues of spiritual independence and national religion in the private tripartite discussions on Presbyterian reunion held in the 1890s.

These issues could only be tackled, however, if the agenda was union rather than co-operation. The way in which so many issues were bundled up together is aptly illustrated in Dr John White's correspondence after the debate on Scott's motion on closer co-operation in the Edinburgh Presbytery on 27 March 1907. White criticised the rough draft of Scott's overture on Union for not being broad enough.[32] Two days later he received a letter from James Cooper, Regius Professor of Ecclesiastical History in Glasgow and a founder of the Scottish Church Society, praising his initiative and saying that 'the only safe union – and the only fair one for our Church to propose, is one that shall embrace all the children of the Reformation of 1560'; in other words, to include the continuing Free Church and the Scottish Episcopalians. Cooper feared that a union merely with the United Free Church would mean 'the abandonment of Establishment – National Religion; . . . a big sect instead of a National Church, and . . . the leadership of all the dissenters throughout Christendom'. White replied that he had opposed Scott because his proposal was '*not sufficiently comprehensive*', and because it gave undue prominence to endowments, whereas what was needed was a statement of 'the *underlying* truth of Establishment'. He hoped that the Church would be able to state its 'desire to remove any difficulties in the way of stating the Establishment principle that might hinder union, but at the same time giving a definition of Establishment that wd keep intact Christ's Headship *of* the Church & *over* the Nation'.[33]

MacEwen and his friend, Dr James Kidd, also drafted the resolution passed by the United Presbyterian Synod in 1896 which proposed discussions about union in response to the Free Church's invitation to consider closer co-operation: Cairns, *Life of MacEwen*, 182–7.

[32] Muir, *John White*, 105–9.

[33] Cooper to White, 29 March 1907; White to Cooper, 3 April 1907, White Papers, Box 1/11. Cooper said Scott's proposal was worse than he feared, because 'the surrender of the Establishment principle is hardly so much as veiled', and offered his support to White, suggesting that his friend (and later biographer) H. J. Wotherspoon would support him too, Cooper to White, 4 April 1907. For Cooper's view, see his *Confessions of Faith and Formulas of Subscription* (Glasgow, 1907); H. J. Wotherspoon's 1905 MacLeod Memorial Lecture to the Scottish Church Society, *Creed and Confession*, (reprinted, Coatbridge, 1931) reflects the same position.

The two central issues in the subsequent discussions were the spiritual independence of the Church and the national recognition of religion. The term 'spiritual independence' was gradually dropped in favour of 'spiritual freedom' as it became clear that no Church, whatever its legal status, could be independent of the State.[34] Church and State seemed to be inextricably tied together.

Part of the problem lay in the intricate statutory background to the history of the Church in Scotland. The facts were not in dispute, but their interpretation was. The Scots Confession of 1560 was accepted by the Estates of Scotland, not upon the authority of the Church but because they viewed it as expressing scriptural truth. Seven years later the Parliament passed the Act anent the true and holy Kirk, which not only acknowledged the Reformed Church, but also established it as 'the *only* true and Holy Kirk of Jesus Christ within this realm'. Subscription to the Confession was made obligatory in 1572, and the Presbyterian order of the Church was established in 1592.[35] For defenders of establishment this demonstrated that the Church of Scotland was firmly grounded in statute law. For others, like Taylor Innes, the acknowledged expert on the law of creeds in Scotland, this showed that Parliament accepted what the Church had prepared; that is, the statutory backing for ecclesiastical jurisdiction in 1567 was a recognition of what the Church had been doing for seven years.

Innes's argument was even sharper in relation to the Westminster Confession. The General Assembly of the Church of Scotland adopted the Confession in 1647, even though no single sentence or proposition was identical to those in the Scottish Confession.[36] It was approved by the Scottish Parliament in 1649; and although that Act was rescinded in 1660, the Confession remained in regular

---

[34] Sjölinder, *Presbyterian Reunion*, 153.

[35] A.T. Innes, *The Law of Creeds in Scotland* (Edinburgh, 1867), 11–54. A second edition, which took account of the legal developments since 1867, was published just after the formation of the United Free Church and the Court of Session's decision on the legal case, in 1902. It was frequently referred to in the hearing in the House of Lords.

[36] Cooper disagreed, arguing that any doubt about the meaning of the Westminster Confession must be resolved by reference to the 1560 Confession: indeed he suggested that it was not clear that subscription to the Westminster Confession was enforced, unlike subscription to the National Covenant which included the Scots Confession; *Confessions of Faith*, 37–8.

use. It was ratified by statute as the public confession of the Church in 1690, made binding on all ministers by an Act of 1693, and incorporated into the conditions of the Treaty of Union of 1707. So although the Church had demonstrated by its actions in relation to the Westminster Confession that it was free to change its Confession, subsequent statutes restricted that freedom.[37]

In the final section of the 1867 edition of his influential *Law of Creeds in Scotland*, Innes noted that the Free Church had claimed and acted upon the right to amend the terms of subscription, and in this respect it was not noticeably different from the United Presbyterian Church. (This was before the passing of the Declaratory Acts by either Church.) But a Church could not abandon a doctrine which was fundamental to it, and even if it claimed to do so, the law would be bound to prevent it. Innes shrewdly noted that the Churches most likely to assert loudly their freedom to change their doctrine were those least likely to do so. On the other hand he said that, if by its constitution a Church was free to change its confession, such a change would be recognised by the law. Even so there were important underlying questions about a Church's relation to its history. 'The question for law would come to be, Can you arrive at a separate knowledge of a Church's *principles*, disentangling them from, first, its documents; second, its history, and third, its doctrines?'[38] By 1902 these questions had been removed, and the conclusion is much more confident, though recognising that the principles were not yet quite settled.[39]

Nevertheless Innes revealed he had always been unhappy about a union of Churches which did not first establish the right to amend basic doctrine. As early as 1873, when he had been consulted about a possible union between the Free Church and the United

---

[37] Innes, *Law of Creeds*, 58–118, especially 64–5, 70–2, 76–82. However, Innes noted that Scottish statutes, unlike English ones, could lapse by desuetude: *Studies in Scottish History*, 247. Cooper emphasised that the General Assembly's Act of 1711 concerning the formula of subscription was an attempt to avert the reintroduction of patronage and the possible infiltration of episcopalian views (favoured by Queen Anne) into the Church of Scotland: Cooper, *Confessions of Faith*, 61–8. Sands argued similarly in relation to the 1693 statute: Sands, *Archibald Scott*, 106–7.

[38] Innes, *Law of Creeds*, 435–52; the quotation is from 452.

[39] Ibid., 2nd edn, 326.

Presbyterians, he had expressed doubts about 'the legal safety of going straight on to the union'.[40] In the union discussions of the 1890s he warned of the legal dangers to property, if the right to change the Church's Confession was not first established.[41]

The House of Lords' judgement in the Free Church Case of 1904 confirmed the legal necessity of facing these issues. In the words of the Law Reports,

> The identity of a religious community described as a Church consists in the identity of its doctrines, creeds, confessions, formularies, and tests.
>
> The bond of union of a Christian association may contain a power in some recognised body to control, alter, or modify the tenets or principles at one time professed by the association; but the existence of such a power must be proved.[42]

It was held that the establishment principle and the Westminster Confession were distinctive tenets of the Free Church; that the Free Church did not have the power, where property was concerned, to alter or vary the doctrine of the Church; that there was no true union in 1900 because the United Free Church had not preserved its identity with the Free Church; and so the appellants were entitled to the property held by the Free Church before union.[43]

The Law Lords' ruling that it was necessary for an association to prove that it possessed the power to change its principles led directly to the United Free Church's Act anent Spiritual Independence of 1906, largely drafted by Innes and Rainy. In this Act the United Free Church claimed 'independent and exclusive jurisdiction and power of legislating in all matters of doctrine, worship, discipline and government of the Church'; and so declared and enacted that

> recognising the authority of the Word of God, contained in the Scriptures of the Old and New Testaments, as the supreme un-changeable Standard, and looking to the Head of the Church for the

[40] He had privately warned Rainy about it before his book was published in 1867; Innes, *Chapters of Reminiscence*, 204, 209.

[41] Innes, *Chapters of Reminiscence*, 224–32.

[42] *Law Reports: Appeal Cases*, 1904, 515.

[43] Ibid., 516.

promised guidance of the Holy Spirit, this Church has the sole and exclusive right and power from time to time, as duty may require, through her Courts to alter, change, add to, or modify, her constitution and laws, Subordinate Standards, and Formulas, and to determine and declare what these are.[44]

But Innes also recognised the necessity of parliamentary action. Typically, Reformation confessions had ascribed supreme authority to Scripture and asserted that the Church and its Councils might err. John Knox, for example, when presenting the Scots Confession to the Estates of Scotland in 1560, had urged anyone who saw anything in the Confession which was repugnant to God's holy word to inform the authors in writing, so that the point in question might either be proved or corrected. Thus Innes claimed that the right of the Church to amend its Confession was established by precedent. But in view of the House of Lords' requirement that a power of amendment must be demonstrable and the withdrawal of the case concerning the Free Church Model Trust Deed, the law on that point remained undefined. Innes therefore argued that it was essential for Parliament to intervene to ensure justice.[45] The Churches (Scotland) Act of 1905 accordingly provided for a proportionate distribution of property between the United Free Church and the continuing Free Church.

Nevertheless, a significant shift had taken place. The United Free Church had made it clear that it 'did not accept the "trust-deed" view of the Church's constitution'. Marcus Dods went so far as to assert that 'it is essential to the very nature of a Confession that a Church has a right to change it. A Church's confession must be the real expression of the Church, as presently existing'. Such a view would be a commonplace today, but as Kenneth Ross has recently pointed out, the difficulty was 'that such words were not spoken, and could not conceivably have been spoken, by the men who had formed the Free Church in 1843'.[46]

[44] Innes, *Chapters of Reminiscence*, 241–6; Act I, United Free Church Acts 1906: see Sjölinder, *Presbyterian Reunion*, 381–2.

[45] Innes, *Hibbert Journal*, iii (January 1905), 220–32.

[46] M. Dods, 'Address at the Induction of the United Free Church Professors', *The Scotsman*, 29 June 1904; Ross, *Church and Creed in Scotland*, 273–4. Dods wrote on 6 September 1904, 'I am clear from our members we have no right to

Thus, despite his firm belief in the Church's right to amend, Innes recognised that the House of Lords had questioned the previous assumption that the provision for future union in the Free Church Model Trust Deed was an adequate basis on which to proceed. By contrast, James Barr later argued that the law of trusts was sufficient for the Church, if deeds were properly framed to provide for Christian progress; 'to define freedom is to limit it', he wrote. He preferred 'an associated body of Christian believers' to 'a compelling State Establishment'. 'I had rather be under Trust Law than under Statute Law.'[47] Such a view seemed increasingly risky. The Lord Chancellor's judgement suggested that even the Free Church Assembly's Declaratory Act of 1892 concerning subscription to the Westminster Confession was *ultra vires*.[48] Hence in 1905 the Church of Scotland secured statutory recognition of the Assembly's power to change the formula of subscription to the Confession. The majority of the United Free Church were rapidly won over to the view that parliamentary legislation was needed to secure the Church's freedom.[49]

The Anglican, Neville Figgis, drew similar conclusions in a lecture on 'A Free Church in a Free State' given in 1911. 'The very notion of the Church as an independent entity is denied explicitly or implicitly in much of the current controversial writing', he said, 'and is surrendered too often even by her own representatives.'[50]

---

ask any confession save that they accept Christ as their *living* King. But it seems reasonable that from those who teach some guarantee should be taken that they will not teach deleterious nonsense. The question is, How much can you ask? Must you not largely trust men in this as in all other departments?' M. Dods (ed.), *Later Letters of Marcus Dods* (London, 1911), 136.

[47] J. Barr, *The Scottish Church Question* (London, 1920), 255, 257. The context was his opposition to statutory recognition of the Church of Scotland's Articles Declaratory.

[48] Orr, *Free Church of Scotland Appeals*, 568–72; C. Graham (ed.), *Crown Him Lord of All* (Edinburgh, 1993), 19.

[49] Churches (Scotland) Act 1905, 5 Edward VII, ch. 12, §5; the Act also repealed relevant parts of the Acts of 1693 and 1707. For the Church of Scotland's sensitivity to the implications of the House of Lords' judgement, see Sands, *Archibald Scott*, 132–62; but the government decided to use the United Free Church bill for this purpose, not the Church of Scotland. For the United Free Church, see Cairns, *Life of MacEwen*, 253–6.

[50] J. N. Figgis, *Churches in the Modern State* (London, 1913), 4–5.

Indeed, 'mere disestablishment would not of itself ensure liberty'. Although at the beginning of James I's reign, the term 'established' referred 'not to the origin of the Church, but to its control', by the end of the eighteenth century, it came 'to have the meaning of "privileged", or, officially, the State religion, as distinct from those bodies which, though tolerated and in one sense established (as Lord Mansfield said), were private in their nature, partaking of no official or national character'. Even so prominent a constitutional lawyer as Professor Dicey seemed, in Figgis's view, to deprecate 'the notion that the Christian Church can have a higher law than that of the State'.[51]

That is why the Free Church Case was important. Although neither Church was established, the legal judgements of 1904 demonstrated the restricted nature of the freedom of the Church in a free State. No Church, argued Figgis, could admit that 'its entity is derived from the State'.[52] The central issue, therefore, was 'not so much whether or no a religious body be in the technical sense established, but whether or no it be conceived as possessing any living power of self-development, or whether it is conceived either as a creature of the State, or if allowed a private title is to be held rigidly under the trust-deeds of her foundation, thereby enslaved to the dead'.[53] In other words, were corporate societies to be understood as real personalities or fictitious ones? Did they have a life which was greater than the sum of the individuals which composed the body and therefore not 'merely a matter of contract'? Lord James had specifically said that 'the Church is not a positive, defined entity, as would be the case if it were a corporation created by law. It is a body of men united only by the possession of common opinions, and if this community of opinion ceases to exist the foundations of the Church give way'.[54] Figgis noted that jurists such as Gierke and Maitland supported a more positive view, but concluded that 'free Churches are not so free as they had supposed, so long as this doctrine of State omnipotence remains unconquered'.[55]

---

[51] Ibid., 8, 9, 10–11, 15.
[52] Ibid., 37.
[53] Ibid., 39.
[54] Orr, *Free Church Appeals*, 585.
[55] Figgis, *Churches in the Modern State*, 41, 50.

This was the issue the Joint Conference had to tackle. Some strong establishment figures in the Church of Scotland were alarmed by the boldness of the United Free Church's 1906 Act. The apparently unrestrained liberty to change alarmed high churchmen like Professor Cooper.[56] But even an old-fashioned conservative like Lord Balfour of Burleigh had argued in 1898 that

> the State recognizes a jurisdiction as inherent in the Church, and while adding to it and providing means whereby it can be carried into effect, does not profess to confer it *ab initio*; and further that within her sphere the Church of Scotland possesses legislative power to regulate her own affairs as may from time to time be necessary without reference to any external authority whatsoever.[57]

Marcus Dods, on the United Free Church side, thought that the English had made no advance since the time of the *Mayflower*: 'there is as deep an intolerance – as true an inability to see and admit that the Church has a legislation of her own, and that in their religious convictions men should be free from State control'.[58]

The Memorandum of 1912 was intended to resolve this problem. The opening rounds of the discussions had retrodden familiar ground. The Church of Scotland emphasised the benefits of the link between Church and State; the United Free Church looked for a national recognition of religion which did not privilege one Church above another. By October 1910 Lord Balfour of Burleigh, Joint Convener, was beginning to feel that it would be difficult to reach agreement without creating divisions in the Church of Scotland.[59] In response C. N. Johnston, the Church of

---

[56] Cooper, *Confessions of Faith*, 105–6. Cooper regarded the creeds of the undivided Church as unalterable and also strongly rebutted Innes's interpretation of the 1693 formula as not intending to imply that the Confession was the personal belief of the subscriber but that of the Church, *Confessions of Faith*, 51, cf. Innes, *Law of Creeds*, 1st edn, 78.

[57] C. Gore (ed.), *Essays in Aid of the Reform of the Church* (London, 1898), 100. Innes picked out precisely these words for criticism in *Law of Creeds*, 2nd edn, 130–1, and added as an extended footnote what he had written in the 1st edn, 187–96.

[58] Dods, *Later Letters of Marcus Dods*, 184–5.

[59] Archibald Fleming, minister in London, had written to White in January that he thought there were signs of 'a cleavage of opinion among the delegates of the other Church, of which we shall be wise to take full advantage'; but that depended on there being no corresponding cleavage on their own side: Fleming to White, 11 January 1910, White Papers, Box 2/6.

Scotland's Procurator, sought to disarm criticism of establishment in general by arguing a case for Scotland in particular. It was crucial that the united Church should 'be bound only by its freely adopted Constitution, and that its power to modify this Constitution should depend solely upon the provisions of the Constitution itself'. That was not inconsistent with as free and firm an adherence to the faith as Cooper desired. But, he continued, 'we must be bound by our own Constitution as a Church, and not by our special relation to the State'. If there was any external interference, 'it must be by a Court of Law interpreting our own Constitution as might happen equally to a purely voluntary Church'. Johnston acknowledged that there were a few fanatics who longed for complete disestablishment, but he did not think they counted for much. On the other hand, there was a very considerable 'left centre', typified by Professor Alexander Martin of New College, Edinburgh (who had dissented from the 1910 Report), with whom it was absolutely essential to have a *modus vivendi* if the union were to be successful. Such people would never recognise that 'any form of special state recognition is desirable. The only hope with them is to get them to acquiesce in the opinion that our case is special in Scotland.' This could be done by affirming the historical continuity of the Church in Scotland, and by modifying the constitution of the Church of Scotland so as to remove those features which limited its spiritual liberty. Indeed it would be best if they could avoid using either the term 'establishment' or 'disestablishment'.[60]

By 1911–12 'matters seemed drifting to an *impasse*'.[61] The Memorandum broke this by shifting the emphasis from principles to process. Each side had assumed that the process would accord with its own presuppositions: thus the Church of Scotland representatives had thought in terms of some legislative authorisation of changes in the Church of Scotland's constitution to facilitate union, while United Free Church representatives thought in

[60] Johnston to Balfour of Burleigh, 21 October 1910, White Papers, Box 2/6. Both this letter and the Notes by Lord Balfour to which it is a response are in White's hand, and are therefore presumably either drafts or copies.
[61] Lord Sands, *Life of Andrew Wallace Williamson* (Edinburgh, 1929), 255. Characteristically Sands does not indicate that he was the one who sought 'to make an effort to break up the cloud of generalities by a concrete proposal'.

terms of autonomous actions by the two churches.[62] But the House of Lords' judgement had made the latter position untenable. Significantly, when the United Methodist Church was formed in England in 1907, an Act of Parliament was secured to authorise the union.[63]

Johnston proposed that the two Churches should work out an acceptable constitution for a united Church and secure its approval by their respective presbyteries and synods. This constitution should be adopted by the Church of Scotland, and recognised (but not formally approved) by Parliament. A parliamentary commission should make arrangements to secure the ancient endowments for the continued use of the Church. With these measures in place, the formal steps towards union could be taken by the two Churches.[64] In essence this was what ultimately happened, and the pattern has influenced subsequent Church unions in Britain. Both the Methodist reunion in 1933 and the formation of the United Reformed Church in 1972 were acts of the uniting Churches, accompanied by parliamentary approval for the changes in the terms on which the Churches' property was held.

Cooper and A. W. Wotherspoon responded to the Memorandum by submitting a Minority Report to the Church of Scotland Assembly. They suggested that the Assembly was being asked to buy a pig in a poke: the new constitution was undefined; the provision for endowments was vague; and the Memorandum said nothing about doctrine. In the Assembly, however, Johnston met their arguments so effectively that they withdrew their motion and the Majority Report was approved unanimously. Ironically the fact that the Memorandum was suggestive rather than definitive helped the United Free Church Assembly to approve it and only thirteen votes were cast in favour of an amendment requiring complete disestablishment as a precondition of union.[65]

---

[62] Cf. Lord Sands, 'Church Union in Scotland', *Quarterly Review*, ccxxxiii, 462 (January 1920), 214.

[63] 7 Edward VII, ch. lxxv. The Methodist precedent was referred to positively by W. A. Curtis, 'Reunion in the Scottish Church and the Proposed Articles', *Hibbert Journal*, xviii (January 1920), 257–8, but deplored by Barr, *Scottish Church Question*, 254–5.

[64] *Reports on the Schemes of the Church of Scotland*, 1912, 1216–21.

[65] Sjölinder, *Presbyterian Reunion*, 220–33; G. M. Reith, *Reminiscences of the United Free Church General Assembly* (Edinburgh, 1933), 134–6.

Then it was necessary to define the meaning of the national recognition of religion. Archibald Fleming had regarded the crucial points as 'the King's protestantism, the provision of Religious Ordinances in the Navy and Army, and the giving of Religious Instruction in Schools'.[66] The last point is a reminder of the keen debate in England between 1906 and 1908 about modifying the 1902 Education Act. Johnston laid great emphasis on the existence of a mean between establishment and disestablishment.[67] He pointed out that the word 'establishment' was variously defined: for example, Chalmers regarded State endowment as essential, whereas Lord Selborne emphasised State recognition of ecclesiastical jurisdiction. In the seventeenth century the State had not chosen one out of several competing Churches for a special position: rather it had established Presbyterian Church government in the (one) Church in Scotland.[68] Barr certainly claimed that their Church of Scotland supporters justified the proposals on the grounds that they maintained establishment. J. R. Fleming noted that 'almost without knowing it staunch Conservative Churchmen abandoned the old Erastian policy that had hitherto prevailed ... They imagined that the cause of establishment was being strengthened, and did not duly estimate the new freedom that was guaranteed.'[69]

The Church of Scotland's case was probably not helped by the way it was used by protagonists of self-government for the Church of England. Lord Halifax and Viscount Wolmer had been impressed by the Memorandum and sought to secure for the Church of England the same freedom as the Church of Scotland. A. J. Balfour wrote to the Archbishop of Canterbury in January 1914 that he was 'strongly in favour of the principle of spiritual independence' and had 'never admitted any fundamental inconsistency between this and the principle of establishment'.[70] The Selborne Committee on Church and State, set up by

[66] Fleming to White, 11 January 1910, White Papers, Box 2/6.

[67] Sands, *Quarterly Review* (January 1920), 215; *Review of the Churches* (October 1925), 569.

[68] Sands, *Quarterly Review* (January 1920), 222.

[69] Barr, *Scottish Church Question*, 179–81; Fleming, *History of the Church in Scotland, 1875–1929*, 106–7.

[70] G. K. A. Bell, *Randall Davidson*, 3rd edn (London, 1952), 956–8; cf. D. M. Thompson, 'The Politics of the Enabling Act', *Studies in Church History*, xii, 383–5.

the archbishops in 1913, defined its task as 'how to secure a due measure of spiritual independence on the basis of establishment'.[71]

Johnston's success in winning over moderate opinion on the United Free Church side is shown by two papers prepared for the meeting of 7 November 1912. In the first of these, MacEwen viewed the proposed State recognition of a United Church as preserving continuity with the Church of the Reformation. Following Innes, MacEwen argued that the Estates' adoption of the Confession of Faith in 1560 did not involve the establishment or recognition of a Church. But 'manifestly the powers and jurisdiction conferred in 1567, and confirmed with specification in 1592, cannot be taken into a re-united Church' because 'the enactment was not incidentally but deliberately exclusive'. He therefore welcomed the Memorandum's proposal for 'a "statutory disclaimer" – a general clause disclaiming and abolishing such Statutes and enactments as confer monopolising and exclusive privileges' – which would achieve all that was required. Furthermore, the proposal in the draft preamble that the provisions of the Treaty of Union for the security of the doctrine, government, worship and discipline of the Church of Scotland were ratified *in that regard*, indicated that the exclusive establishment of Presbyterian government by the Treaty was not to be pressed.[72]

In the second paper Professor Martin considered the claim for nationality. He argued that 'the legal character of the Church in Scotland as the National Church is to be found in the series of decisions from the first Auchterarder Case in 1838 to the Stewarton Case in 1843, *and nowhere else*'. The decisions in those cases represented a choice from among three previously held views: first, the view that the ancient statutes authoritatively acknowledged the inherent powers of the Church; second, the view that there was a compact between Church and State, whereby in return for State protection the Church allowed an abridgement of her powers by the State; and third, the view 'that the Church as recognised by the

[71] *Report of the Archbishops' Committee on Church and State* (London, 1917), 39. The origin of the Committee was a motion in the Representative Church Council, which noted that 'there is in principle no inconsistency between a national recognition of religion and the spiritual independence of the Church'.

[72] 'Professor MacEwen's Notes' (7 November 1912), White Papers, Box 98, pp. 1, 2, 6, 8, 9.

State was an institution of the State'. The civil courts declared this third view to be the authoritative one, entailing that the Church's rights and powers were derived from parliament, prescribed by statute, and to be interpreted by the civil courts. Even the 'independent jurisdiction' which the Church was allowed was assigned and limited by statute. But the view of the United Free Church was

> that it is for the State to recognise, or to acknowledge, the Church, (that is, the Church Catholic) in its inherent God-given character and rights, and on the other hand that it is no part of the State's duty to render the Church (or any branch of the Church) in any sense a civil institution, vesting in it rights and powers which are its own, or else are nothing.

Hence Martin suggested that the national recognition of religion involved three things: the public recognition of God's providence in the care and guidance of the nation; the protection of the Church (Catholic) in the exercise of her functions; and 'the retention of Presbytery not necessarily as the exclusive organ, but as predominantly the organ of the National worship, in that sense and degree, which its size, power, and history render proper, and even inevitable'. On these terms an agreement with the Church of Scotland should not be impossible and would perhaps be 'a new thing in history'.[73]

The United Free Church Committee decided by 30 votes to 11 to recommend acceptance of the Church of Scotland's proposal to work on a draft constitution. In the United Free Church Assembly of 1912 the dissentient amendments were eventually withdrawn and the Report accepted unanimously; nevertheless 'the unanimity was only on the surface: there were strong undercurrents'.[74] But the growing warmth of the relationship was marked by the first official visit of the Moderator of the General Assembly of the Church of Scotland to the United Free Church Assembly, an impromptu personal initiative of Wallace Williamson, who had become Joint Convener of the Church of Scotland Committee on the death of Norman MacLeod in 1911.[75]

[73] 'Notes of Professor Martin's Speech, 7 November 1912', White Papers, Box 98, 1, 2, 3-4, 6, 9-10 (italics mine): cf. Cairns, *Life of MacEwen*, 254.

[74] Reith, *Reminiscences*, 145.

[75] Sands, *Williamson*, 227-8.

The drafting of the constitution suggested in the Memorandum took the form of a series of articles eventually termed, The Articles Declaratory of the Constitution of the Church of Scotland in Matters Spiritual. Now doctrinal questions really came out into the open. How was the adjustment of theology to historical and scientific criticism to be reflected in the formal doctrinal statements of the Church? Two issues were involved: first, the place of the classical creeds and confessions and the way they should be understood; and secondly, the liberty of the Church to change its doctrinal position.

IV

Both matters had arisen in the Free Church Case of 1903–4. The Rev. John Watson (of the Presbyterian Church of England) and Neville Figgis (of the Community of the Resurrection) had each likened the discussion of the Westminster Confession in the House of Lords to *Alice in Wonderland*.[76] The exchanges between R. B. Haldane and the Law Lords had revealed the difficulty of applying legal principles to theological statements. This had been seen particularly in the discussion of whether the Free Church Declaratory Act of 1892, in allowing diversity of opinion on the doctrine of predestination in the Westminster Confession, had in effect repudiated the Confession itself. These difficulties had illustrated the legal preference for literal interpretations in doctrinal matters and, in effect, brought the issue of tradition *versus* modernism to the fore.[77]

But the law was only part of the problem. Any reader of the discussion of Scottish church union in the contemporary periodicals cannot but be struck by the sense of conflict over doctrine in the surrounding articles.[78] The title of Innes's article of 1906, 'The Creed *Crisis* in Scotland', was indicative. This was also the period

---

[76] J. Watson, 'The Church Crisis in Scotland', *Hibbert Journal*, iii (January 1905), 249; Figgis, *Churches in the Modern State*, 35.

[77] Orr, *Free Church Appeals*, 480–524; cf. Sands, *Life of Scott*, 110.

[78] In the January 1914 issue of the *Hibbert Journal* (xii, 2), an article by R. L. Orr on 'The Scottish Church Question' was preceded by Maud Petre on 'The Advantages and Disadvantages of Authority in Religion' and followed by W. A. Curtis on 'The Value of Confessions of Faith' and H. Handley on 'Ought there to be a Broad Church Disruption?'

of the Modernist crisis in the Roman Catholic Church. Further, the implications of gospel criticism for traditional Christological affirmations were felt in the Church of England and the English Free Churches, typified, for example, by P. T. Forsyth's *The Person and Place of Jesus Christ* in response to R. J. Campbell's *New Theology* in 1909. It is interesting that the *Hibbert Journal* carried several articles about reunion in Scotland in its first twenty years. This quarterly first appeared in October 1902 from a Unitarian stable. Its editors did not deplore the differences of opinion in religious thought nor seek to reconcile them. Among extant varieties of religious thought they selected none 'as the type to which the rest should conform'. But they had no interest in '*dead* forms of religious thought' and 'those which have lost the power to outgrow their own limitations'.[79]

James Cooper's fight over the Articles Declaratory was dominated by doctrinal considerations. In 1907 he had warned John White of 'great *in*security for the *Faith*' in union discussions with the United Free Church alone. H. J. Wotherspoon supported him, criticising Scott's draft overture on union because it 'takes no safeguards for anything & reserves nothing: which on the face of it is to give Taylor Innes what he asks – that all questions be open'.[80] Both Cooper and Wotherspoon saw establishment as a safeguard for Christian orthodoxy. The subsequent definition of the Church's freedom in relation to creeds in 1910 drew substantially on the United Free Church Act anent Spiritual Independence of 1906, but added a clause that the freedom asserted was maintained 'in fidelity to the substance of the Reformed Faith ... and in order to secure their living and effective testimony to the same'.[81] This attempt to conciliate Cooper and Wotherspoon, by referring to the fundamentals of the faith

---

[79] *Hibbert Journal*, i (October 1902), 1. Most of the set of the *Journal* in the library of the Cambridge University Divinity Faculty came from A. J. Balfour (Prime Minister 1902–5), who acted as a parliamentary link for those working for reunion in Scotland.

[80] Cooper to White, 29 March 1907; Wotherspoon to White, 23 April [1907], White Papers, Box 1/11. Innes argued that the Church was not founded on creed, which probably explains Cooper's worry: Innes, *Studies in Scottish History*, 232.

[81] Report of 1911, *Reports on the Schemes of the Church of Scotland*, 1911, 931; Sjölinder, *Presbyterian Reunion*, 170–80.

contained in the catholic creeds, was substantially modified in discussion.

Cooper, however, kept up the pressure. In a letter to White in March 1911, he referred to an article by James Denney, which he thought 'has given our conveners another chance to stand firm for the Catholic Faith in its fulness – including *Chalcedon* as well as *Nicaea*'. He was not prepared to accept union 'except on the ground of our continued maintenance of, and testimony to, the Faith in its integrity and purity'. Almost apocalyptically he suggested that 'peace got by a surrender of the truth, or of the "forms of sound words" in which for fourteen hundred years the whole Church has expressed the fundamental verities of the Trinity and Incarnation, would leave us vague, and powerless against the armaments which we can see converging on us from any point of the horizon'. He did not think 'that Dr Henderson and his friends *dare* let Scotland know that "the professors" of whom they are so proud are shaky on these points'; and added that Dr Scott had urged him 'to agree to this Conference – in the first instance – "to save those poor fellows from *Socinianism*"'. It was up to the Conveners 'to save them; and to save *Scotland* from a calamity she has never yet been called upon to suffer – a large Church professedly "indifferent" to orthodox belief. Think what a Unitarian UF Church would be!'[82]

The first of the Articles Declaratory, which was later given an entrenched status, defined the Church of Scotland's commitment to the doctrines of the Trinity and the Incarnation. Cooper relentlessly pressed for a fuller statement of those doctrines. Although the Minority report which he and A. W. Wotherspoon signed in 1914 received little support in the Assembly, the wording of Article 1 was changed subsequently to incorporate much of what he had suggested. (In what follows, the final version is in bold type, words included in 1914 but subsequently omitted are in ordinary type, and words inserted in 1918 but removed in 1919 are in italics: changes made in 1918 are marked with one asterisk and those in 1919 with two.)

---

[82] Cooper to White, 3 March 1911, White Papers, Box 3/1. Cooper's distrust of German criticism and philosophy is illustrated in a letter of 11 June 1915, though it may have been affected by the war: H. J. Wotherspoon, *James Cooper* (London, 1926), 275–6.

The Church of Scotland is [a branch] part*
of the Holy Catholic or Universal Church
[, believing in one God the Father Almighty, and in Jesus Christ His
only begotten Son Incarnate for our salvation, and in the Holy Ghost,
three Persons in the unity of the Godhead];
worshipping* [*the Father, the Son, and the Holy Ghost,**]
one God, Almighty, all-wise and all-loving, in the Trinity of the Father,
the Son, and the Holy Ghost**,
the same in substance, equal in power and glory*; [owning obedience
to its once crucified, now risen and glorified Lord, as the sole King
and Head of His Church;]
adoring the Father, infinite in Majesty, of whom are all things*;
confessing the eternal Son our Lord Jesus Christ, made very man for
our salvation; glorying in His Cross and Resurrection, and [*adoring
Him**] owning obedience to Him** as the head over all things to His
Church*;
trusting in the promised renewal and guidance of the Holy Spirit;*
proclaiming the forgiveness of sins and acceptance with God through
faith in Christ, [the renewing of the Holy Spirit] and the gift of*
[e]Eternal life;
and labouring for the advancement of the Kingdom of God throughout the world.
The Church of Scotland adheres to the [Protestant] Scottish*
Reformation; receives the Word of God which is contained in the
Scriptures of the Old and New Testaments as its supreme rule of
faith and life; and avows the fundamental doctrines of the [*Christian*]
Catholic** faith founded thereupon and contained in its own
Confession*.

(The last sentence was a reformulation of the first three sentences
of Article 2 of 1914).[83]
Cooper was completely won over by the changes made, though
it may have helped that he was Moderator of the General Assembly
in 1917. By June 1918 he was writing to a friend that 'our union
with the UF's, so far from hindering the progress of Catholic
worship and doctrine and a reunion with the Anglicans, is positively opening new doors for effort in both these directions'; his
biographer wrote that 'the idea of union – almost the name – was
in itself sacred to him'.[84]

[83] Sjölinder, *Presbyterian Reunion*, Appendices V–VII, 386–91.
[84] Wotherspoon, *James Cooper*, 272, 297–8, 306.

Not all were so easily convinced. Donald MacMillan of Glasgow had been another firm defender of the establishment principle. He remained deeply concerned about the later Articles on spiritual freedom. Article IV affirmed the Church's spiritual freedom, and stated that recognition of this freedom by the civil authority did not affect the character of the Church's government and jurisdiction as derived from Christ. Article V affirmed the Church's right to frame its subordinate standards of belief and define the sense in which they were to be understood.[85] Article VI concerned the reciprocal relations of Church and State. Article VII concerned the obligation to seek and promote union with other Christian Churches. Article VIII affirmed the Church's right to interpret the Articles, and in its enlarged form of 1919 made detailed provision for the way in which they might be amended.[86] The reference to Presbyterianism as the only form of government of the Church of Scotland, which was included in the 1914 draft, was subsequently dropped. Article IX ratified and confirmed the constitution of the Church of Scotland in matters spiritual, subject to the provisions of the preceding articles.

In 1909 MacMillan had suggested that the unacknowledged reasons for the search for union were the financial weakness of the United Free Church and the fears of the Church of Scotland about disestablishment.[87] Two years later he had argued that there was no real enthusiasm for union and that the concept of outward unity on the Roman model was misconceived; rather it was necessary to seek first 'that inward unity of spirit which is the bond of peace'.[88] He protested against what he regarded as a misconceived notion of spiritual freedom: 'There never was a church spiritually independent in the sense that [the United Free Church] desires, nor was there ever national religion that was not established by the state.'[89] In 1919 he claimed that the draft Articles

---

[85] This was Article VI in the 1914 draft; in 1918 the former Articles IV and V were combined, and a new Article VI on the civil magistrate inserted.

[86] Prof. W. A. Curtis pointed out that the majorities required to amend the Articles were more stringent than those required by the ancient Barrier Act procedure of the Church of Scotland: *Hibbert Journal*, xviii (January 1920), 256.

[87] D. MacMillan, *The Aberdeen Doctors* (London, 1909), 200–1.

[88] D. MacMillan, *Hibbert Journal*, ix (January 1911), 406–10 (quotation from p. 410).

[89] Ibid., 406; cf. letter from MacMillan to Lord Balfour of Burleigh, 24 November 1913, quoted in Sjölinder, *Presbyterian Reunion*, 264.

would replace the present freedom in belief guaranteed by statute with a power granted to the General Assembly to 'modify, add to, or change the doctrines of the Church' against which there would be no appeal. MacMillan believed that the Church of Scotland 'had fallen into the hands of political intriguers', suggesting that there was significant silent opposition to the proposals.[90] This opposition remained silent, and the Articles were approved by the Church of Scotland General Assembly of 1919 as a basis upon which to approach Parliament. They became a Schedule to the Church of Scotland Act of 1921, which required that all existing statutes be interpreted in a way which was compatible with the Articles Declaratory. This both proved and disproved MacMillan's point: the Act provided for judicial interpretation, demonstrating that there was no escape from statute, but any interpretation had to be consistent with the Articles. The Articles were formally adopted by the General Assembly of the Church of Scotland in 1926, and the plan of union then followed. Contrary to MacMillan's dire predictions, religious strife did not break out all over Scotland.

The final stage was the formulation of the proposals for union. In his history of the Scottish union movement, Sjölinder scarcely referred to the long wrangle over endowments, perhaps because he viewed reunion in essentially ecclesial terms. But his neglect of the endowment question also reflected the consistent playing down of the traditional establishment issue. MacMillan had regarded the question of endowments as a crucial test. W. R. Thomson, replying to MacMillan from the United Free Church side, argued that as a truly national Church, the reunited Church would be justified in its continuing possession of the Church of Scotland's endowments.[91] But although Thomson's view represented the majority position in the United Free Church, the Disestablishment Council still made its voice heard; and it was assisted by the fact

[90] D. MacMillan, 'Presbyterian Reunion in Scotland: the Draft Articles', *Hibbert Journal*, xvii (January 1919), 309–18 (quotation from p. 318). He pointed out that only 24 out of 210 attended the meeting of the Glasgow presbytery to discuss the articles on 3 December 1918. W. R. Thomson denied that there was silent hostility: 'Presbyterian Reunion in Scotland', *Hibbert Journal*, xvii (April 1919), 451.

[91] Macmillan, *Hibbert Journal*, xvii (January 1919), 311–12, 317–18; Thomson, *Hibbert Journal*, xvii (April 1919), 455.

that the Church of Scotland Bill was presented in Parliament as making no fundamental change in the Church's position.

In a statement for the Joint Committee meeting on 26 January 1922, Barr cited the statements in parliament by Balfour, that the Act made 'no fundamental alteration in the relations of Church and State', and Wolmer, that it was 'reunion on the basis of Establishment', as evidence of the true nature of the Church of Scotland Act.[92] He objected to Article I as 'a short but rigid creed, and a many-sided test of doctrine'. He continued:

> It is a mistake for the Church to bind herself permanently to any form of words; still more to pledge herself to the State never to depart from them. Why should we make our thoughts compulsory on genera-tions yet unborn? . . . It does not give free play to the conviction that 'the Lord hath ever more truth and light to break forth out of His Holy Word'. It runs counter alike to the Thirty-First Chapter of the Confession of Faith, and to the historic symbol of the Reformation, known as Knox's Confession. How, with an unalterable Article, can we promise any man 'reformation of that which he shall prove to be amisse'?[93]

Finally he objected that every special privilege for the Church of Scotland in the Act inevitably prejudiced the full recognition of the liberties of other Churches.

This indeed had been a continual problem with what became Article VII. One of Johnston's earliest drafts of the constitution stated that the Church

> recognises other Churches in Scotland in which the word is purely preached and the sacraments rightly administered as Christian Churches having their own place in the religious life of the nation, sanctions and approves of Conference with representatives of these Churches on matters affecting the spiritual and moral wellbeing of the community, and welcomes the participation in religious services on special occasions of the ministers of such Churches in accordance with the usages of this Church in worship.[94]

In the 1914 draft constitution this recognition had been modified to a simple acknowledgement of their rich contribution to the

---

[92] Draft Statement by Mr James Barr on the Present Position in the light of the passing of the Church of Scotland Act 1921, White Papers, Box 98, 1, citing Hansard H.C. 22 June 1921, 1439 and 1468.

[93] Ibid., 7.

[94] Sketch Constitution C, art. 12, c.November 1913, White Papers, Box 99.

spiritual life of the nation. Later even this acknowledgement was omitted as being patronising.

Barr was not alone in his negative interpretation of the Church of Scotland Act. Dr John Young resigned as Joint Convener of the United Free Church Committee. In November 1921 he wrote (according to a United Free Church report)

> that he had latterly *found himself out of harmony with the course of action*, or inaction, which was being followed by the Committee: that, in his judgment, a new situation had been created by the passing of the recent *Church of Scotland Act*, which, as viewed by its official supporters in both Houses of Parliament, *strengthened establishment and did not secure freedom*; that the Committee, as he considered, were not facing the danger for the unity of the Church occasioned thereby, and that the circumstances registered the complete failure of the work to which he had given himself during the thirteen years of his service on the Committee, and rendered impossible his concurrence in the *policy of compromise and surrender of the principles* to which he adhered, which seemed now to guide the Committee.[95]

Young had previously expressed concern over the future disposal of endowments.[96]

On endowments, the Church of Scotland had to accept a compromise, and the parliamentary Act of 1925 did not immediately secure complete control over the endowments for the Church. Nevertheless Dr Welch could affirm: 'The State has lifted its hand from the Church of Scotland. That Church is now recognised as an autonomous communion with power to determine its own creed and with liberty to use its property according to the commands of its supreme Head.' Hence 'the last great obstacle to reunion has been removed'.[97]

[95] 'Dr Young's Retirement', marked 'Z', White Papers, Box 98 (underlinings by White). Young's letter specifically cited Balfour's remarks in the House of Commons.

[96] Minutes of meetings of the United Free Church of Scotland Committee for Conference with the Church of Scotland, 29 September and 3 November 1921.

[97] A. C. Welch, 'Church Union in Scotland', *Review of the Churches*, n.s. ii (October 1925), 575. Albert Bogle noted shrewdly that if the continuing United Free Church had taken the question of the allocation of property to the courts, it could have embarrassed the reunited Church of Scotland by securing a ruling

V

Was the reunited Church more representative of the nation, as supporters on both sides claimed? The existence of a Presbyterian majority in Scotland was never in doubt, but Cooper may have been right to worry about the theological effect of the absence of Episcopalians.[98] Subsequent history shows that the Church of Scotland has found it difficult to think ecumenically in any other terms than absorption. The Scottish Multilateral Conversations from the mid-1960s did much interesting and valuable work, but the fundamental question of whether the Church of Scotland could alter its nature to accommodate other Christians was not faced.

If that was true for other Protestant Churches, it was even more true for Roman Catholics. Not much could have been expected in 1929, when in the previous year the papal encyclical, *Mortalium Animos*, had declared it unlawful for Catholics to encourage or support the infant ecumenical movement. But John White unequivocally identified national religion with Protestantism. 'Rome prevented the growth of nationalities,' he wrote, adding, 'the revival of the sentiment of nationality is one of the achievements of modern civilisation.'[99] In a handwritten note on a memo deploring the Malines Conversations as a waste of precious time, White wrote, 'There is no immediate hope of fellowship between the Roman Catholic and the Protestant Churches. We are worlds apart in faith and government. The Protestant protests against the Roman Catholic in this world; the Roman Catholic protests against the Protestant in the next.'[100] When Sir John MacLeod reported to White on a survey he had made of Scottish MPs in 1924, he divided

---

as to whether it counted as a disestablished Church or not, A. Bogle, 'James Barr, B.D., M.P.', *Records of the Scottish Church History Society*, xxi (1982), 202.

[98] Innes commented that changing the establishment minority into a majority would not meet the moral question: *Studies in Scottish History*, 325.

[99] 'Note on Nationality' (undated), White Papers, Box 97. Fleming's first point in the definition of national religion in 1910 had been the King's Protestantism; see n. 66 above.

[100] 'The Cause of Reunion is being retarded by Grandiose Schemes' (undated), White Papers, Box 97.

the Labour party into two sections, Labour and Socialists, and also noted that some of them were Roman Catholics.[101]

More disturbing still was the way White, as Convener of the Church and Nation Committee of the Church of Scotland, campaigned against Irish Roman Catholic immigration into Scotland from 1923 onwards. Professor Brown has suggested that the reunion movement in Scotland was thereby associated with 'an exclusivist racial nationalism', that manifested itself in a campaign against Irish Catholic immigration.[102] The Edinburgh Faith and Order Conference in 1937 expressed concern about 'a national Church which hallows the common life of a given people, but is at the same time exposed to the perils of an exclusive provincialism or of domination by the secular state'.[103] There is an important ecclesial and ecumenical question here, which is a timely reminder that Cooper's work to make the first Article Declaratory clearly Catholic did not alter those socio-political realities.

Perhaps then, the conference was not as unrestricted as might initially be supposed. The right to amend the Articles Declaratory was conceded, but with what safeguards? Is the protection for Presbyterian government guaranteed in the Treaty of Union of 1707 ruled out by the requirement to interpret previous legislation in the light of the Church of Scotland Act (as MacEwen hypothesised in 1912), or does the international status of the Treaty affect the situation? Do the Articles Declaratory commit the Church of Scotland only to union 'without loss of identity' (Article VIII)? If so, where does that leave the questions of episcopacy or a new relationship with Rome? How far have the underlying questions of fundamental doctrine been tackled? It is striking that the Church of Scotland has not gone so far in reconsidering the status of the Westminster Confession as the Presbyterian Church of England, which produced a new Statement

---

[101] 'Notes on a visit to London by Sir John M. MacLeod, 31 July 1924', White Papers, Box 98.

[102] S. J. Brown, 'The Social Vision of Scottish Presbyterianism and the Union of 1929', *Records of the Scottish Church History Society*, xxiv (1990), 91–4.

[103] Hodgson, *Second World Conference on Faith and Order*, 258. Whilst it would be tempting to say that the Edinburgh Conference had Nazi Germany in mind, the context makes it clear that it had a wider concern.

of Faith in 1956, or even the Presbyterian Church in Ireland, which in the late 1970s formally renounced the Confession's view that the Pope was AntiChrist. Several of the underlying issues which were contested in the aftermath of 1900 remain alive as the Church enters the next millennium.

Chapter 10

Establishing Disestablishment: Some Reflections on Wales and Scotland

Keith Robbins

I

IN 1967 the late David Nicholls apologised in his preface to the collection of writings published with the title *Church and State in Britain since 1820*. The only justification for 'yet another book on Church and State', he wrote, was that it was not really *another* book but rather source material to which he was providing an introduction.[1] It is not altogether clear, however, why he felt a need to apologise. There have in fact been relatively few books which have systematically tackled the issue, at least as far as twentieth-century *Britain*, even more the United Kingdom, is concerned. To some extent, notwithstanding the title of his book, the Anglocentricity of the material which Nicholls himself selected serves to confirm the point. He included extracts from Thomas Chalmers, Gladstone on disestablishment in Ireland and Scotland, and Lloyd George and Charles Gore on Welsh disestablishment – but the remaining twenty-three writings or speeches concerned themselves, in a book on 'Church and State in Britain', with the position in England. Further, in his own stimulating twenty-five page introduction to the selected documents, Nicholls refers to the position of the Established Church in Scotland in but one paragraph, and nowhere alludes to Wales. His discussion of what may be said for or against establishment inevitably refers entirely to England and not to Britain. Indeed, the complexity and variety of the arrangements between Church and State within

[1] D. Nicholls, *Church and State in Britain Since 1820* (London, 1967), ix.

the constituent countries of the present United Kingdom may help to explain why most ecclesiastical historians have shied away from attempting anything which could properly be called a full study of 'Church and State in twentieth-century Britain'. It is not, therefore, so much an apology for *another* book which seems appropriate. He might rather have lamented the lack of *any* book which offers a comprehensive treatment of this topic.

The student will be hard put to it to find much illumination on 'Church and State' from general historians of twentieth-century Britain – a few examples will illustrate the point. Amongst well-known writers of an earlier generation it is perhaps asking too much to look to my own former tutor, A. J. P. Taylor, for illumination on the subject of ecclesiastical establishment. In his well-known *English History 1914–1945* he devoted a paragraph to the Revised Prayer Book controversy in 1927 and 1928, but only to conclude that the outcry was 'the echo of dead themes'. Moreover, 'England had ceased to be, in any real sense, a Christian nation. Only a minority of Englishmen attended any Church, Roman, Anglican or Free. The politicians who exercised themselves on this matter were living in the past.'[2] The question of why the non-churchgoing majority nevertheless acquiesced in or perhaps even welcomed the continuance of 'establishment' did not engage his attention. C. L. Mowat contented himself in his *Britain between the Wars* with the remark that 'dis-establishment, though often talked of, was never a real issue'.[3] He, likewise, did not pursue matters further and ask why this was the case – if, indeed, it was true that England had ceased to be 'in any real sense, a Christian nation'.

More recently, Jeremy Black, arguing that the gradual 'virtual disestablishment' of the Church of England has been gathering pace in recent decades, simply remarks that such a process is 'a parallel to the process of disestablishment that has already taken place on much of the Continent'.[4] In fact, even on 'much of the Continent' disestablishment has taken many forms – and parallels

[2] A. J. P. Taylor, *English History 1914–1945* (Oxford, 1965), 259.

[3] C. L. Mowat, *Britain between the Wars 1918–1940* (London, 1956), 224.

[4] J. Black, *A History of the British Isles* (London, 1996), 295. Black refers, in his discussion of churchgoing, to both the Church of England and the Scottish Episcopal Church being 'badly hit'. It is possible that he may be thinking of the Church of Scotland rather than the Scottish Episcopal Church.

are difficult to draw. However, looking back over the twentieth century as a whole, it is not so much falling into line with 'the Continent' that strikes the historian of twentieth-century Britain, as the fact that it is only at its very end that some kind of 'parallel' seems evident. General historians may indeed not be much interested, but it is the case that 'Establishment', whatever it may mean, has remained a distinctive facet of the life of both England and Scotland (though not Wales) long after formal separations of Church and State, to greater or lesser degree, have occurred in other parts of Europe.

Another recent historian, Peter Clarke, observes that 'Great set-piece debates about Church and State, such as the Victorians relished, were rare after the First World War.' He does add, however, that 'The position of the established Churches, each with a different theology north and south of the border . . . was not quite so anachronistic as it looked at first sight'. To many people, Clarke suggests, the Church of England was a familiar, hierarchical and periodically useful national institution. And he devotes particular attention to the fate of bishops – who were dragged down market, in the era of life peers, as he puts it. Until that date, he adds, they had contrived to draw stipends which enabled them to rub shoulders with the remnants of the landed interest. However, this interesting sociological observation apart, he does not probe 'establishment' any further or reflect on specific ways in which the Church of England remained a 'periodically useful national institution'. He does not ask himself whether the Church of England could even 'periodically' be considered a useful national institution as far as the British (as opposed to English) nation as a whole is concerned.[5]

Brian Harrison's recent study of the British political system concludes, however, that in the 1990s 'what we now call multiculturalism has proceeded so far as to render disestablishment of the Church of England a mere tidying-up operation, congenial even to many Anglicans'.[6] However, his otherwise perceptive analysis of the British constitution does not offer any guidance on what role establishment may still have played earlier in the

---

[5] P. Clarke, *Hope and Glory: Britain 1900–1990* (London, 1996), 163–6.
[6] B. Harrison, *The Transformation of British Politics 1860–1995* (Oxford, 1996), 360.

twentieth century. It is evident that he takes it as axiomatic that multiculturalism (however the term is to be understood) renders unacceptable any specific recognition of Anglicanism. All that is left to do, on this reading, is 'tidy up' a blatant anachronism. He does not say, however, whether this operation, whenever it finally takes place, must entail the withdrawal of any privileged recognition on the part of the State accorded to any religious tradition or whether 'multiculturalism' entails an equal recognition extended to all religious traditions present in significant strength in the United Kingdom. While there can be no dispute about the presence of many religions in contemporary Britain and, one hopes, no dispute about freedom of worship, the act of disestablishment, arguably, does nevertheless represent formal national severance from a long 'Christian past'. As such it may be thought to have deeper social and psychological consequences for 'national identity' than is perhaps implied by a term like 'tidying up'.

Some social historians have indeed recognised that the matter is rather complicated. For example, the French historian, François Bédarida, after recounting 'the inexorable retreat of traditional religious practice', nevertheless felt it important not to exaggerate the extent of English irreligion. He noted that 'public life continued under the aegis of a State Church, and, more importantly, the Church was closely interwoven with the whole fabric of national existence'.[7] In his *British Society 1914–45* (1984) John Stevenson drew attention similarly to what might appear a paradoxical situation. He noted that Britain emerged into the post-1945 world with legislation in areas such as drink, sex and Sunday observance 'which reflected a Christian outlook no longer shared by the majority of the population'. However, he pointed to the paradox that an increasingly secular society, aware of its religious or areligious diversity, 'still found it necessary to turn to Christian ritual and imagery for expression'. This was especially so in the organs of the State where 'at least formal Christianity remained a significant part of the culture'.[8] These remarks, of course, at once take us into the interpretation of just how a 'secular society' might

---

[7] F. Bédarida, *A Social History of England 1851–1975* (London, 1979), 244–5.

[8] J. Stevenson, *The Pelican Social History of Britain: British Society 1914–45* (Harmondsworth, 1984), 370.

be defined. Sociologists, theologians and historians have all attempted answers but it remains a term fraught with difficulty. What is meant by 'formal Christianity'? Is it the antithesis of 'real Christianity' or its ally? The 'many Anglicans' referred to by Harrison who favour disestablishment have often given as reason that the association with the 'organs of state' obscures the mission of the Church of England. Some of them might go further and argue that the sooner the Church extracts itself from 'the whole fabric of national existence' the better.

Not unexpectedly, Church historians have given some attention to the issues involved – though not on an 'all-British' basis.[9] Adrian Hastings in his *History of English Christianity 1920–1990* (1991) and in his lectures *Church and State: the English Experience* (1991) has illuminatingly touched on some central issues but, as their titles indicate, his writings are concerned with England not Britain, and what is happening outside England receives only parenthetical reference. He remarks, for example, concerning the situation in England after the First World War, that the disestablishment of the Church of England in Wales 'showed close at hand what might be done', but quite reasonably, it is beyond his brief to consider the Welsh situation in any detail.[10] There may well be many of his readers who know little of what actually happened to the Church of England in Wales and therefore how far it was or was not a model for what might have been done in England. Indeed, in general, both Churchmen and Church historians – in England, Scotland and Wales – have tended to retain a single country perspective in what they have produced. Books which are in some sense 'standard' from an earlier generation have been written very much from within particular ecclesiastical/national folds. For example, Cyril Garbett's *Church and State in England* (1950)

---

[9] An exception is the volume edited by P. Badham, *Religion, State and Society in Modern Britain* (Lampeter, 1989) but even here the contributors deal discretely rather than comparatively with the countries of Britain. I have touched on some of these matters, though never systematically, in articles collected in *History, Religion and Identity in Modern Britain* (London, 1993); in an essay 'Religion and Community in Scotland and Wales since 1800', in S. Gilley and W. J. Sheils (eds), *A History of Religion in Britain* (Oxford, 1994), 363–80; in *Great Britain: Identities, Institutions and the Idea of Britishness* (London, 1998).

[10] A. Hastings, *Church and State: The English Experience* (Exeter, 1991), 61.

remains an informative example of a particular kind of 'established' English approach to establishment. And, in the preface to his *A Church History of Scotland* (1960) J. H. S. Burleigh argued that for Presbyterianism 'the idea of a National Church has not been seriously questioned'. And, despite its 'unceasing and confident propaganda' the Roman Catholic Church in Scotland in his opinion was 'still to the mass of Scots a strange and alien community'.[11]

If ecclesiastical historians have not been to the fore in trying to look comparatively at what Establishment/Disestablishment really entails and signifies in twentieth-century Britain, the topic has also been neglected by those historians and political scientists who have been interested in constitutional diversity within the British State. I illustrate the point by reference to two books on regionalism and devolution published in 1978 and 1998 respectively.[12] Neither pays any attention to the extent to which, in the past, though perhaps now residually, it has been religious allegiance which has buttressed national/regional identity or even defined it.

The rather sketchy attention to these matters by historians and political scientists – incomplete though this survey has admittedly been – does not therefore take us very far. It would seem likely to be the case that the whole of the relationship between the Church of England and the State will again come under review. Indeed, one commentator has identified three choices open to the Church of England. The first is complete disestablishment – which would bring it into line with its sister churches of the Anglican Communion elsewhere in the British Isles. The second is that it should become completely self-governing, while remaining the Established Church – that is to say the Queen would remain the Supreme Governor of the Church of England, but be advised on all matters ecclesiastical by her archbishops, bishops and synod and not by her Prime Minister, ministers and Parliament. The third is the status quo, with the government of the day continuing to have the ultimate power over appointments.[13] These options, or variants

[11] J. H. S. Burleigh, *A Church History of Scotland* (Oxford, 1960), vii.
[12] M. Kolinsky (ed.), *Divided Loyalties: British Regional Assertion and European Integration* (Manchester, 1978); J. Bradbury and J. Mawson, *British Regionalism and Devolution: The Challenges of State Reform and European Integration* (London, 1997).
[13] Lord Rees-Mogg, 'Faith, Hope and political meddling', *The Times*, 13 April 1998.

of them, have, of course, been discussed before. What gives them some fresh interest is that they are raised at a time when Britain itself is going through a period of great and rapid constitutional change. It is pertinent, therefore, to focus for a moment on the country in Great Britain which has experienced disestablishment in this century – Wales. The final section of this essay, however, considers the issues raised by disestablishment in a Scottish context and draws on the position in Wales to make observations on the contemporary situation in Scotland.

II

Reflection on the experience of Wales, specifically on its first quarter of a century as a 'disestablished' country, offers a perspective which is relevant to current debate in Britain as a whole. If, as J. H. Shakespeare powerfully but not very successfully argued in 1918, the Churches were at the cross-roads, this was even more the case in Wales.[14] Even here, however, a thorough historical analysis is as yet lacking. No study, so far as I am aware, has specifically set out to address the issue of the difference disestablishment has actually made in the life of Wales. This chapter will address the first twenty years of 'disestablished life' though it does not pretend to be comprehensive. In contrast to the situation after the First World War, a great deal of attention has been given to the campaign for disestablishment from the mid-nineteenth century onwards.[15] The particular context of that campaign does, however, need some initial rehearsal.

Critics of establishment in both England and Scotland in the nineteenth century confronted a Church of England and a Church of Scotland. The position in Wales was more complicated. There,

[14] J. H. Shakespeare, *The Churches at the Cross-Roads: A Study in Church Unity* (London, 1918).

[15] To be found, amongst other accounts, in P. M. H. Bell, *Disestablishment in Ireland and Wales* (London, 1969): K. O. Morgan, 'The Campaign for Welsh Disestablishment', in *Modern Wales: Politics, Places and People* (Cardiff, 1995), 142–76: W. B. George, 'Welsh Disestablishment and Welsh Nationalism', *Journal of the Historical Society of the Church in Wales*, xx, no. 25 (1970), 77–91. Rather different nineteenth-century perspectives are offered in I. Gwynedd Jones, *Explorations & Explanations: Essays in the Social History of Victorian Wales* (Llandysul, 1981) and M. Cragoe, *An Anglican Aristocracy: The Moral Economy of the Landed Estate in Carmarthenshire 1832–1895* (Oxford, 1996).

critics of establishment did not confront a Church of Wales, for it did not exist. The four Welsh dioceses were an integral part of the Province of Canterbury. There was thus a distinctive national/ecclesiastical complexity about the struggle for Welsh Disestablishment which marked it off from the situation in either England or Scotland. The ecclesiastical issue was bound up with complicated relationships across 'England and Wales' at a time when formal institutional manifestations of Welsh identity were either non-existent or embryonic (University, National Library, National Museum). So, what was at stake, was not only 'Establishment' as a principle, right or wrong, but the existence or otherwise of 'Wales' as an entity within which it might take place. Basil Jones, Bishop of St Davids, had unwisely committed himself to the view that Wales was 'a geographical expression'.

Although there had been endless argument surrounding the precise significance of the 1851 religious census in Wales and whether or not there had been cheating during its compilation, it proved impossible to argue convincingly thereafter against the fact that adherents of the Established Church constituted a minority (around a fifth to a quarter) of Christian worshippers in Wales. In itself, such a minority position constituted in the eyes of the Church's opponents an intolerable unfairness. If there was a case for Establishment at all, which many Welsh critics declined to admit, it could only rest on the reality that the Church which was established had a majority either of worshippers in its ranks or, more fundamentally, a majority of the nation. That was manifestly not the case with the Church of England in Wales, at least as far as adherents were concerned. If the disestablishment campaign succeeded, the Church of England in 'England and Wales' would fragment and a new Anglican province might emerge. On the other hand, however, the case was argued by defenders of the existing establishment that, ecclesiastically, there was an Anglo-Welsh continuum, as there was in so many other areas of the life of 'England and Wales' at that time. It was argued that if 'England and Wales' was an ecclesiastical as well as a political unit then it was preponderantly Anglican and could therefore be justified. English Nonconformists, enthusiastic for disestablishment in England, were even sometimes not unsympathetic to a Welsh Anglican 'England and Wales' perspective, reasoning that disestablishment might be achievable in 'England and Wales' as a result of the combined pressure of Nonconformity in England and Wales. If Wales were treated as a special case, however, the chances of Nonconformist success in England would greatly diminish because it was only in Wales that there was a Nonconformist majority.

The disestablishment campaign in Wales entered what looked like its final phase after the Liberal electoral victory of 1906. It could hardly be otherwise, it seemed, since every Welsh MP (a majority being Nonconformists) favoured both disestablishment and disendowment of the Church. Lloyd George, champion of Welsh dissent (or so his record suggested), was Chancellor of the Exchequer. Triumph/justice appeared to be at hand. Yet it took a long time to arrive. The Liberal government, taken in the round, had other priorities than a specifically Welsh measure. A Royal Commission to investigate the 'Church of England and other Religious Bodies in Wales and Monmouthshire' offered an excuse for delay – and was set up after private consultations held by Lloyd George with the Bishop of St Asaph and the Archbishop of Canterbury. In due course it produced the most detailed of reports. However, in Wales itself, as Churchill for one knew, issues of health, housing and work in the troubled coalfields had come to the fore, pushing religious grievances into the background. Even so, the issue continued to engage ecclesiastical passions. Attempts to find compromise were fiercely denounced on both sides as treachery. Even some English Tory politicians revealed hitherto unsuspected ecclesiastical commitments. G. K. Chesterton famously called upon F. E. Smith, purportedly spokesman for the conscience of 'every Christian community in Europe', to 'chuck it'. It was not until 1912 that the third Welsh disestablishment bill was introduced in the Commons by Reginald McKenna, the Home Secretary, who sat, perhaps appropriately, for (North) Monmouthshire, a county still deemed to be awkwardly poised between England and Wales. It finally passed through the Commons in January 1913. The Lords rejected it, as they did a second time in the summer. It started on its third passage in 1914 and reached the statute book in September 1914 – by which time other matters claimed the attention of the country. There was a proviso, however, that the measure would not be enacted until a year after the cessation of hostilities.

The fact that disestablishment was achieved in such circumstances meant that it was not quite the event which both advocates and opponents had supposed likely before 1914. As things turned out, the Church was to have some years to get used to the prospect before it, while wartime was hardly the moment for Nonconformists to engage in triumphant celebration. Neither Church nor Chapel could have any real grasp of the social and spiritual impact of the war itself. The dislocations it caused, both physical and mental, had a profound impact on all denominations so that 'pre-1914' seemed a world away in 1919.[16] And it was not exactly clear what there was to celebrate. To some extent, whatever great moral principle 'Disestablishment' represented was obscured by the haggling over 'Disendowment'. Charges of 'plunder and sacrilege' were met by claims that it would only be a just outcome if an 'alien church' were relieved of its past ill-gotten gains. Clergy and ministers seemed to find excoriating each other, and each other's respective flocks, a pleasurable activity. The public platform which the campaign provided, could seem more exciting than routine pastoral duties. Listening to extreme language uttered by both sides in Wales itself, it was tempting to suppose that Church and Chapel stood in solid and perpetually polarised opposition. Beneath the public rhetoric, however, lay a complex pattern of relationships, often family relationships, within Welsh life which cut across the divide or at least softened its significance in private dealings.[17] And, although separation of 'religion' and 'politics' is never easy, the tensions reflected social, cultural and linguistic uncertainties in the Wales of that era as much as they did ecclesiastical or theological differences. In addition, at the very moment of its triumph, when that marriage between 'Welshness' and 'Nonconformity', so

[16] There is an account of Welsh Christianity's response to the Great War in Dewi Eirug Davies, *Byddin y Brenin: Cymru a'i Chrefydd yn y Rhyfel Mawr* (Llandysul, 1988): D. Densil Morgan, '"Christ and the War": Some Aspects of the Welsh Experience, 1914–18', *Journal of Welsh Ecclesiastical History*, 5 (1997), 73–92. I am indebted to Dr D. Densil Morgan for further information on this subject, and indeed on Welsh religion in general after 1914. See his *The Span of the Cross: Christian Religion and Society in Wales 1914–2000* (Cardiff, 1999).

[17] R. L. Brown, 'Traitors and Compromisers: The Shadow Side of the Church's Fight against Disestablishment', *Journal of Welsh Religious History*, 3 (1995), 35–53.

sedulously cultivated since mid-century seemed to be consummated, Nonconformity was in difficulty.

An optimistic reading, that disestablished Wales would see the inexorable but 'non-official' ascendancy of Nonconformity now that the Church had been stripped of its privileged provision, already looked unlikely. The new post-war constitutional position brought out afresh the obvious fact that 'Nonconformity' was not a single body. The relationship between its main components – Baptists, Congregationalists/Independents, Wesleyan Methodists and Calvinistic Methodists (Presbyterians) – had locally been strengthened by ministerial/congregational participation against the Church but that rather frail unity had never removed differences of ecclesiology and theology. These could now have full rein once more, though there were occasional voices who argued that there should be one Free Evangelical Church in Wales. While there was sometimes sage agreement that the time for sectarianism was past, it did not lead to the taking of any effective steps to achieving unity. It was easier to send congratulatory telegrams to Presbyterians in Scotland and Methodists in England than to follow their example.

In addition, all of the organisational and practical issues posed by the existence of two languages further complicated the standpoints of each denomination, especially as the scale of the decline in the Welsh language became apparent. It would be wrong, some said, to insist on the maintenance of Welsh services at the cost of the 'spiritual welfare of our own flesh and blood'.[18] Others thought, or at least felt, differently. The only truly Welsh-generated denomination, and the largest, that of the Calvinistic Methodists – four-fifths of whose churches were Welsh-speaking in 1935 – was itself not altogether certain about a central position in 'Nonconformity', given that final separation from the Church of England had only occurred in 1811. It was not, therefore, as the others were, a Welsh expression and adaptation of an earlier English Dissent. Although, in the 1920s, reinforcements from Scotland came regularly to address the annual conference of the English-speaking Presbyterians, doubt lingered on the subject of Presbyterianism.

[18] Cited in R. Buick Knox, *Voices from the Past: History of the English Conference of the Presbyterian Church of Wales 1889–1938* (Llandysul, 1969), 14.

The Connexion might have adopted it as a form of government but its soul and spirit lay in its Methodism.[19] A further complicating factor lay in the fact that individual denominations were strong in some parts of Wales and relatively weak in others.[20] This pattern both reflected and reinforced tensions in Wales itself which we can broadly describe as North/South and rural/industrial.

In these circumstances, both within and outside its ranks, the 'victory' soon appeared hollow. Pre-1914 social issues have already been alluded to and their importance grew in the 1920s. Chapels struggled to reorientate their mission in a social and intellectual climate which was indifferent if not hostile to a 'Nonconformist Conscience' which appeared to have ossified at the end of the previous century.[21] Some of their ministers did not find it easy to eschew the public role that the 'Campaign' had provided. The lure of full-time politics proved attractive. At the same time, however, the Liberal Party was itself in internal crisis – the other side of the coin. And there was growing anxiety, present to greater or lesser degree in all the denominations, about future recruitment to the ministry. There was alarm, for example, that few sons of ministers seemed to have heard the call to preach (a circumstance which admitted of an uncomfortable explanation) – a situation which allegedly contrasted with Scotland.[22] And it remained the case that some of the most eloquent and able of Welsh ministers found themselves, without undue regret, called to occupy pulpits in England. At another level, the burden imposed on subsequent generations by an earlier zeal for chapel building was already apparent. It was compounded by population drift and outward migration from Wales itself, a country hit hard by unemployment.[23]

[19] Cited in ibid., 18.

[20] M. Watts has helpfully mapped the distribution of all worshippers in Wales in 1851, the distribution of Anglicans, and Nonconformists (both as a whole and of individual denominations) in his *The Dissenters Volume II: The Expansion of Evangelical Nonconformity 1791–1859* (Oxford, 1995), 863–70.

[21] These matters are pursued thoroughly in R. Pope, *Building Jerusalem: Nonconformity, Labour and the Social Question in Wales, 1906–39* (Cardiff, 1998); D. Ben Rees, *Chapels in the Valley: A Study in the Sociology of Welsh Nonconformity* (Upton, Wirral, 1975) studies the Aberdare Valley.

[22] Knox, *Voices from the Past*, 38.

[23] The Royal Commission in 1910 noted that 'religious accommodation is largely in excess of any reasonable expectation of attendance'; cited in C. Williams, *Democratic Rhondda: Politics and Society 1885–1951* (Cardiff,

Cumulatively, therefore, Nonconformity in the inter-war period was in an uncomfortable and uneasy position. One historian, reflecting on the situation back in 1906, has written that 'the French disestablishment of 1905 offered an exciting precedent for British politics' but it was not a precedent which motivated Welsh Nonconformists.[24] Separation of Church and State in France reflected the gulf in French life between clericalism and anti-clericalism, between Catholicism and an articulate and self-conscious 'secularism'. That gulf did not yet exist in Wales. Disestablishment was not seen as the first step towards the 'secular State' or the marginalisation of the Church/es. It was, rather, merely the removal from a privileged position accorded by the British State to one (minority) Church in Wales. Potentially, at least, it offered the prospect that Welsh society would become more Christian, a desirable condition, rather than less, because endorsement by the State was a hindrance rather than a help to Christian mission.[25] We have already noted, however, many of the factors which made it difficult to realise in practice in a dis-established Wales the deeply-held notion, amongst Nonconformists and often outside Wales, that the country was in fact a nation of Nonconformists. In addition, there was an issue of nomenclature still unresolved to this day. How was it possible to be a Non-conformist in a country which had no State Church? To speak of 'the Free Churches' made no sense when all churches were 'free'. The fact that no collective alternative nomenclature was found speaks volumes concerning the failure to grasp what life in a disestablished country should have entailed.

1996). It is only for a brief period, in the late nineteenth century, that Williams, contrary to other writers, is prepared to concede that Nonconformist preachers became 'the natural leaders of Rhondda society' (p. 241). Robin Gill studies Glan-Llyn in rural Merionethshire in his *The Myth of the Empty Church* (London, 1993), 52–71.

[24] P. Jenkins, *A History of Modern Wales* (London, 1992), 340.

[25] There would have been endorsement of P. T. Forsyth's claim that 'as a National Church is one of the great impediments to missionary success, so an Established Church, uttering as it does law rather than grace or Gospel, is, qua established, in standing contradiction to the first principle of the religion for which it exists'. P. T. Forsyth, *The Charter of the Church: The Spiritual Principle of Nonconformity* (London, 1896), p. vi.

Even so, despite its difficulties, it would be wrong to exaggerate the eclipse of Nonconformity in the early post-disestablishment decades, at least in 'Welsh' Wales. Formal public avowals of atheism or agnosticism were relatively rare but were nonetheless present in private. New ex-Nonconformist nonconformists revolted against the 'Nonconformist Establishment' and it was not always necessary to attend the University of Oxford to do so, though it helped. Some writers did rage publicly against what they believed to be the joyless bible-black barbarism of Nonconformity which had captured Wales in the previous century and from which it needed to be released. A start could be made by burning every chapel to the ground.[26] However, there appears to be no evidence of chapel-burning! Perhaps a more typical mixed reaction can be found in the thoughts of Idris Davies, the poet of industrial South Wales. He combined attendance at his local Baptist chapel with the belief in 1936 that what Wales needed was the eradication of Christianity within her borders. Christianity should die. It would die.[27] For their part, some Welsh Communists remained in active membership of their chapels, although there is record that one Welsh miner specifically joined the Communist Party on hearing news of the Soviet persecution of Russian Baptists.[28] Such a gesture apart, the capacity to live in two 'worlds' at once was widespread, perhaps even characteristic, of an influential sector of Welsh society at this juncture.

Adjustment to a disestablished Wales naturally posed quite different issues for the four Anglican bishops. They would no longer sit in the House of Lords and no longer be appointed by the Crown. There was bitterness about the loss of endowments. The fate of churchyards was a matter of special angst. An Amending Act of 1919 brought some amelioration from the Church perspective but clergy and people, for the most part, had not wanted the freedom they now possessed. The prospect, clutched

[26] A. Jones, *Welsh Chapels* (Stroud, 1996) demonstrates that there is more to be said about this 'folk architecture' than is often supposed and J. Harvey demonstrates that not all aspects of Nonconformity were bible-black in his *The Art of Piety: The Visual Culture of Welsh Nonconformity* (Cardiff, 1995).

[27] Ambiguity, too, is present in 'Capel Hebron' in I. Davies, *The Angry Summer: A Poem of 1926* (London, 1953), 53. See D. Johnston (ed.), *The Complete Poems of Idris Davies* (Cardiff, 1994), xxxvii.

[28] H. Francis, *Miners against Fascism* (London, 1984), 60.

at by some, that a Conservative government would reverse what had happened, was soon abandoned. Was the formation of a separate province for Wales evitable or inevitable, desirable or undesirable? Committees and Conventions had been discussing forms and procedures since 1915. A new province of the Anglican Communion emerged with its own Archbishop, Governing Body and Representative Body. Delicate issues of balance between North and South had to be attended to. The question of the name of the Church was pregnant with significance, a significance not always appreciated by those who discussed it. Few, however, had any disposition to equate the new legal equality of all Churches/denominations with ecclesiastical parity. What had happened, in the eyes of the first archbishop was that 'the most ancient Christian Church' in the island of Britain had been severed from the State. It was, in his opinion, 'the first part of the Church in Great Britain' to suffer this fate.[29] It was, however, still self-evidently *the* Church. Some supposed, therefore, that it should call itself 'The Welsh Church', though it was unclear whether the stress should fall upon '*The*' or upon '*Welsh*'. There was strong advocacy of 'The Church of Wales' but, faced with the fact that the Welsh Church Act had used the form 'The Church in Wales', the latter was accepted in 1921. The first Archbishop was enthroned (by the Archbishop of Canterbury) in St Asaph Cathedral in June 1920. There were six thousand people encamped on the cathedral lawns. Prince Arthur of Connaught did duty for the Prince of Wales who happened to be in the Far East. The Prime Minister was present – the Welsh-speaking David Lloyd George whose sceptical ecumenism in receiving communion shocked Anglican and Nonconformist alike. The congregation thus reflected the ironies and complexities of the situation. The Archbishop, writing later, claimed that although Wales in the past might have been disunited now 'the nation arose and thronging voices of approval came from far and wide. It was the thought of Wales "a nation" that thrilled her people'.[30]

For some, failure to adopt the title 'Church of Wales' meant the loss of a golden opportunity to make 'a most effective appeal to the principle and sentiment of nationality' and to make clear that the Church would be coming towards the Welsh people 'in its

---

[29] The Archbishop of Wales (A. G. Edwards), *Memories* (London, 1927), 1.
[30] Edwards, *Memories*, 321.

corporate national capacity'. 'The supreme question', another contemporary writer suggested, 'for the Church in Wales is the combination of its religion with the modern progress of Wales.' Allied to this regret was a complaint that the deciding Convention had been too much in the hands of the upper and middle classes. How could such a Church appeal with any degree of success to Welsh Nonconformists 'with their markedly democratic leanings'?[31] However, although as Charles Green, a subsequent Archbishop of Wales, claimed in 1937, the Constitution of the Church in Wales was 'the result of consultation and co-operation between the Welsh Bishops and their Clergy and Laity', episcopal authority remained absolute. The Church, he wrote, was a theocracy not a democracy. And, it appeared, theocracy was to be equated with the episcopal office. From the chancellor to the bell ringer, all derived their authority from the bishop.[32] It is not surprising to read that thirty years earlier he had told the Royal Commission that he had never been inside a Nonconformist chapel – and had done little, if anything, to repair the omission in the interval. If, therefore, as some claimed, nonconformity would fall apart, was it really the case that 'the people' would 'come back' to the 'mother Church'? Would this 'Church in Wales' come to be, in time, the embodiment of national Christianity in a country which recognised no Church, though that country/nation remained part of a State which in England and Scotland still recognised established churches? Lord Sankey, architect of the constitution, reminded members (addressing them as 'Ladies and Gentlemen' not 'Sisters and Brethren') that the Church in Wales was 'a Catholic and National Church'. It was not easy to hold these two principles in balance.

Historians in general have expressed high praise for the way in which the Church in Wales 'established' itself in its new

---

[31] Dr Maurice Jones, later Principal of St David's College, Lampeter, cited in D. T. W. Price, *A History of the Church in Wales in the Twentieth Century* (Penarth, 1990), 10–11; J. Vyrnwy Morgan, *The Church in Wales in the Light of History* (London, 1918), 214.

[32] C. A. H. Green, *The Setting of the Constitution of the Church in Wales* (London, 1937), 13–15. This work was published as Green was preparing to attend the Coronation of King George VI. He thoughtfully gave copies at his own expense to every member of the Governing Body and Representative Body of the Church in Wales. The *Western Mail* hailed the volume as having said everything that could possibly be worth saying about the Church in Wales – perhaps an ambiguous comment?

circumstances. They have pointed to the creation of two new dioceses – of Monmouth and of Swansea and Brecon. It set about raising funds to replace its lost endowments with vigour.[33] Yet there remained substantial doubt as to how far it had mentally adjusted itself to what disestablishment really entailed. Some of its leading figures continued to assert, and were to do so for decades, that bishops spent more time regretting their 'English' pasts than in welcoming the future. It perhaps did not help that Archbishop Edwards remained in post until 1934, by which date he had reached his 86th year. He himself confessed that he had dreaded the loss of unity. The dismemberment of the Church of England, as he put it, had for the Church in Wales 'severed the arteries through which the life of that Church pulsed'. It was, indeed, thankfully the case that the amputated part had demonstrated a passionate belief in the potentiality of independent life. Nevertheless, he remained convinced that a backward step had been taken: 'It was a lapse from a national to a racial ideal.'[34] However, his successor, Archbishop Charles Green of Bangor spoke thus at the Church Congress at Bournemouth in October 1935: 'You ask me, Is all well? I believe it is.' Such optimism from a product of Charterhouse and Oxford was not universally shared in all parts of Wales. Green was helpfully keen to point out that there was still free communication between England and Wales.[35] His biographer is right to observe that he 'never really faced up to the implications of disestablishment for the Church in Wales' and 'still wanted to retain what he regarded as "the rightful privileges of the Establishment"'.[36] In part this was, and remained, a matter of social assumption and convention. Disestablishment may have been accomplished by law but in 'neutral' social situations bishops and clergy still assumed (and were sometimes granted) a certain precedence.

There was no rush, in a small church, to innovate. Although the Church in Wales had the right to alter its worship and produce a new Prayer Book, it retained the 1662 *Book of Common Prayer*

[33] For an entertaining account of fund-raising as experienced at local level see D. Richards, *Honest Memories* (Llandybie, 1985), 55.

[34] Edwards, *Memories*, 328–31.

[35] A. J. Edwards, *Archbishop Green: His Life and Opinions* (Llandysul, 1986), 87–8.

[36] Edwards, *Archbishop Green*, 81.

'according to the use of the Church of England' until the 1950s.[37] A strong 'Catholic' emphasis to be found in parts of the Church seemed to rule out any engagement with 'Nonconformity'. It was, it seemed, simply a matter of waiting for its demise to occur and to 'win over' as many ministers as possible in the meantime. Frank Morgan, the able lay chief executive of the Church in Wales, reported to the Church and State Commission in the year of his death in service that the Free Churches in Wales, from his perspective were 'undoubtedly less aggressive than they were before the Disestablishment Act was passed'. It was noteworthy, he mentioned, 'that the number of Nonconformist ministers seeking Holy Orders has enormously increased, especially during the last five years'. They at least helped the Church in Wales to recover somewhat from a shortage of clergy in its first decade of independent existence. Some Church in Wales clergy addressed the annual English Presbyterian conference but no Welsh bishop did so before the conferences ended in 1938. Archbishop Green attacked the supporters of ecumenical gatherings with gusto and warned that if Church people 'found no difference in faith and practice between themselves and the divers denominations which were around them, then the sooner they dissolved their ecclesiastical polity and disappeared from the field, the better for themselves, and the better for Wales'.[38]

The strength of such opinions in part reflected a new concern – the apparent growth of Roman Catholicism – and the need to protect the Church in Wales from Roman dismissal of its catholicity. A Roman suggestion that Welsh cathedrals stood cold and empty until such time as they could be once more used for the purpose for which they were erected, was not well received. Another element was complicating the pre-1914 dichotomy between Church and Chapel. Roman Catholicism's pre-1914 role could be dismissed as marginal and 'foreign' and in some measure it remained so. However, the conversion of young men and women, indubitably Welsh, was another matter. The most notable was the writer Saunders Lewis, himself scion of a notable Nonconformist family. The issues they raised took debate and

---

[37] Price, *Church in Wales*, 21.
[38] Edwards, *Archbishop Green*, 83–4.

discussion into new regions, beyond the scope of 'Disestablishment' as it had been considered before 1914.

We may conclude this broad survey, therefore, by suggesting that 'Disestablishment' did not occasion a fundamental appraisal, in any ecclesiastical quarter, of what it meant for the Churches in their relation with either nation or State in Wales. Of course, the fact that 'nation' and 'State' were different complicated the picture. The institutional embodiments of Welsh nationality remained weak. Even if they had been capable of making a collective 'new beginning' in Wales they could still only do so in a political context in which Wales remained firmly within the structures of an undevolved British State. There might be disestablishment in Wales but there was not in England and the 'establishment' ethos of England still remained a potent influence on Welsh ecclesiastical life. 'Isolation' was not desirable. And, contrary to the hopes of those who supposed that disestablishment would enhance Wales as a 'Christian country', it would appear, over a longer perspective, that currently Wales has significantly smaller a 'Church community', defined as the proportion of people who have some kind of affinity to a Christian denomination, than any other nation within the United Kingdom, even it seems, than the 'pagan' English who featured in a certain kind of Welsh mythology.[39]

III

It is apparent at the end of the twentieth century, however, that the relationship between Church and State in both England and Scotland, apparently stable for many decades, will be caught up in the constitutional upheavals that have followed from the election of a Labour government in 1997. In Wales, also, after three-quarters of a century in which the Churches have related to the Welsh nation but also to an undevolved British State that position will change with the establishment of the National Assembly for Wales. While historians have become accustomed to asking in the

---

[39] D. P. Davies, *Against the Tide* (Llandysul, 1995), 6, notes that it is now an established fact that there are more Moslems than Methodists in Wales. He reflects on a situation in which 'Christianity – in its institutional form at any rate – is a matter of complete indifference to nine out of ten of the population of this so-called Christian country'. The UK cross-national picture is according to *Research Trends* as reported in the *Church Times*, 14 November 1997.

past, if inadequately, how the British State has accommodated different Church–State relations within its territory – on the assumption that the State itself was stable – that assumption can now no longer be maintained. The precise form that change will take is not yet clear, but it is evident that what 'establishment' signifies has once again returned to the political and ecclesiastical agenda, but in a new constitutional context for the British State itself.

Alec Cheyne will at once recognise that we live in very different circumstances from those appertaining in Scotland in 1843 at the time of the Disruption. Likewise, the contemporary mood in England is far removed from the expectations of the 728 delegates who assembled in the Crown and Anchor in the Strand in April 1844 to found the British Anti-State Church Association. The hopes of that Association (later the Liberation Society) were not fulfilled and indeed one study has recently endorsed the view that the campaign could never have succeeded. Perhaps only ten per cent of the population in mid-Victorian England actively favoured the disestablishment of the Church of England.[40]

It may be conceded at once that it is no easy matter, as successive enquiries have found, to define what constitutes 'establishment' and 'disestablishment', and therein lies a major difficulty. Successive enquiries into Church–State relations in England have clearly wrestled with this problem.[41] In his evidence to the Archbishops' Commission on the relations between Church and State in 1935 the Cambridge Congregationalist historian, Bernard Lord Manning, admitted that 'establishment of religion and of Churches is a matter of degree'. English Free Churchmen had for the most part ceased to believe that the problem of establishment was a

---

[40] Watts, *The Dissenters*, 548.

[41] The Commissioners, in their introduction to the 1970 Report on *Church and State*, indicated that they had tried, where possible, to avoid using the term 'establishment' because it was used in more than one sense. They also found the term 'Church as by law established' of little utility. It had been used to distinguish the legality of the national Church from other Churches which were then unlawful but that distinction had now disappeared. All Churches now had a basis in law. Yet, as they concluded, the legal situation of the Church of England was still different from that of other Churches – and went on to provide a historical explanation. *Church and State: Report of the Archbishops' Commission* (London, 1970), 1–2 and Appendix A.

perfectly simple one to be settled by the reiteration of a phrase like 'a Free Church in a Free State'. He instanced that as long as any kind of Christianity was taught in State schools, any part of Christianity upheld in State courts, or Christian institutions like Sunday and great feasts legally recognised, all Christian bodies were to a certain extent 'established'.[42] He was, of course, writing at a time when it was evident from developments both in the Soviet Union and in Germany that a State could refuse to give such recognition.

However, the combination of Erastianism with injustice to non-Christians, which Manning believed was 'the actual issue of Establishment in a modern State' – he found repulsive. While he accepted that public recognition of religion had many great advantages, they were not worth getting at that price. At the same time, he conceded, though reluctantly, that something which was rationally indefensible might yet serve a useful purpose in England if it offered a check on unrestrained episcopal government. Inasmuch as establishment curbed episcopacy he wished it well – as an Englishman as much as a Free Churchman. In all these matters, he suggested that in the long run public opinion ruled and it would be best if the whole Church, and not just the Free Churches, could say to anti-clericals and non-Christians that it owed nothing to them.[43] Such evidence, however, did not shake the Commission in its belief that the history of Church and nation in England was 'so closely intertwined that the separation could not be effected without injury to both of a kind impossible to forecast or to forestall'. Perhaps particularly mindful of the *Kirchenkampf* in the Germany of the day, it asserted that 'if England, by Disestablishment, should seem to become neutral in the fight between faith and unfaith in Christianity, that would be a calamity for our own people and, indeed, for the whole world'.[44]

The 'Scottish Solution' did indeed receive attention in the Commission's report. Indeed, perhaps a little optimistically, it was stated that the Church of Scotland Act, 1921, deserved 'the most careful study, not only of every member of the Church of England,

[42] *Church & State: Report of the Archbishops' Commission on the Relations between Church and State 1935*, ii, 79–80.
[43] *Church & State*, ii, 86–91.
[44] *Church & State*, i, 49.

but of every citizen'. Rehearsing a little of its antecedent history, and of the Scottish ecclesiastical union of 1929, the Commission concluded that the Act showed that complete spiritual freedom of the Church was not incompatible with establishment. The Crown in Parliament, for its part, had solemnly ratified the principles on which the Scottish settlement was explicitly based. While the history and conditions of the two countries and the two Churches were not the same and therefore the Scottish settlement could not be an exact model for what should be done in England, it could be inferred that the Crown in Parliament would concede to the Church of England what it had granted or confirmed to the Church of Scotland. What was right for the Church of Scotland could not be in principle wrong for the Church of England. Yet there were those who wondered (Bernard Lord Manning among them) whether the Church of Scotland was really 'established' at all – in their understanding of the term.

Whether or not this was the case, the 'Established Church' in Scotland took unto itself for many decades, through the Church and Nation Committee, a prominent role in pronouncing upon political and social issues, by turns contentious or accommodating, in the eyes of observers and commentators. This is not the place to examine its performance in detail. It is, however, pertinent to probe the basis on which this role was assumed and the complications which surrounded it. Was the voice of the Church of Scotland to be heard within the context of the British State because the Church of Scotland expressed the corporate faith of the Scottish nation? In what sense did it 'speak for Scotland'? The Church of Scotland was indeed 'national' in that it ministered to the Scottish people in every parish but that belied the fact that Scotland had long been an ecclesiastically-riven society. The Catholic presence, although still sometimes perceived, as we have noted, as an alien wedge, was indisputable and growing. It challenged the self-image of the Scots as a Protestant people. The complication which this presented necessarily had its consequences when the Kirk confronted the issue of self-government in Scotland.

Here a paradox seems apparent. The 'Established' voice which the Church of Scotland possessed stemmed in part at least from the lack of self-government in Scotland itself. The Church fulfilled a role as a major national institution, to some extent the embodiment of 'Scottishness', in the absence of a parliament. The

London-based press, on the rare occasions in which it took note of the proceedings of the General Assembly, would help readers by referring to it as 'Scotland's Parliament'. It was on this assumption that British cabinet ministers occasionally appeared before it, culminating in the address by Margaret Thatcher as Prime Minister in 1988. At the same time, however, strong, though never unanimous, support had been given, from the time of the Scottish Covenant movement onwards, by leading ministers to the campaign for a Scottish Parliament. The fluctuating fortunes of that campaign need no repetition here before, at length, we come to the present and its possibilities and disadvantages for an 'Established Church'.

In 1990 one writer expressed the view that in the event of the drive for self-government reaching a successful conclusion, the Church of Scotland might well 'emerge from its limbo-like existence to play a far from negligible role in helping Scottish civil society to adapt to shouldering new responsibilities'.[45] There have been a number of prominent churchmen, one might think, whose existence, where the cause of Scottish self-government is concerned, has been far from limbo-like. The creative, constructive and critical role which they have played is unlikely to fade away. The new political framework in Scotland offers many possibilities. However, perhaps to a degree not yet fully recognised, it also places a question mark over 'establishment' as it has been perceived within the Scotland-in-Britain constitutional structure which has functioned hitherto in the twentieth century. The presence of a real Parliament may well marginalise the make-believe Parliament which the General Assembly has been. A 'prophetic' role may become more complicated when the wielders of power in domestic matters are at hand rather than in distant London. And there is a further point. The existing nature of establishment may have been a necessary carrier of Scottish identity and accepted as such, if somewhat querulously, by non-Presbyterians and non-Christians, but with the creation of a Parliament its pretensions, long since somewhat bogus, now stand out as anomalous, even offensive, to other

[45] T. Gallagher, 'Scottish Protestantism and Politics: the Church Dimension in the Present Century', in G. Walker and T. Gallagher (eds), *Sermons and Battle Hymns: Protestant Popular Culture in Modern Scotland* (Edinburgh, 1990), 108.

Christians and to adherents of other faiths, the indifferent, or atheists. Insofar as the emphasis, in the structures of government in Scotland, are upon 'inclusiveness' and 'representativeness' an 'establishment' that caters for the reality of contemporary Christian Scotland looks likely to need urgent reformulation.

In this regard the interim 1998 publication of the Scottish Church Initiative for Union group breaks new ground. The outcome of talks between the Church of Scotland, the Scottish Episcopal Church, the United Reformed Church, the Congregational and Methodist Churches in Scotland, it reflects on thirty years of national and international consultations. It offers at least the possibility of new structures and assumptions which could overcome centuries of division. There is no prospect that it would be a union which could be joined at any early juncture by the Roman Catholic Church, although a Roman Catholic observer has been present during the discussions. While progress in creating a national Church council would need to take into account 'the status of the Church of Scotland as a national Church' the report also argues that it was important that 'the united Church would be constitutionally rooted in the Scotland of the present, where Scottishness is defined in terms of citizenship and the pluralist nature of the nation is accepted'. In commenting on the proposals the English-produced *Church Times* commented in April 1998 that with Scotland's constitution in the melting-pot, 'If the General Assembly and the presbyteries are willing to modify their unique status, an ecclesiastical revolution might indeed follow on the heels of secular devolution.'[46] Whether or not these particular proposals find favour, some new phase in Church–State relations in a devolved Scotland seems inescapable. Our interpretation of the sterility of post-disestablishment Wales leads one to hope that immobilism will not be repeated. It remains to be seen, after the dust has settled, whenever that will be, whether the result will still constitute some kind of 'Establishment' – and, no doubt, the elasticity of that word has already become plain enough in this chapter!

---

[46] *Church Times*, 3 April 1998: Of course, in all parts of Britain, all of these issues can no longer be considered simply from a Christian perspective and there is much to be gained from reflection on debates and discussions in the contemporary United States, as for example in C. E. Cochran, *Religion in Public and Private Life* (New York and London, 1995).

Chapter 11

Presbyterians and Catholics in Twentieth-Century Scotland

Stewart J. Brown

I

IN May 1923, a committee of the General Assembly of the national Church of Scotland issued a report on the subject of Irish immigration and the Education Act of 1918.[1] Appearing under the names of forty-two prominent Churchmen, the report opened with expressions of 'alarm and anxiety' over the 'incursion' into Scotland of a large Roman Catholic population from Ireland. This population, the committee claimed, was alien both in race and creed; its presence constituted a 'menace', with 'a very sinister meaning for the future of our race'.[2] These Catholics of Irish background diminished the moral tone of society by their intemperance, improvidence, Sabbath-breaking, and criminal behaviour. They enlarged the poor relief rolls, and filled state-supported hospitals and prisons – increasing the burden of taxation. They took employment from native Protestant Scots, forcing tens of thousands of young Scots – 'the flower of the nation' – to emigrate, and thus threatening the survival of a Scottish Protestant culture. 'Irish immigrants' were responsible for much of the industrial and social unrest in post-war Scotland. Further, encouraged by this flood of Irish Catholics, the Roman Catholic Church in Scotland had grown in confidence and had 'definitely committed herself to converting the Scottish nation'.

[1] 'Report of the Committee to Consider Overtures . . . on "Irish Immigration and the Education Act of 1918"', in *Reports of the Schemes of the Church of Scotland* (1923), 750–63.
[2] Ibid., 756.

The report concluded by dismissing the argument that 'Christ died for all' and 'we are all the children of One Heavenly Father'. It appealed instead to the duty of a national Church to preserve national racial purity. 'God', the committee insisted,

> placed the people of this world in families, and history, which is the narrative of His providence, tells us that when kingdoms are divided against themselves they cannot stand. The nations that are homogenous in Faith and ideas, that have maintained unity of race, have ever been the most prosperous, and to them the Almighty had committed the highest tasks, and has granted the largest measure of success in achieving them.[3]

In short, God had willed the separation and the purity of the races, and far from being a virtue, toleration of Catholics of Irish background was a sin against the covenant, which would arouse God's righteous anger and cause him to withdraw his favour from Scotland. The Church of Scotland was called to lead the Scottish nation in 'taking whatever steps may be necessary' to eliminate the Irish Catholic menace.[4] Speaking in support of the report in the General Assembly, one elder argued that the West of Scotland was 'so permeated by foreign nationalities' that the democratic processes there were no longer valid, while a minister complained that the trade unions and labour organisations were controlled by Irish Catholics. The General Assembly accepted the report with gratitude and instructed the standing Church and Nation Committee, created four years earlier, to initiate action for the protection of Scottish nationality. [5]

This action marked the beginning of a national campaign by the Presbyterian Church of Scotland intended to marginalise and reduce the Roman Catholic population in Scotland – a campaign which was conducted for the next fifteen years and which involved many leaders in the national Church. In this campaign, Church of Scotland leaders and committees worked to incite popular hostility towards Catholics of Irish background and to win parliamentary support for a programme that would include the disenfranchisement and the forced expatriation of much of the Catholic population in Scotland to the Irish Free State. The

---

[3] Ibid., 761–2.
[4] Ibid., 756.
[5] *Glasgow Herald*, 30 May 1923.

campaign was overtly sectarian and racist in its language, identifying Catholicism as alien to Scotland and asserting that the Scottish and Irish peoples were two distinct races, that should be kept separate. The campaign was not directed toward the conversion or assimilation of the Catholic population in Scotland, but rather toward isolating and driving off that population. It contributed to an atmosphere of ethnic tension, and, in the summer of 1935, to mob violence directed against Catholics in Edinburgh. In time, however, the campaign also forced Presbyterians in Scotland to recognise the darker side of national religion and this contributed to fundamental changes in Presbyterian attitudes toward Catholics.

This chapter will explore the relations of Presbyterians and Catholics in Scotland during the twentieth century, giving particular attention to the changing attitudes in the Presbyterian Church of Scotland, the Established Church in Scotland, toward the Catholic population in Scotland. It will show how the Church of Scotland moved from a position of confrontation, viewing the Catholic Church as a 'menace', to one of co-operation and respect. There is a considerable literature on the growth and assimilation of the Catholic community in Scotland, including work by John McCaffrey, Tom Gallagher, Bernard Aspinwall, Steve Bruce and Owen Dudley Edwards.[6] Recently, the issue of sectarianism has been explored in a volume, *Scotland's Shame*, prompted by a controversial lecture by the Scottish composer, James Macmillan, and edited by the historian, Tom Devine.[7] This chapter will focus on the responses of the Presbyterian Church of Scotland to the challenge posed by an increasingly confident Catholic community in Scotland.

[6] J. F. McCaffrey, 'Roman Catholics in Scotland in the 19th and 20th Centuries', *Records of the Scottish Church History Society*, xxi (1983), 275–300; T. Gallagher, *Glasgow: The Uneasy Peace. Religious Tension in Modern Scotland* (Manchester, 1987); S. Bruce, *No Pope of Rome: Militant Protestantism in Modern Scotland* (Edinburgh, 1985); O. D. Edwards, 'The Catholic Press in Scotland since the Restoration of the Hierarchy', *Innes Review*, xxix (1978), 156–82; I. Maver, 'The Catholic Community', in T. M. Devine and R. J. Finlay (eds), *Scotland in the Twentieth Century* (Edinburgh, 1996), 269–84; R. Boyle and P. Lynch (eds), *Out of the Ghetto? The Catholic Community in Modern Scotland* (Edinburgh, 1998).

[7] T. M. Devine (ed.), *Scotland's Shame? Bigotry and Sectarianism in Modern Scotland* (Edinburgh, 2000).

II

In the early years of the twentieth century, Scotland was an overwhelmingly Protestant, and more particularly a Presbyterian, nation. The Presbyterian Church of Scotland was the Established Church, which had emerged at the Scottish Reformation and was modelled on the social and ecclesiastical system of Calvin's Geneva. From its beginnings, the Presbyterian Church of Scotland had embraced the idea of the 'godly commonwealth', in which Church and State would co-operate to establish and preserve a godly social order. Scotland was divided territorially into some 1,000 parishes, and placed under the supervision of an hierarchical system of ecclesiastical courts – parish kirk sessions, presbyteries, synods and General Assembly – which had responsibility for ensuring religious observances as well as providing education, poor relief and moral discipline. Presbyterianism had played a major role in defining the national identity of early modern Scotland, which included a strict, Bible-based piety, a theology rooted in Augustine and Calvin, a communal culture based in the parish, and a rejection of episcopalian Church government. The seventeenth-century Covenants, by which the nation had covenanted together under God for the defence of the Presbyterian Church and their ancient liberties, remained potent national symbols.

In the course of the nineteenth century, the Presbyterian ideal of the godly commonwealth had waned – the victim of divisions in the national Church of Scotland, of the dislocations of the parish system resulting from rapid industrialisation and urbanisation, and of new, secular attractions, including popular entertainment and professional sport. Presbyterian leaders had grown concerned over the waning social influence and authority of Presbyterianism, and their anxieties increased with the growth of the labour movement and the emergence of a serious socialist alternative to traditional Presbyterian social teachings after about 1890. This had contributed to a late-nineteenth-century movement to revive the social authority of Presbyterianism. The movement included a commitment to the social gospel, with Church leaders calling for improved housing, a reduction of social inequality, greater understanding between social classes and better relations between management and labour. It also included an effort to heal the schisms in Scottish Presbyterianism and reunite the branches of the Presbyterian Church. In 1900, the two largest non-Established Presbyterian Churches – the Free Church and the United Presbyterian Church – combined to form the United Free Church. Then in 1908, the national Church of Scotland and the United Free Church began formal negotiations for a union which promised to restore the national Presbyterian Church of Scotland to its former authority in national life.

The effort to restore the influence and authority of a national Presbyterianism led to a confrontation with the Catholic community in Scotland. That Catholic community had experienced a significant growth in late-nineteenth-century Scotland, especially in the Lowland central belt, where industrialisation had attracted tens of thousands of migrants from Ireland to meet the pressing need for cheap, unskilled and semi-skilled labour. While many of these Irish migrants were Protestant, the large majority, perhaps three-quarters, were Catholic. Impoverished and ill-educated, the Irish migrants had generally encountered hostility, not only from the Presbyterian majority, but also from the small body of indigenous Scottish Catholics that had survived centuries of pressure to conform to Protestantism. In response to this nativist hostility, Irish Catholic migrant communities in Scotland had tended to turn inward, developing their own communal welfare provision and preserving a distinct identity. In politics, their attention remained focused on Ireland; they supported the Irish home rule movement and the Liberal party because of its commitment to Irish home rule after 1886. The novels of Patrick MacGill, such as the *Children of the Dead End* (1914) and *The Rat-Pit* (1915), convey the isolation, hostility and exploitation that many Irish Catholic migrant labourers experienced in Presbyterian Scotland.[8]

There was, however, a perceptible change in attitudes within the Catholic community in Scotland after 1900 – the beginning of the century brought a new communal confidence and assertiveness among Catholics. In 1900 there were about 450,000 Catholics in Scotland, representing about ten per cent of the Scottish

---

[8] See P. Reilly, 'Catholics and Scottish Literature 1878–1978', in D. McRoberts (ed.), *Modern Scottish Catholicism 1878–1978* (Glasgow, 1979), 183–203.

population. About 200,000 of these were Irish-born.[9] Significantly, Catholics were heavily concentrated in the West of Scotland, where their numbers gave them a political weight, especially following the expansion of the franchise among working-class males in 1884. By 1900, many Catholic families of Irish background had been in Scotland for a generation or longer, and they increasingly perceived themselves as Scottish as well as Irish, and took an active interest in Scottish politics. The growth of the labour movement in Scotland drew many of these 'Scoto-Irish' Catholics to trade union activity and labour politics, and Catholics like John Wheatley and Patrick Dolan rose to positions of leadership in the Glasgow labour movement.[10] The Catholic Church also strengthened its position in Scotland. The territorial hierarchy in Scotland had been restored in 1878. In the last three decades of the nineteenth century, the number of priests in the Glasgow archdiocese increased from 74 to 234, there was considerable new building of churches and schools, and the Catholic community was served by a growing number of Catholic benefit associations.[11]

While there were sectarian tensions between the Catholic and Presbyterian communities, especially in the West of Scotland, those tensions were muted in the early years of the twentieth century. This is not to say all was peace and harmony. But the economy was reasonably healthy and Catholic labour was vital to the strength of Scottish industry. Presbyterian Church leaders were more focused on their own movements for Presbyterian Church reunion and on securing social improvements through the social gospel, than on conversionist activity among Catholics in Scotland. The increasing attention to Scottish historical studies, associated with the establishment of new chairs of Scottish history and the founding of the *Scottish Historical Review* in 1903, encouraged interest in early Christian and medieval Scotland and the contributions of the pre-Reformation Church to shaping Scottish national identity. With the beginning of the First World War in 1914, Catholic bishops and priests in Scotland joined with

[9] Maver, 'The Catholic Community', 271; McCaffrey, 'Roman Catholics in Scotland in the 19th and 20th Centuries', 277.

[10] J. F. McCaffrey, 'Politics and the Catholic Community since 1878', in McRoberts (ed.), *Modern Scottish Catholicism*, 140–55.

[11] Maver, 'The Catholic Community', 273.

Presbyterian ministers in publicly supporting the British war effort, and tens of thousands of Scottish Catholics enlisted in the British armed forces. Soon the pages of the Catholic *Glasgow Observer* were filled with the names of Catholic volunteers dying on the Western Front, and these deaths signalled the degree to which the Catholic community in Scotland had become assimilated into the Scottish, and indeed, the British nation.

The sense of acceptance of the Catholic community into national life found expression near the end of the war, with the Education Act of 1918 for Scotland, which brought denominational schools, especially Roman Catholic schools, into the rate-supported system of national education. Catholic and other denominational schools were able to provide religious instruction and Catholic clergy continued to exercise considerable control over the general curriculum. Catholics, noted Robert Munro, Secretary of State for Scotland, in introducing the bill for its second reading in the Commons, now represented one-seventh of the school age population of Scotland, and in some districts a third. 'It is clearly not in the national interest', he insisted, 'that such a proportion of the population in Scotland should be left out of account in our endeavour to raise the general level of education for the mass of the people.'[12] For the British State, the Catholics of Scotland were an integral part of Scottish national life, and should not be left out of the new society which would be constructed in the post-war era.

III

Not everyone in Scotland, however, shared this commitment. While liberal Presbyterians had welcomed the Education Act of 1918, other Presbyterians had bitterly opposed it, and a Committee of the General Assembly lobbied for the exclusion of members of religious orders from teaching in State-supported schools. In June 1918, *Life & Work*, the magazine of the Church of Scotland, denounced the Roman Catholic Church as 'the enemy of Great Britain and the friend, more or less avowed, of Germany', and as responsible for numerous 'outrages [against] international right

[12] R. Munro, *Looking Back: Fugitive Writings and Sayings* (London, n.d.), 232–3.

and human liberty since the beginning of the war'.[13] The implication was clear: regardless of the sacrifices of thousands of young Scottish Catholics, the Catholic Church was an enemy within, an alien and potentially treacherous presence. In the last two years of the war, meanwhile, the two main Presbyterian Churches both pledged themselves to programmes of sweeping social reconstruction aimed at achieving a Christian commonwealth; a Christian social ethic would be reflected in improved standards of living, greater social equality and increased co-operation between labour and management. The Presbyterian Churches held conferences on housing and industrial organisation, published reports and sought to co-operate closely with the government on reconstruction. Early in 1919, they co-sponsored a 'National Mission of Rededication', calling for the recognition of Christ's supremacy in all spheres of national life. At the General Assembly of the Church of Scotland in May 1919, the Moderator, Professor W. P. Paterson of Edinburgh University, summoned the Scottish nation to 'covenant together' in shared commitment to ensure that the sacrifices of the war would lead to the achievement of a Protestant commonwealth in Scotland.[14] At the same time, they revived the negotiations for Presbyterian Church union.

The hopes of social reconstruction, however, were soon frustrated in the grim post-war environment. The Conservative-dominated Coalition government, elected in late 1918, withdrew from many of the promises of State-supported social reconstruction and began dismantling war-time economic controls, creating widespread social dislocation and misery.[15] The economy was in serious difficulties, weakened by years of war and the loss of markets; the industrial base in the West of Scotland faced collapse, at the same time as hundreds of thousands of men were demobilised and desperate for work. There was industrial and political unrest.

[13] 'The Cloven Foot once More', *Life & Work* (June 1918), 84.

[14] W. P. Paterson, *Recent History and the Call to Brotherhood: Address delivered at the Close of the General Assembly, May 29, 1919* (Edinburgh, 1919).

[15] R. H. Tawney, 'The Abolition of Economic Controls, 1918–1921', *Economic History Review*, xiii (1943), 1–30; P. Abrams, 'The Failure of Social Reform, 1918–1920', *Past and Present*, 24 (1963), 43–64; K. O. Morgan, *Consensus and Disunity: The Lloyd George Coalition Government 1918–1922* (Oxford, 1979), 88–105.

By the early 1920s, tens of thousands of Scots were leaving the country for the United States or the colonies. The Liberal party had been shattered during the war, and politics increasingly became divided along the fault lines of social class, between a Conservative or Unionist party, representing the propertied classes, and the Labour party, representing the propertiless. With the creation of the Irish Free State in 1922, Catholics in Scotland shifted their support from the Liberal party, the party of Irish home rule, to the Labour party. Benefiting from Catholic support, Labour achieved its major breakthrough in Scottish politics in the general election of November 1922, winning twenty-nine of Scotland's seventy-four seats, including ten of the fifteen Glasgow area seats. The 'Clydeside' MPs sent down to Westminster soon established a reputation for their uncompromising socialism. The Russian Revolution and Civil War raised fears among the propertied classes of revolutionary upheaval in Britain. The formation of the Free State in 1922 created fears for the future of the Empire and bitter resentments among many Scots, who had viewed the Irish nationalist struggle from the Easter Rising of 1916 as a treacherous attack on the United Kingdom in its time of trial. Presbyterian leaders found the post-war tensions and unrest especially difficult. This was not what had been expected when Field Marshal Douglas Haig, an elder of the Church of Scotland, had visited the General Assembly in 1919 and received a hero's welcome, or when the Moderator of the General Assembly of 1919 had called on the nation to convenant together in building the new social order. The war-time sacrifices had led to neither a renewal of the covenant nor a reconstruction of society.

Amid this post-war disillusionment and frustration, many within the Presbyterian Churches in Scotland turned upon the Catholic population of Irish ethnic background as an evil presence that was somehow responsible for the failures of post-war reconstruction.[16] In May 1922, the General Assembly of the Church of Scotland received overtures from the Synod of Glasgow and Ayr and the Presbytery of Glasgow, calling on the Church to take action against both Catholics of Irish background living in the West of

---

[16] For a more detailed account of the Presbyterian campaign, see S. J. Brown, '"Outside the Covenant": The Scottish Presbyterian Churches and Irish Immigration, 1922–1938', *Innes Review*, xlii (1991), 19–45.

Scotland and the Education Act of 1918. The Assembly agreed to appoint a special committee of prominent Church ministers and elders to explore the problem, and on receiving that committee's notorious report, the General Assembly of 1923 remitted the matter of 'Irish immigration' to the Church and Nation Committee, with instructions to organise a Church-led national campaign against the 'menace'. A permanent sub-committee on Irish immigration was set up, and began collecting statistics. The other major Presbyterian denominations in Scotland, the United Free Church and the Free Church, were drawn into the campaign, and a so-called 'Joint Committee of the Scottish Churches' was created: Presbyterian unity would be forged in reviving the Protestant commonwealth against the Catholic 'Other'. In late 1925, John White, co-convener of the Church and Nation Committee and Moderator of the General Assembly of the Church of Scotland, wrote to Sir John Gilmour, the Scottish Secretary, on behalf of the Church. The Church's investigations, he claimed, had revealed that Irish immigrants were flooding into Scotland at a rate of 9,000 per year, that Irish foremen controlled many workplaces and employed only 'Irish' Catholics, and that while 'Irish' Catholics accounted for only 25% of the population of Glasgow, they consumed over 70% of public and private relief funds. He asserted that a 'superior race' was being supplanted in Scotland by an 'inferior race'.[17] A deputation of the 'Joint Committee' met with the Scottish Secretary in late 1926 to demand legislation aimed at curbing Irish immigration, with John White insisting on this occasion that the Presbyterian Churches were pressing the issue 'entirely as a racial and not as a religious question'.[18] Nonetheless, the deputation then proceeded to protest against the government's Catholic Relief Bill, which would legalise Catholic outdoor processions under certain conditions; for the deputation, it made no difference whether these processions were conducted by Catholics of the Scottish or Irish 'race'.

While Presbyterian Church committees gathered statistics and pressed the government for legislation, the Scottish Reformation Society, the Scottish Protestant League, Orange Lodges and other

---

[17] Cited in *Reports on the Schemes of the Church of Scotland* (1926), 619–23.
[18] *The Scotsman*, 6 November 1926.

associations organised mass meetings in support of the Church's initiative in Scottish towns and cities. These meetings employed inflammatory language, aimed at inciting popular resentment against Scoto-Irish Catholics. At a meeting in Paisley in October 1926, for example, the Rev. Duncan Cameron, minister of Kilsyth and a leading member of the Church of Scotland's sub-committee on Irish Immigration, exclaimed that in Catholics of Irish background, native Scots 'were faced with a menace more insidious by far, and more formidable, than the menace of the German Empire and his multitudinous legions'. True Scots, he maintained, could not be expected to live alongside Catholics of Irish extraction, people whom he described as 'weeds' – presumably fit only to be uprooted and destroyed.[19] At another meeting late in 1927, Cameron predicted that 'a racial and religious struggle was a certain consequence of the immense growth of the Irish population in Scotland'.[20] At a meeting in 1928, John White maintained that the Presbyterian campaign was being conducted on the 'high moral ground' of protecting the Scottish race from being 'corrupted by the introduction of a horde of Irish immigrants'.[21]

The Presbyterian 'Joint Committee' defined its demands for legislation to the government in July 1928. They insisted that immigration from the Irish Free State into Scotland must be severely restricted, that all Irish-born persons who received welfare assistance, or who had been convicted of a crime, should be deported to the Free State, that the right to vote of Irish-born persons should be restricted, and that preference should be given to native Scots in all public works projects and government employment. The 'Joint Committee' claimed that it had the support of 80% of the Scottish population.[22] The Presbyterian Churches placed increasing pressure on the government over the coming year. The Church of Scotland and United Free Church were

[19] *Paisley Daily Express*, 27 October 1926.

[20] *Glasgow Herald*, 8 December 1927.

[21] 'Notes for Speeches' [1928], John White Papers, New College Library, Edinburgh, 'Irish Immigration' box.

[22] 'Note of Proceedings at a Deputation to the Home Secretary and the Secretary of State for Scotland from the Church of Scotland, the United Free Church and the Free Church, 19 July 1928, Scottish Records Office, Edinburgh, HH.1.551; Cabinet Memorandum, 1928, SRO, HH.1.55; *Glasgow Herald*, 20 July 1928.

proceeding to the final stages of the Presbyterian reunion, which was to be celebrated in 1929. The hope of John White and other Presbyterian leaders was that they would combine Presbyterian Church reunion with a public announcement that, in response to the Presbyterian initiative, the government had agreed to sponsor a programme of legislation aimed at reducing the Catholic population of Irish ethnic background. This would demonstrate the power and influence of the reunited national Church, as the defender of both Scottish racial purity and the idea of the covenanted Protestant nation.

White and his fellow Presbyterian Church leaders, however, were disappointed in their demand for legislation. The Scottish Office proved unsupportive. In fact, the Scottish Office had begun collecting statistics in 1923, and by late 1926 those enquiries had revealed that the Presbyterian claims about Irish immigration were greatly exaggerated. The percentage of Irish-born persons in Scotland had declined from 6.18% in 1871 to 3.26% in 1921. Statistics from steamship companies revealed that migration from Ireland to Scotland in the mid-1920s was about 1,600 a year, and not 9,000 a year as the Presbyterian Churches claimed. The numbers of Irish-born persons on the relief rolls had fallen from 11.9% in 1907 to 7.6% in 1927, and Irish-born persons represented only 7.3% of those employed in public works in 1927.[23] The statistics demonstrated that Irish migration to Scotland had fallen off sharply following the collapse of Scottish industries in the post-war years and that Scottish welfare provision was hardly so generous as to attract migrants into the country. The Scottish Office frankly informed a Presbyterian deputation in July 1928 that government statistics did not support the Presbyterian claims. These government statistics were confirmed by statistics collected through an independent enquiry conducted by the Glasgow Herald newspaper and published as a series of five articles in March 1929, in the lead-up to the Presbyterian reunion of 1929.[24]

Catholics, meanwhile, were not shy about denouncing the Presbyterian campaign as based on both bigotry and dubious ideas

[23] Cabinet Memorandum, 1928, SRO, HH.1.55; Scottish Board of Health Memorandum, 3 March 1926, SRO, HH.1.541.

[24] 'The Irish in Scotland: An Inquiry into the Facts', Glasgow Herald, 20, 21, 22, 23, 25 March 1929.

about racial purity. One correspondent in the *Glasgow Herald* in July 1928 noted the recent death of the actress, Ellen Terry, who had been born to an Irish father and Scottish mother. Surely her illustrious career was an eloquent testimony against those who would argue that 'mixed marriages' served to pollute racial purity.[25] Others called attention to the large numbers of Scoto-Irish Catholics who had fought and died for Britain during the Great War. The Catholic hierarchy, on the whole, maintained a dignified silence on the Presbyterian campaign, which was probably the most eloquent response possible.

The Presbyterian Church reunion was finally achieved in October 1929. The formidable John White, architect of Church union and leader of the campaign against Irish Catholic immigration, became the first Moderator of the General Assembly of the reunited Church of Scotland. For Presbyterian leaders, the events of 1929 had restored the unity of Scotland's national Church, and they looked confidently for the restoration of the influence and authority of that national Church over the Scottish people. But in one sense the triumph had not been complete, for Church reunion in 1929 had not been accompanied by the announcement of co-operation of Church and State for the reduction of Scotland's large Catholic minority. The reunited national Church had not fulfilled its self-appointed task as the guardian of Scottish racial nationalism against the 'Irish' Catholics.

The campaign of the 1920s had represented a significant change in Presbyterian attitudes toward the Catholic population in Scotland. In the nineteenth century, Presbyterian home missionaries had frequently endeavoured to convert Irish Catholic migrants to a Presbyterian faith, which they regarded as more scriptural and more rational. In the 1920s, however, the Presbyterian Churches showed no conversionist zeal; rather, they sought to marginalise the Catholic community, to define them as alien in race and creed, and render them vulnerable – to drive them off rather than convert and assimilate them. Many Presbyterians no doubt believed that the 'Irish' Catholics were responsible for most of Scotland's post-war difficulties. Despite British victory in the war, Scotland experienced industrial decline, social unrest, mass emigration and rapid change in moral behaviour. It was all too easy for some to

[25] *Glasgow Herald*, 25 July 1928.

make scapegoats of the Catholic minority, and to believe that if only this minority could be isolated and driven off, national unity and harmony could be restored, along with a common religious faith. Such notions were of course affecting other countries and other Churches in Europe at this time.

The Presbyterian campaign may well have been a response to the extent to which Catholics in Scotland were being assimilated into national life. The campaign was steeped in a fear that Scotland was losing its Presbyterian national identity. Through their involvement in Labour politics and trade unions – and following the passing of the Education Act of 1918 and the Catholic Relief Act of 1926 – Catholics in Scotland were becoming more confident, more assertive and more active in Scottish politics and cultural life. By raising the outcry against 'Irish immigration', Presbyterian Church leaders evidently hoped to halt and reverse this process of Catholic assimilation into Scottish life, by portraying Catholics as 'Irish' and a 'foreign element', which because of their 'race' could never be assimilated.

IV

Despite the government's refusal to announce legislation against the 'Irish menace' in 1929, the year of Presbyterian reunion, the newly united Church of Scotland continued its campaign against the 'Irish' Catholics. John White, the first Moderator of the General Assembly of the united Church, proclaimed in February 1930 that combating the 'menace' of Irish immigration and Catholicism would remain a priority for the national Church.[26] Church leaders and committees spread reports that Irish Catholics were controlling employment at public works projects, and they called on Scottish employers to take on only native Scots. In 1931, as it grew clear that Irish immigration had virtually ceased with the economic slump, the Presbyterian Church of Scotland embarked on a new initiative. In response to a set of proposals agreed at a public meeting held in Edinburgh, the General Assembly formed a new standing committee, the 'Church Interests Committee', which was charged to preserve the Scottish Protestant heritage. Along with

---

[26] 'Spread of Romanism in Scotland. Moderator's Call to the Church', *Glasgow Herald*, 26 February 1930; see also *Glasgow Herald*, 21 January 1930.

the campaign against Irish immigration and the Education Act of 1918, the Church Interests Committee was also to carry on a propaganda campaign against the Catholic Church. It began by conducting an enquiry into the numbers and racial composition of all Catholics residing in Scotland. In 1933, it advocated Scottish Presbyterian affiliation with the 'International League for the Defence and Furtherance of Protestantism', a recently-formed Berlin-based association which combined both anti-Catholicism and anti-Semitism in its literature.

Nevertheless, by the mid-1930s wider Presbyterian support for the anti-Catholic campaign was waning. It was becoming unclear what the Presbyterian campaign could hope to achieve. The government was not prepared to legislate against Irish migration to Scotland or to rescind the Education Act of 1918. In his *History of the Church in Scotland 1875–1929* (1933), the Presbyterian historian, J. R. Fleming, lamented the presence of Catholics of Irish background, 'an alien and unmixable element [that] has altered things for the worse'. Nonetheless, he acknowledged, 'it does not seem likely that any agitation for the disenfranchisement or repatriation of Irish immigrants will be successful'.[27] Whatever their origins, Catholics were becoming rooted in Scotland. They were benefiting from the improved educational opportunities. While in 1919 only 8.5% of the Catholic school population went on to some form of post-elementary education, by 1939 that proportion had increased to over 13%.[28] In 1931, the writer and Catholic convert, Compton Mackenzie, was elected Rector of Glasgow University on a Scottish nationalist platform. By the mid-1930s, moreover, the international situation was growing ominous, with the consolidation of Fascism in Italy, Stalinist Communism in Russia and Nazism in Germany. Some suggested that the day might soon come when all Christian Churches would have to stand together against a 'sheer paganism not only beyond the Rhine but in their own midst'.[29]

[27] J. R. Fleming, *History of the Church in Scotland 1875–1929* (Edinburgh, 1933), 150.

[28] McCaffrey, 'Roman Catholics in Scotland in the 19th and 20th Centuries', 298.

[29] *Proceedings and Debates of the General Assembly of the Church of Scotland* (1935), 409–13.

Events in Edinburgh in the spring and summer of 1935 further undermined the Presbyterian anti-Catholic campaign, by demonstrating where such activities could lead. In April 1935, a militant, Edinburgh-based anti-Catholic association, Protestant Action, under the leadership of John Cormack, gathered a mob of 10,000 to disrupt a civic reception hosted by the Edinburgh City Council in honour of the Catholic Young Men's Association. In June, Cormack's organisation led a mob attack on another civic reception, this time in honour of the Australian prime minister, who was a Roman Catholic. Far worse violence followed later in June, when Protestant Action orchestrated mob attacks on the Catholic Eucharistic Congress being held in Edinburgh. Over two days, thousands of Protestant Action supporters attacked the Congress, fought with mounted police, and stoned coaches filled with Catholic women and children. Throughout the summer, gangs of thugs attacked Catholics in the streets, while Catholic parishioners mounted all-night vigils to protect their churches from arson.[30] While no Presbyterian clergymen were directly involved in the anti-Catholic rioting in Edinburgh, it was clear that the Presbyterian campaign since 1922 had contributed to the feeling among many Protestants that racist and sectarian violence was acceptable Christian behaviour.

In the aftermath of the violence in 1935, the Church of Scotland gradually brought its campaign against the Scoto-Irish Catholics to an end. The anti-Catholic Church Interests Committee was dissolved in 1937, and its work remitted back to the Church and Nation Committee. Although a few stalwarts endeavoured to keep the campaign alive in the later 1930s, they found dwindling interest in the Church, especially among younger ministers and lay members, who were more concerned over issues of social justice at home, and Fascism and Nazism on the Continent, than with struggles for ecclesiastical dominance. Younger Scottish Presbyterian leaders, including John Baillie and George MacLeod, were active in the Oxford Faith and Order Conference on 'Church, Community and State', which marked a major advance both in

---

[30] T. Gallagher, *Edinburgh Divided: John Cormack and No Popery in the 1930s* (Edinburgh, 1987), 35–61; *The Scotsman*, 27 June 1935; see also T. Gallagher, 'Protestant Extremism in Urban Scotland 1930–1939', *Scottish Historical Review*, lxiv (1985), 143–67.

the ecumenical movement and in the call on the Churches to work for the elimination of oppression and racism at the international level.[31] This was far from the ethos of the Presbyterian campaign against 'Irish immigration'. In 1938, George Macleod's formation of the Iona Community – with its aims of restoring the monastic buildings on Iona and conducting a vigorous home mission in the industrial cities – represented a conscious effort to connect a socially active Reformed Church with the traditions of early Scottish Christianity. At the local level, moreover, friendships between Presbyterian ministers and Catholic priests, could act as solvents to the walls separating the communities. In his memoir, the Church of Scotland minister, Harry Whitley, later minister of St Giles, Edinburgh, recalled how in his early ministry in the 1930s in Newark, near Port Glasgow, he had developed a friendship with the local Catholic priest, the Irish-born Fr Simon Keane. Their shared good humour and abiding humanity overcame their denominational differences. Whitley recalled being called by the police inspector one Saturday night, and asked to collect Fr Keane and try to break up a mêlée between Protestant and Catholic rival mobs. 'Five minutes later', Whitley wrote,

> we were striding side by side towards a mob of two or three hundred men – there was a no-man's-land of the Glen Burn between them. I was scared. Father Simon had a strong walking-stick in his hand and he showed not a trace of fear. 'Come on', he said, 'we'll deal with my flock first.' Right in among them he went, flailing right and left with his stick and cursing them in the broadest Irish imaginable. In next to no time they began to scatter. Some faces he recognized, and his powerful voice called out: 'Go on, Paddy, get home, you scoundrel. I've brought the bloody minister to scare you if this stick doesn't.' One side of the road was cleared. Then we moved to the other. Beside me he whispered, 'Perhaps you should try a word of prayer.' But there was no need – like sheep they scattered.

The vision of minister and priest working together to halt sectarian and ethnic violence had its effect. 'There was never', Whitley added, 'to be another riot in the Glen.'[32]

[31] J. H. Oldham (ed.), *The Churches Survey their Task: the Report of the Conference at Oxford, July 1937, on Church, Community and State* (London, 1937); K. Clements, *Faith on the Frontier: A Life of J. H. Oldham* (Edinburgh, 1999), 307–31.

[32] H. C. Whitley, *Laughter in Heaven* (London, 1962), 48–9.

With the outbreak of the Second World War in 1939, ecclesiastical rivalries were subsumed under the larger cause of defeating Nazism and Fascism. Patrick Dolan, the activist war-time Lord Provost of Glasgow, was a Catholic and gained broad support for his leadership. There was co-operation and mutual respect among Presbyterian and Roman Catholic chaplains among the troops.[33] The novel, *All Glorious Within*, published in 1944 by the Scottish Catholic writer, Bruce Marshall, captured the growing acceptance of the Catholic Church in early twentieth-century Scotland, with the shared experiences of the First and Second World Wars helping to break down prejudices. In the final scene, the formerly bitter anti-Catholic Councillor Thompson, chairman of the 'Protestant Action Society', was found among the mourners at the bedside of the dying Father Smith following the blitz that destroyed the Catholic Cathedral.[34] During the war, the Church of Scotland's Commission on God's Will in the Present Crisis, under the convenorship of John Baillie, redefined the role of the national Church in Scottish society, emphasising its responsibilities within an open society, and calling for an end to claims by the national Church to exercise social authority. After the war, attention focused instead on the ideological struggle with an atheistic Communism in Russia and Eastern Europe, and all religious denominations in Scotland experienced a revival in the post-war years.

V

The post-war years brought a gradual reorientation, though not, to be sure, without tensions, in relations between the Presbyterian and Catholic communities in Scotland. The inter-war Presbyterian effort to reassert its former social authority, revive the idea of the covenanted commonwealth, and marginalise the Catholic community, had failed, and the Church of Scotland now had to adjust to a role in an increasingly pluralistic society. There was a final effort to revive the confrontation with the Catholic Church in Scotland. In May 1951, a few months before the death of the still formidable John White, the General Assembly instructed the Church and Nation Committee to consider again the growth of Roman Catholicism and its implications. The Committee reported

[33] Ibid., 105; C. L. Warr, *The Glimmering Landscape* (London, 1960), 240.
[34] B. Marshall, *All Glorious Within* (London, 1944).

to the Assembly of 1952, expressing alarm and dismay over the growth of Catholicism, and attempting to portray Catholics as an alien presence. 'In Scotland', it observed, 'the Roman Catholic Church forms a compact community largely of alien origin with interests of its own. Its policy is to keep its people as far as possible apart from the general community, the better to serve those interests.' While the Committee recognised the right of a 'minority' to exist in a 'free democratic society', it also maintained that 'the belief that the Roman Church is coming to exercise an undue influence over public life is widespread and is undoubtedly causing uneasiness even to many who shrink from giving public expression to it'. How 'undue influence' was to be defined, or how the Committee was so certain of the views of those who did not give 'public expression' of their views, was not clarified. The Committee cited the work of an American journalist, Paul Blanshard, who argued that Roman Catholicism was not adaptable to liberal society, and it raised the old song that Scotland's 'Protestant heritage' was 'being definitely menaced'. But apart from reminding Presbyterians of their 'duty' to confront Catholicism and defend the 'native Scottish element', the Committee recommended no further action.[35] There was, in truth, little that the Church of Scotland could do, and the conservative authors of this report seem to have recognised this.

The Catholic community, as the Church and Nation Committee bitterly observed, was increasingly confident in the post-war years. Catholics were taking advantage of the educational opportunities introduced after the war, including the new comprehensive high schools and the university grants system. For the first time, Catholics began entering the professions in substantial numbers. The Catholic descendants of Irish migrants, moreover, became ever more assimilated into Scottish national life. Gordon Gray, consecrated Catholic Archbishop of Edinburgh and St Andrews in 1950, was committed to emphasising the Scottish character of the Catholic Church in Scotland. He banned, for example, the sale of *The Irish Weekly*, a magazine directed to Irish immigrants, at the back of churches in his archdioceses.[36] The formation of the

[35] 'Church Interests. The Growth of Roman Catholicism', *Reports to the General Assembly of the Church of Scotland* (1952), 328–30.
[36] Gallagher, *Glasgow: The Uneasy Peace*, 235.

Scottish Catholic Historical Association in 1949, and the beginning of its journal, the *Innes Review*, the following year, encouraged the view of Catholicism as an integral part of Scottish history and culture. Sectarian divisions continued, aggravated by football rivalries and by the simmering civil strife across the narrow North Channel in Northern Ireland. But it was clear that the Catholics of Scotland were an integral part of Scottish society. 'The Catholic population of Glasgow', wrote the Catholic journalist, Colm Brogan, in 1954, 'is bedded down. It is there, it is large, it is growing, and it cannot be got rid of by any methods short of those favoured by Herr Himmler.'[37]

By the 1970s, sectarian tensions in Scotland had eased considerably. The 1960s had brought a significant improvement in Catholic secondary schools, and more and more Catholics went on to university and entered the professions.[38] There was an increase in 'mixed' marriages between Catholics and Protestants, from 36% of all marriages involving a Catholic in 1966 to 48% of such marriages in 1977.[39] The Second Vatican Council (1962–5) had brought changes to Catholic liturgy, including the use of the vernacular rather than Latin, which reduced the differences between Catholic and Protestant Churches in public worship. Vatican II also encouraged ecumenical co-operation between Catholics and other Churches, especially in work for social justice and human rights. When Archbishop Gordon Gray, a leading proponent of ecumenical dialogue, was made Cardinal in 1969, the news was welcomed by his friends within the Church of Scotland.[40] The beginning of the Troubles in Northern Ireland in 1968 may well have promoted closer relations between leaders of the Church of Scotland and Roman Catholic Church, who were united in condemning acts of violence from both sides of the sectarian divide. Perhaps most important, as the historian Callum Brown has demonstrated, the decade of the 1960s witnessed a significant decline in church attendance for all Christian

---

[37] Cited in Gallagher, *Glasgow: The Uneasy Peace*, 256.
[38] L. Paterson, 'Salvation through Education? The Changing Social Status of Scottish Catholics', in Devine (ed.), *Scotland's Shame?*, 146.
[39] I. R. Paterson, 'The Pulpit and the Ballot Box: Catholic Assimilation and the Decline of Church Influence', in Devine (ed.), *Scotland's Shame?*, 223.
[40] M. Turnbull, *Cardinal Gordon Joseph Gray* (Edinburgh, 1994), 80–7.

denominations in Scotland, as people responded to the end of post-war austerity by embracing new forms of leisure activities that had no connection with the Churches. Many were influenced by a growing trans-Atlantic youth culture with emphasis on a rejection of traditional authorities and traditional values.[41] From the 1960s, the Churches, Protestant and Catholic, found themselves confronting common challenges in an increasingly secular society, impatient of all forms of organised religion; they had more in common with one another than with the predominantly secular society surrounding them.

The improved relations between the Church of Scotland and Catholic Church were given public expression in May 1975, when Thomas Winning, the young and dynamic Archbishop of Glasgow, was invited to address the General Assembly of the Church of Scotland. Despite protests from the Grand Orange Lodge of Scotland and angry expressions from the Free Church General Assembly, Winning addressed a packed Assembly Hall on 21 May, appealing for continued dialogue and co-operation between the Churches. Following his address, he received a warm handclasp from the Moderator, James Matheson, who told him simply and powerfully, 'You have won our hearts.'[42] 'A generation ago', observed *The Scotsman*'s lead editorial on 22 May, 'it would have seemed beyond belief that such fraternal courtesies would ever be exchanged.'[43]

Four years later, in 1979, these improved relations between Scottish Presbyterians and Catholics were put to the test, with the controversy surrounding the appointment of a Roman Catholic to the chair of divinity at the University of Edinburgh. At the time, the public perception of the Faculty of Divinity at the University of Edinburgh, located since 1935 in New College, was that it was primarily a seminary for the training of ministers in the Church of Scotland. For many Presbyterians, New College on the Mound was a citadel of Reformed orthodoxy – symbolised by the statue of John Knox in the courtyard and by buildings associated with Thomas Chalmers and the Disruption of 1843. The Chair of

[41] C. G. Brown, *Religion and Society in Scotland since 1707* (Edinburgh, 1997), 158–76.
[42] *The Scotsman*, 20, 21, 22 May 1975; *Glasgow Herald*, 22 May 1975.
[43] *The Scotsman*, 22 May 1975.

Christian Dogmatics was to become vacant with the retirement of the highly respected and highly orthodox Reformed theologian and Presbyterian Church leader, Thomas F. Torrance, due to retire in September 1979. The Faculty renamed the Dogmatics Chair the Thomas Chalmers Chair of Divinity, after the great nineteenth-century Scottish Presbyterian leader, a move that further emphasised its Presbyterian roots. It was advertised in late 1978. A nominating committee made up of six University of Edinburgh representatives and six Church of Scotland representatives, and chaired by the Acting Principal of the University, Professor John McIntyre of New College, reviewed applications and interviewed candidates in the spring of 1979. In May, the committee conveyed to the University Court its recommendation that the chair be offered to James P. Mackey.

This was a bold move, and one which reflected the changed attitudes among many Scottish Presbyterians. For James Mackey was also a Catholic – a married Irish Catholic priest and a professor at a Jesuit University. Born in Waterford in 1934, Mackey had been educated at the Roman Catholic College of Maynooth, and had taught at Maynooth, at Queen's University, Belfast, and at St John's College, Waterford, before becoming an associate professor of theology at the University of San Francisco in California. He had received a papal dispensation to marry, and had two children. His most recent book was *Jesus, the Man and the Myth*, in which he maintained that the scriptural references did not provide convincing proof of the physical resurrection, and that by resurrection the New Testament writers sought to convey an understanding of Jesus as an exalting power in human lives. This book, as with his previous works, was based on solid, probing and considered theological scholarship.

Before the University Court met to consider the recommendation of Mackey, the General Assembly of the Church of Scotland convened for its annual meeting in the Assembly Hall, adjacent to New College. Rumours of the recommendation of the nomination committee, which were already circulating through the halls of New College, were soon also circulating in the corridors of the Assembly Hall. They caused an immediate uproar. How could a Catholic, and an Irish Catholic at that, be recommended for appointment to the major theological chair at one of the leading seminaries for the training of the ministry of the Church of

Scotland? How could a Catholic hold a chair now named after the celebrated Presbyterian divine, Thomas Chalmers? With one newspaper dubbing the twelve-person nomination committee the 'dirty dozen', the General Assembly immediately voted to summon the Church members of the selection committee to appear at the bar of the Assembly and explain themselves. Five of the six Church members duly appeared, but insisted that they could not discuss the nomination, as their recommendation had not yet been considered by the University Court. To members of the Assembly, unfamiliar with University procedures, this seemed like dissembling on the part of their representatives, and the anger increased.

John R. Gray, minister of Dunblane and a former Moderator (and no relation to the Cardinal) now took the lead in the movement to block Mackey's appointment. 'It seemed', he commented to the press, 'a curious criticism of the Scottish faculties of divinity that they were unable to produce one theologian to fill the chair.'[44] By a large majority, the Assembly passed a motion demanding that the University Court not ratify the appointment of a Roman Catholic to the chair. The Court, the Assembly insisted, must reject the nomination and re-advertise the post. The Edinburgh University Faculty of Divinity, according to the majority of the Assembly, was a Reformed theological hall. If the University persisted in appointing a Catholic to the chair, some Church leaders threatened to withdraw all Church of Scotland candidates from the University of Edinburgh and establish an independent seminary. Presbyterian students, proclaimed John Gray, could not in conscience attend the lectures of a Catholic. In the Free Church General Assembly, meeting at the same time next door, Professor Donald MacLeod of the Free Church College also condemned the appointment of a Roman Catholic to a New College chair, and insisted that if the University Court persisted, there should be a new Disruption, with the Church of Scotland breaking from the University and setting up its own ministerial training college.[45] Conservatives in the Church of Scotland Assembly sought to capitalise on the perceived anti-Catholic mood by moving a censure of the former Moderator, Peter Brodie, for having visited Rome the previous year to attend the installation of Pope John Paul II. The motion

[44] *Glasgow Herald*, 26 May 1979.
[45] *The Scotsman*, 25 May 1979.

was overwhelmingly rejected by the Assembly, which, whatever its feelings about the divinity chair, was not prepared to join in a general anti-Catholic witch-hunt.[46]

Leading academics within New College were not slow to speak out. Of these voices, perhaps the most influential was that of A. C. Cheyne, Professor of Ecclesiastical History since 1964 and a highly respected representative of the liberal evangelical wing of the Church. A son of the manse, of a distinguished family that contributed numerous ministers and professors to the Scottish Church, Cheyne's Presbyterian credentials were unquestionable. But he rejected the idea that New College chairs should be reserved for Reformed theologians, as if Church of Scotland candidates could not be expected to study under professors of a different faith. 'Education', Cheyne argued, 'is not indoctrination. I suggest that an educator doesn't need to hold the same position as those he is educating in order to help them understand.'[47] These sentiments were echoed by the recently elected Rector of the University of Edinburgh, the Roman Catholic priest, Anthony Ross. 'People who teach in theological faculties . . .', he maintained, 'are no longer teaching safe doctrine'. 'They are there', he continued, 'to make people think about their faith and about Christianity, instead of parrot repetition from text books handed down for hundreds of years.'[48] Hugh Anderson, Professor of New Testament at New College, who had been profoundly influenced by the civil rights movement in the southern United States through his association with Duke University in North Carolina, spoke in the General Assembly of the importance of exposing students to traditions other than their own.[49] Cardinal Gray, while expressing understanding for the concerns expressed by members of the General Assembly, nonetheless observed that the appointment was in the hands of the University officials and not the Church of Scotland.[50]

The University Court, meanwhile, considered the concerns of the General Assembly, but supported the nominating committee. At its next regular meeting, which occurred a few days after the

[46] *The Scotsman*, 24 May 1979.
[47] *Glasgow Herald*, 24 May 1979.
[48] Ibid.
[49] *Glasgow Herald*, 26 May 1979.
[50] *Glasgow Herald*, 28 May 1979.

meeting of the General Assembly, it confirmed the appointment of Mackey. In the course of the debate in the General Assembly and the press, it had become clear that candidates for the Church of Scotland ministry now represented less than a quarter of the students in the Divinity Faculty. That Faculty had an inter-denominational and international student body, and no longer viewed itself as a confessional college or a denominational seminary. James Mackey was duly appointed to the post. A furious John Gray responded on 30 May by arguing that appointment boards to church vacancies should no longer even consider New College students; such students, he maintained, would be corrupted by their exposure to a Roman Catholic professor.[51] But others took a more liberal view, combined with a healthy sense of humour. In a letter to the editor of the *Glasgow Herald*, Ian Whyte, Church of Scotland minister in Paisley (and later Chaplain of the University of St Andrews and of the University of Edinburgh), suggested that the statue of John Knox in the New College Quad might well have smiled over the General Assembly's behaviour. 'For if Dr Gray's motion carried any power', Whyte explained, 'Mr Knox would himself have been declared ineligible for the post on account of being an ex-priest.'[52] The Church of Scotland in the event did not withdraw its students from New College, nor did Church nomination boards exclude New College students from consideration for Church appointments. Within five years of his appointment, Professor Mackey was Dean of the Faculty of Divinity. Liberal Presbyterians, as we have seen, welcomed the appointment. But for many older members of the Assembly, including those whose views had been shaped in the Church of John White and the campaign against 'Irish immigration', it was a humiliating defeat. The General Assembly's protests had been ignored in the appointment of a theological professor, and a Roman Catholic and an Irishman was appointed to one of the most important chairs in the leading theological faculty in Scotland. It was the end of the old idea of the Presbyterian commonwealth.

Three years later, in the late spring of 1982, Pope John Paul II briefly visited Scotland, as part of a British tour. It proved to be an extraordinary event. A youth rally in Edinburgh's Murrayfield

---

[51] *Glasgow Herald*, 30 May 1979.
[52] Ibid.

stadium attracted some 45,000 young people. The next day, the Pope addressed an estimated 250,000 in Glasgow's Bellahouston Park – the largest crowd ever assembled in Scotland. Eighteen years later, Thomas Winning would report that, apart from his visits to Poland, the Pope considered 'the welcome he received from Scots that June day in 1982 was the warmest he has ever felt'.[53] It was a watershed for Scotland. In its enthusiastic welcome to the pontiff, the Scottish Catholic community was proclaiming its emergence from the ghetto and its full integration into the Scottish nation, while many non-Catholics joined in and signalled their approval.

For Presbyterians, the most memorable event of the forty-hour visit was the Pope's fraternal meeting with the Moderator of the General Assembly of the Church of Scotland, Professor John McIntyre, which took place in the quadrangle of New College, under the statue of John Knox. McIntyre, it will be recalled, had been Acting Principal of Edinburgh University at the time of James Mackey's appointment. The simple handshake between the two Church leaders was a major step toward reconciliation between the two Christian communions, and toward improved relations in the future. John McIntyre expressed the hope that it would lead to increased dialogue, 'not only on subjects of disagreement but also on the joint themes on which we agree in the face of a hostile world'.[54]

The meeting on the Mound was also a public acknowledgement on the part of the Church of Scotland that the Catholic Church was a Christian society deserving of respect, that it was a major part of Scottish national life and that it was in Scotland to stay. The time when the Presbyterian Church of Scotland claimed to exercise authority over the moral and religious life of the Scottish people had now passed, along with the idea of Scotland as a covenanted Protestant nation. No longer would the Church of Scotland seek to isolate and marginalise Catholics by defining them as an alien racial or ethnic group, as immigrants who did not belong in Scotland. For Catholics, their place in Scottish life and culture was now assured, and they could claim Scotland's Christian history as their own. For many Scottish Presbyterians, this ceasing

---

[53] *The Scotsman*, 18 May 2000.
[54] *The Scotsman*, 1 June 1982.

to be the dominant national Church has probably been a liberating experience, the removal after many centuries of a heavy weight. The Church of Scotland was now able to cease being the representative of national religion and to become something higher, a Church of Christ, carrying on a mission to people in Scotland in a spirit of humility, as servants of Christ. Nor was the Catholic leadership in 1982 interested in seeking dominance in Scotland. In the aftermath of the Pope's visit, Cardinal Gray was asked if recent events did not mean that the Catholic Church was poised to assume the ecclesiastical ascendancy in Scotland. 'I sincerely hope not', he replied. 'We've surely got to work together in unity and friendship. We have to give our best talents for the good of the *whole* community, independent of race or creed, so that the Catholic Church may be a more committed Church.'[55] Sectarian tensions would certainly continue after 1982. And there would be significant differences between Presbyterians and Catholics on such vital issues as abortion and homosexuality. But the relations between the Church of Scotland and Roman Catholic Church have, on the whole, remained cordial, neither wishing to establish an ascendancy, however tempting a return to the seventeenth century might be for the one, or a return to the fifteenth century for the other. Both are in the best sense national Churches, embracing a sense of responsibility for the religious education of the Scottish people. And as Professor Cheyne observed at the height of the Mackey affair in 1979, 'education is not indoctrination', but involves a growth in understanding which can come through interaction with other traditions in a pluralist society.

---

[55] Turnbull, *Cardinal Gray*, 117.

Chapter 12

Scotland and Malawi, 1859–1964

Andrew C. Ross

I

Its all very well for you Nyasas, when we complain no one listens, when you complain so does Scotland.

THIS is what Nathan Shamiyarira, then a young Southern Rhodesian journalist, now a Zimbabwean cabinet minister, said to the writer in Salisbury (now Harare) in 1963. The words have stayed with me because they encapsulate the more than a century-old link between Scotland and Nyasaland/Malawi. Of course when the African people of Southern Rhodesia complained about their unjust treatment there were groups of people in Britain who listened. They were, however, that body of radicals who were critics of all colonialism – so that, for them, Southern Rhodesia was just another case. Where Nathan hit the nail on the head was in his insistence that Malawi was different. When in 1948 the people of Malawi began a campaign first to prevent the setting up of the Central African Federation and then to get Malawi out of it and on the road to independence, a number of individuals initiated a parallel campaign in Scotland. It was a campaign that was specific to 'the land of the lake' and which came to embrace people of many different political persuasions, Unionists and Scottish Nationalists, Communists and Tories, Labour activists and the apolitical. This was not new phenomenon. Rather it was another episode in the story of a relationship which began with a campaign in Scotland that united Tory and Liberal, Free Kirk and Auld Kirk.

Their aim was to persuade the British Government to prevent Malawi falling into the hands of the Arabs, the Portuguese or that empire-builder supreme, Cecil Rhodes. In 1916 and then again in the late 1920s and late 1930s Scottish opinion was active in attempting to influence British colonial policy with regard to Malawi.

How did this connection begin? The legend has it that it all began with Livingstone and so it did but not in a straightforward sense. It was only when Livingstone, while leading the disastrous Zambesi Expedition, found that he could not get a steamer through the Cabora Bassa gorge on the Zambesi in 1858 that he went up the Shire into what is now Malawi. In the Shire Highlands, south of Lake Malawi, he thought he had found the very spot for the missionary and commercial settlement that would be the catalyst in initiating what we would now call the development of Central Africa. Even before the Expedition ended in 1864, increased Swahili and Portuguese slave raiding had destroyed the peace of Malawi and driven away the Universities' Mission to Central Africa, the High Church Anglican Society that alone had responded to the call of that most independent of Independent Christians.

James Stewart, later Principal of Lovedale, did visit the Expedition to see if there was an opening for a Free Kirk mission but he had left disillusioned with Livingstone whom he dismissed as an unreliable dreamer.

All was very different when Stewart joined the massed ranks of the great and the good that turned up at Westminster Abbey in April 1874 for the funeral of Livingstone, by then Scotland's great hero. Building on the nationwide publicity created by this event, Stewart, on 19 May of that year, made an appeal to the General Assembly of the Free Kirk for the initiation of a mission to the Lake Malawi area. The Foreign Mission Committee (FMC) of the Free Kirk had been toying with the idea of an East African mission, probably in Somalia, without receiving much of a response from the Scottish public.[1] The FMC of the Free Kirk now supported Stewart's idea, and a special fund-raising committee of Glasgow industrialists, including Livingstone's oldest and dearest friend,

---

[1] See J. McCracken, *Politics and Christianity in Malawi 1875–1940* (Cambridge, 1977), 17–33, for a thorough study of the founding of the Livingstonia Mission.

James 'Paraffin' Young, was set up.[2] A missionary party was rapidly recruited with a young, United Presbyterian, medically qualified minister, Robert Laws, as second in command to E. D. Young. Young, a naval officer, was appointed simply to lead the party to its destination and arrange the first settlement. He then returned to the United Kingdom. So from 1877 until his retirement in 1927 Robert Laws was Head of the Livingstonia Mission, achieving almost mythic status in Malawi.[3]

Dr John Macrae, Auld Kirk minister of Hawick, had been persistently advocating the setting up of a mission to the Lake Malawi area as a memorial to Livingstone ever since news of the hero's death had reached Scotland in 1873. He even approached E. D. Young some weeks before the Free Kirk did to ask Young to head the projected new Blantyre mission. Since, at that time, Macrae had no staff appointed and no real preparations made, Young accepted the other offer. Although the Auld Kirk's General Assembly of May 1874 approved the setting up of the mission, six months later, in November 1874, Macrae was appealing in desperate tones in the *Mission Record*: 'Will no successors from Scotland be found to tread the path of her Christian Warrior? No Volunteers of Scotland to go forth to endure the hardness as becomes the soldiers of Christ?'[4]

To Macrae's relief a young man, Henry Henderson,[5] volunteered for service in time to go to Malawi with the Livingstonia party. Young and Laws fixed their first station on Cape Maclear at the south end of Lake Malawi. Henderson, accompanied by Tom Bokwito, an evangelist trained at Lovedale and lent to Henderson by the Livingstonia Mission, looked for a site suitable for the Kirk's Blantyre Mission in the Shire Highlands to the south. This initial co-operation between the missions was to continue in many different ways until 1901, when the African Churches founded by these missions united to form the Church of Central Africa

---

[2] In 1877 they became in practice a sub-committee of the FMC and were the 'home' base of the mission until 1914 when the situation was regularised under the FMC.

[3] In the 1950s and 1960s I was told stories by old people of the miracles of healing and rainmaking that he had performed.

[4] *Church of Scotland Home and Foreign Mission Record*, 9 (November 1874).

[5] A High School with a long list distinguished alumni commemorates him in Blantyre, Malawi, today.

Presbyterian (CCAP) – twenty-eight years before their 'mother' churches re-united in Scotland.

Henderson and Bokwito chose as a suitable site for the new mission the lower slopes of Nyambadwe hill on the lands of Chief Kapeni, close to Ndirande Mountain.[6] Strangely this was the site that Livingstone had suggested to the Universities' Mission to Central Africa mission under Bishop Mackenzie (the bishop had chosen to go to Magomero instead).[7]

In 1878 the Livingstonia Mission moved their headquarters north to Bandawe on the Lakeshore in what is now the Northern Province of Malawi. That Province plus part of what is now the Central Province became their area of concern, leaving what is now the Ntcheu District of the Central province and all of what is now the Southern Province to Blantyre. The Scots came to accept that they could not effectively work the central districts that lay between their two spheres. As a result the Free Kirk invited the Cape Synod of the Nederduits Gereformeerde Kerk van Suid Afrika to help, and its missionaries, led by members of the Murray family, came to Malawi in 1886 to work in the under-developed centre of the country.

A third Scottish connection was initiated at this time. A group of Glasgow businessmen associated with the Free Kirk formed the African Lakes Company in 1878. It began trading with the Lake Malawi area via the Zambesi/Shire route; their task was to provide the commercial side of Livingstone's 'Christianity and Commerce' vision.

The first years of the Blantyre Mission were almost a total disaster and in 1880 a majority of the staff were dismissed. In 1881 David Clement Scott had to begin the work again, almost from scratch. This time a secure foundation was created and good relations were built up with chiefs in the Highlands as far north as the southern Ngoni paramount chief in Ntcheu.[8] This was at a time when the Livingstonia Mission under Laws was building up

---

[6] W. P. Livingstone in his *Laws of Livingstonia* and A. J. Hanna in *The Beginnings of Nyasaland and North-Eastern Rhodesia* get the story of the siting of the Blantyre Mission completely wrong.

[7] The story of the Universities Mission to Central Africa and its brief tenure of Magomero is told in O. Chadwick, *Mackenzie's Grave* (London, 1959).

[8] A. C. Ross, *Blantyre Mission and the Making of Modern Malawi* (Blantyre, 1996), chapters 1–3.

good relations with the local Tonga and Tumbuka peoples as well as the paramount chief of the Northern Ngoni kingdom.[9]

Their work and the associated commercial developments initiated by the African Lakes Company were soon under threat. Before we discuss this threat to their work, we need to review what the missionaries conceived their purpose to be. It was not simply to convert individual Africans to the Christian faith, though they intended to do that. They were also committed to the understanding that they, together with the African Lakes Company, were to form the Scottish settlements of which Livingstone had consistently written. They were to initiate the economic and social transformation of the region.

Their work and indeed their continued existence came under threat from two sources. The first was the increase in Swahili-inspired slave-raiding, which culminated in a Swahili slaver, Mlozi, attempting to set up a new Swahili-controlled state based at Karonga at the north end of the Lake. The second threat came from the Portuguese in Mozambique who claimed that all of what is now the Southern Province fell within the area of Portuguese sovereignty.

The threat from Portugal was the more formidable in the long run, but Mlozi's threat was the more immediate. It was the war between forces raised by the African Lakes Company and the local Ngonde people on one side, and Mlozi and his people on the other, that first roused Scottish public opinion in general to take an interest in Malawi.[10] Although they were not directly involved, the Portuguese loomed large in this conflict, because, according to international law, they had a strong claim to be able to cut off the Scots from the outside world. This situation had developed because, despite much searching, no clear way had been found from the sea through the delta of the Zambesi into the river proper. Therefore, goods had to be landed first – that is, landed on Portuguese soil and only then loaded onto a riverboat for the

[9] The Southern and Northern Ngoni states were kingdoms created in the 1860s by Nguni groups who had fled Chaka's expansionist policies in what is now the RSA and through their superior military organisation had created a number of small kingdoms in present day Mozambique, Zambia and Malawi.

[10] H. Macmillan, 'The Origin and Development of the African Lakes Company', University of Edinburgh PhD thesis, [1970], 297.

journey to Malawi. It was not until in January 1889 that D. J. Rankin[11] discovered the Chinde mouth of the Zambesi. Only then could the Zambesi/Shire route be legally recognised as an international waterway.

The presence of the African Lakes Company and the two Scottish Missions in Malawi was seen by some Portuguese officials in both Lisbon and Mozambique as an obstacle to the fulfilment of the old dream of a great Portuguese dominion stretching from coast to coast. Portuguese discontent was increased when, as a result of pressure from the Free Kirk and the African Lakes Company, the Foreign Office appointed a consul 'to the chiefs in the Lake Nyasa region'. His job was to encourage legitimate trade and discourage the slave trade. This consul was pointedly not accredited to the Portuguese authorities in Mozambique. The consul's presence was, however, a mere token and he had no real power. He had no means, save diplomacy, of attacking the slave trade, as London made it clear that it had no intention of committing any force to a region so inaccessible. Just when the Consul, Hawes, was at his most depressed because of the ineffectiveness of his position a crisis arose which changed everything.

As we have seen, Mlozi at Karonga began, in 1886, seeking to impose his authority over the local Ngonde people who resisted him and a war broke out. Ngonde refugees fled to the African Lakes Company station at Karonga for protection and called on the Scots as their friends to aid them in the fight. Hawes, on the other hand, insisted that the African Lakes Company and the missions should stay out of the conflict, an attitude which showed his inability to understand the *raison d'être* of the African Lakes Company and the aims of the Scottish missions. The Livingstonia Mission backed up the African Lakes Company in siding with the Ngonde people, and its supporters in Scotland through the press and the pulpit told Scotland that this war was one in which Scots were standing shoulder to shoulder with the African people against an attack by Arab[12] slavers. Initially the Blantyre Mission was very cool in response to requests for support of this venture. However, when O'Neill, Consul at Mozambique, in a private

---

[11] Rankin had been for a time a member of the staff of the Blantyre Mission.
[12] At the time these Muslim Swahili were always referred to as Arabs.

capacity[13] went to lead the allied forces in the north and then persuaded Captain Lugard[14] to succeed him as leader of the allied forces, Scott and company joined in supporting the war. From 1887 until 1889 there was desultory fighting at Karonga. The Ngonde and the Scots could not take the stockaded strongholds of Mlozi, while he in turn failed to subdue the Ngonde or drive off their Scottish allies.

Just at this time the newly active Portuguese authorities decided to intervene. In March 1888 the Portuguese detained the African Lakes Company steamer at Quilemane stating that it would have to be transferred to Portuguese ownership since there could only be Portuguese traffic on the Zambesi and Shire. The Portuguese also reiterated their claim to sovereignty over all the territory between the Zambesi and southern end of Lake Malawi. The African Lakes Company, the Scottish missions and their African allies and friends appeared to be helpless between the jaws of the Swahili–Portuguese nutcracker.

In response to this crisis, members of the Free and Auld Kirks came together, in the spring of 1888, in a way unprecedented since the Disruption. They initiated a massive campaign to arouse Scottish public opinion, gaining cross-party Liberal and Tory support. The two Scottish Churches together set up a meeting of all Scottish members of both Houses of Parliament that was well attended by both Liberals and Tories. At the meeting it was agreed to ask the Foreign Secretary to press for the free navigation of the Zambesi and for Malawi north of the Ruo river to be declared a British sphere of interest. The result of this meeting was that the Prime Minister, Lord Salisbury, granted an interview to a Scottish delegation. One of the Auld Kirk representatives on the delegation, in his capacity as a Kirk elder, was Lord Balfour of Burleigh, a leading Tory member of the House of Lords.[15] The leading Scottish Liberal peer, Lord Rosebery, fully supported this action though

[13] O'Neill was consul at Mozambique and a fervent campaigner against the slave trade. He went to Karonga in a private capacity which greatly upset the Portuguese and certainly broke diplomatic protocol.

[14] F. D. Lugard, later Lord Lugard, would play a key role in the creation of Uganda and was later Governor of Northern Nigeria.

[15] Lord Balfour was later to serve as Secretary of State for Scotland in A. J. Balfour's Tory government of 1902.

did not join the delegation. Salisbury received the delegation with courtesy but offered no help.

'Salisbury in 1888 was at one with his predecessors in thinking that these missionary concerns were no good reason to extend British rule over Nyasa.'[16] Where Professors Robinson and Gallagher went awry in this otherwise accurate comment was to use the word 'rule'. As John McCracken makes very clear, the missions at no time asked for British rule over the area. What they wanted was intervention by the British Imperial State to ensure that the Portuguese and Swahili were not allowed to take over the area.[17]

Both the moment of greatest danger in Malawi and the climax of the Scottish campaign came in 1889. In Malawi the Ngonde and their Scottish allies were very much on the defensive early in the year and the Scots were unclear about how much longer they could continue the struggle. That ability was further weakened by Portuguese political initiatives. The first of these was, as we have noted, their impounding of the African Lakes Company steamer as part of their policy of Portuguese-only traffic on the rivers. The second occurred when Lt Cardoso, in January 1889, led a body of Portuguese troops up to the Ruo, preparatory to occupying the country 'in order to protect the missionaries'.

All of this led to a great intensification of activity in Scotland which culminated in well-attended public meetings in Glasgow, Edinburgh, Dundee and Aberdeen during April and May of 1889. The Tory aristocrat, Balfour of Burleigh, by now a member of Lord Salisbury's cabinet, chaired some of these meetings, even in Liberal strongholds. He then led the delegation which presented Lord Salisbury with a monster petition signed by 11,000 ministers and elders of the United Presbyterian, Free and Auld Kirks, who demanded British intervention in the Lake Malawi area.

It is an interesting question as to how far Salisbury welcomed and even encouraged this Scottish pressure. In November 1888, Salisbury had appointed H. H. Johnston to succeed O'Neill as consul at Mozambique. Before he went to his post, Salisbury sent Johnston to negotiate a settlement of the Zambesi/Malawi problem

---

[16] R. E. Robinson and J. A. Gallagher, *Africa and the Victorians* (London, 1961), 223.

[17] McCracken, *Politics and Christianity in Malawi*, 157–9.

with the Portuguese government in Lisbon. Most authorities[18] are agreed that Salisbury's aim was to gain what is now Zimbabwe for Britain and persuade the Portuguese to stay out of Malawi. On 9 April 1889, Salisbury received Johnston's report with annotations by senior Foreign Office officials in support of its conclusions. The draft agreement gained for Britain Mashonaland, Manicaland and all of what is now Zambia plus the lands adjoining the west coast of Lake Malawi. However, all of southern Malawi, including Blantyre and the Shire Highlands, were to go to Portugal. Salisbury then sent Johnston to sell this scheme to the Scots.

Johnston's arrival in Scotland in May coincided with the campaign in Scotland preparing the monster petition for British intervention. What Johnston now tried to 'sell' to the Scots infuriated them further. Did Salisbury intend this to happen so he could tell the Portuguese that Scotland was imposing such massive popular pressure that he had to do something to placate it? We cannot be certain from the existing archival material. However, the timing was certainly fortuitous and there were hints that Salisbury wanted the furore. How else can we explain the role in the campaign played by Burleigh, a member of Salisbury's cabinet? There is at least one piece of documentary evidence. This is a letter from Dr McMurtrie to D. C. Scott, in which the Convenor of the FMC wrote

> In a conversation I had with Balfour, his Lordship spoke very guardedly, as was right in his position, but he left the impression on my mind – which I state to you in confidence – that Lord Salisbury is really bringing pressure to bear on Portugal and that Portugal will retrace her steps. Be good enough to withhold Lord Burleigh's name as confidential.[19]

W. P. Livingstone, in his biography of Alexander Hetherwick, asserts unambiguously that Salisbury actively encouraged the Scottish campaign, even quoting a conversation in the House of Lords between Balfour and Salisbury in support of this contention. However, he cites no authority for this conversation.[20]

[18] A. J. Hanna, *The Beginnings of Nyasaland and North-Eastern Rhodesia* (Oxford, 1956); R. Oliver, *The Missionary Factor in East Africa* (London, 1957); Robinson and Gallagher, *Africa and the Victorians*.

[19] Quoted in W. P. Livingstone, *A Prince of Missionaries* (London, 1931), 52.

[20] Ibid., 51–2.

In July, Cecil Rhodes made it clear that in return for a Charter, his British South Africa Company would take over what is now Zambia as well as Mashonaland and Manicaland. The Company was also willing to pay for the British administration of what is now Malawi even if the latter was not included in the Charter – at least at first.[21] Salisbury was by this stroke free of Treasury restrictions on his policy making.

He ordered Johnston to go from Quilemane via the Chinde mouth of the Zambesi and proceed via the Zambesi and Shire to southern Malawi, thus establishing the international status of the waterway. Having arrived at Blantyre, Johnston then went northwards to make treaties of friendship with various chiefs, including Mlozi. While he was away, the Vice-Consul, John Buchanan,[22] was faced with the advance of Portuguese troops led by Serpa Pinto up the Shire valley. He hoisted the Union Jack at Blantyre and declared the Makololo country in the Shire Valley together with the Shire Highlands to be under British Protection. This declaration, however, did not stop Serpa Pinto's askari from advancing and engaging in heavy fighting with the Makololo. Most of the Makololo chiefs and their retinues now fled to Blantyre mission in the highlands. It was only an ultimatum from Salisbury to the government in Lisbon in February 1890 that forced the withdrawal of Portuguese troops.

In all of this long period of campaigning the Scottish lobbyists adopted a consistent line in their approaches to the government in London. The issue, they insisted again and again, was not simply a Church concern. The future of the land and people of the Lake Malawi area was a Scottish issue, uniting Scots of different Churches and of different political persuasions.

Finally in May 1891 Malawi was declared a British Protectorate and H. H. Johnston was named as Commissioner.[23] In the interim there was a great deal of speculation by the Scots in the African Lakes Company and the two missions about what the

---

[21] Cawston to Herbert, 1 July 1889, Public Records Office, London, FO 403/III.

[22] Buchanan had been a member of the original 1875 Blantyre Mission party but had resigned to become a coffee planter, though he remained supportive of the Mission.

[23] It was called the British Central African Protectorate initially and then in 1907, the Nyasaland Protectorate.

future was to hold. The Blantyre Missionaries led by David Clement Scott were adamant that rule by a Chartered Company was no real aid to their goal of bringing both the Gospel and 'development' to Africa. David Scott wrote to a friend during this period of uncertainty:

> We have heard nothing of any sort of government for this place beyond the Chartered Company. If we have no independent Commissioner to whom to appeal for the natives' sake and for the mission, then I fear we may look forward to years of darkness from which the only escape will be in agitation and political revolution. When government bars the way with legislation, it really means revolution to get it removed: we want help before the legislation bars the way.[24]

Scott and Alexander Hetherwick campaigned against Company rule, even after the declaration of a Protectorate. They persevered in this campaign because they knew of the extraordinary situation whereby the Imperial administration of the new Protectorate was only maintained by a subvention from Rhodes who believed that after three years Malawi would come to the Company. Scott was greatly helped in this fight by John Moir[25] who passed confidential information to Scott confirming his fears that in 1894 the Company was to get Malawi. The direct connection of the Blantyre leaders through Dr McMurtrie to Lord Burleigh and on to Salisbury was a vital element in guaranteeing that in 1894 the Protectorate was confirmed and did not revert to being part of a greater Rhodesia. This confirmation was made by Lord Rosebery's Liberal Administration but Salisbury had made the decision before demitting office late in 1892.

This struggle to resist a Rhodesian take-over became a recurring theme of Malawi history and a recurring theme of Scottish–Malawi relations. In this first victory over Rhodesian advance the vital role played by the Scottish Blantyre Missionaries was summed up by Nyasaland's first British administrator. H. H. Johnston, though later to become a critic of Rhodes, at that time still wished the Rhodesian take-over to succeed. In 1893 he wrote to Rhodes:

[24] D. C. Scott to James Robertson, 18 August 1890, Edinburgh University Library, MS. 717/10.
[25] One of the African Lakes Company Directors who was in negotiation with the British South African Company over the latter's take-over bid.

I don't think you have ever realised the bitter hatred borne you by these Scotch missionaries of Blantyre. They hate you because you are an Englishman, because you threaten to overshadow their own petty meddling and muddling with grander schemes that will outshine mission work in popular favour. Remember that it was mainly Scott and Hetherwick who balked the scheme of 1890 of all B.C.A. coming under the Company's Charter. They are now up and at it again and are the most serious enemies you possess.[26]

II

The next crisis calling forth Scottish efforts to change British policy came over the so-called Native Rising of 1915. The rebellion was led by the brilliant Malawi independent pastor, John Chilembwe, the subject of Shepperson and Price's classic work, *Independent African*.[27] In the aftermath of the suppression of the Rising it became clear that the white settlers' lobby and many officials firmly believed that the Scottish missions were to blame for the Rising. The Commission of Enquiry into the Rising set out as part of its agenda an enquiry into mission schools in general, an ominous matter when the Blantyre schools and the even larger Livingstonia school system were together twice as big as all the schools of the other missions together. Scottish fears were confirmed when one of the commissioners, a Mr Metcalfe of the British Central Africa Company, wrote to Hetherwick[28] in a letter heavily marked as confidential and private: 'I am certain this Enquiry will not be, nor is intended by Government that it should be, "a complete and impartial" one.'[29]

It rapidly became clear that the settlers and key officials wanted all mission schools closed that were not closely supervised by whites. (The other missions said their schools were already so supervised and were praised for it.) The Government's move to impose close white supervision would have been a disaster for the Blantyre and Livingstonia missions, whose widespread school

---

[26] Johnston to Rhodes, 7 June 1893, Harare, Zimbabwe National Archives, CT/1/16/4/1.

[27] G. Shepperson and T. Price, *Independent African* (Edinburgh, 1958).

[28] Alexander Hetherwick succeeded D. C. Scott as Head of Mission in 1898.

[29] Metcalfe to Hetherwick, 25 May 1915, Malawi Archives, Zomba, Hetherwick Correspondence.

systems simply could not be supervised in the way the Commission wanted. This was indeed the nub of the issue. The Scottish missions believed they could trust their teachers to get on with the job of teaching and preaching, their opponents believed that the autonomy the Scots gave to their ministers and teachers was subversive of good order.[30]

Despite the fact that most people in the United Kingdom in the midst of the Great War looked on this trouble in Malawi as an irrelevant side-show, the leaders of the United Free and Auld Kirks joined together to lobby the Colonial Office. They were able to use Steele-Maitland, the Under-Secretary at the Colonial Office, a Scot and a Kirk elder who helped guarantee that although the Report of the Commission was critical of Africans being allowed to teach and preach unsupervised by Europeans, no action was taken to close the so-called 'unsupervised' schools of the Church of Central Africa. In the United Kingdom this was mainly a Scottish affair; the Rising caused no significant reaction otherwise in British Church or political circles at that time, though it did have long-term effects on Colonial Office attitudes to 'fringe' missionary societies like the Watch Tower movement.

In the 1920s and 1930s there was no major crisis in the affairs of Malawi that provoked any kind of significant political action in Scotland – until the eve of the Second World War. However, that period witnessed a strong new movement for the amalgamation of the two Rhodesias and Nyasaland. This idea was strongly advocated in some circles of the Colonial Service and was almost universally supported by the white settlers in the region.

In 1927 the Hilton Young Commission was set up to investigate the possibility of closer political union among the Central and East African Territories. Initially the members of the Commission were sympathetic to the settlers' position that they, as 'men on the spot', should control 'native policy'. However, two leading members of the Commission, Sir George Schuster and J. H. Oldham, were converted by evidence presented to them by Scottish missionaries in Nyasaland to a different position – to which they

---

[30] At that date it was only the Blantyre and Livingstonia Presbyteries of the Church of Central Africa Presbyterian that had ordained Africans to the Christian ministry in all of Central Africa.

won over the other members of the Commission but failed to move its chairman, Sir Edward Hilton Young.[31] As a result the Chairman wrote what was in effect the minority report and the other members of the Commission wrote the majority report. In the latter report the majority of the Commission members opposed amalgamation and, perhaps even more important, they opposed responsible government being granted to a white electorate, as had been done already in Southern Rhodesia. They observed that 'experience has taught mankind that a man, however just and honourable, ought not to be made judge in his own cause'.[32] They were also influenced by the evidence given in Nyasaland by the leaders of the Native Associations, organisations of educated Africans keen to affect the future of their country. Robert Laws, before he retired, had played a major role in helping them to organise and, even more importantly, in persuading the Colonial authorities not to suppress them.[33]

In 1930, Lord Passfield, the Colonial Secretary, published his famous Memorandum asserting the principle that in all territories north of the Zambesi the primacy of 'native' interests would be maintained over those of immigrant races. This created a new situation. From then on the white settler leaders in Nyasaland and Northern Rhodesia were committed to seeking amalgamation with the white-settler-ruled Southern Rhodesia in order to escape control from London.

The powerful British Empire Producers' Organisation threw its weight behind the proponents of amalgamation, while in the early 1930s the Governors of both Nyasaland and Northern Rhodesia were sympathetic to the idea. The Southern Rhodesian government, supported by the white settler leaders in Northern Rhodesia, petitioned London three times – in 1933, 1935 and 1936 – for a conference on amalgamation. In response the Native Associations

---

[31] See L. Gann and P. Duignan (eds), *The History and Politics of Colonialism* (Cambridge, 1970), 66.

[32] Cmd 3234, *Report of the Commission on Closer Union of the Dependencies of Eastern and Central Africa* (The Hilton Young Report) (HMSO, 1929), 83.

[33] These Associations came together to form the Nyasaland African National Congress under the inspiration and leadership of a Blantyre Church elder, James F. Sangala, though the first President was a Livingstonia man, Levi Mumba, who had given evidence to the Hilton Young Commission in 1927.

in Nyasaland began to marshal support for a campaign opposing amalgamation. As early as August 1935, the Blantyre Native Association formally petitioned the Governor to resist any suggestion of amalgamation with Southern Rhodesia. They insisted that many Nyasas had worked there and they knew what conditions were like for Africans south of the Zambesi.[34]

In January 1938, the Government appointed a Royal Commission, made up of six members and headed by Lord Bledisloe, to consider the issues. It spent three months taking evidence in the three territories and published its report early in 1939. Unlike the Hilton Young Commission there was no minority report but a number of individual members insisted on appending long personal notes to the final report. The one thing every member was agreed upon was that African opposition to amalgamation, indeed to any closer relationship to Southern Rhodesia, was overwhelming in Nyasaland and Northern Rhodesia. In Nyasaland the Scottish Missionaries assured the Commission that amalgamation was against both the wishes and interest of the African people of the Protectorate. In 1938 the missionaries gained support from the 1938 General Assembly of the now re-united Church of Scotland in warning the Government against pressing amalgamation against the opposition of the African people of Nyasaland.

As early as 1935, J. A. Rodgers of Blantyre Mission wrote an important article in a journal read in Malawi by Africans as well as in Scotland by mission supporters. In it he made clear the parallel between the contemporary situation in Central Africa and that leading up to the creation of the Union of South Africa in 1910. He emphasised how soon after the inception of the Union all of the special rights previously enjoyed by Cape Africans and supposedly guaranteed in the new constitution by the Imperial government had been swept away. This precedent would be raised again in the new discussions about closer association that took place after the war.

The Bledisloe Report initiated a great deal of discussion. Sir John Harris of the Aborigines Protection Society insisted that the very integrity of British colonial policy was at stake. The outbreak of the Second World War soon diverted attention in Scotland away

---

[34] Minutes of the Executive Council of Nyasaland Protectorate for 1935. Minute 166, Malawi Archives, Zomba.

from this issue. The war, however, did not distract the Rhodesian whites to the same extent. Throughout the conflict the Government of Southern Rhodesia and the settler leaders in Northern Rhodesia continually reminded the Imperial government that they sought amalgamation of the three territories. In 1941, for instance, Sir Godfrey Huggins, the Southern Rhodesian Prime Minister, and Roy Welensky, the leader of the Northern Rhodesian whites, both requested the British Government to agree at least in principle to the future amalgamation of the three territories. In 1943 they received encouragement when the Central Africa Council, consisting of the three Governors plus a leading white politician from each territory, was set up to co-ordinate co-operation between the three territories.

The coming of the Labour party to power in 1945 did not end the matter. Huggins and Welensky continued their lobbying. In 1948 when they were both in the United Kingdom, they persuaded Arthur Creech Jones, the Colonial Secretary, to agree that, although he opposed amalgamation, some form of federation might be possible. Huggins and Welensky were delighted and now pressed ahead with a campaign to create a Federation of the three territories. Their aim was eventual Dominion status. Then, just as the Government of the new Union of South Africa had done in the 1920s, they could jettison whatever safeguards for the indigenous population the Imperial Government might write into the constitution of the new Dominion. Huggins himself made that very clear when addressing his constituents at a later time. Speaking of constitutional changes which he hoped would bring Dominion status to the Federation, he noted that 'once the Imperial Government have granted this Constitution they have lost all control – don't forget that'.[35]

In January 1949 a conference was held at the Victoria Falls to inaugurate the new campaign for federation. The first formal step was withdrawal from the Central Africa Council of the Southern Rhodesian Government on the grounds that it was totally inadequate to deal with the region's problems. However, the pro-federation forces experienced a set-back when Creech-Jones declined to call a conference to discuss the federation of the three

[35] Quoted in C. Leys and C. Pratt (eds), *A New Deal in Central Africa* (London, 1964), 28.

territories. At this point events in British politics, which bore no relation to Africa's problems, intervened. The general election of 1950 saw the Labour party returned to power with only a paper-thin majority. Creech-Jones lost his seat and James Griffith became Colonial Secretary. Unlike his predecessor, Griffith, a tough trade union negotiator, had no experience of Colonial matters. While some Labour members saw federation as a way of raising African living standards in the three territories, a Labour administration fighting for its life did not see the possible federation of the African territories as a central issue.

Huggins pressed Griffith for a conference of officials to consider what such a federation might look like and Griffith fell for the bait. He insisted that such a conference did not commit the government to anything but what was the point of having a group of senior officials explore a constitution for a federation if you were not going to have one? In January 1951 a group of civil servants from the Commonwealth Relations Office (CRO), the Colonial Office and each of the three territories began their work under the chairmanship of a convinced federation supporter, G. H. Baxter of the CRO. They soon discovered that there was a fundamental block to progress, the profound difference in 'Native Policy' between Southern Rhodesia on the one hand and the two northern territories on the other. This, as most observers at the time and since have pointed out, was the key issue.[36] In their working paper they made the following declaration and then went on as if the problem was solved: 'The most striking conclusion which we draw from our examination of the survey is the degree of similarity between the policy and the practice of the three Governments, rather than the degree of difference.'[37]

Griff Jones, a District Commissioner in Nyasaland at the time, wrote later that the officials knew this was 'rubbish', but that the statement let them get on with their constitution making.[38] Welensky and Huggins were delighted with the report and, ominously for the opponents of federation, the Tory leadership in the United Kingdom also welcomed it. Indeed in the House of Lords, Lord Altrincham insisted on the fundamental importance

[36] Ibid., 20; G. Jones, *Britain and Nyasaland* (London, 1964), 135–7.
[37] *Comparative Survey of Native Policy*, Public Records Office, London, Cmd 8235.
[38] Jones, *Britain and Nyasaland*, 136–7.

for the future of this report by experienced men 'whose impartiality could not be doubted'. Griffith decided to go to Nyasaland himself to canvass African opinion and he was impressed at the unanimity of African opposition to federation, from young Congressmen to traditional headmen. He nonetheless agreed to yet another Victoria Falls conference of politicians from all three territories in September of that year. He and the Commonwealth Secretary attended, while Nyasaland Africans sent three delegates who pointed out fiercely that their presence was intended simply to reiterate the total opposition of the Nyasaland people to any closer association with Southern Rhodesia.[39]

III

The Conservatives won the British general election in 1951 with a substantial majority. The friends of Welensky and Huggins were now in power. The new Colonial Secretary was Oliver Lyttelton, who agreed enthusiastically with proponents of federation. It was simply a matter of when not whether the federation of the three territories would come about.

But the opposition to federation had begun to organise in the United Kingdom. A key weapon in this fight was a pamphlet written by Harry Nkumbula of Northern Rhodesia, a student at the London School of Economics, and Dr H. Kamuzu Banda of Nyasaland, who had left the Protectorate before the First World War. The pamphlet, entitled *Federation in Central Africa*, made clear their view, based on what white politicians in the Rhodesias were saying at meetings and in the local press, that federation was simply the first step to amalgamation and Dominion status. With that achieved then, as in South Africa after 1910, all built-in protections for African rights could be swept aside. As David Williams commented in his history of Malawi, this was not unusually perceptive but almost no one in the British Parliament saw it.[40] Those who were pro-federation trotted out the same old arguments that had been used in the negotiations for the 1910 union, that these white leaders were fine upstanding men who could be trusted to do the right thing.

[39] B. Pachai, *Malawi: The History of the Nation* (London, 1973), 260.
[40] T. D. Williams, *Malawi: The Politics of Despair* (Ithica, New York, 1978), 141.

There were three pressures that seemed overwhelming to most Labour politicians, as well as Tories. The first was the need to help the ailing British economy, the second was the need to raise the standard of living of the people of the three territories and the third was the alarm created by the massive victory of the National party in South Africa in 1948. With regard to the economy, Sir Stafford Cripps had said: 'The whole future of the sterling group and its ability to survive depends on the quick and extensive development of our African resources.'[41]

Welensky had pointed out to the British Government that if the British wanted to benefit from the mineral and other resources of the Central African Territories, they should support the creation of a stable and friendly state run by white settlers. Although Professor Arthur Hazlewood has pointed out that the economic advantages to the people of Central Africa of the new state were always declared to be self-evident, they were in truth not at all that obvious and no one bothered to explain them systematically.[42] Although the issue of the protection of the rights of Africans was raised by Labour politicians, they gave the appearance of being ready grudgingly to accept federation and to ask Africans in the two northern territories to help make it work. Liberal Tories like Lord Alport even comforted themselves by insisting that the new federation 'would curb the worst excesses of extreme white and black nationalists'.[43] Partnership and the advance of Africans were to be guaranteed by a scheme that had to be imposed against almost universal African opposition in the northern territories.

It was in Scotland that opposition to the scheme was most clear-cut and well organised. Dr Banda was welcomed at a number of public meetings in Edinburgh and Glasgow. The Blantyre Missionary Council published a very strong statement about the situation and a significant cross-section of Scottish opinion came out against the federal scheme. A key group in keeping Nyasaland at the centre of Scottish concern was a group led by Kenneth Mackenzie, the Scottish Council on African Questions, which we will look at in more detail later.

[41] Jones, *Britain and Nyasaland*, 136.
[42] A. Hazlewood, 'The Economics of Federation and Dissolution', in A. Hazlewood (ed.), *African Integration and Disintegration* (Oxford, 1967), 185–250.
[43] Leys and Pratt (eds), *New Deal in Central Africa*, 52.

It is interesting to contrast the attitude of a senior Labour party MP, Patrick Gordon Walker, with that of a Scotsman, Mr. W. Young, teaching at Gordonstoun School, hardly a hotbed of left-wing radicalism. Gordon Walker hoped that the proposed federation would be a successful experiment in race relations and make a contribution to a multi-racial Commonwealth. It was in this area of race-relations, he went on, that Soviet Communism most successfully challenged the West and the Soviet challenge was particularly real in Africa.[44] Mr W. Young from Gordonstoun wrote to *The Scotsman* on 7 November 1952. He insisted that there were plenty of intelligent Nyasas with experience of the wider world outside their villages. They opposed closer links with the South for good reasons and they deserved to be listened to. Even if the economic arguments being bandied about were valid, Young insisted that:

> The Africans are concerned about deeper issues, the rights of free men in a free society. It is because these rights are denied in practice and the emphasis laid on economic values that the Africans are afraid for their future in a federation which must be European dominated.

The pressure in Scotland was so persuasive that the first leader in the editorial columns of *The Scotsman* of 4 November 1952 opposed the scheme. It quoted the published memorandum of the Blantyre Mission Council which declared that the present discussion of federation had so affected African opinion in Nyasaland that its imposition would destroy any hope of good race relations. The editorial then went on to say that proposed federation should be postponed until Nyasaland Africans could be persuaded of its worth by clear practical steps in areas such as conditions of employment. The editor knew full well about the strict industrial and other forms of 'colour bar' in Southern Rhodesia.

In 1952 there was a clearer and firmer opposition in Scotland to the imposition of the new federation on Nyasaland than in the parliamentary Labour opposition. We have already seen what Patrick Gordon Walker thought. Even more significant was James Griffith, who insisted in the Commons on 4 March 1953 that the

[44] Gordon Walker's attitude is summarised in Williams, *Malawi: The Politics of Despair*, 147–8.

problem was not federation itself, which was good in principle, but was rather how to get it with African assent!

All of this was to no avail. The scheme went ahead with both the Government and Opposition taking the paternalist view that they knew best and setting aside the African opposition to the scheme in Nyasaland. Lord Llewellyn took up his post as Governor General of the new Federal state in September 1953. In Nyasaland, however, a programme of civil disobedience was instituted by Congress which soon tipped over into violence in Ntcheu and across the Southern Province. By September this had been crushed and various leaders sent into internal exile. The Nyasaland African National Congress now tried a period of reluctant co-operation, putting up candidates for the Federal Parliament and trying to make partnership work. Even Andrew Doig who had written the Blantyre Mission statement of 1952 accepted an appointment to the African Affairs Board of the Federal Parliament. The African Affairs Board was meant to protect African interests and be able to refer any measure passed by the Federal Assembly to London if they deemed it detrimental to African interests.

The crisis for this policy came in 1957. Although in Nyasaland Legislative Council a revitalised Congress had captured all the African seats and demanded Nyasaland's withdrawal from the Federation, in the Federal capital they tolerated Doig's work. But this changed with two federal bills, the Constitutional Amendment Bill and the Federal Electoral Bill. The Board referred both to London to be disallowed as discriminatory. They were not aware that the Federal Prime Minister, Welensky, had in April concluded a deal with the British Government, which implied that in 1960 the workings of the Federation would be reviewed and Dominion status granted if all was well. The real situation became clear when the appeal of the African Affairs Board was turned down in London and the two bills became law. Andrew Doig now resigned from the African Affairs Board, saying that 'in my opinion, further service on the Board is useless. I feel we have gone past the point of "no return" as far as an approach to real partnership is concerned.'[45]

The African people in Nyasaland felt fundamentally betrayed, and lost all hope that the British Government would not desert

[45] Quoted in C. Sanger, *Central African Emergency* (London, 1960), 170.

them. The sense of betrayal was also widespread in Scotland. One result was the setting up at the General Assembly of the Kirk in May 1958 of a Special Committee on Central Africa chaired by Dr George Macleod with Kenneth Mackenzie as Secretary. This immediate response was due partly to the fact that Scottish public opinion had been kept well informed since 1953 by the Scottish Council on African Questions. The driving force behind this was the same Kenneth Mackenzie who had served as a missionary in both Malawi and Zambia. He had an extraordinary gift of holding together people of diverse backgrounds and opinions. For example, he included on his team Sir Gordon Letham, previously Governor of British Guiana, as well as senior Trade Union figures and the Episcopal Bishop of Edinburgh.

In Nyasaland the new leadership of NANC called Dr H. K. Banda back to his homeland to lead the movement. These NANC leaders were too young – in their late twenties and early thirties – to command the unambiguous respect of traditional village elders that Banda certainly could. After his return to Malawi, Congress began preparing a programme of civil disobedience to force the British Government to pay attention to African opinion and withdraw them from the Federation. The Federal Government and the Governor of Nyasaland, Sir Robert Armitage, had no option but to accede to their demands or crush them. The decision was made to crush them. In 'Operation Sunrise' on 3 March 1959, three hundred Nyasalanders were detained without trial in a dawn swoop by security forces, including all-white Rhodesian territorial units. The response in Nyasaland was one of astonishment. Crowds gathered and they were dispersed only with great difficulty and some fifty-one people were killed. As a result many more people were then put into detention. As Griff Jones, himself a District Commissioner at the time, put it later in his book:

> emergency powers had never been employed in Nyasaland before; sudden arrests on a large scale were without precedent. Congress was apparently flourishing; Dr Banda was being treated by the government as the leader of political opinion among Africans and the Government was in the middle of discussions with him on constitutional reform.[46]

---

[46] Jones, *Britain and Nyasaland*, 241.

People in Scotland were also taken aback and the Scottish Council on African Questions bombarded them with pamphlets and letters to the newspapers on a vast scale. The correspondence columns of *The Scotsman* and the *Glasgow Herald* during March and April 1959 each took up a whole page rather than the more usual two columns. Seventy-nine newspapers in Scotland are listed in the records of SCAQ in Edinburgh University Library as being offered articles and fed with letters. A key pamphlet was also produced and delivered across Scotland through the parish and other churches. Entitled *Our Brothers in Revolt*, it emphasised the long-term links between Nyasaland and Scotland, insisting that this special relationship was one starting with Livingstone binding the two nations together with the aim of bettering the lot of the people of Nyasaland. Professor Shepperson suggested to a class in the University of Edinburgh that for the Scottish people Nyasaland was the success that had made up for the failure of the late-seventeenth-century colonial venture at Darien, and London must not be allowed to do down Scotland again.

The anger in Scotland came at a time when the Opposition in Parliament was pressing the Government hard over a number of other colonial issues, notably the appalling treatment of detainees at Hola Camp in Kenya. The result was that the Government appointed a Commission of Enquiry, the Devlin Commission, to review the situation in Nyasaland. While it was only one among many issues dividing the Government and Opposition in Great Britain, Nyasaland became *the* issue in Scotland and Scottish public opinion became something like a one-issue lobby group. We can see this clearly on 12 May 1959, when a speech in the Commons by the veteran Scottish Labour MP, Margaret Herbison, in which she defended the stand taken by the Kirk's Special Committee on Central Africa, was printed almost in full in *The Scotsman*, taking up most of its front page. This was at a time when *The Scotsman* was in no way a pro-Labour newspaper.

The importance of Scottish anti-Federation opinion was also clearly recognised by the authorities in Central Africa, who expended considerable time and energy attempting to discredit it. The Government Secretariat in Zomba produced a special report, marked 'Secret and Confidential, Not to be Published', entitled *The Church of Central Africa Presbyterian*. This was sent to help Whitehall deal with the Scots as well as to the Federal Government in Salisbury. It described the Church of Central Africa as a tool of the Scots, and it maintained that the African ministers and elders in both the Livingstonia and Blantyre Synods who had passed motions opposing the continuance of Federation were unable to think for themselves. This was its concluding paragraph:

> The Church of Scotland and their Foreign Missions Committee in the United Kingdom are directly responsible for the attitude of their Church [meaning the CCAP] with regard to the Federation issue in that
>
> a) They have sent into the Mission field in Nyasaland persons with extreme left-wing political views who have had the effect of greatly exacerbating African opposition to Government, and of impairing race relations generally.
>
> b) The Moderator of the General Assembly of the Church of Scotland in 1958 openly advocated participation in politics as a Christian duty.
>
> c) By promising to consider the views on the Federation issue of the Christian Action group in Blantyre before the General Assembly of the Church of Scotland they have actively encouraged those opposing Federation to look to the Church of Scotland in the United Kingdom for assistance.[47]

The Federal Information Service then set up a 'front' committee of concerned people who circulated a document that the Information Service had produced based on the secret report. This was entitled *The New Face of the Kirk in Nyasaland*. It went further than the Nyasaland Government Report in asserting that the Kirk had sent communists as missionaries to Nyasaland. This committee then made a serious error of judgement. In May 1959 the General Assembly of the Kirk was to discuss the Report of its Special Committee on Central Africa and a supplementary report produced after Operation Sunrise. Feelings reached boiling point when it was announced in the morning of 25 May, the day of the debate, that a copy of *The New Face of the Kirk* had been placed by 'an outside agency' in the mailbox of each of the 1,500 commissioners. This did not help the pro-Federation cause, annoying, as it did, many commissioners who felt the dignity of the Assembly had been offended.

[47] A copy of this document is in the possession of the writer who is not sure if it is now available in the Public Records Office, London.

The Scotsman of 26 May reported the debate on its front page as well as inside and commented in its leader column. The reporter said he had not seen such a full or tense house since the debates in the late 1920s that had led up to the Church Union of 1929. It is important to remember that in 1959 the membership of the Church of Scotland had reached a peak for modern times and represented a community of about two-and-a-half million people. The British Government took the Scottish situation so seriously that the Home Secretary, 'Rab' Butler, who had addressed the Assembly earlier in the day, stayed on to listen to the whole Central African debate from the Gallery. He was accompanied there by Lord Home, Minister at the Commonwealth Office.

What they witnessed was a long emotionally-charged debate in which the Special Committee won vote after vote. The first vote set the scene; it was on a motion put by the two prominent laymen who led the 'Federal' case throughout the day. They moved that the Special Committee be thanked and discharged. In a House of around fifteen hundred Commissioners they gained fewer than fifty votes for their motion. Of the ten 'deliverances' of the Committee accepted by the Assembly, two effectively called for the end of the Federation. The two key deliverances were

5. The General Assembly request H.M. Government that at the 1960 Conference there be no development in the direction of Dominion status for the Federation *without the consent of the majority of the inhabitants.*

9. The General Assembly, recognising that the time has come for a radical revision of the Territorial Constitution for Nyasaland, earnestly recommend to Her Majesty's Government *that effective power be given to the African community in that land,* which admits the possibility of an African majority in the Legislative Council.[48]

In 1959 the General Assembly represented a large cross-section of the Scottish population, including many who would normally vote Tory. Butler and Home got the message and took it south. Meanwhile the Scottish Council on African Questions kept up its production of pamphlets, letters to the press, and lobbying of MPs of all parties. The Devlin Commission Report with its

---

[48] *Reports to the General Assembly of the Church of Scotland* (1959), 683. The italics are mine.

trenchant critique of the policies that had led to the crisis in Central Africa appeared as a heaven-sent ally. The result was that in the run-up to the British General Election of 1959, colonial policy, in particular African policy, was central.[49] This was also the time when Macmillan was selecting the membership of the Commission to review the situation of the Federation in 1960. This was the Commission that Federation leaders had expected would recommend Commonwealth status for the Federation; indeed Welensky in his autobiography insisted that this had been promised as early as 1953.

Welensky, Federal Prime Minister by this time, knew that things were changing. His anger made him very aggressive in negotiating with London. As a result Macmillan and his advisers began to become irritated with Welensky and his supporters, particularly their attempts to divert Macmillan from appointing whom he wanted to the Commission. It was under these circumstances that Macmillan appointed the brilliant young Scotsman, Ian Macleod, as Colonial Secretary. Whether or not Macleod was the most powerful holder of the office since Joseph Chamberlain in the previous century (as Welensky was to say later), he certainly had a privileged position with Macmillan. This is seen most clearly in his decision to free Dr Banda from detention in April 1960 and to deal with him from then on as representative of the Malawi (as Congress had by now decided should be their country's name) people. This was Macleod's decision alone and Macmillan confirmed it against the advice of his official advisers and of the senior Colonial Office figures in Central Africa as well as over protests by senior members of the Cabinet.[50] Malawi was then on the road to independence. The subsequent story of the conferences and diplomacy that led to the secession of Malawi from the Federation and its gaining of independence in July 1964 inevitably followed on from Macmillan's support for his new Colonial Secretary.

During these years from 1948 to 1964 there had been steady support in Scotland across party lines for the expressed wishes of the Malawi people. Some of it was paternalistic but it was not all so – as can be seen from the publications of the Scottish Council on African Questions, the debates in the Church of Scotland

---

[49] See Boyle's 'Introduction' to N. Fisher, *Ian Macleod* (London, 1973).
[50] Fisher, *Ian Macleod*, 155ff.

General Assembly, and the famous General Assembly deliverances of 1959. This active support was part of a relationship that was not one way and was seen by Malawians as one of comradeship and not paternalism. This is clear in the cable sent to the Moderator by Kanyama Chiume on behalf of the banned NANC on the day of critical debate. It read:

> In this perilous time in the history of my country when the civil liberties and freedom of my people are shamefully scorned and suppressed, may I, as a member of the Church, assure you of the unfailing friendship and brotherhood between the peoples of Scotland and Nyasaland.[51]

It was also exemplified by the role Scots in Malawi and the United Kingdom played in both resistance to and support for the tyrannical regime imposed by Dr Kamuzu Banda in 1965 – a regime finally brought to an end, mainly without violence by the people of Malawi, in the years 1992 to 1994.[52] In all those years people in Malawi on both sides of the bitter divide looked to Scotland for support, presuming on this enduring connection. How the ups and downs of the relationship went during these years forms another chapter, still to be written.

[51] *The Scotsman*, 26 May 1959.
[52] To understand this period of Malawi history there are two important studies produced by Kachere Publications in Malawi: M. S. Nzunda and K. Ross (eds), *Church, Law and Political Transition in Malawi* (Blantyre, 1995), and K. Ross (ed.), *God, People and Power in Malawi* (Blantyre, 1996).

Contributors

STEWART J. BROWN is Professor of Ecclesiastical History and Dean of the Faculty of Divinity at the University of Edinburgh. He is the author of *Thomas Chalmers and the Godly Commonwealth in Scotland*, and editor of *Scotland in the Age of the Disruption*, *William Robertson and the Expansion of Europe*, and *Piety and Power in Ireland 1760–1960*.

IAN CAMPBELL is Professor of Scottish and Victorian Literature at the University of Edinburgh. Among his many books are *Thomas Carlyle*, *Carlyle and Europe*, *Kailyard* and *Lewis Grassic Gibbon*.

OWEN CHADWICK is Regius Professor Emeritus of Modern History at the University of Cambridge. His numerous books include *The Mind of the Oxford Movement*, *The Victorian Church*, *The Secularization of the European Mind*, *Michael Ramsay: A Life*, and *Acton and History*.

WILLIAM FERGUSON retired as Reader in Scottish History at the University of Edinburgh and is now an Honorary Fellow in the Department of Scottish History. His publications include *Scotland, 1689 to the Present*, *Scotland's Relations with England* and *The Identity of the Scottish Nation*.

KENNETH J. FIELDING is Professor Emeritus of English Literature at the University of Edinburgh, senior editor of the Duke–Edinburgh edition of *The Collected Letters of Thomas and Jane*

Welsh Carlyle, co-editor of the Pilgrim edition of Charles Dickens's *Letters* and co-editor of the *Selected Letters of Jane Welsh Carlyle.* He has also edited Dickens's *Speeches.*

JOHN F. MCCAFFREY recently retired as Senior Lecturer in Scottish History at the University of Glasgow and is now an Honorary Research Fellow in Glasgow's Department of Scottish History. He is the author of *Scotland in the Nineteenth Century,* along with numerous articles on modern Scottish history.

BARBARA MACHAFFIE is Israel Ward Andrews and Molly C. Putnam Associate Professor of History and Religion at Marietta College, Marietta, Ohio. Her books include *Her Story: Women in Christian Tradition* and *Readings in Her Story.*

PETER MATHESON is Principal of the Theological Hall, Ormond College, Melbourne, and Senior Fellow of the Department of History, University of Melbourne. His books include *Argula von Grumbach, The Rhetoric of the Reformation,* and *The Imaginative World of the Reformation.*

GEORGE NEWLANDS is Professor of Theology at the University of Glasgow. He is the author of *Theology and the Love of God, Making Christian Decisions, God in Christian Perspective* and *Generosity and the Christian Future.*

KEITH ROBBINS is Vice-Chancellor of the University of Wales, Lampeter, and currently Senior Vice-Chancellor of the federal University of Wales. He is President of the Welsh Religious History Society, a former President of the Ecclesiastical History Society and a former President of the Historical Association. His numerous books include *The Eclipse of a Great Power: Modern Britain, 1870–1975, History, Religion and Identity in Modern Britain* and *Great Britain: Identities, Institutions and the Idea of Britishness.*

ANDREW C. ROSS recently retired as Senior Lecturer in the History and Theology of Christian Missions at the University of Edinburgh. A former Dean of the Faculty of Divinity at Edinburgh, he is currently an Honorary Fellow in the Faculty of Divinity. His books include *John Philip: Missions, Race and Politics in South Africa,*

A Vision Betrayed: The Jesuits in Japan and China, 1542–1742, and *Blantyre Mission and the Making of Modern Malawi*.

D. W. D. SHAW is Professor Emeritus of Divinity at the University of St Andrews and a former Dean of the Faculty of Divinity at the University of Edinburgh. He is currently editor of *Theology in Scotland*. His books include *Who is God* and *Dissuaders: Three Explanations of Religion*.

DAVID M. THOMPSON is a Fellow of Fitzwilliam College, University Lecturer in Modern Church History and Director of the Centre for Advanced Religious and Theological Studies at the University of Cambridge. He is the author of numerous articles and editor of *Nonconformity in the Nineteenth Century*.

Index